"I have learned that, like a gas pedal, the applying and pressing in of your faith directly determines the speed and acceleration to your divine breakthrough."
- *Annamarie Strawhand*

FAITH AT FULL SPEED

Your High Performance Manual For Success

Written By: Annamarie Strawhand

Co-Edited By: Jeno Shaw, Karen Aued and Gynti "Goose" Pinon

INTRODUCTION

Can you accelerate your purpose and reach your goals at a much faster pace and still be in God's will and timing for your life? The answer is YES!

Faith At Full Speed is a powerful resource to help you discover your "personal race strategy" to become victorious in your life purpose. Our individual journey on this earth is compared to a "race" many times in the Bible. *Faith At Full Speed* gives you the keys that will add "horsepower" to your own personal journey, along with step by step teachings and easy to apply strategies that are based on the Word of God which have worked successfully for those who have a desire to live a life of victory. By applying these teachings and strategies many have reached their goals and dreams faster than they ever expected!

This book includes decrees and prayer activations in each chapter that you can speak over yourself and your life to build your faith and call forth your destiny.

Faith At Full Speed provides encouragement and inspiration on every page along with inspiring true stories that will motivate you and keep you moving forward while powerfully activating and operating in God's promises for your life, career, business, family, or ministry!

DEDICATION

This book, *Faith At Full Speed,* is dedicated to The Holy Spirit. He is my best friend, co-pilot, crew chief, and spotter. He gets me easily through any wrecks and gives me the strategy to drive myself and others successfully to the finish line and victory EVERY time! **Thank YOU, Holy Spirit!**

IN MEMORIAM

In memory of my earthly father, Carmen Malfitana, who instilled in me a love for high performance cars, speed, and the thrill of victory.

A PERSONAL MESSAGE
FROM ANNAMARIE

Hello, My VICTORIOUS Friend!

I am so excited you are here, and I want to share some of my personal story with you, and to give you a little insight on how this book, *Faith At Full Speed* came about.

Let's take a ride into my *"full speed"* background…

During my 35 plus years of working professionally in the sport of auto racing and around the fast-paced world of motorsports, I was convinced that I was living out my purpose in life. I believed it was my true calling. Motorsports was my passion, the sights, the sounds, the excitement—the adrenaline rush of landing a large sponsor deal for my race car team or driver, not to mention celebrating with them in victory lane when we win a race!

Little did I know the entire time in my motorsports marketing and NASCAR racing career, God was actually preparing me for my true calling and purpose, which I will reveal further in this message to you. My years as a top professional in the auto racing industry were simply the training ground for what God had planned for me. I was at a point in my life where I was entering my 50s, focusing on developing more business in motorsports when most people my age are planning retirement. I loved what I did. It's challenging work, and I thrived in it. I figured it was my divine gift to be good at this. During the last 12 years of my career, my vast experience in the sport brought me into a position of coaching up and coming pro race car drivers to do what it takes for their racing careers to move into the top levels in NASCAR, Indy Car, and Formula One. I was teaching them how to become great leaders, marketers and spokespersons on and off the racetrack. My drivers had great success in attracting the "rides" (winning race cars to drive) and major "sponsors" (corporations that back them financially) into their racing careers. I was sure that I would be doing this to a ripe old age, even if they had to give me my own souped up scooter to get around the racetracks!

But God had something even bigger, something miraculous for me and my life and for others He sent to me.

I had been growing stronger in my faith. I wanted to get closer to God, digging deeper into His Word, and I found myself feeling like He had more for me in this life than racing. I actually began to crave more. I started asking God, "I want to do more for Your Kingdom and Your people. But how, Lord, how do I work in my racing business and have you there with me front and center?"

I consider myself a very bold person, but I was confused and apprehensive about how to share my faith and God's word in my industry of motorsports. Would I be rejected? Would I look unprofessional? More and more, God was showing His goodness to me—my walk with Him became more intimate. I started to hear His voice more clearly. He was blessing me and my family in a big way. I wanted God in EVERY aspect of my life, especially in my career and business, but I could not *see how* to do it.

"For we walk by faith, not by sight." 2 Corinthians 5:7

6

One day, I heard the Lord speak to me LOUDLY in my spirit. It stopped me in my tracks. He said, "Annamarie, you have promoted race drivers, teams, and sponsors. Now, it's time for you to promote ME and MY KINGDOM. It's time for you to show MY PEOPLE how to WIN with the purpose that I have designed for them!"

BOOM! There it was. Hit the brakes and come in for a pit stop! I realized I was called to do God's work. But how? How do I start? Where do I start? I was well-known in motorsports, and I had a good reputation and invested years of my life into this industry. Do I walk away from my racing business? Do I start over? Do I launch a ministry? Not to mention at the time, I was bringing in most of the income in my family. I was like, now God? Do I do this now? I knew that He was Faithful. He had brought me so much blessing, prosperity, and success in my business. He had shown me how to activate my Faith and His word to receive financial miracles and personal breakthroughs for my family—especially with my daughter overcoming getting bullied in school, my husband overcoming health issues, and even bringing us a debt-free house to live in!

But this was a GIANT step. This was GOING PUBLIC with my FAITH and promoting GOD in the *marketplace*.

I LOVE TO THINK BIG. It comes naturally to me, but, I have to tell you honestly, I fought with this new thing that God had revealed that He wanted me to do for months! I was in an internal struggle many times that brought me flat on my face on the floor crying out to God that I needed clarity and His help with this new purpose. How does He want me to start? I didn't know HOW to leave the racing business, it's all I have ever known. Do I do this in racing? The people in racing might not accept this new "faithful" message from me. They might not see me as a "legit" teacher of the Bible. These doubt-filled thoughts kept hitting me left and right. The enemy was working on my mind playing with my own insecurities! (You will know that God has a HUGE blessing for you in the assignment He has asked you to do by the level the enemy comes at you.) But I kept pressing into God. I had a deep desire in my heart to act on this godly assignment. I was passionate about God, His promises, and His goodness more than anything ever in my life. I could not deny it.

"For God has not given us a spirit of fear and timidity, but of power, love, and self-discipline." 2 Timothy 1:7

I was praying fiercely over this. It was a huge step—like being in labor to give birth all over again! That's what it felt like! One afternoon, my husband was out mowing the yard, and I was inside literally laying over the footstool in my bedroom in deep prayer CRYING OUT to God for a breakthrough. I was at a make it or break it point. I could not wait. I was ready. I asked a friend to pray with me over the phone to come to an agreement in my prayer request. Then alone I said, "I surrender to You Father. I trust You." A few minutes later, I was sitting in the chair resting with some tea, and the answer came to me like a download from the Holy Spirit. I heard these words: *"Faith At Full Speed."* It hit me like a bolt! I actually jumped up from the chair! I was so excited! I was yelling YES! YES!!! Thank you, Jesus!!! That's it!

I knew in my heart and soul without a doubt THIS was the name of my new faith teaching program that I would create and my first book I would write.

It made complete sense because, at the time, my motorsports coaching business was called "Marketing At

Full Speed." I immediately saw very clearly that God was telling me, "START WHERE YOU ARE." This is the biggest and best lesson God has ever taught me and to teach to you:

"Start where you are."

Praise God! He is so FAITHFUL! His answers are always so simple. We are the ones who complicate them! I had to SURRENDER to Him and get out from under my own fears! Then He could bring it to me! Woo hooo!

"In the day when I cried out, You answered me, And made me bold with strength in my soul." Psalm 138:3

So I did. I started where I was. I began sharing my faith and praying with my racing clients. In our coaching sessions, I would decree God's word over their race driving careers. We would pray in agreement in Jesus' name and call forth in faith opportunities and finances they were needing to move forward with their goals. I started bringing Biblical Business Strategy into my race team owner clients to help them go to the next level and build their businesses, adding more race cars and expanding their development programs. Even my younger racers, they started asking for prayer and for me to decree over them. They were experiencing quick answers to these prayers! All my doubts and fears faded away. The truth is, when God calls you, He WILL equip you, guide you, and make a path for you! I have learned that by being BOLD in your FAITH it becomes more than an emotion; it becomes a state of your being—because you fully TRUST God.

Soon, my racing clients and I started experiencing amazing breakthroughs. Plus, they were growing stronger in their own faith and walk with God. Then, the miracles started to happen! God wanted to show up in a BIG way. He loves to do this for those who have been obedient to Him. I learned He loves to surprise us too!

The Miracle:

At that time, one of my race car driver coaching clients, Alyssa, was chatting with me through social media messenger in the evening hours. She was in a crisis; she was about to quit and give up her career. She had come far in my program, but she still did not have enough money to buy her race car to begin racing in her chosen series. She was stuck on the sidelines. It seemed like every time she would get ahead, something would come against her and try to pull her back. She was a young woman of faith too, and I really believed in her. I did not want her to give up, and I knew God did not want her to give up either.

I became angry at the enemy coming against her, and I knew we needed to activate BOLD FAITH right at that moment. So, IN ALL CAPS, in the private message to her, I wrote a powerful decree over her racing career, and I called forth a divine breakthrough to come NOW for Alyssa in Jesus' name. She received it and said, "Amen." We released our faith in positive expectation for God to move on her behalf.

Twenty-four hours later, I received an email from a woman in Florida who was producing a large international conference for women in business coming up in a month in West Palm Beach. She said the theme of the conference was "accelerate," and they were going to have all kinds of racing stuff around that event theme—and they were looking for "a dynamic woman of motorsports" to come and speak. That's how she found me on google. I called her that day, and we hit it off right away. I agreed to speak at the conference, and then she asked if I would be willing to bring some of my female race driver clients with me and their race cars to also appear at the event. I said, "Sure." I would have to check with them. It was a great opportunity!

I had a good feeling about this, and I could not help but think this was God working. The old me would have just seen it as coincidence, maybe even too good to be true. The new me in Christ could feel the Holy Spirit all over the first phone call, and I knew God would make it happen.

No coincidences, only God.

The female race car drivers I wanted to ask to come with me to this women's conference were my brightest coaching students—Maddy Ryan, of Virginia, and Mandy Chick, of Kansas. They had race cars to bring but might be tight on timing and finances to get to Florida since they were in the latter part of the racing season. The third driver I wanted to bring was Alyssa, who I prayed with the night before, but she had no race car to display. I told her she could appear and speak with the other drivers—just bring her race helmet, and we would rock it! They all had positive stories to share at the conference. They were working hard in my marketing programs—very motivated and professional. I knew they would be well-received and make good connections for their racing careers.

I talked to Maddy and Mandy and their families, and they were excited for the opportunity. However, Maddy Ryan's family did not have the budget to travel right then, and Mandy's dad was just starting to build a new race car. It would not be done in time. Alyssa was not sure how she could get the time off her day job. I prayed with each of them for God to make a way to get them to this conference.

I spoke to the Lord and I said, "Father, I know You brought this opportunity, and I am certain that You are going to get us all to West Palm Beach for this conference." I released my faith, BIG TIME. God does not bring an opportunity that He won't see through all the way for you. He will make a way. Especially if you release the entire situation in faith to Him and everyone comes together to agree in faith. The power of agreement in prayer is a big key. I prayed that prayer with each driver and their families.

"For where two or three are gathered together in my name, there am I in the midst of them." Matthew 18:20

Things began to fall into place quickly. Everyone said they had the same feeling about this, that God was opening a door, and they had to be there. Maddy Ryan's dad and mom pulled her race car down to Florida on an open trailer to save fuel, and Alyssa and I followed in a rental car. I will never forget it was a Jetta with Jersey plates. I got a great deal on it, too! We drove straight through from Virginia, hit rain halfway through in South Carolina, and the tarp flew off Maddy Ryan's race car about 10 times, but we had so much fun. We still laugh about it to this day. Meanwhile, in Kansas, Mandy Chick's dad finished a complete late model race car from a bare frame to a new body paint and rolling

out in less than 30 days by himself, which is quite a feat. They excused Mandy from school for a few days, and she and dad hauled all night to Florida. Mandy kept calling me to check in along the way. Mandy's mom flew in the next day.

Once we hit the Florida state line, we stopped off the exit to Daytona International Speedway—where every race car driver dreams to race someday. The sun was just setting, and it was a calm and quiet evening—no action on the track. We pulled in the entrance and stood together looking over the beautiful, legendary super speedway. Maddy Ryan's mom said, "I feel the presence of God!" I said, "Let's pray!"

We all joined hands and I prayed for God's blessings and breakthroughs on this trip and thanked Him and praised Him for getting us here. Then Alyssa gave Maddy Ryan a special racing themed Bible she had made for her. It was all so powerful!

"And all things, whatsoever you shall ask in prayer, believing, you shall receive." Matthew 21:22

We continued on our trip south. We met up with Mandy Chick and her dad at the hotel in West Palm Beach where the conference would start the next morning.   I had brought a special gift for each girl—a bracelet with their race car number on it—not just because they were my wonderful students but, most of all, because of their faithfulness to God and as a reminder of this moment together. I had a hard time holding back tears of joy at the great favor God was showing us, but that was just the beginning. God had a HUGE surprise in store!

The next morning, the race cars were on display at the main entrance of the hotel conference center, glistening in the Florida sunshine.   My drivers were dressed in their race driving suits greeting all the attendees coming in the doors to the main hall. They were an instant hit. Everyone was talking about these young women who raced cars! At the time, Mandy Chick was just 14 years old, Maddy Ryan was 16 years old, and Alyssa was 20 years old. I was 50!

Next, I had each driver go up on stage at the opening welcome ceremony and introduce themselves and tell a short inspirational story about their goals and where they wanted to go in their careers. This was their "Elevator Speech." I had prepared them to know this by heart as their coach months before—to be ready for all opportunities! These girls were prepared for such a time as this! They got huge applause. I cried happy tears. I was so proud of them!

The day was filled with great speakers and tons of networking, networking, networking! As a featured speaker myself, I was invited with my group to a luncheon with VIPs. My drivers again were the stars of the show— Maddy Ryan, Mandy and Alyssa! They all became closer friends that day too. It was a very special time together.

At the end of the first conference day a gentleman and his wife came up to me. I could tell he was a well-to-do businessman, and he said to me, "Are you and your drivers going to be here tomorrow after your speech?" I told him yes, we were. He then asked me if we could be near the stage at 2 pm. I said yes, we would be there.

The next day I got up on stage and gave my speech about becoming a woman of influence in an industry mostly known for men and how it compared to mainstream business. I had a blast! I love to speak, and I had everyone revved up in the room. After I was done with my speech, at 2 pm, I gathered my drivers and their families and I said, "We need to be at the stage. They are calling us up for something. I am not sure what it is." We took our places next to the stage as they called us up.

God Shows Up BIG...

Mandy, Maddy Ryan, Alyssa, and I all came up on the stage and faced the audience of well over a thousand professional women entrepreneurs as well as men in business—distinguished authors and speakers—in the Grand Ballroom at the conference there in West Palm Beach. Maddy Ryan and Mandy Chick's parents were below and snapping photos. We had no idea what was about to happen next. It was surreal.

The businessman and his wife were there waiting up on stage for us. My drivers and I held hands in excited anticipation, and I could feel the presence of the Holy Spirit on the stage. The businessman took the microphone and said, "Annamarie, Maddy Ryan, Mandy and Alyssa, we called you back up here to the stage because you all have inspired us greatly. My wife and I would like to give each of your drivers a *sponsorship check* today for their racing careers. We hope that it helps each girl reach their goals and dreams."

Whoa! Wait! What?!

Remember when I said God loves to give us *surprises* when we are faithful? This is exactly what I mean. We were shocked! We never expected this. They handed Maddy, Ryan, and Mandy each checks of $5,000 and Alyssa's check was more—the exact amount she needed to buy her race car. *The exact amount*. She had not told anyone about that. *But God knew.*

When you show up in faith, God will meet you there.

Remember the very first decree and prayer I "spoke" with Alyssa over social media messenger a month before? That prayer and decree, with steadfast faith over the 30 days, no matter what came against us, brought us to this moment of God's grace and provision! What a good Father our God is! Wow! We cried. We rejoiced. We celebrated, and we praised God!

"You will also decide and decree a thing, and it will be established for you; And the light [of God's favor] will shine upon your ways." Job 22:28

God is still in the miracle business. We just have to believe He is. *I know He is.* I have experienced it. My family has experienced it. My clients and students have experienced it. Now, I want YOU to experience it.

Let's Fast Forward a couple of years from that Miracle Day on the Florida stage with my drivers, to May 2017. I made the decision to leave my motorsports career fully and begin my faith coaching ministry. God was calling me to fully serve Him and His Kingdom and I could not deny it. I felt like I was trying to drive two cars at the same time and I was not in full obedience to what God had asked me to do.

It was exciting and a bit scary to walk away from all I ever knew in motorsports and go full-time into serving the Kingdom of God. With the support and encouragement of my Church Pastor, Chuck Mosley, (thank you, Pastor Chuck!) and my husband, Michael, (thank you, Honey!) I hosted and taught my first Faith At Full Speed Seminar at my church. This really was my very first step into ministry and Christian life coaching. I only had a few people show up to the Seminar, and I was feeling discouraged. I had bought enough bagels and pastries to feed at least 100 + people, but, with just 8 people in attendance and my husband and daughter, I pressed on and put my full heart into teaching and preaching to all who were there. Just *one person* came up to me afterward with a notebook filled with notes she had taken from my seminar. She told me how excited she was to use the tools I shared that day. That was all I needed! The one person who was impacted by my stepping out that day on the stage in the church multi-purpose building. *Just one person.* There will always be a time when you are discouraged, thinking nobody cares or supports what God wants you to do, but, if you impact one person, that is all you need to start! Your first seed is planted. Then, you keep going, trusting God to increase it.

I heard this quote, and it encouraged me. I hope it encourages you:

"Your One is depending on you! Who's Your One?"

Kingdom Activation is all about putting your feet to your faith, and getting your mouth, mind, and spirit in alignment with your assignment!

As of that day in May 2017, the KINGDOM of God that is within me was ACTIVATED. I am now walking in my true calling and my divine purpose! But I had to take that first step in obedience. More miracles have happened for me and those around me! I am filled with joy every day! Yes, I loved my old job, but working for the kingdom of God and the Body of Christ blesses me beyond my wildest dreams because I get to help so many more people live their dreams! God brought me to a bigger place and wanted to be able to bless me even more. It was His plan all along!

"For I know the plans and thoughts that I have for you,' says the Lord, plans for peace and well-being and not for disaster, to give you a future and a hope."
Jeremiah 29:11

Since that first day of my KINGDOM ACTIVATION, God has opened every door. He has sent me the answers, helpers, and the provision I have needed every step of the way. My faith and knowledge of God's word and promises has grown, and the Holy Spirit has shown me so much more to teach and impart to others! I communicate with the Holy Spirit 24/7, and, as my relationship has grown with Him, He has grown me to the level of being a prophetic voice for His kingdom. He has given me prophetic words for individuals, regions, and even nations! I have seen these prophetic words come to pass! It's so exciting! We are all meant to walk in these gifts and anointing of the Holy Spirit. Is He calling you for a KINGDOM ACTIVATION? *Your divine calling is calling YOU!*

Our God is so GOOD, and it's no mistake you have this book in your hands at this moment.

God is saying NOW IS YOUR TIME to encounter His goodness and faithfulness immediately in your life! No matter what age you are or where you are, God has an amazing plan to bless you and fulfill what you have been hoping for! Why? Because He wants you to START WHERE YOU ARE.

"And we know that all things work together for good to them that love God, to them who are called according to his purpose." Romans 8:2

I am now a "Faith and Victory Coach" for all God's people, and it feels amazing! God wants YOU to be walking in your true calling and divine purpose! He wants to provide YOU with open doors, divine connections, financial provision, breakthroughs, and miracles for your goals and dreams! It's my purpose to teach you what He has taught me and help you discover, activate, and accelerate your purpose at FULL SPEED!

I am grateful you are now here, my victorious friend! This is exactly where God wants you right now, and He is starting you right where you are, just like He did with me!

This book you are about to read is packed with power for your life! So buckle up, get both hands on the wheel and get ready to fire up the ignition switch.

Ladies and Gentlemen, START YOUR ENGINES!!! Time to go for what God has called you to be and to WIN BIG!

I am cheering you on, and all of heaven is cheering you on!

YOU'VE GOT THIS! Meet YOU in Victory Lane!

Your Faith and Victory Coach,

Annamarie

TABLE OF CONTENTS

CHAPTER 1
YOU ARE BUILT FOR PERFORMANCE

Reaching a major goal of achieving a dream is like a successful racing strategy. God has set us up to WIN if we follow His strategies in complete faith and fully use what He has gifted us with. We will come into our divine purpose with amazing success and *speed*.

Everything in your life is similar to preparing and competing in a race—bringing you to the finish line and ultimate victory. It's up to you how much power you want to activate behind it to speed it up. If you are like me, you want to live a victorious life, fulfill your true purpose, and be able to have the tools, the funds, the resources, and people around you that you need to live your dream with great blessing that overflows for your family and loved ones.

Ask yourself this question: What were you born for? Do you have enough faith to get there? God sees your potential. He designed it for you. It's time to activate it!

I saw this quote on social media recently:

"When you meet Jesus, He activates the destiny blueprint within your spirit." - Lance Wallnau

That quote really spoke to me. Jesus is our master builder. I believe it's no accident that God had His only Son, born in the flesh on earth to save us, to be raised in the house of a carpenter (Joseph). What does a carpenter do? He starts with a design, draws it up (blueprints it), and creates it. A skilled carpenter or builder not only fulfills a need with his creations, it actually can be celebrated as a work of art that stands the test of time and serves many people for many generations. This is a design like no other.

Many times when I pray, I pray these words, ***"Jesus, You are my master builder. Activate the great plans and blueprints you have designed for me and let's build together!"***

In the Bible, Jeremiah Chapter 29 verse 11, God tells Jeremiah this same thing: **"I have great plans for you."**

That means me and YOU, too.

You are designed for superior performance like a high powered racing engine.

When I was a little girl, my earthly father, Carmen Malfitana was a champion drag racer. He had a winning race car, a '55 Chevy Bel Air, that he modified for ultimate speed. This car was legendary around the Upstate NY drag strips. My dad, with this very special race car, set many speed records in the 1960's that stood for years! The track promoters even set up a race with a jet powered car to see if it could break the record against my dad and his '55 Chevy. My dad still won by a smidgen and held his record! As a child, I spent countless hours on a little rolling stool in the garage watching my dad work on his car, handing him wrenches and asking him questions. My Mom tells me that my bedtime story with my dad, Carmen, was reading articles in Hot Rod Magazine and National Speed Sport News, pointing to the beautiful shiny race cars on the pages, while propped on my daddy's knee! No wonder my passion for fast cars! It was instilled in me at a very early age.

But my Dad's biggest pride and joy in that '55 Chevy race car was the custom-built *high performance engine*—a 327 small block that was built by the best engine guy in town. My Dad had collaborated with this engine builder to create a power plant in this race car with "secret" characteristics and components that nobody else was using or knew about. This was to give it that extra pull off the starting line and all the way down the track. Now get this, this engine was so unique it was ***"blueprinted"*** by the engine builder.

In the motorsports world, when an engine is blueprinted that means it's serious. It means you have something so custom that when the engine performs, the engine builder wants to have a blueprint to keep recreating that same super fast performance for you. Building upon the original and keeping the specs unique to you, his special customer. When you win, he wins. Because more customers will come wanting a special engine designed for them, too. Blueprinting an engine is also a winning edge for the racer because he or she can keep the blueprint as a document for safe keeping for their race engine that nobody else can copy.

The purpose in you is blueprinted for the winning edge like nobody else! Jesus wants to collaborate with you to take what He uniquely blueprinted and designed in you— your specialized divine gifts and talents! All to make great things happen through you in your life! He wants to ADVANCE you and advance those around you through you and your unique calling! When you succeed and give Him the glory you inspire more people to turn in faith to God for their lives too! When you win, He (God) wins!

"A man's gift makes room for him, And brings him before great men." Proverbs 18:16

Here's the deal. A high performance engine is no good sitting on the engine stand in the garage. It might *look fast* and powerful, but, unless it's "activated" with a proper vessel (chassis), tires, gas and the rest of the components it needs to run and win, it's just there collecting dust, and it will never win a single race!

Is your high performance purpose collecting dust? Is your engine just sitting there on a "stand" waiting for you to start putting it to use?

Have you tried to put your gifts, purpose, and calling to use, but it never seems to get going or it needs to pick up some serious speed?

Are you ready to rev up your purpose and activate your gifts so you can step off the starting line full speed into your divine calling?

If the answer is YES then take a deep breath, close your eyes, hands on your heart, and DECLARE this out loud:

"Father, I am ready to use the gifts you have put inside me and activate the divine purpose you have designed me for! I say YES to my calling right now in Jesus' name, Amen!"

Did you feel it? Did you feel your spirit power up inside you?

Remember what Jesus said: *"The Kingdom Is Within You!" (Luke 17:21)*

You just activated God's Kingdom with its unlimited power in you with your words! The power of life and death are in the tongue! You will learn as you go along in this book the words that come out of your mouth are either added horsepower or dead weight to your purpose! I want more horsepower. How about you? YES!

Okay, now here are your Start Up Power Keys To Your Purpose (Your High Performance Engine):

- Inner Components (God's Kingdom is within you!)
- Timing/Alignment (God's Plan—you were made for such a time as this!)
- Spark Plugs (Holy Spirit—the fire that sparks you and drives you.)
- Oil (Anointing—the gift that sets you apart for the purposes of God, with His divine hand of favor, power, and grace upon you.)
- Water (Living Water—the spirit inside of you that you pour out to others.)
- Air (Word of God—living and breathing into you)
- Fuel (Your Faith and Prayer Life)

Every engine needs these things to be able to perform up to the FULL potential it was built for!

I have been around many racing engines in my motorsports career, and I will tell you this, the highest powered ones sound so awesome when you fire that baby up! It's the coolest thing! The power moves you and shakes you from head to toe! It captures the attention of everyone within earshot and people come running to check it out! That's going to be your unique SOUND in the world!

TIME TO REVVVVVV IT UP!!!!!

Wait! We need more than just an engine to win our race, right? We have to start putting everything else we need together with our engine to get in the race and go for the VICTORY! We will take that next step in Chapter 2, but, first, let's get this engine (purpose) fired up with speaking this Activation Prayer out loud. You want the angels of the Lord on assignment that are waiting around you to be activated.   That's why it's so much more powerful and important to pray out loud!

Activation Prayer:

"Father, I thank You for giving me gifts and talents. I thank You Father for the plan and purpose You have for my life. I trust you completely Father. According to Your promise in Romans 8:28, You are working all things for my good. I take all my fears, worries, and doubts from my mind, heart, spirit, and soul right now and put them all at the foot of the cross of Jesus. I surrender myself to You right now, Father God. I agree with Your Plan, Your Blueprint for me, and Your promises to prosper me with my calling and my future. Show me my purpose and direct my steps. You alone, God, know all the hopes and dreams of my heart. I know you want to advance me in my purpose, and I thank you, Father. I invite Your Holy Spirit to come inside me right now! I will be obedient and listen to Your voice showing me and guiding me, and I will take action when You direct me. Today is the day I become all You have designed me to be! I am certain that You are bringing me everything I need to activate and carry out my purpose. I thank You, Jesus, for being my Master Builder!

Father God, I am excited to see the work you do in me and through me for Your glory, in Jesus' Name, Amen!"

WOOO HOOO!

CHAPTER 2
GARAGE TIME!

The first thing that a successful racing team does is go into the garage to build, plan, and strategize for the upcoming season. They want to be the fastest, yes, but, more so, to have a unique performance edge to win races and ultimately a championship season, which secures repeated victories and top finishes.

When I was working in motorsports, especially NASCAR, this "garage time" of building and prepping the race car was a top-secret time. The public was not allowed to come around and see what the team was doing with the cars. That area of the shop was closed off, and, many times, the teams worked into the night hours. It was a time of intense dedication. Everyone had to support the team, even their family members. The crew went without vacations or seeing their families at suppertime. Many times, the families of the crew would stop by with pizza for dinner or, if late, coffees for all of us. I can even remember being in the office next to the race shop working until midnight on sponsorship proposals and contracts to get that one last sponsor finalized for our season opening race at Daytona.

This "garage time" was understood by all of us on the team as the most crucial time for our overall success, and everyone had to be on board with it. If not, you were fired by the crew chief, and you were rolling your toolbox out the door!

I remember this dedicated, intense, top-secret "garage time" being *so* worth it. Usually this was the three winter months during the "off season." The entire team, no matter what position you were part of, was blessed by it all later with the accolades we received from success on the track. Not to mention the team bonuses in our paychecks when we won a race or finished in the top ten! Even I got a bonus in my check, and I was the team PR and Marketing person. My toolbox consisted of a flip phone, a notepad and pen, Kodak Instamatic camera, laptop case, comfy running shoes, and a good attitude! (It was the 90's and flip phones were cutting edge tech, ha!)

What You Do In Secret, God Rewards Openly!

God created YOU to be a Champion with your calling on this earth! The key to your "garage time" is to "build and prepare yourself" with direction from God into becoming a lean, mean, fast machine for your divine purpose—to be victorious in each assignment and level completing what He has called you to do.

One of my favorite quotes from Boxing Champion, Joe Frazier, reflects this crucial time of building and preparation:

"Champions aren't made in the ring, they're recognized there. What you work on in the early light of the morning will show up in the ring under the bright lights."

You might be saying to yourself: *"But Annamarie, I know what my purpose is, and I want to get out there now and get going, not be in the garage waiting for it to happen!"*

Yes, I know you are chomping at the bit to get to that finish line and be victoriously living in your goals and dreams, but we need to understand one thing first. *In order to be fast out of the box, we must go into our box to prepare.* This is where we receive our winning strategy from the Holy Spirit, who is our divine coach and crew chief! I have learned the hard way after racing ahead without consulting and getting confirmation from God's Holy Spirit. Trust me, it will not be pretty! You will end up in more delay and frustration! God has a plan waaayyyy better than what we could ever devise by ourselves for achieving the goals and dreams in your heart! You want to do this according to God's brilliant strategy in a *partnership* with Him. I have tried plans and ideas before on my own I thought were "right" without God, and I just ended up spinning out or hitting a wall! I always say, "Put God first in everything you do, and you will never be last."

The "garage time" strategy will give you clarity, speed, and power toward your goals while being fully aligned with God and His will so when you emerge, watch out, you are like a bolt of lightning! Everything you set your hand to will be from a position of divine power that will flow to you and through you consistently, speedily and smoothly. You will know exactly, without a doubt, what God's plan is for you and that His favor is on it. YOU CAN'T LOSE. Your goal must be to get more and more into His presence because everything comes from the strength of your relationship with God. The stronger your relationship, the better the outcome.

I have truly come to believe there is no "Plan B" for us with God, only "Plan A". We are the ones who veer off course and keep trying to take off on our own path without the guidance of the Holy Spirit—often spinning out or crashing in our own plans and devices! Unwisely, we end up taking up valuable time that could have been strategic, divinely guided steps to our goals, BUT God is faithful and never forsakes us even when we don't listen! (I have been there, LOL....) He keeps reeling us back in and back on track! Thank you, Father! We have a SURPLUS of Grace for our mistakes because of Jesus, so don't be afraid to get started. Jesus rigged it and set up this race *in your favor!*

God wants to prepare you for YOUR SEASON so you can SHINE and HE can SHINE through YOU. When you celebrate your victories, share your story of faith, you become a testimony for God's GOODNESS and GLORY.

Over the years, I always coached my racing drivers that if God prospers you and you win races and championships— or any good thing you are celebrating—don't forget to praise God in Victory Lane because God takes PLEASURE in our victories. When you praise His Goodness, He will give you even more!

"Let them shout for joy and be glad, who favor my righteous cause; and let them say continually, "Let the Lord be magnified, who has pleasure in the prosperity of His servant." Psalm 35:27

How awesome is this! God WANTS us to WIN with our gifts and purpose! He is a proud Father when we do!

So HOW do you get to that point—the point of celebrating your victories and pleasing God?

It all starts with ACKNOWLEDGING without a doubt that God designed you with your own special gifts and divine purpose *in your DNA.* There is NO MISTAKE why these goals and dreams and desires are in your heart. God PUT them there.

"Your eyes saw my unformed body; all my days were written in Your book and ordained for me before one of them came to be." Psalm 139:16

The exciting news is that God designed you for His AWESOME Plan A! Your life is strategically made to get you to fully prosper in your divine purpose. YOU have a scroll (book) that has been written for you in heaven! A divine blueprint written by the author and finisher of your faith—Jesus Christ, the Word, who spoke you into existence. He is the Alpha and the Omega—the Beginning and the End—and, guess what? He sees the end from the beginning! He sends His Holy Spirit to keep you prospering on that plan—that path to your victorious, glorious expected finish.

Your calling is the desire you feel in your heart and soul pulling and tugging at you all the time that there's something more, something bigger and greater for you. Your calling is calling out for you to TAKE ACTION! Your "Garage Time" is to get you perfectly aligned with your Plan A strategy, prepare it, build it, and activate it!

Jesus writes the BEST stories and He is the Master Builder. He is your top-secret Engine Man! When you meet Jesus in your building process (garage time) your scroll and blueprints are being accessed for you in Heaven! I have experienced this firsthand and have seen my own scrolls in dreams and visions. You can ask to see yours too in prayer!

Don't IGNORE the Tugging!

Many people try to squelch down the tugging in their heart and soul because they don't believe they can go after their calling. Or they put off working on their goals and dreams for years because they feel or think they need "special" things or situations to even get started and use that as an excuse. That is a LIE from the enemy trying to hold you back from your divine purpose! Time to kick his butt to the curb! I did! You can too!

Time to kick the devil's butt to the curb!

You are reading this chapter right now because I finally got serious about writing this book—a huge goal and dream I had in my heart for three years! I decided to take a few months of "garage time" to get it written, completed, published, and here it is in your hands! Thank You, Lord! I pray that every word you read inspires, equips, and motivates you but, most of all, *activates* you!

But first, my faith had to be put into action for you to be reading this page right now. If I had not taken my "garage time," this book would still be a bunch of post-it notes piled in a folder on my shelf. I am so grateful I asked the Holy Spirit to help move me into action. What a waste it would have been for my daughter someday to find my notes after I am gone to Heaven and they were never activated into the book God had planned for me to write? It would have been tragic! Your purpose, goals, and dreams must be activated and carried out to completion so your legacy can be established!

Our Father God is a GENERATIONAL THINKER AND PLANNER, so, to be successful, we need to be generational thinkers and planners too! God is thinking about how you will carry out something special He programmed into your DNA that will have a powerful life-changing and miraculous effect on your children and children's children and others in your generation, even if it's just the longevity of your testimony of faith that you record in a book or what you do on this earth that will inspire many generations to come! I've learned that this life is not just about me but what God wants to do *through me*. Like the book of Esther in the Bible, she is faced with a choice that was not for her survival but for the survival of her people. God prepared her for just that moment in time —to take a step in boldness "for such a time as this"—that had an effect that saved the future of the Jewish people. One step, one person—big results. What were you born for? Have you asked God that question?

I believe that in the Bible where it says God will wipe away our tears when we come to Heaven, some of those tears could be from when God tells us what our purpose was, what He planned to do through us, and we never took the time to really partner with Him and see it through. We must not waste our gifts. If we do waste them, I believe we break God's heart, and it's actually disobedience to God when we ignore the tugging and prompting and never seek Him to act upon it or if we never step forward and multiply our gifts because of fear.

Jesus told a powerful "parable of the talents" (Matthew 25:14–30) about how the Kingdom of Heaven works if we bury and never use our gifts and talents—what God has given us to multiply and prosper with. To the one who buried their talents, they were cursed as a "wicked servant." To the ones who used their talents, invested in them and multiplied what they started with, they were blessed and praised—"*well done good and faithful servant.*"

If you are anything like me, I want to hear "well done good and faithful servant" when I meet the Lord in heaven! YES!

Here's what the Holy Spirit has shown me to encourage you:

Start where you are now and use what you have currently available to you! All you need to start creating, activating your dream, and going after that goal, is ALREADY within YOU, and HE will give you everything you need to make it happen and PROSPER! This is God's promise for your life and His TRUTH!

Again, Jesus told us that the kingdom of Heaven is WITHIN us. Heaven's resources are UNLIMITED! We don't need any more than that to start activating our purpose and calling—no fancy gadgets, no jackpot lottery wins, no marrying a rich prince or princess charming. You only need to seek ONE THING to kick this into HIGH gear now, and you already HAVE IT.

"Seek first the kingdom of God and his righteousness, and all these things will be added to you." **Matthew 6:33**

Do you feel your purpose is calling out to you—something bigger tugging in your heart and soul? Then you are ready to rock and roll and activate your purpose! The Holy Spirit has been waiting on you! Some of you think you have been waiting on God, but He may be waiting on YOU.

Each of us have been redeemed and set apart for Go— through Christ Jesus. We are His chosen as sons and daughters! We have access to ALL we need right from our Heavenly Father!

Now, Let's Get In The Garage and Get To Work!

When you look at some of the greatest success stories of our time, they all had very humble beginnings. Many of them *actually started* in a small garage. Harley Davidson Motorcycles, Mattel Toys, Yankee Candles, Steve Jobs of Apple, to name a few, all started in a garage! Many large ministries and churches started in a living room or around the kitchen table! Joyce Meyer's ministry started in her basement! Mine started in a spare bedroom in my house!

"Do not despise these small beginnings for the LORD rejoices to see the work begin!" Zechariah 4:10

Getting into your "garage" means you are getting serious about your goals and what you really want for your life. As a crew chief would say to his race team and pit crew:

"Let's Get 'Er Done!"

Garage Time 10 Step Strategies:

Step 1: Create YOUR Special Workspace
Your "garage" is the place where you pray, talk to God, plan, focus, build, and create. It can be an office, a garden, a special room, or even converting a part of a room, an actual garage, shed, or basement. It's your DIVINE WORKSHOP. This is the place for you and God to work together on your goals.

Step 2: Declare YOUR Vision
Get your pictures of your goals on the walls in front of you and write them down. Make a vision board, journal, and create a desire statement by faith! Scripture instructs us to "Write the vision; make it plain on tablets, so he may run who reads it." Habakkuk 2:2-3

Step 3: Fasting For Clarity and Answers
Fasting helps with focused clarity to hear the Holy Spirit's guidance. This is a time to ask God and write down what He speaks and shows to you.

Step 4: Clean The Junk Out Of Your Trunk

This is where repentance, forgiveness, and soul healing take place. You need to be lightened up spiritually in order to rocket out of the gate carrying out your purpose! When your soul prospers the rest of you prospers! Time to clean the junk out of your trunk and forgive anything and anyone you have been holding inside your soul. Let it go—loose it and release it.

Say this prayer: *"Father, you love my soul and you want me to prosper in life, so, right now, I release all the pain and bitterness that is in my soul upon the cross of Jesus. I forgive anyone who has hurt me, and I release them to you right now, Jesus. Cleanse my soul with your blood, Jesus, wash it clean. I ask the Holy Spirit to restore and refresh my soul today. I am ready for the new things you have planned for me, Father. I am ready to grow, build, prosper, and advance, in Jesus' name, Amen!"*

Step 5: Read the Word!

Soak in the Promises of God. He will take you through scripture into your promised land! Read about Abraham, Joshua, and Caleb. Ask God to give you your mountain just like Caleb did! They believed God's promises and God gave them what He promised them! (Joshua 14:12-15) The Word also keeps your Sword of the Spirit sharp! It's your best weapon against the enemy. Don't let it get rusty!

Step 6: PRAY BOLDLY

Start asking God for what you need by praying **boldly**. Hebrews 4:16 in the Amplified Version says: "Therefore let us [with privilege] approach the throne of grace [that is, the throne of God's gracious favor] with confidence and without fear, so that we may receive mercy [for our failures] and find [His amazing] grace to help in time of need [an appropriate blessing, coming just at the right moment]."

Decree your purpose!

DECLARE IT AS YOURS IN FAITH!

Decree: *"Lord, Your word says, in Jeremiah 29:11, 'For I know the plans I have for you,' declares the LORD, 'plans to prosper you and not to harm you, plans to give you hope and a future.' Lord God, I am ready for your plans for my future right now, and I call forth those plans in Jesus' name!"*

My three-part rule: Declare/prophesy it in the spirit, command it to manifest in the natural, and claim it is yours by saying, "I now possess my promise in Jesus' name!"

Step 7: Prayer Agreement Partner
Ask another person of faith to pray with you over your goals and dreams and come into agreement with you in prayer. In my mentoring programs, my students are matched with an "AB" or "Accountability Buddy" to help encourage each other and help keep each other on track during the building and preparation time.

- Matthew 18:19 says: "Again I say to you, that if two of you agree on earth about anything that they may ask, it shall be done for them by My Father who is in heaven."
- The power of agreement brings Jesus right there in your prayer! Matthew 18:20 says: "For where two

or three are gathered together in my name, there am I in the midst of them."

Step 8: Dedicate All Your Work to The Lord

We dedicate and take vows and commitments to our church, our spouses, and, many times, we have to sign agreements for our jobs. How much more can we be blessed with a commitment with God? He wants to be in covenant with you and your purpose.

When you dedicate and commit all your work, gifts, purpose, and yourself to God, He will prosper it. God loves covenants. He wanted to have one with Abraham whom he called His friend. This is where you enter into a true partnership with the Father. Proverbs 16:3 says: "Commit your works to the LORD, and your plans will be established." Take your vision and write it down or draw it out on paper. Then, lift it up to God and commit it to Him. Ask Him to bless it and prosper it in Jesus name!

Step 9 : Plant Seeds and First Fruit Offerings

For me, this has been life changing! The more I give to my church and other ministries, the more God has blessed me, financed me, and expedited my purpose, goals, and vision.

Seeds are financial offerings that you sow into the kingdom of God that you "name" to produce what you command it to grow into. Isaiah 55:11 says: "So will My word be which goes forth from My mouth; it will not return to Me empty, without accomplishing what I desire, and without succeeding in the matter for which I sent it." First fruits, you give in FAITH ahead of time to God or you give as the first portion of what God has blessed you with at the time of financial breakthrough. I do this in the beginning of the year. I have more in depth teaching on how God will finance your purpose and vision as your divine "sponsor" in Chapter 5.

Step 10: Expect Divine Idea Downloads, Answers, and Doors to OPEN

Ideas and direction will start to come to you! Write them down! Keep a notepad next to your bed. Many times, these answers can come in dreams and while you are getting ready to fall asleep. Keep asking for wisdom, ideas, and downloads from Heaven!

Ask the Holy Spirit for confirmation of these ideas. You will feel God's presence on them and, many times, another person will come forth within a day or two and out of the blue confirm this idea. God will SHOW you what to activate, and He will show you what is hidden and waiting for you. Jeremiah 33:3 says: "Call to Me, and I will answer you, and show you great and mighty things, which you do not know." Proverbs 8:12 talks about wisdom (which is the Holy Spirit coming into your situation): "I wisdom dwell with prudence and find out knowledge of witty inventions."

Take that step that is being shown to you ASAP! Take action! Do not delay! Praise God for His Faithfulness! Give Him all the credit for His ideas and direction and they will keep coming! Walk out the strategy God gives you!

I want to be clear: The popular country song actually has it wrong! It's not "Jesus, Take the Wheel." It's Jesus who is *within YOU* taking the wheel! He wants to work *through* you! God gave us a seat right with Jesus *in Jesus.* Ephesians 2 says we have the authority to do everything through Christ who works *within* us and through us! YOU are in the driver's seat! He gave you all authority to do it with the help of the Holy Spirit who is your co-pilot. It's time to get your "vehicle" (your purpose) ready to be driven to its full potential! It's YOU at the Wheel!

"I Can Do All Things Through Christ Who Strengthens Me." Philippians 4:13

If you are ready to take this "garage time" to take action on these steps to activate your purpose like I outlined above, I am proud of you! But you might be saying you don't know what your purpose is. You will still need to take this "garage time" for God to reveal what He wants you to do. Keep reading. I will be addressing how to get more clarity and help you to pinpoint exactly what your "Plan A" is and the steps HOW to activate it.

You might be thinking, "How long do I need to stay in my "garage time?" Weeks? Months? Can God launch me in a day?" God can move things suddenly for you, whenever He wants. I have experienced it. I have found when you get an unexpected "suddenly," it's meant to push or shift you into the next level of your purpose and God's plan. However, if you are not ready to GO because you are still dealing with "junk in your trunk," you might get left behind when He opens that door of opportunity for you, or, even worse, you may not *recognize* that door is *for you*, putting you back even further. Windows of opportunity can pass by if you don't move into them because of fear or disobedience to God's calling. This is what I want to make sure I show you—how NOT to miss this! I also want to make sure you are prepared to launch!

What Holds You Back?

Question: What is the "junk in your trunk" that will hold you back and tie you down from accelerating into your next level?

Answer: Sin, un-forgiveness, bitterness, and guilt from your past and soul wounds

Solution: (Soul-u-tion) Repentance, forgiveness, soul cleaning, and healing takes care of that junk and gunk in your trunk!

You may have expected me to say ***prayer***—that prayer will accelerate things. Praying is a very important part of this, but, in my experience and in those I have counseled and coached, repenting from your sin and healing your past soul wounds is like dropping pounds and pounds of weight off your race car and off of you. *It's like going from a dump truck to a corvette!*

"Beloved, I pray that in all respects you may prosper and be in good health, just as your soul prospers." 3 John 1:2

I know PERSONALLY, for a FACT, that this is true. I healed my soul wounds by repenting of my sin and forgiving all in my past, including myself. Some were very deep traumatic wounds from those who hurt me by abuse over the years. But by repenting of my own long-held bitterness, forgiving them, and speaking a blessing over all those people, I could actually feel the weight lift off me! Soon, EVERYTHING in my life started to exponentially improve, including my marriage, my business, my finances, and even my attitude. Stress and anxiety became almost non-existent. I started quickly experiencing great breakthroughs for my goals.

My soul had to prosper first before the rest of me could. Why? The wounds in your soul from your past and from sin and trauma, if not healed, give the devil a foothold to keep you stuck in your past—stuck and spinning your wheels and going nowhere! This is why so many people are praying and praying for breakthroughs and are still waiting and waiting in frustration. You are not moving forward because there is still too much junk in your soul holding you back. It's like you are dealing with a car with all kinds of mechanical issues.

I don't know about you, but I don't want anything blocking me or slowing me down from God being able to move on my needs and requests, nor do I want the enemy sticking his foot in my way trying to slow me down or trip me up! I want to leave the enemy in my dust with tire marks over him! That's exactly what I did! I am teaching you now how to do this!

Jesus has to work *in us* before He can work *through us*.

I asked Jesus to help me take control of my own soul and through His blood and resurrection power I am restoring my soul all shiny and new and running like a top! It's ONLY through Jesus we can do this and that's the key to this entire Victory! We are victorious *through* Him. What an awesome gift! You as a believer in Christ Jesus have this gift and can do this too! That is how GOOD God is!

Jesus said, "I came that they may have life and have it abundantly." Meaning a complete life full of purpose and victory! (John 10:10).

If you have not accepted Jesus Christ as your Lord and Savior, NOW, is the time! Before you can prosper your soul and in your life, Jesus must live in you! It's good to also pray this to reconfirm your commitment to Christ.

Prayer to accept Jesus Christ as your Lord and Savior:

"Lord Jesus, for too long I've kept you out of my life. I know that I am a sinner and that I cannot save myself. I repent of all my sins. No longer will I close the door when I hear you knocking. By faith, I gratefully receive your gift of salvation. I am ready to trust You, Jesus, as my Lord and Savior. I believe Your words are true, Lord. I repent for my sins, and I ask you, Jesus, to wash away and cover all my sins and iniquities with Your blood. Come into my heart and my life, Lord Jesus, and be my Savior and my King. Thank You, Lord Jesus, for coming to earth to redeem us. I believe You are the Son of God who died on the cross for my sins, took the keys of hell and the grave, then rose from the dead on the third day. I believe that You, Jesus, then walked the earth in your glorified body and ascended into heaven. I believe You, Lord Jesus, are seated at the right hand of the Father right now ruling and reigning over all! Thank You, Jesus, that You paid the price so I could be seated with You next to the Father and become a son/daughter of God, too. I am truly sorry for my sins against God the Father and His word and grateful that they are now all covered by Your Blood, Jesus. I will not look back! I have been redeemed by the blood of Jesus Christ out of the hand of the Devil and set apart for the plans and purposes of God! Thank you Lord Jesus for taking on all my sins and giving me the gift of eternal life with You and access to Your Kingdom. Thank you, Father God, for Your grace, mercy, and love. Because of Your Son, Jesus. my sins are forgiven, cleansed, and remembered no more for Your sake. Father God, I now invite Your Holy Spirit to come and heal my soul, heal all my soul wounds and live inside of me and beside me and be my helper as I move forward doing what You have called me to do for the kingdom and Your glory, In Jesus name, Amen."

Now, let's start on getting your soul healed and prospering because Jesus made it possible:

1. Repent for any known sins and unknown sins and ask God for forgiveness.
2. Forgive anyone who has hurt you and forgive yourself.
3. Ask Jesus to wash all these sins, hurts, and bitterness with His blood.
4. Thank God for His grace, mercy, and forgiveness.
5. Ask God to remember your sins no more (wipe them out).
6. Ask God to erase the sins and bitterness from your memory (wipe them out).
7. Ask the Holy Spirit, with His resurrection power, to heal your soul wounds and prosper your soul.

Getting your soul cleaned up from sin, unforgiveness, bitterness, and past hurts is like cleaning the clutter and gunk out of your trunk! It's that cumbersome heavy stuff you have been carrying in your soul that slows you down and holds you back!

"Therefore, since we are surrounded by such a great cloud of witnesses, let us throw off everything that hinders and the sin that so easily entangles. And let us run with perseverance the race marked out for us, 2 fixing our eyes on Jesus, the pioneer and perfecter of faith." Hebrews 12

Thank Jesus and Praise Him.   Praise God for His forgiveness, grace and mercy! Focus on God's presence and talking with Him daily. Start every day covering yourself and your purpose with the blood of Jesus.

Invite the Holy Spirit to align with your spirit and soul. Speak to your soul to be well like the old hymns "All Is Well With My Soul" and "Bless The Lord Oh My Soul". (Daily praise music and singing helps me so much). King David actually called his soul "darling." He understood that you must love it as God loves it. Jesus is the lover of your soul, and that is His reward. That's why He wants to prosper your soul. It's like a shiny precious diamond to Him, and it should be to you too.

If your soul shines, you shine! It's better than Minwax!

Ask God daily to release a *fresh* anointing on you—clarity, wisdom and heavenly downloads—and show you what's in front of you. "Holy Spirit, pour fresh oil on me today in Jesus Name!" The Holy Spirit must be "invited in" to be able to fill you with His powerful presence so you can have access to God's thoughts, plans, and unlimited resources. Start your day working in this divine partnership, and God will show you exactly what you need to do. He WANTS to partner with you in your work! Think about Moses—40 days on the mountain in the presence of God. One man partnering with God saved a nation! What more can He do with you?

Alone Time With God = Strong Relationship

Do you have questions? Maybe you are not sure what your purpose is, how to start, or what to do. It's time to go through the steps I have outlined in this chapter and ASK GOD. The answers will come! Asking God for help is a sign of wisdom not weakness.

Pray this out loud: *"Father, I know you are even more passionate about my gifts and purpose than what I am.*

You want it more for me than anyone! Thank you, Father, for creating me! Today, I ask You to show me what my gifts and purpose are, and show me how to activate them according to your beautiful plans. I love you and trust you, Father! I praise You for Your goodness! I am excited to receive and carry out all you have for me in my life, in Jesus name, Amen."

God does not want to leave you lost and wandering with no direction!

"He found him out in the wilderness, in an empty, windswept wasteland. He threw his arms around him, lavished attention on him, guarding him as the apple of his eye. He was like an eagle hovering over its nest, overshadowing its young. Then, spreading its wings, lifting them into the air, teaching them to fly. God alone led him; there was not a foreign god in sight." Deuteronomy 32:10-11

LET GOD LEAD YOU! He loves you and will put every step and door in front of you. He will give you the map and every strategy. Some of them are same day miracles and breakthroughs.

EVERY promise of God is available to you! You have to agree with these promises and receive them, and let God know you are serious about becoming all He planned for you, so He can move for you in a BIG WAY. If all your efforts originate in the place of His presence and promises, you will be unstoppable!

"Work willingly at whatever you do, as though you were working for the Lord rather than for people. Remember that the Lord will give you an inheritance as your reward, and that the Master you are serving is Christ." Colossians 3:23-24

You are NOW making it happen with the power of God behind you!! This may seem like a lot to do while you are in your garage time, but it's so worth it. You will see the results!! The main thing is your own relationship with the Lord is growing stronger and stronger. But we also need the support of those around us, from our family, friends and church.

Good Ground Support Speeds Things Up:

It's good to ask for prayer support from others while you are in your garage time. Sit down with those closest to you and let them know you are getting serious about your goals and dreams, and be very clear and specific to tell them how and what to pray for you. The power of agreement is even more powerful. If there are many prayers going up to Heaven for you, make sure they are clear that they are praying for the *same thing* for you.

Cancel Any 'Soulish" Prayers, Negative Words and Curses:

Sometimes there are people around us who love us and want the best for us, but they may be praying their own will, opinions, or religious beliefs over your life and causing major *entanglements* with your progress. These are called "soulish" prayers. These are prayers and words being spoken over you, but, however the intention, can be coming against your prayers and worse, against God's word and will for your life. The spirit realm responds to what is being spoken over you, good or bad!

These "soulish" prayers, negative words, and curses spoken about you or over you—even the ones you have spoken yourself—can be working against what you are praying for now. It's like a "spider's web." These negative words and prayers are in the atmosphere and are trying to entangle our prayers and decrees. We need to break down any webs or entanglements in the spirit realm now. We need to cancel any negative words or soulish prayers anyone has prayed for us that is not in alignment with our prayers and decrees and forgive the people who did it. Then, ask the Angelic Hosts of Heaven to come and get our prayers and decrees out of any entanglements and expedite them to our Father God to be fulfilled in Jesus' name and ask God to release his Holy Fire to burn up the webs so your prayers never get entangled again!

For about a year, I found myself making progress with my prayer life and my breakthroughs. Then there would be times of great stalling. I kept rebuking the enemy and still much stalling. I asked the Holy Spirit to show me what was going on. One morning, I saw a *praying mantis* caught in a web outside my bedroom window right near my place of prayer! I heard the Holy Spirit say to me that I was asking the wrong people to pray for me and my prayers were caught up in a web—getting entangled and not going anywhere. There were well meaning people in my life praying "soulish prayers." They were praying for their own will, opinions, and religious beliefs on me! These people meant well and some were in my own family! However, it was totally coming against and throwing confusion into the spirit realm against my own prayers.

Now, I don't ask *certain people* to pray for me anymore, or I tell them how to specifically pray for me! I realized in a conversation with my Mom that she had been inadvertently praying something completely different for me than I had been praying! She meant well—BUT NO—it was stalling me. I asked her to pray like this: "Mom, just say, Lord, I come into agreement with what my daughter is praying for at this time." She happily agreed to do that. I also realized that prayers prayed on the rosary to Mary (and catholic saints) were actually religious prayers and UNBIBLICAL.

We are supposed to pray directly to the Father in the name of Jesus, as Jesus instructed us to. Soulish prayers that I had prayed in the past when I was "religious," were still in the spirit and causing *entanglements* with my new prayer life as a Born Again Believer.

Those old soulish prayers were holding things back!! I was alarmed at the fact that all these soulish and religious prayers needed to be cancelled and renounced immediately. If not cancelled, you could be stalled and stalled and stalled. I know you are here to learn about acceleration of blessing and breakthroughs in your life, and this could be a major thing coming against it! I want to be clear, I honor Mary and her faith and all the faithful ones who went before me. However, we are *all* saints as believers and followers of Christ. We are all Kings and Priests. I do not need the intercession of a saint in Heaven with God when Jesus clearly said He is the only one between us and the Father! We do have a "cloud of witnesses" that the Bible states in Hebrews 12. They are witnessing Jesus *Christ's* intercession for us. They are cheering for us to fulfill our assignments on the earth for Jesus to receive His reward and us to receive our rewards in Heaven. We do not need them to go to the Father for us —only Jesus Christ. He is our High Priest. We agree with what *Jesus* prays about us to the Father.

I might offend some of you with deep set religious beliefs. I had to overcome these old beliefs myself. I will tell you, I love all believers in Christ. I love all people. I know many Holy Spirit filled Catholics. No matter what Church or denomination you attend, I pray for the guidance of the Holy Spirit and for you to fulfill what God has called you to do. I believe Jesus is dealing with all the religious denominations right now and getting His church back as "one" like it was in the Book of Acts. I want each person to hear from Jesus themselves on this matter, as I have. Jesus said we will know everything by its fruit. Jesus also did not like "religious law." He was all about the kingdom and revealing who He was and is for us. I want to tell you, as soon as I cancelled these soulish and religious prayers off my life I had a huge breakthrough, great fruit, and acceleration. Confirmation! Thank You Jesus!

Pray this prayer to get these soulish prayers canceled ASAP:

"Father in the name of Your Son, Jesus, I thank You for Your grace and mercy and hearing my prayers. Right now, I cancel and mark null and void any soulish, superstitious, or religious prayers that have been prayed by myself or others over me and my life! I repent for these types of prayers because they are not in accordance with your word and your will. Lord Jesus, cover these sins and soulish prayers with Your blood. I ask that all these soulish, superstitious, opinionated, judgemental, religious, and false prayers are now washed from the atmosphere, blotted out of the record books, and wiped away forever by Your blood, Lord Jesus! I forgive those who have been praying these soulish, religious, and opinionated prayers. I ask Your Holy Spirit to guide me in my prayer life. I ask that all soulish, religious, and opinionated prayers coming against my breakthrough be completely removed, cancelled, and marked null and void forever! I decree today that my true prayer is this_____. I ask that this prayer come directly to You Father in the name of Jesus, and I ask for my own prayers and decrees according to Your will, Father, that have been held up in the spirit realm be released now directly to Your throne, Father God, and I ask for restoration of any time that was held back or stalled. Thank you, Holy Spirit, for revealing this to me! I ask for

Your angels to be assigned, Father God, to block any soulish, religious, or opinionated prayers being prayed against me and God's will for me, so they will never entangle or come against my prayers or decrees again, in Jesus' name! I decree I am no longer in agreement with the prayers of _____. I cancel them in the name of Jesus! Holy Spirit, please go to these people and give them guidance in their prayer life with the truth. Also, alert me any time a soulish prayer is coming against me and who I need to not ask for prayer from. I believe in the power of agreement in your word, Father, and I will now ask for my advocate, the Holy Spirit, to come into agreement with my prayers today. I also ask for Holy Spirit filled prayer intercessors to come into my life who pray according to your will, Father, and in agreement with my personal prayers and decrees and I with theirs. I also come into agreement with your intercession for me, Lord Jesus! Thank You for your mercy and grace, Father, I am excited to see Your glory at work in my life, in Jesus' name! Amen!" (If the Holy Spirit shows you a specific person in your life who is praying soulish, opinionated, or religious prayers over you, ask that their prayers be cancelled in Jesus' name!)

Canceling Curses and Negative Words Decree:

"In the name of Jesus, I rebuke and renounce every assignment of the enemy and cancel every curse or negative word ever spoken over me or my family right now! I cover every negative word in the Blood of Jesus Christ, including every negative word I have ever spoken over myself. I repent for speaking any negative words over myself or anyone else. I decree that every negative word and every curse spoken against me is now null and void in Jesus name! I decree I am blessed, redeemed, and covered in the blood of Jesus! I have been set apart for

the plans and purposes of Almighty God as a blood-bought believer in Jesus Christ! I decree the favor of God surrounds me as a shield! I decree the glory of God is my covering! I also keep up my shield of faith and extinguish every fiery dart coming against me. No weapon formed against me shall prosper, and I command every curse of witchcraft sent to harm me be returned back to the place it was sent, in Jesus' mighty name and by the power of His blood that covers me and protects me! Amen and so be it!"

Get Laser Targeted:

Recently, I had another conversation about prayer with my mom, and she said, "Annamarie, you are my daughter and I want to pray for you." Then I asked her, "*What* do you want to pray for me?" She told me very basic prayers like health, safety etc. I told her; "Mom, right now, I need a breakthrough on a very specific thing." I then gave her my direction and strategy and she was very excited to be able to pray that specifically for me! Now, she can celebrate with me when the breakthrough comes! It's awesome having my mom asking me to send her specific prayers and it's a beautiful thing we share together! She knows now to pray directly to the Father in Jesus' name. We have seen great breakthroughs together!

If you have a specific prayer strategy and then *multiply* it with more people praying for you in unity with laser targeting on a detailed specific prayer, it's going to add power to your request to God like high octane rocket fuel! This is the *power of agreement.*

"Pray for us, that the word of the Lord may speed ahead and be honored, as happened among you." 2 Thessalonians 3:1

Wow, this has already been some good "garage time" so far! I have been giving you some major strategies to get you cleaned up, scrubbed down to the nuts and bolts, and ready to rebuild and restore even better than before—a lean mean faster machine, right?   Are things coming to mind for you at this very moment that are getting you excited to get fully into your "garage-time" mode? Awesome!

Remember when I said it's already in your DNA to have divine gifts and a purpose?   It made me think about the traits of determination and the gifts for boldness in my family bloodline.   Draw some inspiration from that!   God puts blessings on family bloodlines! Everyone talks about a family bloodline curse but never thinks of the family blessing! That's an actual *anointing*—fully activated divine gift with the power of the Holy Spirit upon it—and even a *mantel*—a divine covering/authority of the Holy Spirit for a specific kingdom purpose—that can be passed from generation to generation! Think of the late Reverend Billy Graham, now his son and daughter and grandsons and granddaughters are carrying on his powerful ministry! Think for a moment, do you have a relative or an ancestor who did something really amazing by using their gifts? Who overcame adversity to reach a great goal?

God had your family purposes planned since the beginning of time!   Maybe it's YOU that is destined to become the one who will inspire your descendants to do great things for generations to come! Be that one!

USE YOUR GIFTS FEARLESSLY SO THE THE NEXT GENERATIONS ARE INSPIRED BY YOUR FAITH!

Your family may have paved a way in the past for you or not, but NOTHING can compare to what you have available to you *now*! As a born again believer in Jesus Christ, you now have *His DNA,* and you are grafted into the blessings and promises God made to Abraham, whom God calls a "Father to all the families of the earth." Abraham obeyed and agreed with God and became a *very* prosperous and *very* wealthy man. You now have access to all this inheritance!

"And if you belong to Christ, then you are Abraham's descendants, heirs according to promise." Galatians 3:29

Set Up Your GOOD WORK Environment:

When Moses went up on the mountain for 40 days, the Israelites started acting up like hoodlums without his leadership. When Moses came back down, all heck was breaking loose with golden idols and rebellion! Chaos is the last thing you need going on around you when you are working in your "garage time." If you are in a leadership position in your household and everyone relies on you, it's important to sit everyone down and have a talk before you go into your "garage time." Let them know you are taking some very important time to work on your goals, and you need their FULL support and THEY have to take on some leadership and responsibility so you can focus on the next step God has for you. Explain how this will bless everyone if they are obedient with you and God. Pray a prayer of agreement together as a family that you all will work together to help and support each other while you take this time to do what you need to do.

I had to ask my husband and daughter to take on the responsibilities of the house—laundry, dinner, errands, etc —while I was working on this book and my new ministry.

Trust me, there were times that I had to put "do not disturb" notes on my door and not freak out if they were eating potato chips and ice cream for supper! LOL!

But God came through for us. I stayed in peace and focused on my work, and my family was very supportive through the process. This is also a great example I am setting for my daughter on how she can activate her goals and dreams too!

Those of you who need to take time off from work to do this, give up family vacation time, give up hobbies or even give up stuff you enjoy for a while, do not hesitate—give it up and get into your "garage time!" God will bless you doubly for your trouble later when you obey Him on this *now*. Your divine purpose is waiting on *you*! You may be activating a huge financial breakthrough waiting for you and your family too!

Fear Is the Enemy of Your Victory

Are you experiencing fear or hesitation? Maybe something is holding you back from moving forward on your "garage time." Fear is a lie from the enemy to stop you from your God given purpose. Speak this scripture over yourself every time you feel fear:

"For God has not given me a spirit of fear, but of power and of love and of a sound mind." 2 Timothy 1:7

If you are experiencing fear, hesitation in getting started, or dealing with roadblocks, that is not from God! Take authority in Christ over your fears, hindrances, and any roadblocks right now, in Jesus' name! You are on a mission from God in this race! I have a chapter coming up where I show you how to overcome all these roadblocks and drive through these issues with ease.

You KNOW you want to get started right? You know it's TIME to make this happen! I want this to happen for you RIGHT NOW. It's time to get into your garage and no more waiting on your goals, dreams and ideas! It's time to work on them and put them into action!

Begin Your Daily Strategy To Be Productive In Your 'Garage Time':

1. **Suit UP** (Put on Your Armor of God and Take Your Seat of Authority in Christ)
2. **Remove Distractions** (TV, News, Social Media)
3. **Get Into God's Frequency** - Play a recording of the Shofar or Praise Music
4. **Listen For Downloads** from the Holy Spirit
5. **Watch For Signs** from the Holy Spirit
6. **Journal** (Write down what God is showing and speaking to you! Record your dreams. Look for repeating colors and numbers you are seeing. Is there a scripture that is standing out on a certain day? These are all guiding messages from the Holy Spirit. This is the way to connect the dots and get your divine strategies. I use a composition notebook so I can draw and write what is being shown to me. It's amazing how many answers and steps I have been able to receive from God!
7. **Outline Your Vision** and goals and get it posted up where you can see it daily
8. **Ask For Confirmation** (Prepping for each assignment and ultimately to be fully walking in your purpose comes easily with step by step instructions from the Holy Spirit. Don't be shy in asking the Holy Spirit for confirmation with each step. Jesus said the Holy Spirit is your helper and will reveal things to you! Ask Him, "Holy Spirit,

show me a color, animal, number etc to confirm to me that this is the right step and it's from God.")

9. **Be Obedient** (Apply What God Shows You - Take the steps - put your feet to your faith)
10. **Declare and decree** over your vision!   Call it forth in Jesus name!

Declare: *"Father God I believe You will accelerate Your will for my life because I put my trust in You!   I believe Your word is Your will for me.   Father, Your word says in Mark 11:24, 'Therefore I tell you, whatever you ask for in prayer, believe that you have received it, and it will be yours.'   So, Father, this is my desire of my heart: this is what I am asking for in prayer right now_____.   I believe I have received it by faith in Jesus' name!"*

Keep decreeing and standing firm on the word of God. Don't allow anyone to discourage you or make you feel guilty for taking this time to prepare. God First. When you put God first you will never be last! Your obedience brings supernatural breakthroughs.

BE ENCOURAGED!   GOD WILL REWARD YOUR FAITH AND TIME YOU TOOK WORKING WITH HIM IN YOUR "GARAGE'" PREPARING FOR THE "RACE"

Stay Seated In Christ Jesus!

Our Champion and King, Jesus Christ, is working through us! Jesus already did all the heavy lifting on the Cross for us, so trust Him to pull you through the hard stuff! Take your seat of Authority in Christ Jesus every day! It makes a HUGE difference!

I highly recommend the book, *The Authority of the Believer,* by Dr. Billye Brim.   It changed my life when I realized the level of authority I truly have and that Jesus paid for! The enemy hardly ever can mess with me anymore. My daily productivity went from about 4 to 10 when I began to take my daily seat of authority in Christ Jesus, and I put everything from the kingdom of darkness under my feet! Now I tell Satan where to go—far below me —because I am seated in the NAME ABOVE ALL NAMES! You know that's right!

We Overcome By The Blood of The Lamb and The Word of Our Testimony

This "garage time" will be the most powerful story and testimony of your life! I know you want to inspire others, and that's my most favorite thing—to hear stories of people like you and me who believed in going after their dream and had the faith and fortitude to get serious and get it done!

I have some inspiration for you too! I would like to share a wonderful true story of my uncle who decided to take his own "garage time" (actually in his basement). This is a modern David and Goliath story that will change the way you look at yourself and your situation, read on….

Uncle Dan - Basement Millionaire

I was much younger when this amazing thing happened for my Uncle Daniel Malfitana, a retired Navy Chief. In the early 80's, after leaving the Navy, my Uncle had tried his hand at many different jobs and businesses looking to create something good for his family, including running a farm stand during the summers where we would go and help stack watermelons and lettuce. We had so much fun working with him and our cousins. Uncle Dan was a hard worker. He always put 110% into everything he did. He was a leader. He loved people and was good at creating solutions for others. These were his God-given gifts.

One year in the mid 1980's, my Uncle Dan was working a 9-5 job at a well-known electric and technology corporation in Upstate New York. He was building and organizing their computer systems and client training, which included military contracts. He had done a great job for them, and they sent him and his family to the west coast to build a program for the company. He threw himself into it—created the program, hired people, and had everything in place. He purchased a home and bought furniture, ready for his family to move in, and they were on the way.

A few days later, the company executives came to him out of the blue and said they wanted to drop the program out west with no real explanation. My Uncle could not understand why, because everything was all set up perfectly and ready to go. He went and had meetings with them, and, no matter what he did, he could not convince them to keep it. They wanted him to just shut it down and move back east. This really upset my Uncle, and he looked at the company executives in the face and said, "Well, I resign from this company and I will go and get these contracts myself!" The company executives laughed at him! This made my Uncle even more determined, and he told them, "Watch me."

Uncle Dan and his family moved back home to Syracuse, New York to a rented house. My aunt was working in a shoe store to make ends meet. She started to see her husband go down in the basement every day into a makeshift office with a phone and an old desktop computer and spend hours on end working on something top secret. One day, he came upstairs and said, "Maryellen, I am going to go and get these military training contracts. I am going to go up against all the other big companies and get it. I am going to be working on my proposal, and I just need you to make me coffee and meals and be patient while I do this."

My aunt was always a devoted military wife and fully supported her husband on this next adventure. She trusted in his gifts and believed he could do it.

As for me, in my early twenties at the time, I remember when my uncle was taking this serious "basement time" because, when I went over there to hang out with my cousins, my uncle came upstairs and it looked like he had not slept for weeks! He was wearing a rumpled T-shirt and his beard was all grown out. I hardly recognized him!

My Aunt said to us, "Try to be quiet because your uncle is working on something very important. Please do not disturb him."

At the time, I really did not "get" what was going on or the importance of it until later in life.

One day, just a few weeks later, my aunt said my uncle got up early in the morning, shaved off his beard, put on a nice suit, and, with his finished proposal, he told my aunt, "Maryellen, when I go out this door today we could become millionaires or not, but I am going to give this everything I've got." He was off to his meeting to present his proposal to the government to go up against all the corporate big guns.

Now that is FAITH and knowing without a doubt you have the gift to do something great with no fear.

A week or so later, an official letter came from the US Government; my Uncle Dan opened it. It was good news. He got the military contracts. He beat out his former employer and the other big corporations! My aunt said he held up the letter and yelled, "Maryellen, we are millionaires; go quit your job at the shoe store!"

I remember things changed quickly for my Uncle Dan and his family, and there were celebrations and joyful happenings at their house with lots of food! Uncle Dan went on for many successful years performing and serving on these military contracts. They traveled to Spain and lived there for a year for my uncle to do consulting, and even took my grandmother on a trip to Italy. My cousins all got new computers almost every Christmas, and they moved to a beautiful big house in Maryland. He retired years later to Virginia Beach with a nice nest egg and was asked back into the Navy as a Master Chief, which is one of the Navy's highest honors, to serve as a mentor to other officers and upcoming officers.

I loved my uncle and I looked up to him, but I did not realize the lesson in all this and the impact of what he had done back in that "basement time." I was young and all I saw was one day he was wearing an old T-shirt and growing a beard, and the next day he was driving a brand new Lincoln Continental and going out for steak and lobster. Looking back, I really wish I had taken the time to understand what was really happening—asked more questions and learned more for my young mind.

In 2011, my Uncle Daniel Malfitana sadly passed away from cancer. He knew when his time was near so he told my Aunt Maryellen to take him to the Navy Hospital where the doctors and nurses all stood up and saluted him "Master Chief" as he left this world. At his funeral, they told the story in detail on how he got the big government contracts—the time in the basement and what he was preparing down there. I was absolutely floored. I was so inspired and so encouraged by the fact that he knew what his gifts were, and he was upset that the people he worked for would not use and appreciate his gifts! He knew he was meant for something greater, and he had enough faith and determination to go up against the biggest corporations in America! Uncle Dan used what he had at hand, had faith, and took his "garage time" (basement time) to make it happen. Uncle Dan, by great determination, went up against the giant corporations and defeated them. Who's laughing now?

I come from that strong and bold family bloodline and DNA, but I now also have the DNA of the King of Kings, Jesus Christ. As I sat in that funeral saying goodbye to my Uncle Dan, in his very last moment on earth, he left me a huge gift—I knew I could do anything and I could defeat any giants in front of me! I could get that big dream no matter what was against me and no matter who laughed at me. Yes I can! It changed my life when I came to this realization. Plus, I have GOD! What can a mere man do to me? Ha! It's fixed in my favor!

We are meant to use our God-given gifts fearlessly, even if people laugh at us. If God is behind it, nothing can come against it.

Think, what is GOOD in your DNA—who in your family did something extraordinary and brave? What did God put into your family bloodline that you also have? Most of all, WHO lives inside of you now? The KINGDOM of God is within you. You have the Spirit of Almighty God—King of the Universe is with you! Time for you to RUN towards that Giant. You will take the giant down and you will win!

"David said to the Philistine, 'You come against me with sword and spear and javelin, but I come against you in the name of the Lord Almighty, the God of the armies of Israel, whom you have defied.'" 1 Samuel 17:45

Activation Prayer:

"Father, I thank You for bringing me to this moment. I am excited to start working on my goals and getting serious about them. Father, your word says in Proverbs 16:3, that if I commit my work to You, my plans will be established.

Today, I commit all my work to You, Father God! I invite Your Holy Spirit, Father, to come and help me get everything I need to create my workspace. Bring me the tools and strategies I need to succeed! Give me downloads from Heaven, Lord! I ask for complete clarity and focus for the task at hand, in the name of Jesus! Father, I trust the great plans you have for me. I say, 'YES, I am ready to get to work today!' Help me with my loved ones, Father, so they can understand and support me during this time. I also ask for provision and protection over me and my household as I build and work on the gifts, goals, assignments, and calling that You, Father, have given me in my life. I will boldly work with no excuses or distractions because I know Your Holy Spirit is with me, Father. I can do all things through Christ who strengthens me! I decree my "garage" work time WILL have abundantly fruitful results that shall multiply and bless my household for years to come! I give You all the glory and praise, Father, for this opportunity to work with You in our *garage" time together. With You, Father, nothing is impossible! I thank, YOU, Father God, for the coming breakthrough and blessing from this work time. It starts NOW, in Jesus' Name! Amen"

Let's get 'er done and roll outta this garage ready to rock and take the win!

CHAPTER 3
SEE YOUR VICTORY!

Since this is a book about faith, not just normal faith, high powered *FAITH AT FULL SPEED*, I want to talk about your ultimate win—your victory that comes because of your faith. It's inevitable. The victory will happen, but you must **see it** before you achieve it.

"Now faith is the substance of things hoped for, the evidence of things not seen." Hebrews 1:11

I like to call this, seeing your "victorious result" before it happens.

Fear looks back. Faith looks forward.

Let's talk about looking forward, BOLDLY.

When a driver straps into their race car before a race, they must have the mindset that they are going for the win, nothing else. Drivers prepare as if they are ready for battle. There is no sense going into a battle if you don't have a winning mindset. This begins with what you see and believe is in front of you and that victory IS attainable without a doubt. The most successful race drivers I have worked with over the years have a winning mindset. They see their victory even before they hit the track. This also applies to you, your calling, and your purpose.

"The horse is made ready for the day of battle, but victory rests with the LORD." Proverbs 21:31

The first thing you need to do is make a decision to be BOLD with your goals, and take that first step to prepare for your own "race" to victory. Many of you have a lot of fear moving forward. I know, because I used to have a lot of fear. My bible teacher and mentor in NASCAR, "Miss Jackie" (Jackie Pegram) said to me, "You can't have faith and fear at the same time - you must choose one or the other." That was a huge teaching moment for me. I never looked at fear again as an uncontrollable emotion. I focused on cancelling it out with faith. That is my daily goal, as it should be yours. Faith trumps fear every time! As soon as I start to feel fear creep up on me, I remember Miss Jackie's lesson, and I go to the word of God. God's promises embolden my faith to move forward fearlessly!

Ask yourself, do you need to cancel some fears? What's keeping you from starting on your goals, visualizing and reaching your victory? When you give in to fear towards your goals, it's like swimming in the ocean to your treasure island, you start out strong but eventually you start to bleed "fear" and the sharks are attracted to it - and start to circle you, waiting to take you out! You stop focusing on the treasure in front of you and instead on the sharks. The wounds from your past are causing fear in your soul! The enemy uses fear against you, to stop you, block you and slow you down from reaching your God given destiny! Hindering rewards of the kingdom that the Lord has promised you! It's a common tactic in the military to find out the weaknesses of your opponent and use those weaknesses to undermine them. The biggest weakness is to play on their fears in order to beat them. You know you want to win; you know what you desire - but it's that fear, distractions, excuses or plain old lack of FAITH that gets in your way! Faith is a sink or swim deal in your life. It just is.

"If you do not stand firm in your faith, you will not stand at all." - Isaiah 7:9

Standing Strong In Faith:

I want to encourage you! God has the battle plan and has your Victory waiting for you. He tells us exactly HOW to win by Faith. He shows us how to apply our faith strategically and He sends us all the help we need. I have discovered this and want to share this in some easy steps for you.

In the old testament, the Israelites knew they were facing giants, unknown territories with big armies when God told them to take the Promised Land. They were scared and doubtful. Their lack of faith in God's promises kept them stuck in the desert for 40 years. But it was time, time to move forward. What did God say to their leader, Joshua?

"Have I not commanded you? Be strong and courageous. Do not be afraid; do not be discouraged, for the LORD your God will be with you wherever you go." - Joshua 1:9

THAT WAS THE FIRST THING GOD TOLD JOSHUA!

Not go right or left, go up a hill, or tell this one or that one to do this or that... GOD TOLD HIM NOT TO FEAR.
I totally believe when you replace fear with faith you are unstoppable!

FAITH IS THE VICTORY. It's time to take your Promised Land! Are you ready? Let's do this!

Faith Over Fear - Steps To Your Victory:

1) **Don't worry about what people will think.** Only what God thinks matters, He is the One that will advance you. *"The fear of the LORD is the beginning of wisdom, And the knowledge of the Holy One is understanding. For by Me your days will be multiplied, and years of life will be added to you."* - Proverbs 9:10-11

2) **The competition is irrelevant.** Stay focused on your own race and not what anyone else is doing. *"Do you not know that in a race all the runners run, but only one receives the prize? Run in such a way as to take the prize."* - 1 Corinthians 9:24

3) **You and your unique calling are designed to win - God has fully equipped you.** As I taught you in the first chapter of this book, you are like a high-performance engine, fully equipped inside to successfully achieve your goals, calling and purpose. Your gifts are already designed in you by God. You just need to activate your gifts by faith. *"A man's gift makes room for him and brings him before great men."* - Proverbs 18-16

4) **Believe, trust and take joy in God's promises in His word.** God is looking to advance those who take delight in Him and agree with Him. *"Take*

delight in the LORD, and He will give you the desires of your heart." - Psalm 37:4

5) **Know God is with you ALL the time.** He never leaves you or forsakes you. He even goes ahead of you to make your way safe and prosperous. He encourages you all the way! *"The LORD himself goes before you and will be with you; He will never leave you nor forsake you. Do not be afraid do not be discouraged" - Deuteronomy 31:8*

6) **See and feel the result you desire in your mind, body, heart and spirit.** Visualize your goals and dreams, it's yours for the taking! *"Now faith is the substance of things hoped for, the evidence of things not seen." Hebrews 11:1*

7) **Praise God ahead of time for the victory!** God inhabits the praises of His people. Your praise brings Him close. Praising Him for what you are believing for is a testament to your great faith in Him. It shows you want to celebrate HIS goodness coming in your life. *"Sing and rejoice, O daughter of Zion: for, lo, I come, and I will dwell in the midst of thee, saith the LORD." – Zechariah 2:10*

8) **Put God first and you will never be last.** God wants you to be victorious because He created you

to be. When you put Him First, you bring in all the promises of the Kingdom God has for you. Love God more than your dream or vision. Serve God not your purpose. Your purpose is a gift from God. Love your Gift Giver, your Heavenly Father - He is the source of all your skills, supply and needs. *"And Jesus answered him, "It is written: Worship the Lord your God and serve Him only." - Luke 4-8 "Seek the Kingdom of God above all else, and live righteously, and He will give you everything you need." Matthew 6:33*

9) **Do everything from a place of love in Christ Jesus through all rewards come.** Your purpose, calling and gifts should always be done in a way to honor God and His son, Jesus Christ. We are Jesus' reward for what He did on the cross. We are His - He is ours. The rewards for us as believers, working our divine purpose in the name of Jesus, come both on earth and in heaven! The Apostle Paul even tells of a crown that is waiting for him! I want to work towards that crown, don't you? *"I have fought the good fight, I have finished the race, I have kept the faith. From now on the crown of righteousness is laid up for me, which the Lord, the righteous judge, will award to me on that day - and not only to me, but to all who crave His appearing." - 2 Timothy 4:7-8*

10) **God will make a way where there is no way.** Your victory has very little to do with what you see

in the natural world, and more to do with what is happening in your supernatural walk with God. He has already "framed" your life out for you from the beginning of time. It's all already there waiting for you - you and your life are God's work of art, His framed masterpiece! *"By faith we understand that the universe was framed by the word of God, so that things that are seen were not made out of things which are visible." - Hebrews 11:3*

Your Cheering Section:

I have more good news for you! Just like the race car driver going for the win - you have a huge group of fans in the grandstands cheering you on! Yes, it's true!! My favorite thing to say at the end of my teaching videos is "All of Heaven Is Cheering You On!" Because they are!

"Therefore, having so vast a cloud of witnesses surrounding us, and throwing off everything that hinders us and especially the sin that so easily entangles us, let us keep running with endurance the race set before us." - Hebrews 12:1

There you go! The cloud of witnesses in heaven is your cheering section! How awesome is this!! Whooo hooo!!

Time To Clear Your Windshield:

The next step is getting clear with your vision. It's time to throw out that rear view mirror - you will not be needing it anymore! Your windshield is now your key focus.

There is a great scene in the 1970's movie, "Cannonball Run" with actor Raul Julia playing an Italian racing driver. In the scene, Franco (Raul Julia) is revving up his Ferrari at the gas station with his mechanic in the passenger seat. He then rips off the rear view mirror and throws it on the ground behind the car and says to his mechanic: "The first rule of Italian driving: What's behind me is not important." (spoken in an Italian accent) LOL...

Look up the video of the movie clip on YouTube! I have used this clip to inspire my race car drivers in my teaching conferences and they love it. Raul Julia was always one of my favorite actors, but even in this comedy role - this message is very profound!

Do this right now: Sit in a chair and act as if you are driving a race car - start revving up your engine, and symbolically rip off your rear-view mirror while saying these words: "What's behind me is NOT important!" (Italian accent optional LOL...)
YES!! Now you have put the past behind you! It's time to only look to the future. Straight ahead. Your Creator and Father has great plans for you and wants you to start calling in those plans now by your faith and actions. Time to start showing God you are serious and you believe and agree with the good things He has waiting for you!

Your Desire = Your Vision

It all starts with your vision. The vision you want for your life and that desire you have in your heart is not there by accident. God planted it there. Vision is so important to God - it is actually the difference between life and death. The bible says in Proverbs 29:18 "Where there is no vision, the people perish." What does perish mean? According to Merriam-Webster definition of PERISH is "to become destroyed or ruined, to cease to exist." Now, let's look at the word VISION: "the act or power of seeing, unusual discernment or foresight."

I am going to go a little supernatural here with you because we serve a supernatural God. The phrase "unusual discernment" jumps out at me. I have been working hand in hand with the Holy Spirit for a while now. I remember the first time I felt the presence of God come upon me. It was like love as an oil pouring over me. I felt an amazing peace - and for the first time I could hear that still small voice speaking clearly to me in my spirit. It was not in my head - but coming from my innermost being. I began talking with the Holy Spirit and realizing He was talking to me like a good friend would. The more I conversed with Him like a friend, the more direct and frequent the communication got - the clearer the vision for my future became.

I once heard a great teaching on the Holy Spirit - "The Helper" that Jesus promised us. I don't remember where I heard this teaching - but the Holy Spirit is like a co-pilot in the car with you. You are driving but He has the map and directions (and shortcuts) to your destination. *The Holy Spirit is a person.* The third person of the Holy Trinity. He is the presence of God here on earth. He is always there waiting for us to communicate with Him. Waiting eagerly to help us. We could ride in the car for miles and miles, hours and hours getting lost if we ignore Him. I don't want to ignore my co-pilot and my best friend anymore. But He must be asked to help - invited. He will not force Himself on you. It's our choice and free will to ask Him to help us. I invite the Holy Spirit to come inside me and beside me every day. I ask for wisdom, guidance and answers for that day.

I say: *"Holy Spirit, I surrender myself to your leadership. I want to see what you see, say what you would say, think what you would think, do what you would do. I ask for divine wisdom and downloads from Heaven today, and big breakthroughs for my goals today - I can only do this with Your help Holy Spirit, I ask in Jesus name, Amen!"*

With the word "discernment" this is where you start to get clear on what your gifts are, your purpose, and your true calling and how to move forward with it - step by step. Discernment is your clarity in the voice of God and instruction God is giving you.

Think of the Holy Spirit as your Crew Chief who is riding beside you and above in your race, on the radio with you - telling you what's up ahead - clearing you before the wrecks and keeping you focused and up to full speed all the way to the finish line and VICTORY! You are a powerful team!

How to work with the Holy Spirit and get clarity and guidance for your Goals and Vision:

Ask Him - Do you tell your best friend your innermost hopes and dreams? Who do you confide in? This is the exact way you can talk with the Holy Spirit. Start speaking to Him by speaking your goals, dreams and visions out loud to Him. The Bible tells us to do this in Job 22:28 "You will also declare a thing, and it will be established unto you; and the light will shine upon your ways." (The first thing I always ask for is WISDOM - especially if you are needing financial breakthrough. That is what King Solomon asked God for and He became the richest man the world has ever seen!)

Show Him - This can come in writing and posting up your goals, dreams, desires on a Vision Board and Journal - the Bible tells us to do this in Habakkuk 2:2-3   "Write the vision,
and make it plain on tablets that he who reads it may run. For the vision is yet for an appointed time; but it speaks of the end and does not lie.   If it delays, wait for it; it will surely come, it will not delay." (You can see my vision board teaching on my YouTube Channel).

Surrender to Him - This can be a hard one for those of us who are strong willed. I used to think I had all the answers and ideas, but I wondered why my goals were not happening and I had been working my butt off! It was not until I surrendered these goals (and myself) to the Holy Spirit to solve them. Only after I surrendered did I see a breakthrough with my goal (and usually bigger than expected). God's ways are greater and bigger than our ways. It's as simple as saying, "Yes Lord - I surrender to your ways to get me to this goal, I am ready for you to do this by your power and not my own!"

Hear Him - This is always the question - am I hearing the voice of God or is it my imagination? Here is the best way to know it's God speaking to you through His Holy Spirit: You won't just hear it, you will *feel it* in your spirit. You will get that check in your gut and just know. There are times where I will feel a gentle jolt in my body - when He is really trying to get my attention. Sometimes if you don't get it the first time the Holy Spirit will keep repeating it to you and show you signs throughout your day that your eye is drawn to repeatedly. Many times, I see numbers repeatedly like 111 or 222. Most of the time He will point me to scripture, that is the exact answer I needed that day. He will do everything he can to get his message across and you need to open yourself to this. There will also be confirmation that it's a message coming from God - another person, or a situation will come up to you quickly to confirm what you are hearing. These are not coincidences. This is the Holy Spirit communicating in your life.

Obey Him - Here is the big key - obedience. When the Holy Spirit opens a door, you walk through it, quickly. When He tells you to do something, do it - even if it does not make any sense. You will know the assignment is for you and it came from God because it will take some faith to do it. In my experience every time I have obeyed His steps and prodding to act on certain things - even if it was out of my comfort zone, huge rewards have come from it. God rewards obedience big time.

Take Action - God is all about action - I have learned that He does great things through His people who are action takers. So many people wait for a move of God and pray for a move of God but should realize that God is trying to move YOU on His behalf so He can bring forth your blessing. God created the world for us to thrive in. He takes pleasure in us doing great and mighty things and fills us with His power to do it. Be an action taker and show God you are grateful for this life He has given you. Do not waste another minute. Take a step, and then another. He is with you!

Expect Breakthrough - When you take the steps above you can expect the big breakthroughs that you have been praying for, needing and been obedient for. God is faithful! He will not let your faithfulness go unrewarded! According to His word, He is working all things for our good for those who love Him (Romans 8:28). He must do His word. He must stand by His promises. He WILL do what you have been faithful for! God's laws of His Creation and His Word stand the test every time and work every time! It's up to us to be faithful, agree with His ways, word and promises and work with His Holy Spirit to bring these breakthroughs to us. We are so blessed to have God's success strategy: Ask, Believe, Agree, Obey, Act and Receive! Apply these strategies by standing in unwavering faith!

Prepare The Place For It - You can do this with any goal or result you envision - this is part of activating your faith and shows God you are serious. God is attracted to BOLD faith. It also gets you into the positive expectation mindset pushing you forward.

SEE IT DONE - BELIEVE IT'S ALREADY HERE!

If you don't have bold faith yet, it's OK - Jesus said you can just start out with a bit of faith and get a big result!

"Jesus said to them, " For truly I say to you, if you have faith as a grain of mustard seed, you will say to this mountain, 'Move from here to there,' and it will move. And nothing will be impossible for you." Matthew 17:20

Activating our faith gives God pleasure! The more we activate our faith the more we please God. God rewards your faith! If you want more faith ask God for more!

"But without faith it is impossible to please him: for he that cometh to God must believe that he is, and that he is a rewarder of them that diligently seek him." - Hebrews 11:6

My Vision Truck:

My husband Mike and I really needed a new car. I had an older minivan that was paid for but was starting to fall apart. Mini vans work great when you are a new mom, and you are running kids and groceries (and a couple of big dogs) around. (Note: racing folks call minivans and station wagons "grocery getters" LOL). At the time Mike and I did not have the money for a new car, even though we desperately needed one.

Mike really wanted a pickup truck for our daily vehicle and so did I. We are country folk now, out here in the back roads and big sprawling farmlands of south Virginia Beach, "Creeds" where Mike grew up. Plus, my daughter Landry was taking an interest in horses. My hubby is no small guy - he is 6 foot 5 inches tall and the pickup truck was easier for him to drive. So, we agreed on getting a truck, but we had no credit at the time and not much of a down payment. Mike was doubtful we could get ever approved to buy one. Mike had mustard seed faith. But I was sure God would do this - I had bold faith. Even though we each had a different level of faith, let me tell you God honored our faith in such a very profound way to grow our faith at our own level.

I was working on my first vision board. I decided to go BIG with my vision and my faith for our new truck. I went to the website of the biggest Ford dealership near us and printed out a picture of the truck we were believing God for. It was a brand-new white Ford F150 four door pickup. I pinned it on my board, so I saw it every day - I even took the picture and used it on my screensaver for my laptop.

I started to speak positive words over the truck, such as; "I love my new Ford f-150 truck so much, it's so great to drive in the winter! Etc. I thanked God for it and I was faithful. He already brought it. I was activating "see things that are not as if they are" according to the Bible in Romans 4:17. I started talking about the things that we were doing with the truck with my family. I was not just *seeing* my "Victorious Result" I was also *speaking* it.

"As it is written, I have made you the father of many nations. [He was appointed our father] in the sight of God in Whom he believed, who gives life to the dead and speaks of the nonexistent things that [He has foretold and promised] as if they [already] existed." Romans 4:17 (Amp)

What we decree and declare is very powerful. This is why I add decrees in my activation prayers in these chapters of this book.

I knew I had my mouth and mind in alignment with my faith for this truck, but now it was time to put my FEET to my faith and take ACTION.

I was getting antsy waiting on my husband Mike to agree to go to the dealership with me. Mike was waiting on our financial situation to get better before he would go to a dealership. I was like but Honey, we have God!

A month went by and my husband was still wavering back and forth about it. I needed Mike on board with this 100% - I kept sending the Holy Spirit to Mike to help me! I drew two red hearts on either side of the pinned truck picture, and I said: "Look Honey, two red hearts - me and you together and our new truck!" I got him to smile! Ha! (You can't give up on those you love around you - keep them pumped up and build their faith - and keep sending your

"Helper" the great PR man The Holy Spirit on your behalf to work on your loved one for ya!)

Many times I think my husband (and everyone else) thought I was losing my mind - especially when I stopped on a trip in North Carolina with my clients at a huge Ford dealership to jump out and ask one of them to take a picture of me standing next to the exact truck style I was believing God for, with my hand on the door like it was already mine!   (true story)!!   I used it of course as a teaching moment for my clients! (I told you to be BOLD)... ha!

A few weeks later after returning from North Carolina I felt a strong urge from the Holy Spirit saying: "GO NOW" to local Ford dealerships to look at trucks.   To my joy and astonishment Mike agreed!

We started at the dealership on my vision board. We test drove a few trucks, but when it came to financing, they turned us down.   We went from dealership to dealership and they all ran our credit, and because we had no credit it was worse than having bad credit. Nobody would sell us a truck with financing.   If they did, the payments would be un-affordable through some outside program. (We had not bought anything on credit in over 7 years, and our house was given to us by Mike's family) Mike was not working at the time because of his knee injuries (he was a plumbing contractor for 20 plus years) and I had just been in business a year with my motorsports coaching company "Marketing At Full Speed". Those dealership guys running our credit were looking at us like we were a couple with no realistic options. I was still faithful! I was not going to give up I KNEW God would do this I just KNEW.

After leaving the third dealership rejection in one day, I said to Mike, let's just go get some lunch and regroup and talk over this truck thing. He said Ok. We were about to turn into the parking lot of Wendy's, waiting on a light. I could tell my husband was getting discouraged.

I felt my spirit rise up in me, sitting in my old mini van passenger seat, (thank God it was a long light) I looked up to God, raised up my hands and I said out loud: *"Lord, I believe you are going to bring us our new truck today. I don't know how You are going to do it, I don't know where it's going to come from but I am faithful. You have our truck coming for us today. I completely surrender this truck to You Father, in Jesus name Amen."*

I SURRENDERED.

I looked at Mike and said Amen? He said, "Amen". (Agreement is important in married couples of faith.) We pulled into Wendy's.

Mike had a cheeseburger with fries and I had a salad. I went back up to refill my drink, as we were walking out the door to go back to the minivan, I said to Mike; "Let's try one last dealership." He said, "OK" ….

We headed up the road to our last dealership. I was not giving up and I think at that point Mike was just going with the flow, but a little reluctantly. I knew it was all in God's hands now and I just wanted to see where HE would lead us.

We pulled into the Ford dealership in Chesapeake, VA - walked in the front showroom and saw very few people on staff in the middle of the week. A tall young man walked up to us wearing a camo (camouflage) hunting jacket, trail boots and a camo hat with a metal fish hook on the brim. He looked like one of the country boys that lived out by us in Creeds, Virginia.

"Hey folks, can I help you?" Mike and I must have looked at him surprised, because he then said; "This is my day off and I came by to catch up on some paperwork." We told him what we were looking for in a truck, and if he could run our credit again on their computers. We began to tell him about the roadblocks we had with the other places. (We wanted to be honest about it). He said: "Ok, let's see what I come up with," and we sat with him at the computer.

My husband said, "I hope you can help us out - we can put some money down, and we can make payments if you can get us approved."

The nice 'camo' salesman smiled and kept typing on the keyboard and clicking the mouse - staring diligently at the screen.

I was feeling hopeful. There was something about this young salesman in camouflage, with fish hooks on his hat, something very special. I thought, He must be a fisherman. Jesus' best friends and disciples were fishermen! I was always looking for God clues!

He stopped clicking and typing - cleared his throat, looked at Mike and I, and said; "Hey, let's go talk outside for just a minute." We followed him outside the dealership. It was just starting to mist rain. It was about two o'clock in the afternoon on a January day and unseasonably warm. We stood there and I felt something very surreal about the moment... at the time I was still learning how to discern the presence of God in a situation - looking back this was surely one of those times.

"Don't forget to show hospitality to strangers, for in doing so, some have entertained angels without knowing it." - Hebrews 13:12

The young salesman in 'camo' (as he is now known - we never got a card to remember his name) quietly says, "Listen, a good buddy of mine just bought a really nice truck down at Little Joe's Autos down the street. They will finance you for sure. I think it would be worth your time to go down there and see what's on his lot."

His words hit me like a bolt of lightning coming from the rain clouds. I said, "Oh My Goodness! Little Joe's Autos!" Joe was one of my racing sponsors years ago when I first started working in NASCAR on the #55 racing team. I knew he was here in Virginia, but I never got around to reconnecting with him when I moved here. We had been good friends, we had shared in our team victories on the track, did plenty of successful racing promos and business together but that was years ago! I had not seen him or talked to him since 1998!

We thanked the nice young salesman in camo and jumped in the minivan. As we headed down the Boulevard to Little Joe's Autos, I started to allow some doubt creep in, I don't know why, maybe because I was feeling stupid and little bit of hurt pride because I had not thought of Little Joe's myself? I said to Mike, "I did not think of Little Joe's! I thought he just sold Mitsubishi's now not trucks. I mean I KNOW Joe but I would never think he would have any trucks there."

My hubby Mike was trying to be funny, "Well that's what you get fer thinkin," He said in his Virginian southern drawl and gave me a half smile look. I did not find it amusing. I was trying to keep my brain and my mouth from going into full 'negative nellie' mode.

As we drove, something checked me in my spirit and I thought, "There is a reason that young camo salesman is sending us to Joe's, stay faithful, God has got this now be quiet and stay calm!!" (Thank you, Holy Spirit!)

This is the point where we must trust and watch our mouths in the process. If we allow doubt or pride to well up in us, negative comments can come out of our mouths that can actually cancel what you are believing God for. (I have learned this the hard way.) You must keep that "child like" faith that Jesus tells us we should have. Staying always in positive expectation as God brings you on the journey to where he has your blessing waiting. I have learned to stop myself when I start to doubt or complain and just say 'God's got this' to keep *my mouth* in check!

We got to Little Joe's Autos, it was still misting rain and we pulled in and drove around. I saw all the new Mitsubishi cars that Joe had featured in the front of his lot. We drove further and there were actually a few trucks on the lot! We parked and decided to get out and go walk around and investigate closer. There were about 5 used pickup trucks there, newer and older models, but not really what we needed or were looking for.

Now, Mike looked really discouraged. I pulled myself back into my positive expectation state and I said, "Honey, let's just walk in and talk to someone and tell them what the nice young salesman in camo told us at the other dealership."

So, we walked in and a big smiling guy the size of an NFL linebacker wearing a windbreaker with a "Little Joe's Autos" logo embroidered on it met us at the door.

"Come on in!" He exclaimed. "It's pretty wet out there! Can I offer you some coffee or soda?"

Faith rose within me. Hope was fluttering back all through my mind, body and spirit as I stepped into Joe's small dealership showroom - it seemed so comfortable and familiar to me. Like a childhood friend's house.

Mike explained to the big friendly salesman why we were there and what we were looking for.

The big friendly salesman - whose name was "Torrey", said; "Hmmm, did you look and see what trucks we have on the lot?"

Mike said, "Yes we looked, but we did not see anything that would work for us in price, year or model."

Torrey said, "I am sorry but that's all we have right now, but if you come back in a couple weeks, we might have more trucks."

I looked at Mike and I saw complete defeat in his face.

Mike was like Ok, let's just head home, with one foot out the door. But I did not want to move. I was going to believe God. He was going to bring our truck today. I just knew! I stood firm. I was not leaving.

When it looks impossible, that's when God wants to remind us of His infinite power!

"Ah Lord GOD! Behold, You have made the heavens and the earth by Your great power and by Your outstretched arm! Nothing is too difficult for You!" Jeremiah 32:17

"Wait! I said, "I really would like to say hello to Joe, we are old friends - is he here?"

Torrey answered me; "Go over to the lady at the service window and she will check for you."

I walked over and asked: "Hi, I am an old friend of Joe and his wife from our racing days in NASCAR, I have not seen him in years and would love to say hello."

She said, "Ok, Joe is out but will be back in about 20 minutes, can I take your name?"

"Yes, please just tell him Annamarie from NASCAR team #55." I said.

"Got it, " she said. "Help yourself to coffee or a soda while you are waiting."

Joe must have a coffee and soda deal, I thought. This is the second time I was offered it, or God is really wanting me to take the time to finish a cup of coffee here.

Mike grabbed a chair and started watching the weather channel on the provided TV in the waiting area, and said to me - "I know you want to see Joe, but we need to be home soon for Landry." (Our teen daughter) who was coming home after being with friends after school.

I started pouring a coffee and said, "This shouldn't take long."

I could tell that my husband was just ready to call it a day on the truck thing, but I was staying in faith. We did not come this far for nothing - I felt that God had a plan even still for today at 4pm on that rainy afternoon.

Even still God, even still You are here.

I started walking around the showroom, and I came upon a large glass display case. It was filled with Joe's personal NASCAR memorabilia (Joe was our sponsor but had also owned his own team - actually one he bought into when I was working with him back in the 90's.)

I looked through the glass case and something caught my eye, it was a large 8x10 framed picture of the #55 NASCAR team with our winning driver Tim Fedewa in Victory Lane at Nazareth Speedway in Pennsylvania back in 1995. In the team photo was Joe, his wife Shirley and me! We were all doing the number one sign with our hands! I knew that photo, I had one myself in my scrapbook at home - and remembered that day well!

That moment looking at that Victory Lane photo from years ago was a sure sign from the Lord that we would be victorious today. I started praying quietly and thanking God for His faithfulness.

Suddenly, I hear someone call out, "Hey, Anna Banana!"

I looked up and it was Joe coming down from his office. 'Anna Banana' was my nickname on the race team. I was so surprised he remembered it!

Many things have changed since I saw Joe. I was now married with a child, put on a few more pounds and had colored my hair blonde (from my natural brunette) not to mention my hair was frizzed out from the rain! I must have looked like a sight! But I did not care, I felt God's favor at that moment.

Joe was as I remembered him, tall, slim and thinning more on top of his head - we both looked older, but his personality was still the same as was mine! We opened the conversation about NASCAR racing! (of course) Ha!

I introduced Joe to Mike and then he said, "What brings you guys here today?"

We told him about the truck we were looking for. We were pretty detailed on what we wanted.

Joe looked at us both and said, "Great, I will have your truck here in twenty minutes."

Whoa, What?! I was shocked at his response that quickly.

Then, Joe walked back into his office.

Mike and I took a deep breath and looked at each other. We went over to the front entrance to the dealership and waited.

Approximately twenty minutes later, a beautiful shiny Ford F150 pickup truck pulled up in front of us. It was everything we wanted, mileage, price, year - we had a white color in mind and white was on my vision board - but this one was BRIGHT RED.

The look on my husband's face was priceless - shock, surprise, disbelief. But, I was OVERCOME with JOY of the GOODNESS of GOD.

Our salesman Torrey was beside us and went out with us to check over the truck, "Here you go, take a test drive." He said.

We jumped in the truck, Mike behind the wheel. The truck was used but in almost new condition. It had a V8 motor and had some power which both of us really were excited about. (That was an extra bonus from God because He knows us.) All of the other trucks we test drove at the other dealerships were only V6's.

Mike and I were like two teenagers on our first date test driving that truck. We knew immediately it was perfect.

Wheeling back into Little Joe's, Torrey met us and said, "What do you think?" "WE LOVE IT!" Mike and I said in unison. We could not wipe the smiles off our faces! We were giddy and delirious after all we had been through - it was almost too good to be true.

BUT GOD.

"Ok." Said Torrey, "Let's go over to my desk and get you all set to take her home!"

Within 30 minutes we had the approved financing agreements with affordable payments. While we finalized and signed the paperwork they had taken the truck back to be vacuumed and cleaned up for us to take home.

They even took our old minivan as a trade in.

Praise be to God!

With hugs to Torrey, I wanted to tell Joe thank you, but he had already left the building, so I gave him a big thank you shout out in a tweet later on social media.

I was in a surreal state of God's favor. I felt as if Heaven had opened up and God was watching and orchestrating the scene, and I could feel His presence and pleasure on the entire thing.

That red truck was not on Joe's lot when we got there. But by the steps God had in place, He made sure it showed up when we showed up.

"For we walk by faith and not by sight." - 2 Corinthians 5:7

We left Little Joe's in our new truck and arrived home just in time to surprise our daughter as she was returning home too.

God's timing is impeccable.

I was praising God all the way back home and all night and the next day too! Mike was too. This truck miracle built my husband's faith so much. I was so glad we stayed faithful that day - and boy did GOD show up in a BIG way!

God Loves YOU! God Wants Good For YOU!

If you ask me what my favorite verse is in the Bible, it's Romans 8:28 - the goodness of God.

"And we know that in all things God works for the good of those who love him, who have been called according to his purpose." Romans 8:28

Thank you, Father for bringing our truck!

Every time I see my beautiful red pickup truck in my driveway it's a reminder of God's wonderful promises.

When we agree with God's word, activate our faith with our vision - surrender to Him and follow the steps with the help of the Holy Spirit - we can expect that God has the best coming to us!

God also provided every payment for our truck. Now, as I am writing this we have fully paid off this truck. We own it now, debt free and it still looks beautiful and runs great! If God brings it, he will provide for it! I might add that this truck has carried me to my many land prayer assignments! Why did this all come together so miraculously? Because I surrendered to God for this vehicle, it's from the Kingdom, from God's hand and Mike came into agreement. We trusted God, and when you seek the Kingdom first - ALL things will be added unto you, not just the truck itself, but God has taken care of everything having to do with it since that day!

Because of Jesus Christ and His work on the Cross, we as believers have all God's Kingdom available to us! When God raised Jesus from the dead, and seated Him at His right hand, we were seated with Him. The second most powerful place in the Universe! We were given Kingdom authority in His Name, redeemed back to the Father as sons and daughters of God by the grace and gift of God - through His Son Jesus. This is an amazing and huge gift. I encourage you to take the time to read Ephesians 2 in the Bible and just soak in the incredible greatness of what has been given to us!

Jesus taught Kingdom Strategies for Victory for us all through the Gospels. His teaching pertains to my story. Jesus taught and gave his disciples these three major keys:

- ASK
- SEEK
- KNOCK

"Ask and it will be given to you; seek and you will find; knock and the door will be opened to you. For everyone who asks receives; he who seeks finds; and to him who knocks, the door will be opened. Which of you, if his son asks for bread, will give him a stone? Or if he asks for a fish, will he give him a snake? So if you who are evil know how to give good gifts to your children, how much more will your Father in heaven give good things to those who ask Him!" Matthew 7:7-11

This is how a vision for something you want and need becomes a reality. You need to realize God is your loving father and wants to give you good gifts and follow these keys.

It does not matter how old you are, where you live, or your current financial situation. This is a success strategy given to all of God's children! It's for YOU with the Father's love! You must ASK in Jesus name, SEEK with the Holy Spirit, and KNOCK on Doors in Faith! God will bring you to the destination where he has what you need - but you must keep following his direction from place to place in faith and obedience! Just like we did with our new truck. It just took that last door that day, the door to Little Joe's Auto's -

where God had our truck waiting for us. Imagine if we had not gone there and just decided to blow it off because I thought it was only Mitsubishi's! We would have never got our miracle that day!

Therefore we should not always try to think with our own logic and lean on our own devices and instead trust God's. He knows how to bring what you are envisioning, and He will give us the best! I saw my "Victorious Result" (my truck) in my vision and I asked God for it. I did not tell him HOW to bring it and I did not tell Him WHERE to bring it. I just had to trust that He WOULD bring it. Amen? Amen.

The Father's Good Gifts:

Jesus' words of the Father's good gifts to His children bring me back to thinking about Joshua and Caleb in the Old Testament of the Bible. I love these two faithful men so much! I could read the Book of Joshua over and over! I encourage you to read the full Book of Joshua, too - it will build your faith so much. He and Caleb stood firm on God's promises! They saw the true promised land, a land flowing with milk and honey that God told Moses about. With the 12 scouts, Caleb and Joshua came back to camp excited! What God says is true!! They did not get bothered by the bad stuff that the other scouts with them saw! Tales of big "scary" giants (and the Israelites acted foolishly and believed the bad "giants" report instead, too bad for them!) Joshua and Caleb brought home huge fruit from their scouting trip and stood on God's awesome promise all the way! They chose to look at the fruit instead of the giants. They chose faith over fear. So God advanced Joshua and Caleb for their faithfulness and their agreement with His word! This is what you must do today! Stop looking at the giants in front of you and start looking at the huge blessings instead! Even if others don't see it with you, you can do your best to convince them - but if they don't have faith you could be talking to a brick wall. I encourage you to be like Caleb - even if they don't listen to you, don't let the naysayers pull you down with them! Stand on God's promise!

"And Caleb stilled the people before Moses, and said, " Let us go up at once, and possess it; for we are well able to overcome it!" - Numbers 13:26-30

In modern terms - Caleb is like; "Ummm hellooooo people! Calm down! God said it's ours! Don't you see? Let's go now! GOD has got these guys!"

Can you imagine how Caleb and Joshua felt when all those Israelites just acted like a bunch of 'Debbie Downers' and had no faith to believe even after they had seen all the miracles God had already done for them (parting the Red Sea)? Can you imagine what God was thinking when they acted faithless and un-appreciative of what He was wanting to bless them with? Well, the word says exactly what God thought of those faithless scaredy-cat Israelites who did not trust God and His promises, He kept them in the desert wandering for another 40 years - when they could have gone right then into the promised land! After the faithless way they acted, God made sure that the doubting generation did not get to see the promised land, they all passed away in the desert. Only Caleb and Joshua, and the sons and daughters of the next generation were able to see and take their promised land!

I want Caleb and Joshua's faith! I am ready to see and take the promises God has for my life right now! How about you?

Caleb and Joshua saw the *"Victorious Result"*.

What Do YOU See? Are YOU the Faithful Generation?

The fertile, fruitful and prosperous land and future God promises us reminds me of my great grandparents when they came from Italy to America in the early 1900's. They had barely anything when they arrived here. They worked as sharecroppers in upstate NY on the onion farms. When they earned their US citizenship and enough money to buy their own land most they could afford was swampland. It was muddy, watery, covered in brambles, trees and clumps of tall marsh grass. But they did not see swamp, brambles, clumps and trees - they visualized the fertile farmland beneath it all. They cleared, drained and cultivated the land - resulting in the blackest most fertile soil you have ever seen! It was like black gold - it was called "muckland" and it was prime for growing vegetables and greenhouse flowers.

I still remember the rich smell and the loamy softness of that soil to this day - I loved to dig my hands into it as a little kid. We grew up on fresh lettuce, melons and strawberries! Oh it was scrumptious! My sisters and I helped at the farm and went with Grandpa to sell his produce at his booth at the market. One of my favorite memories is when we would help shine up our farm's vegetables and fruits for the displays at the New York State Fair - winning Blue Ribbons year after year! My great grandparents and grandparents left a legacy for our family because they had a vision for the land - they believed in the promise it held and acted in great faith. They only looked to the future. The giants of the swamp were not even on their radar. They saw the promised result - a fruitful farm. They never doubted or looked back, only forward. Their faith and vision blessed me and our family for generations. What are you looking at with your vision? Swamp or fertile ground - it's what you make of it!

Jesus replied, "No one who puts a hand to the plow and looks back is fit for service in the kingdom of God." Luke 9:62

Good or Great? What do you want to see?

Who in your family had a vision for something great? Did their vision and faith change the course of history for the better for your family and generations to come? I believe it's you! It's YOUR time to see and activate your vision for Victory!

I would rather fight for something GREAT than just settle for GOOD. That's staying stuck in your comfort zone and that's what the Israelites did. God kept bringing the same daily manna to feed them, but they never got to enjoy any fruit because of their lack of faith in His promises. FAITH BRINGS FRUIT.

God wants us to go for the GREAT because that's what pleases Him and that's how He can bring forth the promises He has for your life. God is all about us being FRUITFUL and MULTIPLYING and that was not just about having a bunch of kids and populating. That was about the purposes He gave us to bring His abundant Kingdom to earth through your life's assignment. God has a divine inheritance for you in this life. But you have to believe it's yours.

You are never too old to take your promise and activate your gifts and divine calling!

Caleb was 85 years old and in great shape when he took his promised land! Caleb wanted GREAT and he did not settle for just GOOD. Did you know that Colonel Sanders was in his 70's when he started Kentucky Fried Chicken (KFC) in the middle of the depression? Laura Ingalls Wilder wrote her first Little House on the Prairie book when she was in her 60's! Heck, I was 55 when I published my first book! Praise God!

Go for Great even if you're 18 or 88!

DON'T WAIT TO ACTIVATE!

Imagine getting to Heaven as a Believer in Christ, which is what we all want - thank you Jesus for the gift of salvation! But then Jesus says to you that you had a great promise and purpose in your life that you never activated, or you never sought out? Maybe you believed in God and saw the victorious vision, but you never tried to go after it, or worse you gave up! It's like having a million-dollar inheritance that was waiting for you and you never pursued. Even if you did not need a million dollars or want it, God may have wanted to use you to help other people with it. Let's not be one of those people who are satisfied with "I'm just working the 9 to 5 till I can retire and relax" type. You are made for greater things! As a believer in Christ, you are of the Kingdom of God and you have riches stored up and waiting for you!

"I will give you hidden treasures, riches stored in secret places, so that you may know that I am the LORD, the God of Israel, who summons you by name."
Isaiah 45:3

Notice that the verse does not say that these treasures are stored in heaven for you, they are stored in secret places here - that God will lead you to so that you will know it only came from HIM. This is for your life and to complete the assignments and callings God planned for you right now on earth!

I always thought about the fish with a coin in its mouth that Jesus told Peter to go and fish for. (Matthew 17:27) Jesus already knew where that fish was, just like He knew where the thousands of fish were under the water where He told Peter to cast his net. (John 21:6) Jesus and the Holy Spirit already know where your wealth, treasures, divine connections and breakthroughs are hidden and can bring you straight to them. When you walk in the Kingdom of God you get the hidden strategies by faith and by asking for them!

Trust His Word. Take the first step in faith. He will clear your path ahead! He's Got YOU!

"I will go before you and make the rough places smooth; I will shatter the doors of bronze and cut through their iron bars." Isaiah 45:2

When we pursue our promises in bold faith it pleases God. When we have a hard time seeing the promise or the victorious result, we must ask God to Help us see it!

Have you reached a point where you see no way it can happen for you?

Don't Give Up!

Maybe you have been trying really hard to pursue your dream, with a lot of opposition from the enemy. Maybe unforeseen circumstances have tried to chip away, steal or hold back your goals and dreams. I have been at that point before too! Then I stop and realize that God says in His word, that we should not give up no matter how bad it looks and how much has been coming against us.

I remember when I was coaching my race drivers back in 2015. One particular driver, Joshua Shipley from Parker, Arizona had just signed up for my coaching program. Our first two online sessions were very basic, getting focused on teaching him marketing strategies so he could attract sponsors to back him financially as a race car driver. Joshua was a blue collar guy, came from a hard working family, and his father whom he was very close to had just passed away from cancer. At the time Joshua was driving for the Bishop Racing team in race cars he did not own, and it was around just the smaller dirt tracks on a more local level. He wanted to secure some sponsors so they could run some bigger races together.

About two or three weeks into our coaching sessions, Joshua was racing for the Bishop Team in Tucson, AZ on a Friday night - and had a horrendous crash on the track that resulted in his race car, flipping violently end over end down the back straightaway. Miraculously Joshua walked away from that accident with just a concussion, but the race car was destroyed. His car owner was so shaken up by the incident he told Joshua he was done racing and closing down his team. I was concerned about Joshua too and we took a week off our sessions so he could rest. The doctors did not want him having any screen time with his concussion. During that week, it seemed everything was being lost for Joshua, his race car ride, his hopes of running bigger races, he had no race car to race and he was down to just his personal helmet bag and two shocks! To make matters worse, his girlfriend at the time decided to break up with him and give him back his engagement ring!

Literally, Joshua had everything he had put his hopes in going badly and he was stripped down to almost nothing at that point. He and I had our coaching session video call that next week. Little did I know for both Joshua and I, this call would be a life changing moment that God would use for His glory for years to come.

During our video coaching call, Joshua was telling me everything that was happening to him. I began to encourage him and try to help him get his mind back on what he signed up to learn from my program - how to market himself and get the sponsors he needs to move forward with his racing career goals. I had just started including my faith with my race drivers and Joshua knew I had been praying for him. I understood he was trying to heal from his accident, however he wanted to make sure he did not miss our coaching call that night to continue with what he was learning from me about marketing himself as a pro race driver. I asked Joshua about his goals again and where he wanted to take his marketing and begin to build his brand name as a professional athlete.

Joshua looked down at the table then up to me on the screen and said: "Well I guess I can become well known here in my town of Parker, represent some small businesses here and try to become "Mr. Parker."

Then all of a sudden, for the first time in my life - my mouth opened and God's voice spoke - I had no control it just came out and so powerfully and with authority - and these where the words to Joshua:

"NO! You are thinking too small! You are to GO BIG! You must think BIG! You are meant for BIG THINGS! Your name is JOSHUA! You have been called for greatness and to go after greatness! You will not be Mr. Parker you will be Mr. Arizona!"

Then silence.   I was stunned and so was Joshua.   It seemed for minutes we just sat there looking at each other. Something supernatural had just released through me to him. It had never happened to me before. Looking back, I realized that was the first time the Holy Spirit audibly prophesied through me to another person.

All of a sudden, Joshua rose up straight in his chair and said: "You know what Annamarie, You're right!   I am thinking too small! I am going to GO BIG! Yes! Yes! I am going to THINK BIG! Let's do this!"

Then he took a 'post it' note, and wrote GO BIG on it and said: "I am posting this on my Vision Board right now!"

I got so excited, I could feel the power of the Holy Spirit. I said: "Joshua, I believe God wants you to understand your name has meaning from Joshua in the Bible. You are to lead and be bold and courageous.   You survived this accident for a reason, God is with you and wants to do great things through you!"

Our coaching call took an incredible turn at that moment, we looked at all of Joshua's goals and we decided to make them all much much bigger.

"I have always wanted to own my own race team," He said to me. "Should I go for it? I have been saving money for a house but I feel like now, I should GO BIG with my racing and take a big step of faith and start my own team."

I knew without a doubt this was confirming in my spirit. "YES!" I said. Go forward with this! Start the team - take this BIG STEP. This is going BIG with your faith and I feel this is exactly what you are being guided to do by God right now!"

The two of us were so pumped up and we just felt the power of God in that moment. This is exactly what Joshua did. He took the money he saved for a new house and went and bought his OWN race car with some spare parts. He started in the two car garage he had in the house he was in at the time, a small suburban home. Joshua then started a campaign on his racing social media, using the hashtag #GOBIG and it became a huge hit. The fans followed his progress as he posted on social media encouraging messages of his plan to return BIG to racing after his terrible wreck. Excitement and support was building around him.

As Joshua fully healed from his concussion the doctors gave him the OK to go back racing. With a borrowed trailer, he hauled his newly owned race car (Dirt Sprint Car) to one of the biggest races to be held in the state of Arizona.

When Joshua got to the track, the fans were coming by pointing to him and saying "GO BIG!" (When you act in obedience, God will go ahead of you and multiply what you start.)

Joshua strapped in his car and decided he would document his first race back with an "in-car" camera. He wanted to share in the ride to victory with his fans. Joshua Shipley knew God was with him and he *would* be victorious.

"Be strong and courageous. Do not be afraid; do not be discouraged, for the Lord your God will be with you wherever you go" - Joshua 1:9

Your life has meaning my friends! We are not meant to sit back and let life run us over, we are God's People! Take a moment to understand you are made for Victory and you have God! Take this word from Joshua and receive it for yourself! God's word is HIs true will for you too! Your identity in the Kingdom of God is not limited to what man can do or having a 'basic' life! You have a great destiny and you must think BIG!

Joshua Shipley went on to WIN that first race back that day. When he pulled his race car into Victory Lane, he unstrapped from his seat, and still with his helmet on, he jumped up on top of the race car and raised up his hands giving glory to God.

Since then, Joshua Shipley has kept the "GO BIG" mindset and focus God gave him. Because of his success many bigger sponsors came on board his team from all over Arizona and beyond, he was able to buy that new home with a bigger shop, and purchase another race car to add to his team. Joshua is also focused on GIVING BIG and now has the #1 fundraiser in the country for Researching a Cure for MS, a disease his Mom has been battling. Joshua is also mentoring other racers and youth to be victorious in their lives and careers. He boldly shares his faith in God and his amazing testimony.

I recently interviewed Joshua on my Youtube show and he still has the GO BIG post it note from that coaching call we had together back in 2015 when he was at his lowest point, yet God told him that was the time for him to GO BIG.

Oh and by the way, Joshua did become "Mr. Arizona" He went on to win the 2019 Arizona State Championship for Sprint Car Racing!

We must remember why we fight for Victory and why God wants us to be Victory minded - The Holy Spirit brought me to this scripture:

"The horse is made ready for the day of battle, but victory rests with the LORD." Proverbs 21:31

We have to understand that if we are not victory minded we are not being obedient to God. This is because these are not just our Victories, but they belong to God! If we sit back and not go for it when God tells us to, it means we are not trusting God and keeping Him from getting glory in our lives!

I thank God for that precious teaching moment with Joshua who had a test of faith and passed it with flying colors!

You will have these moments in your life, or maybe you already have. Many heroes of the Bible have taught us what to do in these moments.

Your Ziklag Moment - A Test Of Faith:

King David, in the Bible, had a horrible situation on his hands. God had promised him much and anointed him to be king. However, when returning from a battle, David and his men reached Ziklag, they found it destroyed by fire and their wives and sons and daughters taken captive. All his men were so upset they all wanted to turn against him. They thought all was lost. But David did not give up. He turned to the Lord for help. This is called a "Ziklag

Moment" - when you have a test in your faith.   You can either give up in despair or turn to God.

"David inquired of the LORD, saying, "Shall I pursue this band?   Shall I overtake them?" And God said to him, "Pursue, for you will surely overtake them, and you will surely recover all." - 1 Samuel 30:7

PURSUE - YOU WILL SURELY RECOVER ALL

YES!   With God there is always a way to your Victory - even if you have had a setback.

Your setback is your setup!

When David pursued, not only was he easily victorious and rescued all the wives and children, he recovered all that was stolen and plundered the enemies camp! He ended up with MORE than he lost.   He returned with added livestock and herds of sheep and his men praised him and shouted: "This is David's plunder!" He went from a zero to a hero in the eyes of his men and God made sure he was greatly blessed - giving him double for his trouble! This was all because David chose to trust God and step out in faith. With the plunder from the victory, David made sure he shared the blessing with all his men. This gave Glory to the Lord! Pleasing God and everyone around him! Now, that's leadership and that's the Victory mindset, showing everyone around you how faith works! God LOVES to reward you for your faith so you can be an example to others to put their trust in Him.

God wants to give you double for your trouble when you stay faithful!

"Instead of your shame you will have a double portion, and instead of humiliation they will shout for joy over their portion.   Therefore, they will possess a double portion in their land, Everlasting joy will be theirs. For I, the LORD, love justice." Isaiah 61.7

God never changes.   His word says He is the same yesterday, today and tomorrow. We get to experience God in new and deeper ways as we grow in faith and real relationship with him. God is looking for those who agree with Him to do great and mighty things in the world! You and I have these same victorious promises of Caleb, Joshua and David. Yes, we do!

Listen to me my friend: No matter what your current situation, I am asking you to put your faith in the promises of God for your life.   God has designed your life to be victorious.   Jesus Christ is the author and finisher of our faith. Our life and purpose were written by HIM and Jesus writes the BEST stories for His Glory!   By the grace of God, nothing can come against it.   If it's in your heart's desire to do it, God put it there!   It's not just hopeful dreams, it's your God Given Destiny and it is awesome. CLAIM IT!

OK... Stop right now and do this: Look in front of you: What do you see for your future?   Do you see a VICTORIOUS RESULT?   Write it down.   Tell God you agree with His promises for your life right now. Tell God you are ready to GO and get hold of your promise.   Tell Him you believe that He is with you all the way and you are faithful, and excited. It's already waiting for you!

Activation Prayer:

"Father, you know the desires of my heart, because you put them there. Thank you, Father for designing me to be victorious. Father, today in Jesus name I ask for the spirit of Boldness! I want to have BOLD FAITH! I am ready to advance even if I don't know all of what's ahead - because I know you are with me Father God and you go before me! I believe my Victory is waiting for me and You Lord are giving me more steps as I take each step in faith! I believe by faith that You, Father God have created me to great and mighty things in my lifetime! I am not afraid! By faith I see the Victory! I am willing Lord, to be obedient in acting on the strategies you give me, even if I think they don't make sense, I will carry out the strategies in obedience Lord because You see the end from the beginning and I trust You. I ask now for divine downloads and strategies from Your Holy Spirit! Show me Lord, the way to obtaining my goals, my dreams, and the desires of my heart! I partner with Your Holy Spirit right now. I receive Your brilliant strategies Holy Spirit! Let's do this! I am in faithful expectation of Your daily guidance! My eyes, ears, mind, heart, and spirit are alert and ready to receive instruction Lord! I decree that I have Your Glory as my covering Lord, and Your favor surrounds me as a shield! It's all in my favor as I move forward because of Jesus Christ who lives within me! I believe that this_____shall be my Victorious Result! I win with You Lord and I give You all the Glory! Thank You Father God, in Jesus name so be it! Amen"

CHAPTER 4
BUILD AND EQUIP YOUR TEAM

When you start building your race team - the very first thing you need to do is find a good crew. Because it's such a mental game (dangerous out there) and since you are the one that's going to be behind the wheel in this deal, you need people you can trust and have your best interests at heart. One loose bolt and it could send you spinning and crashing into the wall. This is the same with you going after your goals and dreams.

Taking Authority Over Your Relationships:

Prepare the VIP parking spots in your life for the people you need to arrive! If that space is occupied by someone who is not part of God's plan to advance you - then He cannot bring you the people, finances, resources and opportunities you need.

When it comes to building and equipping your team - you must first look at your environment of the supporters (and non-supporters) you have around you. Is there anyone on your "crew' right now that would send you out on the track with a loose wheel? Would they not care enough to double check your nuts and bolts to make sure all is safe and tight for you? (hypothetically speaking here) Would they keep your windshield dirty, maybe even throw more debris and mud on it when you come in for a pit stop of support? Who around you would not have enough respect and value in your relationship to make sure you are excelling, helping you keep a clear vision and pumping you up for the win? How are they influencing you - are they cheering you on or holding you back?

This is one of the hardest strategies of your success plan - but truly one of the most important. We need to finish this race strong - and when your crew is not for your victory, guess what? There is no way you are going to make it to the finish line, let alone be victorious.

Listen my friend, I know it's hard to separate yourself from certain people and relationships in your life - I have been there!

What we refuse to deal with now will create worse issues later, so rip off the band-aid quickly and get 'er done. It might sting for a minute, but once you do it, you will be relieved. Then you can see things really start to move forward.

It's time to disconnect yourself from negative, unsupportive and critical people. Pray for them but stop putting the time and energy into them. Stop allowing them to walk all over you. Stop allowing them to discourage you. Stop sharing your God given dreams, ideas and goals with them when all they do is chew up and hold back what God wants you to do! Focus on Him and His assignment for your life and purpose - Jesus told us exactly what to do about this situation in the book of Matthew regarding these 'toxic and negative' relationships...

"Do not give dogs what is sacred; do not throw your pearls to pigs. If you do, they may trample them under their feet, and turn and tear you to pieces." Matthew 7:6

You might be thinking; "Jesus also said to love my neighbor... I am supposed to love all people." Yes, that is exactly what He said. Never stop *loving* them. BUT don't allow them to take advantage of you and treat you like a doormat. This is what tough love does, just as a parent does with a child. You love them, but you show them the authority you have in Christ because you are teaching them something that will help them with their own walk with God. You are showing them how to have DISCIPLINE and OBEDIENCE to God. You are representing God's kingdom on earth when you are following His word and purposes for your life. The word "Disciple" is the first part of the word "Discipline" for both you and them.

To be victorious, you must first learn to lead. Leaders first become disciples of Christ and begin to lead like Christ would. Your crew is like your disciples - leaders in the making. Jesus would have run an amazing race team!

So, HOW do you tell the negative people to leave or move them out of your life? How do you approach this without offending them or causing even more issues? Maybe these people are making fun of you, or they are just making things difficult. What if these negative people are family members?! What to do with people that you must be able to LIVE around? We are told by the Apostle Paul in Romans 12:18 "If it is all possible, live at peace with everyone."

It's impossible to build a good team around you (especially when you are going for a goal or embarking on your purpose) when you don't have peace with or the support of the people closest to you!

Let me share how the Holy Spirit led me to do this successfully in my own life. It's a bit uncomfortable the first time, but when you see the blessing and immediate breakthroughs that come from doing this - for both you and them, WOW it's so worth it!

Seek Relationship with God First. "Seek first the Kingdom of God and all these things will be added unto you." I found this to be very true in my own life, the more I build my relationship with the Lord, His word, and seek out His answers and strategies over my own, I have seen Him bring amazing people into my life. These are the kind of people you know will have your back no matter what and you will have theirs. You feel like you have known these people all your life, and you start to see God healing your other relationships. Why? Because your relationship with Him comes first. What He guides you to do comes first. He is a loving Father and already has great people planned out for your life. I call these "divine relationships." God will even set up the "divine appointments" you need to meet these amazing people! (Yes, these are even people who can bring finances and other support.) It starts with you realizing that you have a divine helper, His name is the Holy Spirit. I will explain further in this chapter about the Holy Spirit being your "crew chief". He will teach you exactly how to seek, find and operate completely in the Kingdom of God for your life.

Have An Overcomer in Christ Mindset! Jesus taught us exactly what to do in John 16:33: "I have told you these things, so that in me you may have peace. In this world you will have trouble. But take heart! I have overcome the world." Sometimes I just walk around the house, and decree: *"I am an overcomer in Christ Jesus! I can do all things through Christ who strengthens me!"*

This is a powerful declaration, that you should speak over yourself everyday:

Decree: "I am an overcomer in Christ! I will become all God has designed me to be! Nothing can stop what God has ordained for my life. I believe right now that God is taking the wrong situations out of my life and bringing me into the right situations. I believe that the Holy Spirit is guiding me and I will listen to His promptings. I have nothing to fear because Christ lives within me! In Jesus name so be it, Amen!"

Fear of God Over Fear of Man - One of the most debilitating things in life is fear of man. If you are worried more about what people think of you over pleasing God, you are going to be stuck for a long time. I have a respectful fear of the Lord. Fear of the Lord is actually being in "AWE" of His power and glory and WHO He is as the creator of ALL and having a deeper desire to please your Heavenly Father more than people. It's knowing inside, that you belong to the Kingdom and not to the world, and operating from heavenly strategies rather than societies. I want His Grace and abundant favor all the time... and I pursue it. We all have Grace because Jesus finished work on the Cross. But Favor comes from putting God first in your life. He is more important than any relationship you have. God's favor brings blessing upon blessing and eventually great favor with man as He advances you. Put God First and You Will Never Be Last. Psalm 56:4 says: "Yes, I will trust the promises of God. And since I am trusting him, *what can a mere man do to me*?" The answer is man *cannot* hurt you! NOPE, NO WAY, NADA!!

Agreement with God - Know that He already has the right people lined up for you and the right doors ready to open -

He is waiting for you to agree with Him and say YES. The Bible says that "For the eyes of the Lord move to and fro throughout the earth so that He may support those whose heart is completely His." (2 Chronicles 16:9) That means He is looking to each of us to surrender completely to Him and agree with His plans and purposes - and YES they are way better and faster than ours! In my experience, I simply say: "Father I agree with You and I say YES to Your plans and strategies - I know they are way better than I can even imagine! I want to work side by side with You, Father in Agreement in Jesus' name!" I have found this to be life changing almost instantaneously - God is waiting for us to say: "YES Father I want to do it YOUR way." Then BOOM doors fly open! I challenge you to try it in faith!

Be A Glory Carrier - Moses was a Glory Carrier. He craved to see God in Glory. God finally agreed. When Moses did have an encounter with God to see Him and was taken into His presence, the Glory came on Moses. (Exodus 33:18-20) After that, Moses had to wear a veil over his face because he shone so bright that many people could not handle it. But with the Glory of God came authority, favor, strength, wisdom. The *right people were attracted* to Moses and wanted to mentor under him and assist him in the mission (Joshua). Now as believers, we have the Glory as our *birthright* when we are born-again in Jesus Christ! It's free by grace! All you do is ask for it in Jesus name, say: *"Create in me a clean heart oh Lord and fill me with Your Glory!"* When you carry the Glory, the *right people* recognize it and are attracted to you! The people whose hearts are not right or walking in evil or deception many times cannot look upon the Glory because it intimidates them! I have witnessed this firsthand!

I go places, and individuals come up to me and say; "Wow you have a light about you! I say - "Oh thank you it's the Glory of Jesus Christ - can I pray for you?" They always say YES! Then I end up having a lovely encouraging conversation with them, connect with them, and invite them to my ministry. Many have become my students! Sometimes the Glory comes on so strong, the Lord will give me a Word of Knowledge for them!! Strangers I had never met before started coming up to me, saying; "Excuse me but, there is something about you…. you have such a light on you".... and then introduce themselves to me! I found it fascinating! God was teaching me about being a light in the darkness and being a Glory Carrier. Not everyone will respond to it, but the Glory of Christ is IN and REFLECTING off you like a lighthouse to ships in a dark and foggy sea! Ask in faith to carry it and watch the Glory Light of Christ work the room for you - giving you exactly who He wants to draw to Him and you! The Glory is better than business cards at any old networking event!

GOD IS CONNECTING THE PERSONAL AND BUSINESS RELATIONSHIPS - DRAWING THE RIGHT PEOPLE TO YOU!

Partner with The Holy Spirit - The apostles were fretting when Jesus had to finally leave them and ascend to heaven to be with The Father. But He did not want them to fret, He wanted to let them know He and the Father had it all planned out for them to have THE HOLY SPIRIT come to help them in everything in their mission. (John 14:16) God will never leave you or forsake you, and now, through Jesus Christ you have a full time assistant in all things - His name is HOLY SPIRIT! You are NOT alone. Did you know, you can send the Holy Spirit ahead of you on missions? Yes! He (Holy Spirit is a PERSON) He is in you, beside you, before you and behind you all the way! In this book's strategy, He is your CREW CHIEF. He knows the best set-up for you to be accelerated into your calling, goals, and purpose. The Holy Spirit is a business and marketing genius and a divine relationship connector. Can you send Him to assist you in relationships, ask Him to find and bring you the right team members? Send Him ahead to meetings? YES! I send Him all the time. I ask Him: "Holy Spirit, I am asking you as my helper to go ahead of me to this important meeting to arrange everything to God's will for me, I ask for favor, divine communications and protection. I would like this meeting to be a testimony for God's Glory. If this meeting is not intended for the best for me, then block it from happening. If this meeting is meant to produce good fruit for me and for those around me, then bless it in Jesus name!"

How about sending the Holy Spirit into difficult family situations? Well, for example, when starting my ministry, my hubby was worried and stressed because of finances and he was not really agreeing with what I was being called by God to do. I gave up my successful motorsports business to go into full time ministry and Christian life coaching. Mike and I were NOT seeing eye to eye on this and I knew that I had to be obedient to the Lord. Mike is a good and righteous man - he loves the Lord, but he is very practical when it comes to paying our bills. We were having arguments - I could not make Mike understand why I had to do this! It was stressing me out and I really needed my husband on my team! I asked the Holy Spirit to go to Mike, help him understand what God called me to do and give him peace in all this. It was a game changer! My husband is now fully on board! Thank You, Holy Spirit!

Acknowledge Him Right Now, Say: *"Holy Spirit thank You for being my right hand man! I am sorry if I ever ignored You! Please forgive me! I fully partner with You*

Holy Spirit! I want Your help and I need Your help. I cannot do this without your Holy Spirit! Let's work together right now from this day forward! Get me on the right track Holy Spirit, go and find my divine team members, my new clients, my new students - You know exactly where they are! Thank You Holy Spirit In Jesus name Amen!"

Woo hoo! Get ready for acceleration - the Holy Spirit is the BEST when it comes to aligning you with all the right moves - and takes care of the problems up ahead if you ask! He even brings SWEET SURPRISES along the way to make it fun. The JOY is in the JOURNEY and He is the best road trip Buddy ever! The Holy Spirit rides with you in your fast machine with His tool box - never worry about breaking down - He is your 'ride along' Crew Chief! He's got ya covered!

Sever Any Soul Ties or Old Agreements - This is probably the most hidden and sneaky thing the enemy uses to hold you back, slow you down and cause delays in and problems in building new relationships! It's like being stuck with a leash or a bungee cord that every time you get going forward then ...BAM! Something stops you in your tracks, delay, delay, delay, or the wrong people keep coming around attacking you - or even the worst part - people from your past who you have tried to move forward from keep popping up and harassing you. I am here to tell you; God is your defender! You are in the Army of God and you possess Mighty Spiritual Weapons! It's time to cut that stuff off you! You have the Sword of the Spirit! When you put on your Armor of God (Ephesians 6:10-18) I call it "Suiting Up" and I do it daily! You take your Sword of the Spirit and you name every person you ever had a relationship with, in your past that was negative, both intimate and professional relationships. Name them and sever them off you in the spirit in Jesus name. Make sure you also remove and discard any gifts, letters, pictures, contracts, etc... from these old soul ties. Watch what happens after you do this! It's like being shot out of a cannon. You will see acceleration and new Holy Spirit filled relationships and connections come forward for you like never before! Let me explain, God is a COVENANT God. The only Covenant you should be in is with Him, your husband or (wife). If business contracts and agreements are made, do so with the leading and confirmation of the Holy Spirit. The enemy knows God's word and that He is a COVENANT God. The Word of God says that the accuser of the *brethren* (us as believers in Jesus Christ) accuses us night and day before the Courts of Heaven, using any ungodly covenants we are still connected to in the spirit and the natural - especially those we have had intimate (sexual) relations with. It creates a soul tie, or covenant in the spirit. On earth as it is in Heaven. I could go into an entire teaching on this. It can be for good or bad for you and the other person. You must release them too! This is also for professional relationships and can hold back your business or theirs! I have experience with this. Years ago, I had a very talented woman in marketing who worked with me in my motorsports business for years. I brought her in as an assistant and had her sign a Non-Disclosure Agreement. She was very loyal to me, learned my methods and carried them out just as good as I could. She helped me grow my business exponentially. When I was called to ministry, God told me to give up all my clients and give her the business to carry on what I started. (She is a Christian). I was obedient and gave everything to her. She knew the system I created and established inside and out, and with my verbal blessing started out on her own. Months and weeks went by and she was struggling. I could not understand why, everything was set up to go. She kept getting roadblocks and delays, even attacks on her finances.   She also was having anxiety and confidence issues carrying out the system when she knew it well and did it before easily with me! I was perplexed! I went to the Lord with this, I asked Him why was this happening to her? I had even sent clients her way and then nothing! I had given her my blessing! What could be holding back her success?   Then one day while cleaning out old files, I found the three-year-old Non-Disclosure agreement we had both signed. I felt the power of the Holy Spirit come on me! I pulled up the agreement. The date had run out a year ago. On paper she was free from the agreement. I heard the Holy Spirit say audibly: "You have not released her from this agreement in the spirit and It is holding her back." I was FLOORED! WHAT!? Oh, my goodness! I knew what to do! I put the agreement before the Lord, and I decreed it severed, null and void in the spirit and in the natural, and I release her from this agreement from this day forward, forever in Jesus name! WOW. I am going to tell you honestly, I never told her about that, what God showed me about our agreement.   But just three weeks later, she messaged me that she was having huge breakthroughs and growth with her business! Praise God! Now, you might be thinking ...What if someone in your past has not released you from an agreement or covenant you had together (written or verbal) in the spirit? Whether you have a paper copy or not, just come before the Lord, say what it is you are cancelling and marking null and void in the spirit. Then in the natural, ask Jesus to put His Blood on the agreement and ask it to be wiped from the record books in heaven and earth and that all parties would be released including yourself in Jesus name! Many of you will notice an immediate change, if not, keep asking the Lord if there are any agreements or soul ties you cannot remember, ask Jesus to step in for you and put them on His Cross and cancel them for you. He's your intercessor and attorney in the legal realm in both Heaven and earth!

Forgive, Bless and Release - You cannot start using your gift to its fullest, and expect God to trust you with new people in your life when you hold any un-forgiveness or bitterness in your soul towards any other person.

"Leave your gift there before the altar. First go and be reconciled to your brother; then come and offer your gift." Matthew 5:24

Listen my friends, I have been burned by people in business through the years. I wanted to have success just to "show them" BUT that is for God to make a show to give Him glory as He gives you favor to succeed. No matter how hard this is, take some time before the Lord and repent for un-forgiveness in your heart, forgive everyone, release all bitterness, ask God for forgiveness and grace, ask Jesus to cover your sins in his blood. Then cancel any curses or negative words you have spoken over them or they have over you in Jesus name.

Ask God To Remove and Add - You can depend on God to remove any negative situation. He will fight for you! Romans 12:19 says: "Do not avenge yourselves, beloved, but leave room for God's wrath. For it is written: "Vengeance is Mine, I will repay, says the Lord." You might find this hard to believe, but I was in a physically abusive relationship for many years and I did not know how to get out of it. I was really stuck and had no confidence in myself. I knew God had something better and that I deserved better, but I was very afraid the person would hurt me if I tried to leave. I had my mom that prayed for me, and I began to pray and cry out to God to help me get out and get away safely. God came through, protected me in an amazing way and got me out of that relationship and back home to my loving family.   Right after that God brought me into a completely new circle of friends and supporters, a new dream job in NASCAR racing and very soon a new loving husband and beautiful daughter! Since then, I have had tremendous favor from God - I did get recompense from all those years of abuse and I have been blessed and restored beyond my hopes and dreams. God will fight your battles but you must ask Him to do so. He will remove the bad influences in your life and bring the good. He will rescue you away from abusive situations! I have a prayer at the end of this chapter that you can pray to activate this.

Put Your Energy Into The New - Decree It Forth

If you tried all the steps above and you still do not get a shift in the attitude of negative people or past situations, understand that it is the enemy working against and through these people and it's not the people - the enemy is trying to distract you from your amazing future. Call his bluff! Forgive them and move on. Keep focusing on the future by "Suiting Up" daily and using your Authority in Christ Jesus.   Resist the devil and He will flee!   He is helpless against the Blood of Jesus! So, apply the Blood to your life daily and take your seat of Authority in Christ, putting the enemy under your feet! Know it's God's will to advance you because of your faith and your focus on what you see GOD doing in your life! Continually prophesy over your future, see it, believe it and *call it forth* in Jesus name.

Make a list of powerful decrees to speak over your future daily.   Make a detailed "Want" List of what you are believing God for in a Team and speak it forth in faith! Romans 4:17 says we are to call things that are not as though they are! It's the power of decreeing the words and promises of God over your future that stops the enemy in his tracks! The word of God is always the will of God for your life and it's the sharpest weapon you will ever have! It will accelerate you like a rocket! It will bring forth what God has waiting for you, the team members and the opportunities in a way that nothing will compare. Be vision minded.   Jesus told us to be!   He had to accelerate His ministry and finish His assignment here on earth in just three years.   Whoa, no pressure there!   Jesus was vision minded because our Father is! Jesus called his main team together in just months!   Then the GLORY of the Mission was totally manifesting quickly.   Imagine what God will do for you when you begin to focus on the Glory He has ahead of you!   What would normally take years will take months, what will normally take weeks will take days! YES!!

SPEAK IT BY FAITH! CALL IT FORTH!

Decree: "I see my team Lord, they are here! I decree it by faith and call them forth in Jesus name!"

Vision is KINGDOM MINDSET = Operating in The Glory and Speaking Life into what you SEE by Faith.

Jesus said: "I only do what I SEE the Father doing." - John 5:19-20

That is operating in God's image and heart in which He created you! You are made in His image. you cannot fail when you are operating in the Kingdom.   Kingdom is Vision, Favor, and Glory! Father God framed you before you were born - you were a vision from His heart in a frame, like a masterpiece - then He created you from His vision by speaking you into existence! We need to do this with God in everything in our life!

Ask Him In Prayer: *"Father God, what is Your Vision for me when You created me? Who did you plan on connecting me with in my life? I agree with Your Vision for my future Father! I receive Your planned divine connections now! Show me, reveal to me and I confirm Your will for my life through Your word Father! I believe You Father God put these desires and vision I have for my life in my spirit! Thank You Father! I will proclaim my vision boldly and by faith without fear or hesitation in Jesus' name!"*

Daily Proclaim: *"Father God, Your favor surrounds me as a shield and Your GLORY is my covering in Jesus name! I receive Your Spirit of Boldness today Father to speak as I ought to speak over my life through Your Holy Spirit in Jesus name!"*

Let God Be Your Judge and Your Defender Against Those Who Ridicule You!

Ask God to *remove* relationships in your life that are negative and are coming against the Fruit of The Holy Spirit in your life! God will remove these influences and relationships swiftly if you ask Him to remove them according to His word. The people will not be hurt, it's just the relationship that God removes. I have used this prayer many times and people that I did not want to confront, God did it all peacefully in the Spirit. They just simply walked out of my life.

Pray The Ax Of God's Judgement Prayer:

"Father God, Your word says in Matthew 3:10 that 'Even now the ax of God's judgment is poised, ready to sever the roots of the trees. Yes, every tree that does not produce

*good fruit will be chopped down and thrown into the fire.'
So according to Your word, Father I am asking you to
remove at the roots every negative relationship or
influence, the ones I know of and the ones I may not see
that are coming against my divine calling and purpose, that
are coming against the good fruit of the Holy Spirit in my
life, business, career, family and household. Father God, if
there is anyone on my team or around me that is not here
to produce good fruit, then remove them from my team.
Pluck these relationships and influences at the root and
put them where you want them to be away from me swiftly,
smoothly and without harm to them or me.Burn any bad
fruit that came from these relationships to ashes now,
never to take root again with me or my life, business,
career, family or household in Jesus name. I now accept
the new HOLY SPIRIT FILLED relationships and influences
in my life that will bear good fruit according to your will and
word in Jesus name! Thank You Father God!"*

You will be shocked that suddenly, people you thought
were for you, quickly move on and away from your life!
Don't chase them down! God saw what was really in their
heart for you and they were not there to produce good fruit.
Trust Him on this! Let them go in peace! This is making
room for the new GOOD relationships and team members
to come!

God will also PROMOTE YOU and MAKE A SHOW of it to
those who scoffed at your dreams!

If you have people making fun of your goals and dreams -
or even telling you that you can't do it - understand that it is
the enemy working against you and through them. Don't
take it upon yourself to force the issue or hold a grudge.
Forgive them and move on. But know in the end, the Lord
will show His glory of advancing you because of your faith.

124

Even better, God will use you to change their minds about having big faith!

There is a song by country singing star Toby Keith: "How Do You Like Me Now?" About how a man who had a big dream and was scoffed at, then went on to become very successful. It's a good driving song to play when you want to get yourself pumped up about your future when you are dealing with scoffers.

"How do you like me now
Now that I'm on my way
Do you still think I'm crazy
Standing here today
I couldn't make you love me
But I always dreamed about living in your radio
How do you like me now?" - Toby Keith

I say let's go straight to the Bible with God's songwriter, King David (a Rockstar Musician of his day) :

"You prepare a table before me in the presence of my enemies, my cup overflows." - Psalm 23

Both songs/psalms state the person has overcome those who did not support them early on, and even those who were their enemies. God will promote you and make a SHOW of it!

If you have a dream and you are standing on God's word, that is God's will. NOTHING can stop what God has ordained for your life, There may be attempts to hinder your purpose, but nothing can stop it. You even have the strategy to use my "negative/soulish word canceling prayer' - go straight to that prayer and cancel every negative word they are speaking over you right now! Cut it off at the pass!

Focus on the MAIN thing - Believe GOD over the scoffers and naysayers and keep moving forward in your vision of FAITH and take authority of your VISION, it belongs to You and God!

AGREE WITH GOD - then watch how He advances you in front of those who doubted! He does this for you because He in turn, will be glorified in your success!

"For the eyes of the Lord run to and fro throughout the whole earth, to show Himself strong on behalf of those whose heart is loyal to Him." 2 Chronicles 16:9

Then you will go on to greatness because you agreed with who God said you are, and God will make SURE those who did not believe will see you at the TOP! Whooo hoooo!!

Remember Jesus told us to be Salt and Light - and we cannot allow anyone to dim our light or trample us under their feet, Amen? When we are obedient to God and only allow supportive people to influence us, and have the Holy Spirit filled people around us who are praying and interceding for us and vice versa - God's Glory is manifested in everyone's life!

You are built and designed to be bright and filled with virtue so the right people are attracted to you!

Salt and Light!

"You are the salt of the earth. But if the salt loses its saltiness, how can it be made salty again? It is no longer good for anything, except to be thrown out and trampled underfoot. You are the light of the world. A town built on a hill cannot be hidden. Neither do people light a lamp and put it under a bowl. Instead

they put it on its stand, and it gives light to everyone in the house. In the same way, let your light shine before others, that they may see your good deeds and glorify your Father in heaven." - Matthew 5:13-16

How to Get the RIGHT People Around You:

First, you must decide what you want FOR THEM. Do you want them to enjoy their job? Do you want your success together to bless them? Do you want them to use their gifts in a big way and be ok if they offer their expertise even if you have to step back and let them shine sometimes? In what way? Will these people be people who like to pray and believe in God's Goodness? Do they have a winning mindset? It's about what you are focusing on. Are you focusing on what you want or what you don't want? FOCUS ONLY ON WHAT YOU WANT. You will attract the people you need based on how each person will have a great purpose alongside you and you, them.

I used to laugh when I would see an ad in the paper or on a job posting site for a company looking for a person to fill a position, and they would actually put in the job posting what they "don't want" the person to be. BIG MISTAKE. That's why they have a revolving door of bad employees. You must always focus on what you WANT and expect by Faith.

Jesus said to His disciples, that they must first change the way they think and believe God for the impossible.
Change your THINKING - Change Your LIFE

The Bible also says as a man thinketh, so HE is - what kind of person are you - how do people perceive you? You will attract good trustworthy people based on WHO you are, not so much what you DO.

When I worked on a racing team, we used to say that there were people who really were 'true grit' professionals and those who just wanted to just 'wear the shirt'. The 'true grit' people were the ones who were not afraid to get their hands dirty, work behind the scenes, stick by the team through the good, the bad and the ugly and work all night even if they were not asked to, and go and get coffee for everyone or run and get race car parts even if it's 'not their job'. They never grumble because they see the big picture and are willing to do whatever it takes. The 'wear the shirt' people are those who want to ride your coattails, look cool and just be part of the 'spoils' but complain when the going gets tough. These 'wear the shirt' people need to be weeded out quickly, but sometimes you will not know the wheat from the tares until harvest time.

That's why Jesus said to know people by their fruit. You might have some trial and error. If you are passionate about your purpose, and if YOU exemplify the 'true grit' you will attract people who appreciate and have true grit - and you must appreciate them. BE AUTHENTIC and you will attract authentic people who resonate with you and your goals and dreams. Love these people and thank God for them even before they show up. Just say: "Thank you God for bringing the perfect people that you have planned as part of my team and we can give You all the Glory together."

While I am writing this chapter, I was also teaching an online Bible study on the book of Joshua. It made me think about how God "chose" the people who would go see and live in the Promised Land based on their faith. It ended up that the complainers and grumblers never got to see the Promised Land. If they had just believed in God, they would have been in the Promised Land in a matter of weeks! Instead, their lack of faith caused a major delay! God waited until they all passed away after 40 years and their children got to go and live in the promise! God's team players, like Joshua and Caleb were the faithful ones. They were the only two of the original generation that got to take their promised land. Teamwork makes the dream work. Complainers get more to complain about. Haha! Doesn't that sound like something a parent would say? "Keep on whining and I will give you something to whine about." LOL. Our Father God is a true Father!

So, you need help, you need support and you have the FAITH to go forward now what?

Describe the supporters/help you want!

Holy Spirit Partnership FIRST before any other leaders or supporters in your life - He is your Crew Chief for The Race of Your Completed Purpose.

"And I will ask the Father, and He will give you another Helper (Comforter, Advocate, Intercessor—Counselor, Strengthener, Standby), to be with you forever—the Spirit of Truth, whom the world cannot receive [and take to its heart] because it does not see Him or know Him, but you know Him because He (the Holy Spirit) remains with you continually and will be in you." John 14:16-17 (Amp)

Do you need a breakthrough? Holy Spirit "CTA" Call To Action

1.) Ask For Divine Appointments To Come

2.) Ask For Doors of Opportunity To Open

3.) Acknowledge that He Is Your Source of ALL Your Supply

Decree: *"Everything I need comes easily and frequently with the Help of the Holy Spirit, In Jesus Name!"*

Get An Agreement Partner to Pray with You:

The power of agreement is huge with your prayer partners. I will not do anything major in my business or ministry without first praying about it with my husband who is my agreement partner. If you do not have one, look for a prayer group at church or join an online prayer group. If you are alone, ask the Holy Spirit to be your agreement partner. I have group prayer on my YouTube livestream - join us with your prayer request!

Sowing A Seed For The Team Members You Need:

When giving to the Lord, we have *the tithe* (our obedient 10%) or *an offering* (over and above the tithe that is given with the intent of love for the Lord and believing Him in making good on His promise in Malachi 3:10) *our first fruits* (a first offering to the Lord each year or the first of something new the Lord has done in your life - first paycheck of a new job, first sale of a new book, etc) Then there is a *seed offering* (where you intentionally give unto the kingdom of God and name the offering as a "seed"). When you plant corn you don't get daisies, right? You expect a corn harvest. It's all about being specific with your seed. So, you write your check, or send it via website into a church or ministry, you write what the name of the seed and what the harvest you are expecting by faith. So say you have a $25 seed, you say this prayer over your check or transaction:

Prayer over your seed offering: *"Father, Thank you for this $25. I offer this up to you and plant this as a seed into your Kingdom and I name this seed "Holy Spirit filled personal assistant". I believe by faith that this shall produce a harvest for which it is sent according to Your* *word Father in Isaiah 55:11 that so My word that proceeds from My mouth will not return to Me empty, but it will accomplish what I please, and it will prosper where I send it. In Jesus name, I receive my Holy Spirit filled personal assistant in faith, Thank you Father, Amen"*

You can even put more specific details on the person you are believing for in the prayer - the more specific qualities you need by faith.   God is not impatient if your prayer is longer. He is moved by your faith!

Put Out A Public Challenge or Call To Action - To Pull In Ideal People:

In the book of Joshua, an elderly but still strong and sharp Caleb was just given his 'mountain' and the promise of a large region of land called Hebron.   Caleb had believed God faithfully for over 40 years and was ready to take his promise. Well into his 80's he knew the land was occupied by the enemy and he had to conquer it,   which he easily did. (Joshua 14:6-14) After that Joshua wanted to expand southward toward the Dead Sea along the Jordan River for more territory for Caleb and the tribe of Judah.

This time, Caleb kicked in his leadership skills knowing he had a beautiful daughter who was very special to him, he decided to offer her hand in marriage to whoever would take on this challenge to lead an army to conquer the next level of territory.   He literally 'announced' this in public. (Joshua 15: 13-17) Caleb was being strategic, looking for a way to attract a brave young man who would have the kind of character traits he wanted in a son-in law and eventually someone to be an integral part of his family legacy (or team). This could not be just anybody in Judah. A young and virtuous man by the name of Othaniel jumped at the challenge and succeeded.   Not only did Othaniel get to marry the beautiful Aksah, daughter of Caleb, but he shared in her expansive land inheritance with both upper and lower springs, a gift from her father Caleb. Othaniel went on to be a very respected Judge over the people of Israel - keeping Caleb's legacy honorable. My point here is when you put out a public challenge, with strategic wording in the right circles (in marketing we call this a "call to action" or CTA) you will attract the ideal people for your purpose, and long term!

This is MORE than putting a basic classified ad for helpers! This is calling forth exactly what you want in a person by creating wording by visualizing "who they are" in character and virtue. Your goal is to speak to them personally, their wants, their desires, so that when they read or hear your call to action, (or challenge) it resonates in their soul and spirit . You want them to say "wow - that's totally me!"

An example of a Call To Action Posting For A Team Member:
The Post (CTA) Reads Like This: "You have a dream to be a big part of something successful, challenging, and rewarding. It seems that you have put your heart into many things for others but have not been appreciated for your hard work. You have been looking to work in an atmosphere where God is honored, and your gifts and talents can grow and be recognized. We have been praying for someone like you! We have new exciting opportunities available with generous pay for those who are focused on team success and potential leadership in our company and for the future." Contact us today at 222-222-2222 (example).

This CTA will resonate with the right people you want to bring on your team! They will read it and say to themselves - wow that sounds like me! Then it propels them to take action and contact you.

How To Equip Your Team:

Once you feel confirmed you have the right people in place. Give them some time for them to reveal their strengths and weaknesses to you. Of course, it's important to pray with your team as a whole. One thing that has been shown to me repeatedly, that I have the right team members in place, is if they offer to pray for me as a leader and for the organization as a whole and for others in the organization. That makes all the difference! Then, get them to work in smaller teams, create rotating partnerships or "AB" teams "Accountability Buddies" Give them challenges and projects with clear direction. The "AB" teams take the pressure off of you as a leader to try and keep track of everyone - it keeps you from micromanaging and gives each team member a cheerleader and someone they answer to hold them accountable as they see the project or challenge to completion.

I have used this "AB" strategy for years, even in my motorsports coaching of teams and God confirmed He wanted me to bring this into my ministry and coaching programs. We have seen exponential growth with individuals this way and not only that - they get so excited with what they are able to do to completion that they could never do before on their own - they share their testimony and bring in more great people into the organization.

I start with SPIRITUAL EQUIPPING, then I help people expand their gifts and strengths as they start to emerge. If a person does not know their own value in Christ, they cannot be of value to a team that is operating for the Kingdom and for the success of the team and business! If the Leader is committed to God with the business or team, and a team member just will not ever see their own value It just will not work. Been there done that! Can a team member come in not knowing their full value in Christ? Can they be mentored into their gifts and strengths? Absolutely! In fact, I HIGHLY encourage it.

It should be a Leader's responsibility to observe and evaluate each person as they come along, and begin to allow that person to grow, and work with their AB. They may have been sent to you by God as a place for them to be refined like gold and let their gifts emerge under Godly leadership! I look at myself as a gold miner! I love to watch people grow and pull those gold nuggets forth from them that they never knew were there! It is so rewarding!

Equipping your team should be like shepherding a flock and also like training up disciples - your business and anywhere you are called to lead is your Ministry! Yes even in the secular world! We are called as Christians, as The Body of Christ to take the 7 Mountains of Influence in Society. We are to Occupy Until He (Jesus) comes! (Luke 19:13)

I love how Jesus saw the giftings and attributes in His disciples as He chose and sent them out to do the work of the Kingdom. There is a great book I have read called "Marketing Like Jesus". It's my go-to for building and equipping people and your brand. It's a brilliant book. I highly recommend it. Ask a professional marketer in the secular world of NASCAR racing for over thirty years - I had to re-train myself to market the Kingdom way! God wanted me to take what I learned in motorsports and apply it for Him, however the secular business practices can be very dog eat dog - and I had to learn how to do everything with love, yet wisdom and discernment! You cannot be a doormat and let people take advantage of you- Jesus said do not throw your pearls to the swine (Matthew 7:6)

Jesus also said you must be as shrewd as a serpent and as innocent as doves. (Matthew 10:16) That was the way Jesus equipped His disciples to carry out the great commission for the Gospel. He told them to know their authority, to command a mountain to move, that they also had keys to the kingdom by binding and loosing whatever they needed to on earth. It would be done for them in heaven. Jesus was teaching them to lead like Him! He was teaching them the Kingdom. God told Joshua the very same thing in different terms. Believe and do His commandments and Joshua would be successful.

Leading and equipping your team by God's word is the key to the success of your team. I lead my team by the Bible and my favorite leadership book, "The 21 Irrefutable Laws of Leadership" By John C. Maxwell. I knew that John was a Christian pastor of a church for many years before he began to train leaders and his strategies were Biblical sound. I have every one of my students and team members read his book! This way they understand the way I lead - and we come into the power of agreement, which accelerates your team.

Equipping a team is a responsibility - you must have a love for the person you are equipping and a desire to expand them into greater things, not just for your business or ministry, but for them as individuals. I have found when you do this you not only make a friend for life, but your positive influence on that person becomes a legacy, that they pour into others long after you are gone from this world. This is the Kingdom. This is how Jesus did it. You cannot fail yourself or your team if you follow His lead.

You may not have an impact on every person that comes through your programs, business or ministry. BUT even if you have a positive impact on just one person you must focus on that, not the ones that failed under your leadership, or just never "got it" while you were trying to help them grow and be a part of your mission.

Focus On The Fruit You Hope To See In Your People!

While still working as a Motorsports Coach in 2015, I went to the Las Vegas Motor Speedway - a state of the art auto race track just on the outskirts of Las Vegas, Nevada. They were holding a NASCAR event, with the all famous big-time drivers, sponsors, teams, top professionals and major media in the sport. I was there with my clients who wanted their daughter, a 22-year-old talented female race car driver to get an opportunity to apply for the D4D "NASCAR Drive for Diversity" program. It was a difficult program to make it into - set up for women and minorities who were aspiring professional race car drivers - they had very few openings and each applicant had to go through a resume' selection process that included having some very good references. I had set up everything ahead of time for my clients - especially this young woman, to meet powerful influencers in the industry to get her connected and to create relationships to start building a strong resume' for her future career. My plan was to connect her with people that were decision makers at NASCAR, as well as Chevrolet, Toyota and major media outlets.

As soon as we got to Vegas, I had tons of favor with the parents of this young woman, especially the Mom, paying for everything, a luxury room, steak dinners - they were so excited about the opportunity! However, the daughter did not want anything to do with me and what I had set up for her! I was trying to be patient but inside I was so frustrated with her. I tried to reason with her but all I got was push back. She really did not want to meet or talk to anyone. She tried a few times to shake hands with some powerful meet-ups to make her parents happy, but then ran all the way back to the parking lot and refused to meet anymore people. I tried everything I could think of based on my experience with other racing students - to no avail. She was done, and she would only go back into the track to watch the race if we left her alone. I agreed, but I was very upset.

I felt like a total failure! I apologized to the parents. They were very kind, they were disappointed too. I went back inside the track to make the best of the time I was there at the Vegas Speedway in the busy garage and pit area where the teams were (we had hot passes) to shoot some marketing tip videos for my coaching practice. While I did videos and walked around I saw many people I have helped over the years that had made it to the top, and now acquired great jobs and positions in NASCAR. Some were big time pro drivers now too, including one professional driver (Alex Bowman) that used to come to my marketing classes when he was 13 and now he was 23! When they saw me, they ran up to me and made a point to tell me that their encounter and time working or mentoring with me had made a huge difference in both their professional and personal lives. I was so grateful for that moment - God was showing me not to focus on my failures, but on my successes. I realized that there was so much good fruit in people that had been produced over the years through my time, labor and dedication to pour into them. This fruit through these people were going to keep producing more good fruit in more people that they mentored and encountered someday! What a revelation! Then, I noticed the mountains around the track, I thought about how they built the place in the desert where there was nothing and now such a huge and prosperous place. The track was one of the finest I had ever been to. It was my last big NASCAR race as a professional, Las Vegas. There it was shown to me that from my biggest disappointment of failure came my biggest reveal of success.

"Behold, I am doing a new thing; now it springs forth, do you not perceive it? I will make a way in the wilderness and rivers in the desert. The wild beasts will honor me, the jackals and ostriches, for I give water in the wilderness, rivers in the desert, to give drink to my chosen people, the people whom I formed for myself that they might declare my praise." Isaiah 43:19-21

My Victorious Friend, that day at the Las Vegas Motor Speedway - built in the middle of the desert - I realized that it is all about the good seeds and stewarding of my field, bringing forth good fruit, the good harvest, that keeps replanting into the future. These good seeds are the people you pour yourself into, love and nurture - help them become fruitful so that they will also do the same thing someday. That is your legacy.

God will make a way, provide everything you need, take care of your enemies, too! He is with you through it all as you build with Him from nothing, He will make sure it is successful so You will *give Him praise* for it! WOW.

Many times while stewarding my field in Motorsports, I would get frustrated. Did I even make an impact? Maybe the person had a fleeting connection with me and was only part of my team for a short time. Maybe I had poured a lot into that person and maybe they did not seem to appreciate it. I worked with a lot of people's kids with big dreams, spent many hours traveling away from my own child and family while I mentored young aspiring professionals all over the country. My daughter would cry sometimes, "Mommy don't leave" - but I had a calling at that time, a field to steward, it was where God trained me up for ministry. Even though I did not realize He was training me at the time.

When I was traveling home from that Vegas race I cried out to God and said: "God, I have poured into so many other people and their children, thank you for showing me their successes and the fruits of my labor. I just want the same for my child too! Help me steward her faithfully in the same way!"

I heard God promise me back then: *"Annamarie, what good seeds you have sown into other people's lives, including their children, you will reap in your own."*

I held on to that promise. Today, my daughter, Landry Leigh. She travels with me, assists me in the ministry and we have a very close relationship. God is faithful!

He did it for me, He will do it for you too!

Shortly after that Vegas NASCAR race back in 2015, God called me to build a ministry from scratch - by myself with only *His* help. Something interesting about God using that moment at my last professional race event. He wanted to teach me something for my future and how He wanted me to understand that's how it works for His Kingdom! God is calling leaders like you and me to bring people into His Kingdom and work together as a team. It's all about your perspective, and how He wants us to touch people's lives through our own divine callings. What field are you stewarding? What people are you pouring into? Big teams or little teams - He will multiply the fruit of everyone you sow into faithfully. He is a God of multiplication. Jesus started with the twelve.

I know I am saying it again, but - Teamwork (does) Make The Dream Work - It's not just for individuals - it's for all of us who make up the Body of Christ. Our families, our ministries, our businesses, our field of work and areas of influence. We are the Kingdom Team!

Prayer To Build and Equip Your Team:

"Father, I thank You for who You are! I acknowledge that You care for me and You care about my success. Thank You for all my successes in the past, and for teaching me through my failures! Father, I give You Praise and Glory through it all! Father, I want to build a team of honorable, Holy Spirit filled individuals that can help me grow and I can help them grow. I want to produce good fruit in our personal and professional lives and for Your Kingdom. Father, today I want to partner with Your Holy Spirit to bring forth the people I need right now for my _____. You know exactly where they are Holy Spirit and I trust You to bring them to me and I am prepared to receive them. Holy Spirit help me to be a good and righteous leader like Jesus and have the wisdom to discern properly and quickly how to guide and lead my team, and how to release those who should not be on my team.   I want to be a good steward and Godly mentor of the people You bring to me Holy Spirit! Equip me Holy Spirit so I can properly equip others! Train me Holy Spirit so I can properly train others! Help me to focus on the fruit and not the failures! I am grateful to Father God that You want to build a good _____ with me and build a good team around me! I am excited to advance the Kingdom through what You have called me and my team to do, and for their future teams! Father, I want to have a good and fruitful legacy

that goes on for generations to come for Your Glory in Jesus name, Amen!"

CHAPTER 5
DIVINE SPONSORSHIP

Do you feel God is commissioning you to do something big or unique? Do you have a dream or goal in your heart that you feel God has put there? Will it take FINANCES to do this? Do you pray all the time for the money to come to carry out your calling, build something and live the dream of your heart? Would it be a miracle for you right now if a big check for the amount of what you need to money wise do this show up your mailbox? I am here to tell you in this chapter that God *will fund* your dream, your goals, your calling and purpose. God is your Divine Sponsor!

One of the biggest challenges of my motorsports career was attracting major corporate sponsors to fund my teams and drivers and their racing programs. My drivers and teams had operational budgets ranging from $20,000 to $2,000,000+ per season - depending on the level of their series. Sponsorship is a must for professional automobile racing, most teams cannot run successfully without major sponsors and it's an excellent platform for advertising. For marketing professionals like myself, it was all about "push sales" and "cold calling" and "silly season" when drivers, teams and sponsors were all moving around and you tried to snag their sponsor to come on your team! It was a stressful and very competitive way of doing things, and really not very ethical to say the least!

For over 15 years, I did this the old fashioned way, "the way it was always done" to procure sponsorship for my teams and drivers that I was employed by with some success. However, I never felt good or right about the way I did it. I despised the 'slick sales' tactics and the 'cold calling' that was so humiliating, sometimes getting hung up on - or the schmoozing or sometimes begging to get past the receptionist to the decision makers in that company. That was like pulling teeth! Really, at times I felt like a telemarketer, dialing my fingers to the bone daily, flipping rolodexes, trying to get leads - hoping to get a 'bite' of interest in team sponsorship. Every once and a while I would get that 'bite' and reel in a company. I enjoyed seeing my team and drivers working successfully with their sponsors and I loved marketing them! Then I would be back at it year after year doing the same process to bring in more sponsors - it was exhausting! Business communication back in those days we only had a desk phone, the post office "snail mail" and facsimile "faxing" then eventually email was just starting to come into the fold to send proposals to these potential sponsors. This was the 1980's and early 1990's in NASCAR racing. (giving away my age here, lol)....

The sport was growing, TV exposure was expanding, but the team budgets were also expanding into the tens of millions of dollars - it was harder to get the Fortune 500 companies on board if you did not have a big name 'celebrity' driver. Marketers that procured and managed sponsorships had to be really good at their game, and some were known as sharks and had terrible reputations. There also was a lot of corruption and greed as some (not all) of the team owners were "pocketing" most of the sponsor money and buying boats and fancy homes instead of making sure the sponsorship dollars were spent on operating a good racing team. I refused to stoop to that level and I wanted to keep my excellent reputation in the sport. It was important to me. It was more than getting the 'big money".... it was about integrity making sure that your team and sponsor were getting good results, proper representation for your sponsors with honesty, credibility and accountability.

There HAD to be a better way!

In 1997, while managing and marketing a NASCAR team in Mooresville, North Carolina - I met my husband, Michael Lee Strawhand, a big, tall, kind hearted country boy from Virginia.   Mike was and still is a man of honesty and integrity, and God brought him into my life when I was 35 years old.   (Our first meeting was love at first sight but that's a funny story I will tell you later....)   The timing of meeting and dating Mike prepared me to get off the road working with teams on the weekly circuit so I could spend more time with him.   Mike was not involved in racing, he liked to go as a fan but he was a plumbing contractor by trade.

I decided to set up a home office in my apartment and start a Motorsports Marketing Consulting Company. This way I could consult teams and drivers on procuring and managing their own sponsors and for the first time consult sponsors on finding the right team and driver to meet their needs. I only had to go to a few out of town events a year this way. This was a huge awakening for me. I was now working on both the driver/team side and the sponsor/ corporate side. I worked with all levels of teams and all levels of companies. I learned to understand the money is more easily given by companies for sponsorship when they see the VALUE immediately and the team focuses on the RELATIONSHIP instead of just asking for money to do what they wanted to do.

I started to see a pattern with the teams and drivers and the ones that got more sponsors and more money from these sponsors. These specifically were the teams and drivers who truly knew their own VALUE and how they wanted to share the value they built with their sponsors. Then they commenced sharing that value in a big way. They also put the RELATIONSHIP they had with their fans and sponsors to the utmost importance. I was not just about the race car and going faster. Ultimately - this new way of doing things based ON VALUE AND RELATIONSHIP made their teams get better and faster as an added benefit!

These teams and drivers using this new strategy seemed to have the same sponsors coming back year after year, with more money! Together growing and advancing their company with the team. It was a true partnership. Little did I know was this was GOD training me up to understand how HIS Kingdom works!

Enter the Title "Marketing Partner"...

Instead of calling this a "Sponsorship" I began to use the phrase "Marketing Partner" I realized that the teams and companies that advertise with them and got behind them financially wanted to be treated more like a partner on the team and with the driver who carried their brand name. They wanted to be a part of the team in every aspect, connect personally with the driver and crew. This also worked vice- versa with the driver and team becoming a direct part of the company they had brought on as a "Marketing Partner". Even their employees and customers could benefit from the relationship too. It was something that I began to understand as this was supposed more than a 'business deal" or who's decal on the race car got the most TV time. It was more about how much the team valued the sponsor's company it's leaders, it's people and brand. It was more about the race team putting the need of the sponsor first before the team itself. It was fool proof, it worked and it seemed to attract even more companies to come on board as sponsors - *it multiplied*!

I began to see this as an ATTRACTION of a Sponsor and not a SALE or a slick advertising gimmick. This was like a good healthy marriage of two parties with major benefits for all involved.

Finances for your dream and vision are attracted to you by the value, partnership and long term relationship the person gets for putting their dollars behind you. These teams and drivers have a dream to win races and move up the ladder in the sport. Depending on the level they aspire to advance to it could take millions of dollars. The companies that finance and invest in them have a dream to grow their brand in a positive way - and get a return on their investment into where they market that brand.

The companies are ATTRACTED to the race drivers and teams who believe in *their* dreams! It was not just about the drivers and teams wants and needs. I realized also that the companies were on board quicker when they saw that the driver/team offered something that nobody else was offering and the programs were tailored to meet the companies' goals. This is how God looks at HIS "company" goals! Ask yourself this question: Will partnering with you and your calling, dreams and visions produce the fruit of the Holy Spirit and promote and assist the advancement of the Kingdom? The Kingdom is God's business, Jesus even said, "I go about the Father's business." God is looking throughout the earth for those who will agree with His plans and purposes - there is no mistake you have these goals and dreams and that you want to honor God with them - if you didn't you would not be reading this book!

I know now that God showed me how His Kingdom operates in every area of influence in the earthly realm. It is designed to ATTRACT PARTNERSHIPS. With God and with each other!

Now, before you get concerned about me using the word "attraction" this is NOT new age 'law of attraction' stuff. I left and rebuked the 'new age' lies years ago when Jesus Christ came and saved me out of it and I will never ever go back! Thank You Lord!

The *attraction* I am talking about is this: God wants to put like minded people together for HIS SAKE so He can see fruitfulness in His creation. That includes all areas of the Seven Mountains or "spheres" of Influence in society. Which includes Religion, Family, Education, Government, Media, Arts and Entertainment, Business and Marketplace. God also has given us His word promises and laws - that were HIS to begin with and the devil stole, twisted it and took Jesus Christ out of the picture and made the law of attraction 'new age' when it belonged to GOD FIRST!

Here is my rule with "law of attraction" for you to use to discern things: If Jesus Christ is not worshipped as the only Son of God and God's word does not line up with the 'attraction message' >> RUN AWAY.

There I said it.

Now, to be clear - as I was discovering that sponsorship was a divine attraction process - I realized it had everything to do with God's word and what Jesus Christ Himself taught us about bearing good fruit in our lives, blessing and honoring what God has called us to do, and abiding by the laws of sowing and reaping, from the word.

In this chapter I am going to teach you how to partner with God, operate in His Kingdom finance principles, align with His word to fully understand how this attraction process works - to bring in Godly, Holy Spirit filled financial backers, clients, funding and everything you need financially to do what you have been called to do - and represent the Kingdom of God while doing it. Understanding that God is the source of all your supply and through His Holy Spirit working with you in the marketplace, and through divine strategies and connections - your dream can be fully funded! This now with the understanding when you set out to use your success to Advance the Kingdom, Glorifying God - Your Divine Sponsor! It's a win- win for everyone!

GOD HAS A DREAM FOR HIS KINGDOM ON THE EARTH AND IS LOOKING FOR THOSE WHO WANT TO PARTNER WITH HIM - HE WILL FINANCE YOUR DREAM AS IT ALIGNS WITH HIS DREAM.

Delight yourself also in the Lord, and He shall give you the desires of your heart." - Psalm 37:4

I want to share with you what I discovered about "Sponsor Attraction". I believe now, looking back, God was teaching me how His Kingdom operates from day one in my Motorsports career. He had to show me what did not work first, then bring me into HIS WAY…. I believe now that as I discovered this and with the help of the Holy Spirit created a new way of doing sponsorship for my industry, God was setting me up to teach this to His people to advance the Kingdom on the earth. Let's face it - it takes money to grow a ministry and it takes money to spread the Gospel and advance the Kingdom of God on earth. Why should all the secular stuff out there get all the financial backing when we are at a time of Great Awakening and Outpouring of the Holy Spirit and Great Harvest of Souls for Jesus Christ? Right?

I am tired of the kingdom of darkness taking over these spheres of influence! I want to see Father God, Son Jesus Christ, the Holy Spirit and the Word of God glorified in every single one of these areas! I want to witness the love of Jesus Christ front and center personified in *every* aspect of life!   Schools, Sports, Music, Movies and everything there is!   I believe this is God's Dream!   Thy Kingdom Come, Thy Will Be Done, On Earth As It Is in Heaven! Kingdom Come Lord! Now Lord! YES!! Who is with me?

I used to be focused on super speedway stadiums being filled with race fans, now I want to see these same stadiums filled with people coming to hear the Gospel and giving their lives to Jesus Christ!   JESUS FANS! Wooo hooo!! I know many of you want to be a part of this and dream of starting a ministry, doing mission work or even being able to have successful businesses where you can give generously to the work of the Kingdom of God. This takes FINANCES to see this become a reality.   God's people cannot sit back anymore. It's GO TIME!

I realize now that God was showing me "Sponsor Attraction" as an applicable strategy for His people to work for the Kingdom in bringing forth financial backing and supporters.   It's time for the Transference of Wealth from the wicked to the righteous! To fund the people of God and the good works they will do for the Kingdom in these last days! Now let's go get this! This is the time of the Great Awakening - The Great Harvest for Jesus Christ - right now - straight to us and our legacy for the Lord with our children and those we mentor and disciple for the future!

"A good person leaves an inheritance for their children's children, but a sinner's wealth is stored up for the righteous." - Proverbs 13:22

Let's get to attracting in faith and receiving by faith this transference of wealth!

"The Sponsor Attraction System" was given to me by the Holy Spirit for my company "Marketing at Full Speed" in 2012. I had been developing it years before - but as I became more and more bold with my faith and as a professional in my industry - I knew I had something very unique that had been proven over and over again with my clients - and it was working the same on all levels of motorsports across the board - whether you needed $500 or $5,000,000 the system worked the same with the same principles.

I began to teach this to my clients and students, up and coming professional race car drivers, new team owners and companies wanting to develop products and brands in the sport of auto racing. It became a powerful strategy and easy to apply for my clients once they got into the flow of the system and its strategies. They successfully attracted many companies this way. I created DVD's, wrote articles, did video teachings on YouTube, spoke and taught this at trade shows, conferences and seminars. It was unique and new and people in my industry were taking notice! Why? Because it was working! It was bearing great fruit! It was also a way to do business with integrity, honesty and excellence. A Godly way!

Some of the old cronies and sharks from my industry started to bad mouth me out of jealousy - but I knew in my heart that this was right and I knew that God was behind it.

I kept going and getting the 'Sponsor Attraction System' out there bigtime and it got more and more popular. Racers from all over the world were getting it and applying it easily. I believed in it with all my heart, and it gave me great joy to see my clients and students succeed with it! Plus my own consulting business was booming!

Here are the basics to the "Sponsor Attraction System" that I developed OFFICIALLY in 2012 that brought great results and thousands upon thousands of dollars in sponsorships "Marketing Partnerships" for my racers - see how it aligns with God's word! I did not realize it at the time but now I do! It will be a 'lightbulb' moment for you as you keep reading this chapter to understand how and why God will finance your dreams and goals!

THE SPONSOR ATTRACTION SYSTEM:
(Developed By Annamarie Strawhand For Motorsports - 2012)

1. Know Your Value To Give Value
2. Give Generously To Receive Generously
3. Prepare to RECEIVE Your Partners
4. Get Your Message Out There In a Big Way
5. Be Authentic,Creative,Unique
6. What Sets You Apart From The Rest of the Crowd
7. Be Omni-Present (Visible/Influential Across Many Platforms)
1. Calls To Action (Who Will This Resonate With?)
2. Connect with Like Minded Leaders
3. Build The Relationship - Think Longer Term
4. Treat Them As Part Of Your Team
5. Focus On What You Can Do For Them

6. Align Your Visions - Do You Agree with Their Vision?
7. Give A Sign of Good Will - Pre-Gift Them
8. LKT Rule = Get to Like, Know and Trust each other
9. Go Boldly To Them With Your Proposal
10. Give Three Levels of Options For Them to Grow Into
11. Entry Level, Building Level, Full Title Rights Level
12. Offer Perks They Are Not Getting Anywhere Else
13. Be Clear - Your Cause Aligns with Theirs
14. Give Social Proof - Testimonies
15. Partnership / Co-Branded "As One"
16. Activation Plan In Place and Ready To Carry Forth
17. Your Fans Become Their Fans - Share The List!
18. Share In All Victories Together
19. Offer Perks They Are Not Getting Anywhere Else
20. Be Accountable To Your Word
21. UPOD Rule = Under Promise and Over Deliver

Did you also realize that God wants to give you witty ideas for business and for the marketplace? Yes! Proverbs 8:12 says: "I wisdom dwell with prudence, and find out knowledge of witty inventions." He wants you to stand out and be unique in the marketplace!

Did you know God also gave us - His people the power to "get" (procure/attract) wealth? **YES!**

Deuteronomy 8:18 says: "But remember the Lord your God, for it is he who gives you the ability to produce wealth, and so confirms his covenant, which he swore to your ancestors, as it is today."

I feel we complicate things so much when it comes to money, finances and getting what we need to fund our goals and dreams. We need to remember it's all about our trust in God and His word.

I love to teach the Book of Joshua and in this Book, God basically - very straight to the point - gives Joshua the strategy for success in what He has called Him to do. It is God that commissions our goals, callings, and purposes! So if God commissions it, don't you think He will take care of everything including the finances to do it? We know that as Joshua moved forward boldly in faith and obedience - God gave Joshua and His people all the plunder from the Victories (except from the first one at Jericho) But after that it was all theirs! By the time they got to the promised land, they had gold, silver, fabrics, livestock, you name it - it was more than enough!

Then, when Jesus Christ was born - Father God provided for His Son! The Wise Men came from afar loaded down with treasures! They believed a KING was born - they did not just bring three little tiny boxes of gold, frankincense and myrrh like we see in Christmas nativity scenes! I was shocked when I researched this. The Kings that were born of Jesus' day in the Middle East would have been gifted with a multitude of treasure boxes of gold, jewels, silks, rugs and more! Each wise man would have had a caravan of camels loaded down with gifts and expensive items fit for a king! God made sure that Mary and Joseph could provide for Jesus because soon after that they had to flee to Egypt for years until it was safe for them to return to Nazareth after Herod died.

Yes! God is your divine sponsor for what He has called you to do! He provides all your needs according to His riches and Glory!

But how do you ask for it? How do you align with God's will that you know that you know that you know that HE commissioned you - therefore He will finance it?

How will God bring the finances? How do you attract and get wealth like His word says?

Will a witty idea come for business? Will it come to give you a financial strategy too?

Will God bring you divine connections that are attracted to finance you?

YES, YES and YES!

Let's look again at what God told Joshua as He commissioned him:

God Commissions Joshua:

"Above all, be strong and very courageous. Be careful to observe all the law that My servant Moses commanded you. Do not turn from it to the right or to the left, so that you may prosper wherever you go. This book of the Law must not depart from your mouth; you are to recite it day and night, so that you may carefully observe everything written in it. For then you will prosper and succeed in all you do. Have I not commanded you to be strong and courageous? Do not be afraid; do not be discouraged, for the LORD your God is with you wherever you go." - Joshua Chapter 1

Do you see the KEY here?

- Be Obedient
- Be Bold
- Keep Moving Forward

- Speak The Word of God
- Observe The Word (Have Faith In The Promises)
- Act Upon and Do The Word "Actions"
- Believe God is with You and Goes Before You
- Do Not Doubt
- You WILL Prosper and Succeed in EVERYTHING

YOUR PHYSICAL OBEDIENCE TO GOD BRINGS SUPERNATURAL BREAKTHROUGHS

Do you desire to have Jesus Christ Lord and King over our businesses, products we put into the marketplace, our careers, families, schools and communities? Do we occupy those areas for the Kingdom until He comes? Jesus says in Luke 19:13: "Calling ten of his servants, he gave them ten minas, and said to them, 'Engage in business until I come." Meaning He wanted His Disciples to continue the Father's Business that He started His ministry - and that means us today until His return.

We also know that Jesus talked about the 'Kingdom - His Father's Business". Jesus also said The Kingdom of God is within us - so we operate by Kingdom principles according to the word and promises of God in everything we do! Not just ministry. Your business is your ministry, your family, your career. You walk, talk, operate and do Kingdom minded business. We don't just leave it to the four walls of the church - we are the church!

BOOM THERE IT IS!

You might be thinking: "Yes, I see what you are saying Annamarie, but I still need money to do what God has called me to do. I want to honor God and be obedient but where do I start with all this?"

I am about to give you a step by step strategy. Keep reading. It was important that I laid out the groundwork and background for all this before I got you to the main part! I really, really want you to get this!

Understanding God's Kingdom As Your Source:

To get to the main thing, we must understand the way God the Father looks at our provision, and how He sees us as Sons and Daughters to come and ask for what we need. I had a dream recently where I was in my old home town looking for the bank. I was driving around and driving around and no banks, just a bunch of tourist type shops. I went to the car wash. There after I went through the car wash with my car, my windshield was sparkly clean. I then saw someone I knew who was very successful in their Kingdom business and she came over to me to chat. I said to her: "Where are all the banks? I need money today." She said, "Annamarie, all the banks are North of here!" I knew exactly what she meant. North to me means "Kingdom". I know this because when I put on my Armor of God every morning, and I put on my Belt of Truth, I decree I have the Compass of Almighty God on my belt that points me to "True North, the Kingdom of God." (I don't know why - I just was prompted in the Spirit to say that.)

In the dream I thanked her, pulled out of the car wash and headed North. Soon I came to my Grandparent's neighborhood, where they used to live in a beautiful home on Victoria Park Drive when I was a child. I pulled in the driveway, and the front doors were double doors, they were open and I walked in. There were my clients and students and some new students I did not recognize yet in the living room, singing and worshiping the Lord, one of my clients had a calculator and was putting together numbers for what she was needing to finance her business. She was showing me the numbers and excited because she was about to get the money she needed.

I looked around in the dream and saw on the walls white danish tile with blue windmill designs and blue flowers, a Dutch type Delft design that my grandmother loved to decorate with. I noticed that the home was filled with fine things that my grandparents had when they were in the height of their success in their homebuilding business. I stopped to see that lights were shining on the Blue Delft Tile like it was a priceless artwork and the dream ended.

Now my friends, there is no mistake that God speaks to us in our dreams. The Holy Spirit gives us keys, strategies and clues to answers that we need right at that time. I was writing this chapter on Divine Sponsorship and this was a very timely dream. I quickly opened my laptop after that dream and typed out notes of everything that was shown and said to me in the dream. I then prayed: *"Holy Spirit, I know you were speaking to me about finances in that dream. Please unpack this dream for me, Holy Spirit, and give me exactly what it means so I can understand and use and share the keys you are giving me in Jesus name."*

Have you had some interesting dreams, that you think God is trying to speak to you about something important in your life? This is why I encourage you to write down your dreams and partner with the Holy Spirit to show you exactly what they mean. There are important keys being shown to you! It is fun to do this with the Holy Spirit too, like detective work!

The next day after the dream the Holy Spirit began to download some things to me from the dream. Ask and you shall receive! Always have a way to keep notes because many times it is given to you like a piece to a puzzle, a clue at a time. I went to wash dishes, mindless peaceful work, and that's usually where I get a big download! In my mind He showed me the Blue Delft tiles with the light on them. I heard Him say to me: "What did your grandmother have in her house that was Blue Delft and had a light?" I said, "Well Holy Spirit, her lamp in the kitchen!" I heard, "Yes, and where was that lamp?" I thought - the lamp was one thing left of my grandmother's that is now in my house in the den, next to Mike's chair, but it used to be next to my grandmother's kitchen hutch. Then He said to me, "Good, what was on your grandmother's hutch that you always ran in that house to get?" I knew exactly and my spirit leaped: "THE COOKIE JAR!"

The Cookie Jar. My grandmother's cookie jar. Always filled with fresh baked cookies. When she knew her grandchildren were coming, she made sure the cookie jar was full. My sisters and I would run into grandma's house straight for that hutch and the cookie jar. We would stop for a short second to turn and ask permission as our little hands were poised on the lid - "Grandma, can we have a cookie?" Barely waiting for her to say, "yes" we reached up on tiptoe and I would lift the lid of the big round ceramic jar (I was the oldest) and my sisters and I would reach in and grab a cookie. Sometimes we would have to retreat to the bathroom to wash our hands first if we came in from playing outside. But the KEY here is there were ALWAYS cookies in the cookie jar, and plenty of them. Sometimes they were still warm. The cookies never ever ran out, grandma made sure of that!

I knew the exact financial KEY that was being shown to me in the spirit. I felt God's Fatherly love so powerful at that moment.

YOUR HEAVENLY FATHER HAS EXPECTED YOU TO COME TO HIM FOR WHAT YOU WANT AND NEED. HE

HAS PREPARED UNLIMITED AMOUNTS OF BLESSINGS FOR YOU BECAUSE HE LOVES YOU.

YOU JUST NEED TO GO IN THE DIRECTION OF HIS KINGDOM, COME TO THE FATHER AND ASK.

Are we pointing ourselves and our 'vehicles' (purpose) in the direction of the Kingdom 'north' or are we searching in all the wrong places for our "bank"?

"But seek ye FIRST the kingdom of God, and his righteousness; and ALL these things shall be added unto you." - Matthew 6:3

That was probably the most prophetic dream I have ever had about how the Kingdom of God operates, and the Lord has given me many prophetic messages in my dreams - but this is a very important KEY that came straight from the Father's heart, not just for me but for all of His children, you all too!

So to put it in simple terms, we must look at Father God, as a loving Father, who wants to give His children good things, and like the cookies in the cookie jar, these good things that we need are already there and waiting for us, and it never runs out!

"Every good gift and every perfect gift is from above, and cometh down from the Father of lights, with whom is no variableness, neither shadow of turning." James 1:17

But why do so many of us, who believe what the Bible says, and love God still struggle with finances, still are waiting for what we need financially to achieve our dreams?

I want to tell you why, and this is very personal. It's about you personally and who you believe and see as your source.

God Is the Source of ALL Your Supply!

I want to ask you a serious question: Who do you see as the source of your supply? Is it God?

This chapter is about God as your sponsor. A sponsor is your source, your supplier, your backer, your partner. The one whom you are in covenant and agreement with to cover all your expenses to do what you dream of doing.

When you fully look to God as the source of ALL your supply, that's when everything changes.

God tells us what He owns as your Father, including land and cattle - this was used for a food supply source and represented true wealth: "For every beast of the forest is Mine, and the cattle on a thousand hills." - Psalm 50:10

Who and where do you look to for your supply? Who do you trust first for finances, for all your needs? Your job? Your family? Credit Cards? The Publishers Clearing House Sweepstakes? OR YOUR HEAVENLY FATHER?

Let me tell you something I have learned (yes the hard way).... When you fully surrender to God as the source of all your supply, He can bring exactly what you need from anywhere, anyone and any place he wants!

Whoa....

Expect the unexpected when you surrender all your finances and needs to God!

God LOVES to give us surprises too, not just cookies. Abundant surprises. More than we expect, when we truly trust Him in this.

This is why when someone shows up in my life, even if they are not a believer and want to bless me in some way I receive it all as from God.

Remember in the Bible Joshua? Joseph? Jacob? Jesus?

They all received from unbelievers and sinners, then offered it back up to God and used it to advance the Kingdom.

First you must learn to receive everything as it comes from God.

A good man leaves an inheritance to his children's children, And the wealth of the sinner is stored up for [the hands of] the righteous. Proverbs 13:22

Do you know about Joanna?   One of Jesus's main sponsors of His ministry?

Yes, Jesus had sponsors! The Bible speaks of a particular follower of Jesus, a woman who was married to one of King Herod's Administrators - who gave generously of her finances to Jesus and His ministry.

Joanna is mentioned a mere two times in the Bible, but we can take what is said, and based with historical knowledge of the times - get amazing revelation on how huge this was for this woman to be a "ministry partner" or full out sponsor of Jesus Christ and His mission.

"After this, Jesus traveled about from one town and village to another, proclaiming the good news of the kingdom of God. The Twelve were with him, and also

some women who had been cured of evil spirits and diseases: Mary (called Magdalene) from whom seven demons had come out; Joanna the wife of Cuza, the manager of Herod's household; Susannna; and many others. These women were helping to support them out of their own means." Luke 8:1-3

"When they came back from the tomb, they told all these things to the Eleven and to all the others. It was Mary Magdalene, Joanna, Mary the mother of James, and the others with them who told this to the apostles." Luke 24:9-10

So just imagine, if you had a ministry, and the wife of the President's chief of staff was your biggest supporter and financier!

However, Herod was a corrupt and evil ruler, and not a 'practicing Jew'. King Herod was not a fan of Jesus at the time, and he executed John the Baptist. No matter how much evil was in the house of Herod, God found someone He could use righteously and spoke to the heart of one woman to take what money her husband gave her directly to Jesus Christ! That woman was Joanna, one of Jesus' most generous ministry sponsors!

Just imagine the scenario between Joanna and her Hubby:

Husband: "Joanna my dear, here is 100 shekels to go shopping, buy yourself something nice, a new dress or go get your hair done."

Joanna: "Thank you sweetheart, I know just the place!"

Next scene we see Joanna leaving her home in the morning and running up to where Jesus was preaching, then as the evening falls before she has to return home to hubby, she runs up to Jesus and hands him the 100 shekels! He blesses her, as she quickly runs home to her hubby….

Husband: "Hello dear, did you find something nice to treat yourself today?

Joanna: "Oh yes sweetheart, I feel so refreshed, I might go back tomorrow."

Husband: "Wonderful darling, just let me know what you need, I am going on a business trip with the King, so I want to leave you with enough for several days."

Joanna ponders in her heart how much more she can give Jesus and spend several days with him! She must have been running to her closet and shutting the door so she could yell out wooo hoooo!!!

(I had to add that part in!)

Now, I am not saying you should deceive your husband to give to the church, what I am saying is that those were the times they were living in and Joanna would have to have been discreet, her husband possibly eventually knew and approved of her being a follower of Christ - but the Bible does not say for sure. I believe in my heart her Hubby was OK with it. Interesting that Joanna was one of the women at Jesus tomb when He resurrected. That was an early morning divine appointment - how could her Hubby not have known? I bless him either way! The bible is clear that the husband and wife are one flesh - so as the finances came through him to his wife, then to Jesus - that was a blessing that returned to their household. Hubby's crabby and corrupt boss King Herod was only interested in using Jesus for his own amusement, and when Jesus did not give him a miracle on demand, Herod was furious and sent Jesus to be condemned by Pilate. So it does not matter who you work for, it could be a company that has the worst of unrighteous leadership, what matters is what YOU do with YOUR money once it's transferred to YOU.

Personally, I don't like to work for people who don't honor God. You might feel that way too. But over the years, from Pharaoh to Nebuchadnezzar, to Herod - God used their wealth to go directly to HIS people for HIS purposes! If God wants to do that for your needs - trust Him with it!

My own Hubby, Mike worked for a very mean boss for years, this boss was so difficult and cruel. However, he trusted Mike and gave him tons of favor because Mike is an honorable man and was very good at his job as a plumbing foreman. Mike did not allow the boss to treat him badly, he set the boundaries of respect (Mike is also six foot five, 280 lbs and the boss was just about five foot three, LOL). Mike respected the authority of the boss - the owner of the company that paid his check and fed his family.

But, my husband never stooped to that level of cruelty and hateful attitude back! Instead Mike stayed even tempered, positive as a leader on the jobs himself - always of good character, and was grateful for the work - and the guys that worked with Mike loved him. God used that time with that mean boss to advance my husband financially and also bring him to North Carolina where Mike and I would meet and get married! God uses whoever He wants to get His will done - even the most mean and difficult people in your life! We have forgiven that boss and prayed for him too!

The point here that I am trying to make is how God used a woman of means (Joanna) and spoke to her heart to GIVE to the ministry of His Son - Jesus Christ - and how God uses creative and unusual ways to sponsor what He wants to get done in the Kingdom on earth and through His people like me and you!

Let us look at how God the Father provides earthly sponsorship for us - you and me - His sons and daughters by bringing it from unlikely places. When you press in by faith and step out in obedience, God will activate finances, opportunities, favor, divine connections, buildings, land and even inheritances to be released that has been waiting for you to FULLY carry out your assignment, your purpose and calling for His Kingdom! He can transfer this all from wherever and whatever place or person He wants directly to you!

Declare: *"Father God, I say YES to You! I am ready to receive all that I need to carry out my divine assignment for Your Kingdom. I trust You God in however You want to bring it to me! Like your Son Jesus had sponsors like Joanna, I am ready to receive my sponsors that You have aligned for me! Please help me, the Holy Spirit, to realize and discern who and what is coming from God, so I do not miss it in Jesus name!"*

"A good man leaveth an inheritance to his children's children: and the wealth of the sinner is laid up for the just.

The Amplified Translation says: The wealth of the sinner [finds its way eventually] into the hands of the righteous, for whom it was laid up." - Proverbs 13:22

Understand that we don't put our trust into playing the state lottery, we put our trust in God. We sow our finances and trust into the Kingdom of God, not lottery tickets.

However, if *someone else* wins the lottery, and God wants to move that money to you, then so be it! The key here is for when you receive the finances, you receive it as it is

ALL coming from God and you use it for righteous, Kingdom minded things without ANY compromise.

So if the lottery winners give to you financially and your assignments or callings in faith because they felt they should in their heart, you receive it graciously and bless them. However, do not get into an ungodly covenant with them and start playing the lottery with them! Instead - minister to them about the Kingdom based on what I have taught you here. Use it as an opportunity to share the Kingdom of God, like Jesus did with Joanna.

"Do not be unequally bound together with unbelievers [do not make mismatched alliances with them, inconsistent with your faith]. For what partnership can righteousness have with lawlessness? Or what fellowship can light have with darkness?" 2 Corinthians 6:14 Amplified Bible (AMP)

Do not be yoked "in contract" or in "covenant" with anything sinful or anything that is against God's word or law. This could even be verbal or handshake - because God looks at any agreement as covenant, and so does the accuser, satan. The accuser can accuse you of any unholy covenants in the courts of heaven to hold back your prosperity. We know that the Bible says this in Revelation 12:10 and Jesus Christ blood speaks and shuts the accuser's mouth and casts Him down on our behalf!

Take a moment right now to repent and break off any unholy covenants that you or your ancestors were ever involved in. These are covenants with secret societies, such as the masons, or even way back in your bloodline that people swore or signed their name to allegiance to serve or worship something other than God Almighty. I have learned that these are still held against us in the spirit realm during my prayer time in the Courts of Heaven. But we have our advocate, Jesus Christ who can get these things broken off us and our bloodlines right away! Thank You Jesus!

Prayer To Break Unholy Covenants:

Pray out loud: "Father God, I come to you now in the name of Jesus Christ and repent of any unholy covenants that me or my ancestors have ever agreed or entered into. I ask for grace, mercy and forgiveness. Lord Jesus I ask you as my advocate and savior to cover these sins with your blood, cover these unholy covenants in my life and the life of my ancestors with your blood Lord Jesus. I am no longer in agreement with any of these unholy covenants and I stand in the gap as an intercessor for my ancestors going all the way back to Adam and Eve. I repent for my entire bloodline. Lord Jesus wash me and my family bloodline clean, and break off and sever every unholy covenant Lord. I cancel every unholy covenant, I mark them all null and void in Jesus name! Father God I renounce right now all unholy covenants on behalf of myself and my bloodline, and I decree the only covenant I am in and my household and descendants are in is ONE HOLY COVENANT with YOU Father God through the precious shed blood of Your Son Jesus Christ. Father God, thank You for your grace, mercy and forgiveness, and Father it is written that a curse causeless cannot light, therefore now because these sins are now under the blood of Jesus Christ, all accusations, curses and demonic assignments coming against my prosperity must be removed. Father God, I ask you to strip the accuser of all his accusations and his legal rights in Jesus name. Father God, I ask for all these sins and accusations and any evidence of unholy covenants in my life or my ancestors be wiped from the record books of heaven forever by the Blood of Jesus. Father God, I ask for all the blessings that have been waiting to be released to me and my household now be released to me by your Angels on Assignment and by the power of the Holy Spirit and the Authority of Jesus Christ. I now enter into a complete and full partnership and representation with You Father God and Your Kingdom, in my life, my household, my family, my business, my ministry, my finances, and my destiny as it is in Heaven, now in Jesus name. Thank You Father God! Amen"

Remember, you are a representative of the Kingdom of God, so God and all His righteousness need to be clearly seen through all that you do, and everything you represent through your life. business and ministry.

You might be thinking; "But Annamarie, Jesus sat and ate with sinners." Of course He did, He sat and ate with them to bring HIS influence to them! He was the representation of the Kingdom and He sat with them to turn them from wickedness to follow Him instead. This is the great commission, for all of us as representatives of Christ today. To be the influencers of the GOOD NEWS in every area. The sinners that Jesus sat and ate with may have even given financially to Jesus ministry, along with feeding him a meal, but the key here was, was His influence life changing for them? Yes! God was His sponsor of His mission on earth, and He represented His Father to the fullest! Did He go into a covenant with their lifestyle after they fed him or gave him money? NO! He encouraged them to change, turn from sin, FOLLOW Him and go into covenant with the KINGDOM of God.

Jesus, during His ministry on earth was like the CMO, "Chief Marketing Officer" of the Kingdom! He represented the Kingdom everywhere He went. He was in ACTIVATION MODE. When I was in NASCAR the promotions and events that we did for the sponsors were called "Activation" - It was done in an effort to grow the customer loyalty, fan base, brand identity and increase sales. Jesus was and is still focused on KINGDOM brand loyalty through us!

You never compromise to fall into someone else's sinful lifestyle to get the money you need! You have to discern what God is doing financially, based on the fruit it will produce through you and what you are called to do for the KINGDOM. It's our responsibility to represent, and plant those GOOD seeds into everyone around you. YOU are the influencer attracting and utilizing God's financial backing! You can even speak over the money that you receive to work for the Kingdom.

However, if God sees compromised churches, businesses, buildings, land and places, He can shut them down and bring in His faithful obedient ones into that place! Look what God did with the Promised Land! It was filled with idol worshippers - God intended it for His people. He intends all the earth and the fullness of it for His people! Soon, King Jesus will rule here for 1000 years of peace on the earth and we as believers will rule with him over everything!

In your life right now, God will use the transference of wealth promise from the most unlikely places. It's up to you to take it for the Kingdom and use it for bearing good, Holy Spirit led fruit!

For example if a pornography studio wanted to sponsor you, and said; 'we will give you the money but you must represent us, sign an agreement to market our ideas and sinful message' - you would NOT take that money! The word says do not be in covenant with sin (yoked to unbelievers). However if a pornography studio closes down and you get an opportunity to move into that studio with all the electronic equipment ready for your Christian based business, you will simply move in and repent for that property and equipment being used for sin and dedicate it to God's plans and purposes, anoint the doors and windows, take communion on the property to cleanse the land, and get to work for the Kingdom! This happened exactly for the world renowned prophet of God, Kim Clement! I remember watching a broadcast of Kim Clement's House of Destiny and he was telling a story of how God told him he would have a major television ministry. At the time, Kim was not sure how he would raise the funding to get the studio and equipment to do this. He started faithfully in a small rented space called the "Den" when he arrived in California.

Just a few years later Kim got the opportunity to purchase a huge studio space complete with sound stage, equipment and more for a very low price, (which in California we know normally would be in the millions), only the building had been used for pornographic films! Kim understood the nature of God and His word, and how the wealth of the wicked is transferred to the righteous! They prayed and confirmed with God, repented for the sins on the property and moved in! This expanded Kim Clement's ministry exponentially and some of the most powerful words from the Lord for the nations came from that studio! This was not just an act of the transference of wealth but an act of redemption on that land and property. As Christians we walk in this authority to redeem the land and buildings back to God through the blood of Jesus Christ.

OCCUPY THE LAND (PLACE) AND CLAIM IT FOR GOD'S PLANS AND PURPOSES

"The Lord your God will drive them out from before you and remove them, so you can occupy their land as the Lord your God promised you." - Joshua 23:5

We don't pursue wealth, we pursue and agree with God and ask Him for what we need and desire by faith. We pursue what God's plan is to do with our wealth. Faith moves God and the Kingdom is activated for you through His Holy Spirit and Angels on Assignment when you declare by faith! Our declarations create and activate in the spirit! God set this up for us! The bible says that God has given us the power to create wealth,

I believe that is with our faith, our words and our actions coming into alignment with what God has aligned for us and His angels are standing by waiting for you to speak it and ask for it. Everything you need and want belongs to God already, Angels hearken to the word of the Lord, therefore, it's time to look up, open your mouth and ASK YOUR FATHER GOD for the sponsorship.

Decree: *"My Help Always Comes from the Lord Every Time I Ask Him!"*

> *"I lift up my eyes to the hills. Where does my help come? My help comes from the Lord, who made heaven and earth! - Psalm 121*

There may be a sudden breakthrough when you ask, there may be a waiting period, support and finances WILL come! Don't question it, don't try to over-analyze it and get all panicked and worried! I always tell my coaching students that the easiest way to get stuck or go backwards is when you put yourself into *analysis paralysis* (over thinking)! Instead, ask the Holy Spirit for quick confirmation to keep encouraging you! Continue to call it forth, claim it from God, for God, receive it and glorify Him with it!

Covenant With God Brings Wealth:

Abraham - The Father of our faith. Abraham is listed as a Father of the faith in Hebrews 11. We are to emulate our faith after Abraham. Abraham had a true relationship and friendship with God, walked in obedience to God no matter what. This was God's dream to have with Adam, but Adam dis-obeyed and broke God's heart. God wanted to have a covenant with man again and Abraham's faith and obedience was tested, and every time he passed the test. Pleasing God. The covenant is important to God, and that we do not break that - Abraham stayed true to their agreement and God blessed him with huge wealth, property and for all his descendants. That means because of Abraham sticking by God's word and promises through thick and thin, you and I benefit from his same blessings and promises today, if we come into covenant with God through Jesus Christ, we gain the covenant blessings of Abraham.

Sonship/Daughtership Brings Sponsorship:

Jacob - Even though his father-in-law Laban was controlling and manipulative and trying to keep Jacob under his servitude, Jacob received a brilliant business idea and strategy from God The Father, to breed a special speckled and striped sheep! Jacob ended up having even more sheep than his father-in-law, and when he finally moved with his wife and kids onto his own land that God promised him - Jacob was fully "sponsored" with flocks and flocks of unique and valuable sheep!   This is like you, leaving the "9 to 5" job to go forward into building your own business and Your Daddy - Father God set you up nicely. God set him up for success because Jacob was renamed "Israel" by God way before he got stuck in Laban's house. He carried a promise of God as Son to bear the Sons of Israel - the 12 tribes! God chose him even before he was stuck in his father-in-law's Laban's servitude. No matter how much Jacob went through with being a "slave" to his 'earthly' father-in-law, he remembered who he really was… a "Son" to God! This is something many people have to realize - you are not a slave! You are a Son/Daughter! All the benefits of sonship come with it from your Heavenly Father, no matter what your circumstances are in the natural! Your Daddy God will set you up for greatness! Sons and Daughters carry a promise that nobody can hinder!

Righteousness and Representation:

Moses - Found in a basket as a baby raised in the Pharaoh's palace, kept his love for his Hebrew people, chosen by God to deliver them out of Egypt. Moses *represented* God and God's power to Pharaoh. He then took all the plunder and wealth from the Egyptian people for the Hebrew people when they exited Egypt and slavery. Moses got to see God and had such influence with God he actually convinced God not to punish the people for disobedience!

Daniel - was one person who made both intercession to God and *representation* for God for all the Jewish people even while in captivity himself. While in exile Daniel used his God-given gifts of dream interpretation to gain favor in the house of Babylonian King. Daniel stayed true to his faith in God and represented God's power to pagan King! Daniel made intercession with God for an entire nation of Hebrews in captivity while still gaining favor, status with Babylonian leaders. Angels were dispatched and fought battles for Daniel and God's glory was on him through any persecution that put the fear of God into the pagan Kings.

Imagine now what your intercession can do for your entire family, business, household, community and nation!

Transference of Wealth:

Esther and Mordechai - Jewish Orphan made Queen of Persia with her Cousin Mordechai, gained favor with Persian King to overthrow the plot to kill Jews, saved her people, and Mordechai became a noble man in the King's court. What the enemy meant for evil, God turned for Esther's good and for her entire nation by boldly activating her faith.

Joshua - Was an obedient leader for God. Received all the plunder, gold, livestock from battles won over pagan cities on the way to the Promised Land - Once arriving in Promised Land everyone (millions of Israelites) were set for wealth and prosperity with gold, silver, sheep and they also took over all the land as their own.

Joseph - Went from the prison to the palace in one day by using his God given gift of dream interpretation for Pharaoh. He was named Governor over Egypt - Second in command to Pharaoh, had immense wealth - stayed in Hebrew faith to God and roots to family. Was in charge over all food in Egypt, saved his own people from famine even in a pagan land.

Jesus Christ is ALL of the above, as are we in Christ Jesus. Each person mentioned above stayed true to their faith in God, they did not bow to idols in the situations they found themselves in, and they still received wealth and favor! God used the pagan leaders and land to bless His own people - a transference of wealth! They never compromised their faith and they were even more blessed! God controls where He wants the money to go! God can harden or soften a person's heart like He did Pharaoh and when you stay focused on what God can do instead of man, watch what God does with the people around you to bless you!

I have my own story about God doing this exact thing for me and my family!

I wrote a book about our rescue horse "Pongo". He needed a barn to stay in the winter. At the time we did not have the funds to build a barn. We had Pongo in a smaller paddock on our property. Winter was coming and we prayed for a financial breakthrough to build the barn, we sowed a seed at Church and named it "Pongo's Barn" in faith. We came into agreement as a family and believed God would bring a barn for this horse before winter in Jesus name. Almost a week later, my neighbor behind us stopped over to see Pongo. He was sweet and she liked him right away. She asked us about having a barn for him and we told her we were praying for one. Immediately she offered her beautiful barn just up the lane behind our house. She said she would be thrilled to have Pongo there and we could see him all the time from our back window across the pasture.

Now my neighbor is not a Christian, and she does not have any religious or faith background that she has revealed to us in any way. But, God took our seed that we planted into His Kingdom, and then directly planted a seed into my neighbor's heart to give Pongo a beautiful barn to stay in! We thanked her for her generosity and a few days later Pongo moved over there happily! He is warm, safe and sound and enjoys a huge pasture that comes all the way up to our house. Plus my neighbor enjoys him, too. It's like we have one property together, we even put a gate up to our paddock so he can go back and forth! God showed me that someday Mike and I would buy the property!

What do you think would have happened if I had gotten all religious and self-righteous and not allowed Pongo to go on her property because she was not a believer in Jesus? No! I knew what God was doing here and I was grateful!

We used our Holy Spirit discernment in this situation. "Would it produce good fruit for the Holy Spirit?" Yes! We had a chance to be blessed by our neighbor for our sweet horse and God actually owns all the land! Once Pongo's book was done, my neighbor bought copies for herself and all her friends! It's a book of faith and witnesses the Gospel of Jesus Christ! PONGO (a rescue horse) is an evangelist to my neighbor! He has a beautiful barn to stay in, two donkey pals, huge pasture, training ring and we can walk there every day and have full use of the facility! How cool is God!! He even cares about our pets and livestock! He works in our favor for what we ask and even more! Because it all belongs to and comes from Him! We just have to ask and activate our faith! Because of this wonderful set-up from God through our neighbor, we are able to give away cases of Pongo's books to children and teens who have suffered from bullying! WOW GOD!

"For every beast of the forest is Mine - the cattle on a thousand hills. I know every bird in the mountains, and the creatures of the field are Mine. If I were hungry, I would not tell you, for the world is Mine, and the fullness thereof...." - Psalm 50:11

DIVINE SPONSORSHIP KEYS:

1. Seek First The Kingdom of God
2. God is your source and it's unlimited
3. Partner with the Holy Spirit
4. Ask for What You want and Need
5. Expect divine ideas and strategies for the marketplace
6. The Holy Spirit will connect you with like minded people (Attraction)
7. Receive everything as if God is bringing to you
8. Bless and pray over everything that comes in

9. Use discernment - will this produce fruit of the Holy Spirit?
10. Plant seeds - GIVE
11. Don't be afraid to ASK
12. Watch God move things in your favor!

DIVINE SPONSORSHIP ACCELERATION:

Feel the need for speed? Want to get your financial breakthrough accelerated to you faster?

God has given me an important KEY to Financial Acceleration! You must KNOW this Secret:

Growing up my earthly dad, Carmen was a drag racer. His race car was built for short fast races, down a straight strip. The objective was to just race against one car, beat it off the line and get down the strip before the other car in a shorter time. My dad had many speed records and one of his secrets was a "nitrous oxide" or "Nitro" bottle - a special gas that blasted into his carburetor on the engine that propelled the car like a rocket at the end of the strip to take the win every time.

This was more than 'turbo boost" where you just have a blower on the engine to "force" more air for performance. Nitro was a secret fuel injected ingredient that was an instant powerful blast of power to make any gasoline engine a super jet!

My dad would power down the drag strip, then just before the finish line, he would hit the secret button and a blast of nitro would kick in! It was like instant rocket fuel to the race car, and nobody could beat him.

Soon, almost all the racers caught on to the secret and were using the "nitrous bottle". But my dad was always looking for an edge to be the fastest car out there!

I still enjoy drag racing and I always think about how they dial in these cars like land rockets for short races focused on intense speed, getting to the finish line faster in a shorter time. That's in my nature; "How can we get to the goal faster, better, in less time?" What gives us an edge in our journey in our faith?

I am all about understanding the nature of our Father God, and I know He has many mysteries that He reveals to His people a step at a time. I am one of those daughters of Father God who is always asking Him questions like; "Father God, everyone is always saying that we have to wait for Your timing, but Your timing can be one year, one month, one day or one minute! I would ask, Father, How do I get this faster? How can I see you move suddenly on this for me? Is there something slowing me down? What is the secret to accelerating my breakthrough Father God?" These are the questions I ask God all the time!

One day I began to see the numbers 333 everywhere. The Holy Spirit communicates with me a lot through repeated numbers. I know that when He shows me these numbers over and over again, I am to acknowledge what He is showing me and He always brings me to the word, first. He brought me to Jeremiah 33:3...

"Call to me and I will answer you and tell you great and unsearchable things you do not know." - Jeremiah 33:3

Instantly, I decreed that word, and said: *"Father God, I call unto You now, according to your word in Jeremiah 33:3 and I am asking You to tell me what I do not know and need to know to accelerate my goals and my finances. Thank You Father God, I await your answer faithfully in Jesus name!"*

A few days later I began to see teachings about God's love for Israel and the Jewish people. More and more I kept seeing bible lessons coming into my email about the blessings of Abraham and His descendants. Over and over again this verse kept coming to my attention:

"Whoever blesses Israel will be blessed, And whoever curses Israel will be cursed." Numbers 24:9

Then it all hit me! The blessing of Abraham! God's covenant and promise to His people! The Hebrew people! When we bless Israel we will be blessed! It all connects back to ISRAEL!

SUPPORTING ISRAEL AND THE JEWISH PEOPLE IS LIKE ADDING JET FUEL TO SPEED UP YOUR FINANCIAL BREAKTHROUGHS!

I knew at that moment the Holy Spirit had given me an answer to my question to the Father. This is a powerful key, and God is *very serious* about it, and honors His word!

Quickly I did a mind sweep: "Oh my goodness have I ever done anything against a Jewish person? Have I really blessed God's chosen people?" I repented just in case, and set out to bless God's Chosen People and The Land Of Israel!

I began to press in to God about this, praying into it more - deeply studying this powerful promise of God.

I found some astounding historical facts of blessings and prosperity coming upon nations that supported and blessed Israel. The more I studied about God's Chosen people, the more I fell in love with them too! The more I began to understand God's love for Israel and especially Jerusalem! The more I understand how, we as born again believers in Jesus Christ are 'grafted in' to the blessings, wealth and prosperity of Abraham - but we must be obedient to this word of blessing Israel to receive them!

My heart began to understand and feel the Father's heart. I wanted to support Israel, I began to have a desire to pour my finances and support ministries that supported Holocaust survivors, relocation for Jewish families coming back to Israel (making aliyah) and other support of orphans and more "Messianic" Hebrew charities (Hebrews/Jews who believe in Jesus Christ as Messiah). A fire was lit in me to learn more about my Jesus as a Jewish Savior, Yeshua Messiah! I began to follow the Hebrew feasts, calendar and seasons.

As I sowed my finances, time and desire to learn everything about Israel, I noticed how blessed I felt, how much closer I got to God and understood Him! Then I saw how my own seasons begin to line up with His Hebrew calendar, then my finances began to be blessed and blessed and blessed! I never felt more in alignment with God! This was amazing and wonderful!

Then Mike and I got an opportunity to invest in companies in Israel, we jumped right on it!

It's been an amazing revelation, and it changed my life. Our financial breakthroughs as well as the advancement in my goals and gifts have accelerated exponentially since I started blessing and supporting Israel. My Christian Life Coaching business "Victory Lane Mentoring" has grown quickly as well as my following and sponsors "Faith Partners" with my online live broadcasts "Faith Lane TV" and my new multi-media publishing company has now launched Faith Lane Media, LLC.

I am excited to be fully operating in the Kingdom - in business and ministry. My business finances my ministry. God gave me the strategy to do it this way. If you purchased this book, this is my business - I am an author and publisher. A percentage of the sale of my book goes into the ministry - our outreach. This is not a non-profit. The Lord specifically told me NOT to make my ministry a 501c3. It's an apostolic ministry, fully funded as needed to do exactly what Jesus said to do in the great commission. I am focused on training up those to do the work of Jesus final instructions to His own disciples. He did not tell them to start non-profits. He told them to DISCIPLE PEOPLE.

Go therefore and make disciples of all nations, baptizing them in the name of the Father and of the Son and of the Holy Spirit, teaching them to observe all that I have commanded you. And behold, I am with you always, to the end of the age." Matthew 28:16

My ministry (Annamarie Strawhand Ministries) is set up now on the full premise of the Great Commission, and our goal is to flow what we receive financially to missions that are spreading the gospel, helping those who are in need and to come to know who they are in Christ Jesus. Also to build programs with full scholarships for apostolic training of leaders to be sent out to lead and disciple all nations for Jesus Christ - including Israel. (Our scholarship program we already have been doing this - with Disciples activated in different areas of America so far....) The people of God fund the work of the church, and the church is not a building, it's the Body of Christ at work for the Kingdom. It must be MOVING and MOBILE....

AS MENTORS, COACHES, PASTORS, TEACHERS LEADERS WE MUST TEACH YOU AND RELEASE YOU TO GO AND DO THE WORK OF YOUR KINGDOM CALLING

We are called to be RIVERS of living water, not LAKES. God is all about the flow! The Bible even says God's voice sounds like "many waters".

When you are focused on being a RIVER and not a LAKE for God - more and more finances come. Why? Because that's how God is. He sees the end from the beginning and He wants you to come into agreement with what He and His Son Jesus Christ's goals are for the Kingdom.

I remember when I was really at odds with myself trying to understand how to do a ministry and a business at the same time. Is it possible? Can we do both? YES!

The word came from the Holy Spirit to release me to do BOTH Business and Ministry on August 8, 2018

This is the scripture God showed me to confirm this:

"Fruit trees of all kinds will grow on both banks of the river (Holy Spirit). Their leaves will not wither, nor will their fruit fail. Every month they will bear fruit, because the water from the sanctuary flows to them. Their fruit will serve for food (personal) and their leaves for healing (ministry)." Ezekiel 47:12

MY BUSINESS AND MINISTRY WILL BOTH BEAR FRUIT AND THE LORD WILL SUSTAIN ME AND MY FAMILY'S NEEDS AS I ALSO FLOW TO OTHERS IN NEED (BOTH SIDES OF THE RIVER) AND SO WILL YOURS!

We are meant to be prosperous in our businesses and careers so we can flow the finances into ministries doing the work of Jesus Christ to all the world! This is how the Kingdom of God advances! This is how we are blessed ourselves! Israel is a big key in all this because this is where God's ultimate goal is - for His Son to return there to rule and reign from Jerusalem - and we will reign with Him!

BE A PART OF GOD'S DREAM AND WATCH HIM BLESS YOUR DREAM!

I just don't support Israel because I want faster money or to speed up my goals - that is an added benefit - I do it because I have a true love for what God loves! I *want* to do it! My ministry directly supports Israel, and Mike and I regularly pray for Jerusalem and bless the Jewish people. This is our commitment. God has stood by His promise to this word, and our family, ministry, business and finances have seen the measurable positive results!

I truly have acceleration of what I needed and asked for! Thank You Father God for being Faithful to His Word!

Now, I will tell you that the other side of this is also true, that if you curse Israel you will be cursed. It was amazing how God showed me this! Please carefully pay attention to what I am about to tell you!

While visiting a coaching client in California, she asked me as a prophetic person while I stayed at her place, (a beautiful bed and breakfast and spa) if I would ask the Lord to speak to me about her business and finances. She had been in a very dry financial season with her business and could not understand why.

I stayed in a room that many other prophets of God had stayed in before, and the anointing was strong in the room. The very first night I stayed there the Holy Spirit spoke so powerfully to me! He said: *"This woman is in covenant with a company that curses Israel! Therefore she has brought a curse on her business!"*

What!? Whoa!!

I said, "Holy Spirit, please tell me what it is so I can tell her first thing tomorrow!" He then showed me a vision of some brochures of a bed and breakfast "B&B" online booking service. I recognized the logo of the company - I had seen it on her business promotions that she had "affiliated" her Spa with that "B&B" company! I had also noticed that she had some of their brochures displayed around her own Bed and Breakfast home that was connected to her Spa where I had been staying.

Immediately I went to her spa website (I had my laptop on the bed) and clicked on the link to the "B&B" company she had "affiliated" her company with. I went to the area of their site where it said: "Who we are and what we stand for" - I clicked and read through. I kept reading through the small print, then it jumped out at me: *"We do not support any illegal **Israeli** occupied properties on the west bank."*

Oh No! They were supporters of the BDS movement - a political movement that boycotts and has very negative press about Israel, their products, their land and economy! They literally are 'cursing' Israel's prosperity through their company policies.

BOOM there it is! This is the reason my clients' own spa business and bed and breakfast was having a "dry season"! It was directly affecting her finances negatively! She could not understand why! She was a woman of faith, too!

Remember earlier in this chapter, I led you to a prayer to remove any unholy covenants (agreements) so you could prepare to receive your divine sponsorship from the Kingdom of God?

Understand what my client was involved in looked like just a simple business *agreement!* A simple business affiliation! She thought becoming affiliated with this online "B&B" service would help and grow her business! But it was actually a signed covenant against God and His word!

Because the B&B Company cursed Israel - she was cursed! Her business dried up!

I thanked the Holy Spirit for showing me this so quickly and bringing me to the root of her problem so we could solve it!

He is *so good* like that!

That morning I told her what the Holy Spirit said! She was shocked! She was a Christian and loved Israel, she would never knowingly connect with a company that cursed God's land and people!

I led her through repentance, we threw out all the brochures, and she went online and cancelled her agreement with them right away. She also had paperwork she signed and we canceled that too. All the money that she already gave them in fees, we prayed and decreed it as a seed for the owners of that company to come to know, support and love Israel the way the Father God does! We prayed that they would drop this terrible policy.

Then I had her sow a financial offering into a good Christian - Israel Charity and bless it unto the Lord and for His people and that it would bring an expedited blessing to her business.

WOW! Thank You Lord!!

I am so grateful for that lesson the Holy Spirit showed me! God will not be mocked! He is true to His word. Even though this woman did not realize what she was signing on for, a curse - God was merciful because of her faith in Jesus Christ! The Holy Spirit worked with us to get directly to the answer to get her out from under it!

It was interesting because almost immediately after we did all this, she saw a burst in her spa business - while I was there, she was getting more bookings! Praise God! He hit the "Jet Fuel Button" for her as a sign of His Faithfulness!

It is so wonderful we have the promises of God going all the way back to Abraham because of Jesus Christ. All of God's words are true and alive and working for our prosperity today!

I love how God has shown me this important Israel Financial Blessing Key to share with you! Take a moment to repent for anything you may have ever said or done against Israel or the Jewish people, any negative word - have God show you right down to the fine print if you are connected through an agreement "covenant" with anything that is negative towards Israel or the Jewish people. Let the Holy Spirit guide you to quickly root out anything like this that would come against your financial breakthrough. Remember to read the fine print!

"Therefore know that only those who are of faith are sons of Abraham." Galatians 3:7

The Bible says Abraham was a "Friend of God" - Abraham was in covenant with God, and tithed faithfully into the Kingdom of Salem (Jeru-Salem) therefore God made Abraham a very wealthy man and land owner. Therefore we have the same blessing available to us!

Decree: *Through Jesus Christ The Son of Almighty God and my Messiah, I Love, Bless and Support Israel and the Jewish People! I have been grafted into the blessing of Abraham! I am in faith that my Messiah Jesus Christ is the Jewish Messiah and I honor my Hebrew roots and brotherhood! I decree I am a son/daughter of Abraham through the Blood of Jesus Christ and I receive all the blessings and promises of Abraham in Jesus name!*

My Victorious Friend, when you are in complete faith, stand on ALL the promises of God through Jesus Christ (old and new testament) and love what God loves, stay in covenant with God and be careful not to get into any covenant with anything that God despises - you will see the blessings (and divine financial sponsorship) of God come into your life at *supersonic* speed!

How To Do Kingdom Giving, Banking and Investing - Expecting A Return On Your Investment By Faith:

When giving to the Lord, we have *the tithe* (our obedient 10%) or *an offering* (over and above the tithe that is given with the intent of love for the Lord and believing Him in making good on His promise in Malachi 3:10) *our first fruits* (a first offering to the Lord each year or the first of something new the Lord has done in your life - first paycheck of a new job, first sale of a new book, etc) Then there is a *seed offering:* where you intentionally give unto the kingdom of God and name the offering as a "seed" that you will be expecting a harvest from.

When you plant corn you don't get daisies, right? You expect a corn harvest. It's all about being *specific* with your seed. So you write your check, or send it via website, you write what the name of the seed and what the harvest you are expecting by faith. So you have a $25 seed, you say this prayer over your check or transaction:

"Father, Thank you for this $25. I offer this up to you Father and plant this as a seed into your Kingdom and I name this seed "new car". I believe by faith that this shall produce a harvest for which it is sent according to Your word Father in Isaiah 55:11 that so My word that proceeds from My mouth will not return to Me empty, but it will accomplish what I please, and it will prosper where I send it.. In Jesus name I receive my new car in faith, Thank you Father, Amen"

You can even name your seed "for the salvation of my loved one _____" or "for the restoration of my marriage" or "for the returning home of my prodigal _____"

YOU CANNOT EXPECT A HARVEST OF BREAKTHROUGHS AND FINANCES IF YOU DON'T PLANT ANY SEEDS! (I say this with Love as your coach and mentor…)

God makes it simple and wants us to understand Kingdom Finance and Giving. Once your check or offering is decreed by faith into the Kingdom of God, it changes realms and is not under the earth curse system, but God's unlimited Kingdom, where there is no lack - only abundance.

You also want to make sure the ministries where you "plant" your seed are growing and producing much fruit of the Holy Spirit and advancing the Kingdom of God. You want to sow into "fertile ground".

You can also decree a 1000 fold return on your seed financially. WHEN YOU GIVE - GIVE WITH FAITH AND SAY: I AM BELIEVING GOD FOR 1000 FOLD RETURN ON MY SEED!! ACCORDING DEUT. 1:11 - "Father I sow this seed of $_____ into your Kingdom and decree by faith over this seed that it will be blessed and multiply 1000 fold financial return according to Your promise in Deuteronomy 1:11 for me and my household and the ministry I am sowing it into in Jesus name, Amen!"

There are many teachings out there on Kingdom finances and giving. I have been guided directly by the Holy Spirit on Kingdom giving and I am excited to share this with you because I have received abundantly! He will never steer you wrong and I want to encourage you to seek Him deeper on your finances too! I also find it powerful giving your "FIRST FRUITS" to your loving Heavenly Father. First Fruits is a direct gift of love back to God - and it pleases God. The Holy Spirit has given me a good understanding of how this works and why God set it up this way. It's all very sacred and all very beautiful when giving to the Father and thinking of Him first. The best understanding is this wonderful teaching I heard one time, I cannot remember where I heard it but it has stuck with me......

First Fruits Offering Is Like a Box of Chocolates!

"A father has two young sons, he wants to bless them each with a beautiful box of assorted chocolates. He gives each boy their box of chocolates and tells them he loves them and to enjoy. One boy runs to his room and digs eagerly into the box, and quickly eats up all the candy, chocolate all over his face, and is full and satisfied. The other boy stays near the father, opens the box of chocolates, thanks the father for the gift, and reaches the opened box back up to the father, and says; "Father, would you like the first piece?"

Oh, how I love that little story! It fills my heart with the true relationship of how we are to be with our loving Father God! Even when we get great blessings - He wants to share them with us! This is the First Fruits. I have found when I do this my relationship with God grows deeper, and more good gifts that come from above to share with Him!

James 1:17, KJV: "Every good gift and every perfect gift is from above, and cometh down from the Father of lights, with whom is no variableness, neither shadow of turning."

When God brings your DIVINE SPONSORSHIP, bless Him back with the first part of it. This is a very powerful act, and when you do this with love - you are in the GLORY, covering your finances! God says to TEST Him in your offerings and watch Him pour out a blessing that you can hardly contain!

Malachi 3:10 "Bring the whole tithe into the storehouse, that there may be food in my house. Test me in this," says the Lord Almighty, "and see if I will not throw open the floodgates of heaven and pour out so much blessing that there will not be room enough to store it."

Understanding God's financial laws of sowing and reaping is key to your financial growth and divine sponsorships. Giving to Israel based missions is always important for your expediting finances and blessings and connecting yourself to the promises of Abraham. My ministry directly supports Israel. You should never come to the Altar of the Lord empty handed. You give what you can from the heart. Also understand when you give to a prophetic ministry you are blessed by a "Prophet's Reward". When we give to a prophet (like the Shunamite woman did for

Elisha) you receive major blessings and even miracles. My ministry operates under a prophetic mantle and we have seen so many words come to pass for those the Holy Spirit has spoken through me.. I am so grateful and humbled to operate in this calling and office of the kingdom! God is TRUE to His word!

You have a choice to give an offering or sow a seed where you want. God gives us free will, but we must give with the heart. I have learned it's important to give where you are being fed the most. This is the "fertile ground". I also have been instructed many times by the Lord where and how much He wants me to give. It's important to step out in obedience - God will always return the blessing swiftly to you for your obedience. Obedience brings quick supernatural breakthroughs!

Here is a prayer that I pray over my tithes, seeds and first fruit offerings to the Kingdom:

Tithing Money in the Kingdom - *Declare: "God is my treasure, God is my prosperity and my source of all my supply! God is my security!"*

When you give, give with your heart in the kingdom - give to God. Acknowledge God as my everything and He prospers me!

Lay your hand on the money, envelope or transaction you are giving to God. *Declare: "I acknowledge God as my prosperity and my source! He prospers me!"*

Pray: *"Father, in the name of Jesus, I believe! I believe what YOU say and YOU prosper the work of my hands! My job, my family, my bank accounts, they are not my* *source! You Father God are my source, everything else is a resource! You Father God are my prosperity! I am grateful and I choose to worship You today Father God with my offering! In Jesus name! Amen!"*

A specific need - pray: *"Father God, your word says in Mark 11:24 Therefore I say unto you, What things soever ye desire, when ye pray, believe that ye receive them, and ye shall have them. Therefore, Father I am in need of _____ and I believe I have received it today in Jesus name! Thank you Father God!"*

You might be thinking these stories are great but what about years and seasons of lack in your life? Many Christians have what I call a lack mindset and say things like: *"if it's the Lord's will or I will wait on God's timing".*

GOD'S WORD IS HIS WILL! GOD'S TIMING IS BASED ON YOUR ACTIONS OF FAITH!

The Holy Spirit spoke very powerfully to me on this very issue!

I ASKED GOD: "HOW DO I BREAK OUT OF A SEASON OF LACK INTO A SEASON OF ABUNDANCE?"

This is what was revealed to me:

- Time does not determine my seasons my seed does
- The seeds I sow today determine my tomorrow
- Seeds can break you out of a season of lack into a season of abundance and more seasons of multiplied abundance

- Loose all poverty and lack from your soul and your life and bind God's abundance and blessing to your soul and your life

Word From God: "Then Isaac sowed in that land, and reaped in the same year a hundredfold; and the Lord blessed him. The man began to prosper, and continued prospering until he became very prosperous;" (Genesis 26:12-13)

What seeds are you sowing right now that you are expecting a harvest in the next season?I have learned to sow seeds into the Kingdom of God, into learning, into people, into my children, into my own ministry, others ministries, my own businesses and others businesses. It's all about sowing and reaping for your success!

GIVE GOD YOUR FEW LOAVES AND FISHES! GIVE GOD SOMETHING TO MULTIPLY!

YOUR SEED IS FOR GOD – THE HARVEST IS FOR YOU!

I am learning about this too as the Holy Spirit reveals - I have reaped much fruit from "Banking and Sowing/ Reaping in the Kingdom" and wanting to give to my loving Father who gives so much to me. The key I have found is to use your money for the kingdom as much as possible and if you have to pay into something that is not fully aligned with the kingdom of God, take what you have to pay them and make it a seed unto the Lord for the salvation of the people who own that company you are paying. For example, you meet a friend for lunch one day at a Mexican place that was known for the fresh dishes. While in the place, you notice a lot of pagan decor on the walls, such as Aztec sun gods etc. Just go ahead and pray over your food, enjoy your meal then when you pay for the meal, declare the money as a seed for salvation to Jesus Christ for the owners and all who were employed there! Command your money what you want it to do in Jesus name and take your authority in Christ everywhere you go.

The Kingdom is a lifestyle! When you command your money all day long what you want it to do in Jesus name - you are at a level of GLORY with your finances - watch what God does for you when you come up to this level! There is only "Shalem" (wholeness - fullness - life - peace) nothing lacking, nothing missing, nothing broken when you are fully operating in the Kingdom! Plus it's fun - every day is a Holy Spirit adventure and miracles are a regular occurrence!

I just love to have all my money flowing in for my needs and then put to use for advancing the Kingdom! God is faithful to His word and promises, and if you carry these out by faith - you can expect DIVINE SPONSORSHIP for whatever you need and more!

CHAPTER 6
SET- UPS FOR SPEED

You have been learning about how you are already equipped with a powerful engine inside you, how to build a good team around you and also how to prepare and partner with God to do what He has called you to do and for the finances you need to do it. You are ready to hit the track baby!

So let's get out of the box and roll 'er out. You are ready to take on this race. You might feel a little nervous, not sure if everything you prepped for is going to fly. I know - I have been there!

A million questions are in your mind.....

- Is this really gonna work?
- Will people like and accept it?
- I hope I am being obedient to God?
- What if I heard God wrong?
- What if the enemy tries to attack me?
- Do I need more training?
- What if I fail?
- Am I really prepared to do this?
- Maybe I should wait until _ (insert whatever excuse, LOL)

I will tell you, that if you have done most of the things that I have mapped out for you in the previous chapters you are ready to do the final steps to hit the track! It is time to launch your purpose, assignment and calling that you were born to do - and win!

First, let's address a common problem you may encounter when you hit this stage…

You might feel ready, you believe God - but something is stopping you from launching out. Here is what I teach my mentoring students when they have what I call *"analysis paralysis"*. You might begin to **overthink the situation** to the point that it stops you from moving forward. As soon as God is wanting you to prepare to launch into your purpose, calling and assignment - the enemy comes in to try and stall you, freeze you up with all these negative thoughts. Now, I am not trying to scare you that you will get an attack from the enemy - I want to **prepare** you to easily overcome it! These thoughts people get right before the breakthrough launch It's actually a sign that you are on the right track! But you are designed and built to overcome these attacks, and not only overcome but crush them and go on to Victory!

It's divine timing because just as I was writing this chapter, I did a teaching on being an OVERCOMER on my Youtube Broadcast. These are the days of the sons and daughters of God rising up to do great things in the world and advancing the kingdom of God. Did you know that the Bible says we will "Wear the Victor's Crown" and this is given to those who overcome? YES!

The five crowns for various acts of faithfulness:

1. A "Crown of Rejoicing:" The soul winner's crown - 1 Thessalonians 2:19,20; Proverbs 11:30,31.
2. A "Crown of Righteousness:" given for looking for Christ's return - 2 Timothy 4:8
3. The "Incorruptible Crown:" for living a separated life - 1 Corinthians 9:25-27.
4. A "Crown of Life:" for enduring tests, even faithful unto death; sometimes called the Martyr's Crown. - James 1:12; Revelation 2:10.
5. A "Crown of Glory:" for being faithful in care of the flock...a Pastor's Crown - 1 Peter 5:1-5.

I have asked The Holy Spirit boldly that I would be honored to receive the Crown Of Glory. I asked Him to help me to be obedient and faithful in my purpose and assignment to receive this Crown!

I believe and have seen these crowns in the spirit. In a vision I saw a beautiful crown being handed to me. I reached up and took it. I asked what it was for. The Lord sent me to these scriptures I just gave you about Crowns. I believe many of us are already wearing these in the spirit. Especially those who are fully operating in their Kingdom Assignment here on earth.

Jesus OVERCAME the World - He told us to *occupy* until He comes.

Are you ready to OVERCOME and take your rightful place that God has ordained for you? Now that you are in the set-up to launch time, you may be dealing with some obstacles in front of you. You really want to get started - but there may be a few things holding you back, or keeping you from accelerating once you have launched. My goal is to help you keep your eye on the prize, the VICTORY and these set-ups for speed that I will be outlining in this chapter must first start with your mindset! Yes your MIND. You must have an OVERCOMER MINDSET.

While teaching on the Overcomer Mindset, I came up with the title of a video teaching "Your Mountains will Become Speed Bumps!"

I came up with that title because one of my moderators on the chat as I was teaching live, typed in this awesome quote:

"Speed Bumps Are God's Air Time" - David Piccorillo

That made me laugh so hard when he posted that in the chat because I visualized us as Overcomers behind the wheel of our Purpose - going full out, pedal to the metal over what we used to think were mountains that by faith became these little speed bumps, and as we powered over them full speed ahead we caught some air like the Dukes of Hazzard General Lee car speeding through the backroads of Tennessee and out runnin' Boss Hogg! LOL

Ok yes, I watched the show Dukes of Hazzard in the 80's and I will be honest, one of my favorite movies of all time is Smokey and the Bandit (I grew up a car girl in the 70's and 80's - now I am a faith girl - God has made quite a combination in me over the years!)

I feel the need, the need for speed! How about you?

So let's get set up for SPEED.

First, understand there is no "STRIVING" with God. We do not have to strive and fight for His love, promises and favor to be upon us. It's already there to receive. But what He does want, is our TRUST. The more we trust, the more we overcome, the more we overcome the more we accelerate! So much we are leaping over bridges and canyons, catching air over hills and mountains (speed bumps) and - you guessed it - barrelling through and running over every giant

of doubt and fear that would ever try to stand in our way! Heck - we are even leaving tread marks on the heads of every demon that would be dumb enough to mess with us! YES!

When a race car driver is ready to hit the track, he does the final run-down with the crew chief. Final tweaks and checks are done on the shocks and suspension, charging up the battery, topping the tank off with fuel, adjustments on tire pressures. Checking all the dash instruments and most of all the communications are working over the radio between the driver and crew. The crew chief gets the driver tightened in his seat belts, overlooking the driver's safety equipment and gives some final instructions on race strategy - and of course some words of encouragement. Then the driver gets his gloves on, flips down his helmet visor and gets himself in the Victory 'overcomer' Mindset. This is you with the Holy Spirit. Your vehicle is your purpose and you must trust that you cannot fail - it's rigged in your favor to win because you are on God's team!

You are about to get that famous command: ***"Gentlemen and Ladies, Start Your Engines!"***

Setups For Speed:

- Suit Up - Put On The Full Armor Of God
- Strap in to Your Seat Of Authority in Christ Jesus
- Apply The Blood Of Jesus Over You and Your Purpose
- Ask For Fresh Oil From The Holy Spirit

- Check Communication - Yield To The Holy Spirit
- Thank Jesus For His Intercession For You and Your Purpose
- Agree With God's Strategy
- Take A Deep Breath in The Holy Spirit
- Ask For An Open Heaven and Angelic Hosts To Come and Protect (Psalm 24 and Psalm 91)
- Tell God You Are Ready!
- Declare Who You Are In Faith and BELIEVE it
- Take The First Step In Faith
- Speak What You Want To See Until You See It (call it forth by faith!)
- Praise God! Declare "Father, Your Glory Is My Covering!"
- Keep Showing Up Every Day!
- Stay In Constant Communication with The Holy Spirit
- Stay Focused On The Victory!
- God Will Take Your Steps and Accelerate Them
- Do Not Give Up - Ignore Distractions - Keep Eyes Ahead
- You Do Not Need a Rear View Mirror Only The Windshield
- What's Behind You Is God! He's Got Your Back
- Protect Your Faith at ALL Costs - Keep Belts Tight (Belt of Truth!)
- Set Your Pace - Jesus Set The Pace To Victory - It's All Good Through Him! You Cannot Lose!
- All of Heaven Is Cheering You On! Wave To Your Fans In Heaven!

My friend, you are ready to enter this race and you are set up to win. If you begin to feel fear or anxiety, that is not of God. If you follow the steps I just set up for you, you will be so filled with faith you will be pumped up and ready to rock and roll this deal and ace this race!

Sometimes we do all the steps and we still get stuck - if this happens I tell my mentoring students it's because they have an issue with conditions being "perfect" or wanting everything to be "perfect" that they don't do anything at all. Let me tell you this, that is a tactic of the enemy! Only Jesus is perfect. That's why we need Him. Let me give you some things to remember if you deal with "analysis paralysis" or over thinking stuff that holds up your launch or slows down your momentum.

Write this down and get it where you can see it and declare it :

- I WILL TAKE ACTION EVEN IF IT'S NOT PERFECT!
- IF I MAKE A MISTAKE, I HAVE GRACE AND GOD WILL GET ME BACK ON TRACK!
- FAITHFUL PEOPLE ARE DECISIVE - BECAUSE THEY KNOW GOD HAS THEIR BACK - I AM FAITHFUL, AND DECISIVE BECAUSE GOD HAS MY BACK!
- OBEDIENCE BRINGS BREAKTHROUGH AND I MOVE IN OBEDIENCE QUICKLY WITH NO FEAR!
- JESUS IS WITHIN ME - HE OVERCOMES SO I OVERCOME!
- HOLY SPIRIT GIVES ME EACH STRATEGY I NEED!
- ANGELS ARE ASSISTING ME AND PROTECTING ME!

- GOD GOES BEFORE ME, BESIDE ME AND IS MY REAR GUARD - I AM NOT ALONE!
- I WILL WIN! VICTORY IS MY PORTION IN CHRIST JESUS!

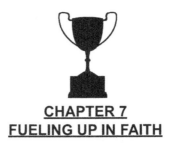

CHAPTER 7
FUELING UP IN FAITH

There is an old hymn we sing in church, and the words go like this:

Faith is the victory!
Faith is the victory!
Oh, glorious victory,
That overcomes the world.

I loved to sing that song! I felt the faith rising up in me and the song would encourage me all day.

When I began writing this book - the Holy Spirit was adamant about doing a chapter on Faith being the Fuel component to our overall victory with our calling and purpose. Without fuel in your tank, you ain't goin' nowhere! You might get a tow truck or a push but that's only a temporary fix.

Let's be clear - in this race of life - your vehicle is your purpose, and you must be driving it. I do dream interpretations in my ministry - anytime anyone is in any kind of vehicle in their dream - that's what it represents - your purpose.

Since I have been in full time ministry and as a prophetic mentor for the Lord - I have had Christians who come on my broadcast and in my classes who have asked me what their dreams mean with a vehicle. Some dreamed they ran out of gas, or had no gas to go somewhere, or they were stuck on the side of the road and had to walk to a gas station, etc. One time I had someone tell me they saw someone in a dream siphoning gas out of their car and wanted to know what that means! You may have guessed correctly, that these were all things that were coming against their faith in God to be able to carry through with their divine purpose. The Holy Spirit lovingly gives us dreams to prompt us that it's time to come to God in prayer to help us strengthen our faith and yes, even ask Him for MORE faith! The Bible says we are all given a portion of faith, but we are told to ask, seek, knock until more is given to us to overcome the situation so we can power forward in our purpose with a *full tank* of faith!

Jesus said that even with faith as small as a mustard seed we can command a mountain to throw itself into the sea. He went on to teach that the mustard seed, although tiny, grew into a big tree! Faith is supposed to GROW into maturity, into FULLNESS. (Luke 17:5)

It's time to fill' er up!

Faith is Fuel, Fuel is Faith - it's what **drives** you and keeps you going ALL THE WAY to the finish line!

You might say, "Well Annamarie, I have passion, my passion drives me."

That's all well and good, I have known plenty of people that are very passionate about what they do. However, when the going gets tough, or they hit some roadblocks I have observed some of the most passionate and gifted people go into a complete slump or lose major momentum - some even give up on their dreams and then years later

say ..."oh if I could have only followed my 'passion'....."
They blame circumstances for coming against their dreams
that never materialized.

Listen to me!   Do not be that person where you think
passion is enough!   It's not about gifts, talent or passion,
it's all about FAITH, and your Faith in God to see you
through everything and to protect you from the sharks in
your path! The ones who want to eat you up and spit you
out!

I have been there.   I am a person who grabs a hold of a
project like a bulldog. I passionately go for it. I was thrilled
to work in the motorsports industry.   I was passionate
about what I did.   But let me tell you this.   I learned the
hard way. I was in a tough, cut throat business, especially
when it came to corporate sponsorship in NASCAR.   My
passion only went so far, until I hit a wall.   Trust me there
were times where I would be tempted to compromise
myself and my morals for a deal. I was very ambitious. I
wanted to rise to the top and I wanted it now.   I was
passionate. I had drive and I was looking to land big time
connections and big time money.   I was a woman in a
man's world, a wide eyed gal with lots of go-getter, eager
to please and wanting to get ahead - and the sharks saw
me coming a mile away. They only saw me as fresh meat.

Many hard lessons happened to me, when my passion
turned into disappointment - when these sharks promised
me all this great stuff and never delivered. They would get
my trust, talk a good talk and then steal my connections.
Many times giving me a sponsor check that would not clear
the bank - leaving me to explain that to my team. *I was so
naive.* The wind came out of my sails.   I was losing my
drive. I did not know who I could trust. I didn't even know
if I could trust myself.   I was not delivering and my team

was in need of a solid sponsorship - the feeling of this pressure just made it worse and I burned myself out desperately trying to fulfill my obligation to my team to land a sponsor. My team owners Diane and Ray Dewitt had moved me down from New York to North Carolina because they believed in me. My driver of the #55 race car at the time - Tim Fedewa - he was the best and he was very good and kind to me, he did not deserve this either. I felt I had let everyone down.

I remember one time I was so worn out, I had not slept, I had been working night and day trying to land a sponsor deal. When I got to the speedway to work my PR job during a race, I could not even stand in the pits with my team to do my job, I thought I would pass out. I had to go and sit in my car in the parking lot and listen to the race on the radio with the air conditioning running. I missed out on getting my team a lot of media that day. I was not able to even do my job properly.

How is that for passion? Passion without faith means plenty of "show" but no "go".

I was exhausted and wondered if I was really cut out to do this. It was my dream. The sharks had a field day taking advantage of me, and I was running out of steam. I cried and cried. I was like, God why would you bring me here just so I could fail? How can I do this? I really want this! I am doing this all wrong! I am afraid to move forward because I don't know who I can trust! I felt fear take over every part of me. I want to do a good job and keep my good reputation. My confidence in everything I knew and loved was under attack and I did not know how to fix it.

Sometimes God has to bring us to the end of ourselves so we can begin with Him.

GOD WILL SEND YOU A DIVINELY ORDAINED MENTOR!

Enter Miss Jackie.

A few weeks later, the Chaplains for the NASCAR Busch Grand National Series, (this was 1995) Motor Racing Outreach (MRO) approached our #55 Team and asked if we could haul their audio equipment to the racing events every weekend. Ron Pegram was one of the ministers to the teams and drivers and his wife Jackie would be helping him and ministering to the women and children of the teams and drivers.

As the weeks went by, I would chat with Ron and Jackie of MRO at our race hauler and they invited me to come to Chapel Service. It was the busiest time for me, and I really wanted to go, but something was holding me back.

Next thing I knew, my driver Tim Fedewa was being invited to everything MRO was doing at the race events. I would accompany him as his PR representative. Everytime I found myself sitting at the same table with Ron and Jackie Pegram.

They began to draw me under their wing. They had fully devoted their lives to Jesus and served Him in the Motorsports Industry. We had interesting conversations. I knew Jesus, I grew up Catholic. I had accepted Jesus as my Lord and Savior as a Senior in High School when I attended a bible study of a friend of my Mom's. I had never felt the presence of the Lord before that time and I was hungry for more. After graduating High School, I had no church or anyone to guide me or mentor me in my faith. I back-slid and my faith became weak, I never really grew or gained a full relationship with Jesus Christ. Now in my 30's Jesus was calling me back to Him. He sent me Miss Jackie.

I wanted to do everything with Miss Jackie. I wanted to be around her all the time hearing her teach about faith and Jesus. She had sparkly blue eyes, a megawatt smile and dressed very colorful and flowy - in beautiful layered fabrics and scarves. Jackie looked like what a Citizen of Heaven would look like on earth. At that time she was in her late-50's but had the energy of a 20 year old. She wore bracelets and dangly earrings that jingled all the time, and was as southern as sweet tea. Jackie threw her head back and clapped her hands when she laughed and she laughed loudly right down to her very soul and people of all ages flocked to her. This woman was filled with life, light, colorful and bright! The joy of the Lord radiated from her and I wanted what she had! I wanted to know and live for Jesus this way!

I began to attend Ladies Bible Club each week that Jackie taught in between race events when we were home in Charlotte, NC. I never knew the Bible, let alone the way Jackie taught it. I had never heard anything like this before. She brought the Bible to life, I could see the characters and understand them in their trials of faith. One day Jackie said she would be holding a special event teaching "Esther" of the Bible and it would be in the evening, and invited our Bible Club ladies to attend.

I was so excited. I didn't even know who Esther was, but knowing Jackie was teaching it would be good.

I arrived at the event at the Church. The place was packed with women of all ages. The lights dimmed. An announcer went to the microphone and with a deep voice addressed the audience: *"Honored Guests, please rise and welcome Her Majesty, Queen Esther of Persia……."*

The music was queued, and an ancient style middle eastern instrumental began to play.

Entering the stage was the most beautiful sight! Jackie, in full costume. She was draped in rich colorful long flowing fabrics and silks, a gold headdress and jewels, beautiful eye makeup, everything trimmed in gold, rings on all her fingers and gold slippers. As she walked regally across the stage, Jackie **became** *Queen Esther the great heroine of the Bible.*

I had never ever seen anything like this in my entire life. I was in *awe*.

Jackie had a microphone headset as she freely walked across the stage, back and forth - and began to tell the story of Esther in the first person. She was Esther, telling her own story, her struggles, her ups and downs, her fate and her faith.

I was undone. I have never heard a story like this. A choice in faith. A moment in time - a Queen with a dilemma that could mean death to millions of people - her people, God's people. Talk about pressure, talk about letting your team down if you don't produce a solution! My problems began to look very small. Esther was called to save a NATION - Israel.

Then Esther (Jackie) turned to the audience and said: *"You shall all come to this choice in your life. Will you be bitter, or will you be better?"*

Then she sang a song I will never ever forget:

"Bitter, better, bitter, better, what shall it be?
The choice is up to me, and one will set us free
Bitter, better, bitter, better, what shall it be?
Bitter or better for me.....
I choose better!"

I was hit in the Spirit - right to my core.

I thought: *"Wow. Here I am with an opportunity in my life too. I have been put here for such a time as this just like Esther. God brought me into a place, now it's up to me to be bold, with no excuses of the circumstances coming against me and know by faith God is with me. If I stay bitter or stressed out about the situation, nothing will be made better for me or anyone else. Esther was bold with her choice. She wanted to make things better for her people because she loved them. She trusted why God had her there at that moment. It was not about her performing as 'queen', or job security. It came down to one bold move in faith because she got her mind off the moment and was willing to take a chance for the future. It was not about her fear of failure - but her faith in action."*

This is the attitude we all have to have. This is faith. Go for what you believe in and know God has you no matter what. Even if you get turned down, it's OK because you know you did it with a pure heart. If people don't understand that, it's too bad and their problem. You must fulfill your destiny to the best of your ability, God will take care of the rest. If He brought you to it, He will see you through it!

I want Esther's faith! I want bold faith! I want Jackie's faith! I want more faith in God! I want the favor of my King Jesus! I want to be able to come to Him boldly and ask! I have a cause! It's my purpose! You have put me here for a reason God and I will see what it is! I will keep going!

I wanted more of my King. Who is He? What does He want from me? I had so many questions! I wanted to hear HIM!

I left that Jackie/Esther dramatic stage teaching with a million questions, because I was starting to see, really see for the first time in my life why we are all here. *For such a time as this.* God plans and positions us, it's up to us to carry out the assignment by faith. He brings us to the point where we must make a choice. We must push past our own logic, our excuses, our bitterness, our fear of man, and come boldly to Him our King, a test of faith. When we do, He reaches His scepter out to us and grants us favor.

He was calling me. I felt it. Maybe you are feeling it right now. Is He calling you? Do you feel like you are here for such a time as this? Are you ready to throw off everything with no fear and go boldly before Him and ask for what you want?

That was a pivotal moment for me.

The next week in Bible Study I had a completely different perspective of Jesus. I wanted to know Him as my Lord, my King. I knew I could ask Him for anything. I wanted to live for Him.

Work was changing too. We got a big win for the #55 Team at Nazareth Speedway in Pennsylvania. I was really getting confident in landing big media exposure for my team and driver and we wer signing several smaller, but good trustworthy sponsors. Opportunities were coming. My hard work and dedication as a PR person was getting noticed and I got offered a job with a major team, the Stanley Tools team. It was a huge opportunity, I would have a chance to learn how to work with a major corporate sponsor. I felt bad leaving my #55 Team, but at the same time my driver Tim, got a bigger opportunity too. I was sad to leave the people who had given me my first break in NASCAR. I went to them and told them how much I appreciated it. To this day I am forever grateful. My team was understanding that I must grow into new opportunities, and even today we are all still friends.

My faith was growing, too. My confidence was coming back. I had plenty of energy to do my job and keep up with the grueling NASCAR Tour schedule. I went to more teachings and events with Jackie. I was learning the Bible. Then my faith was really put to the test.

A friend came to me asking me to take over another Team PR job, that the girl who was in the job left abruptly and the driver Todd Bodine had nobody to manage the sponsor. They were in a bind. The Stanley team that I currently was working for had a main PR person and at the time I was assisting her. She had also hired on more people besides myself to grow her marketing firm. I told her about the situation I was offered, thanked her for all she taught me and went to work with the new team PR Director with Todd Bodine as the driver of the #88 Team. This was mid-season and it was a tremendous amount of work, the Team Sponsor was Canaveral Cruise Lines. They had a huge show car program that traveled to the events and I had to manage a promotional program that had "win a free cruise" booths all over the race track plus do race-day PR for my driver.

It took up all of my time and pulled me away from MRO, Ladies Bible Club and Miss Jackie.

My faith began to waver, the stress level began to come back and the pressure to "produce" was intense. The sponsor paid us by the sales leads generated at the track by the fans. I was working non stop to get more leads and do more events and keep the sponsor checks coming weekly to the team owner so we could keep racing each week. I seemed to have forgotten what I had learned from Jackie and the Bible Study and began to back-slide again! The sharks began circling around me and I felt compromised. I was miserable. The team owners were struggling too and had a hard time paying the team employees including me. We would go to the bank to cash our paychecks and the bank would not cash them. Many times, our driver Todd Bodine would pull money out of his personal account to pay the team when the team owners could not. I would try to keep encouraging the guys on the team, but because we could not pay our bills, team morale was horrible. They had families to feed too. It was a very dark and uncertain time. I was burning out quickly. I literally wanted to walk away from racing and do something else. Walk away from everything I had known and worked for. Walk away from my dream.

STAY CONNECTED TO YOUR FAITH SOURCE - IT'S YOUR FUEL - YOU ARE GONNA NEED IT WHEN YOU LEAST EXPECT IT!

Weeks later the team and I had to race at Charlotte Motor Speedway, it was a huge event. I had show cars and booths manned with college students working leads all over the track facility in high traffic fan areas. I had been up since 5am getting my promotional teams set up outside the track and then back inside the track in time to do team PR. My driver, Todd Bodine was doing well, we were fast in practice and getting ready to qualify for the race. I went to the team hauler to get some notes together for the press and then I was going to head over to the media center. All of a sudden, I saw out of the corner of my eye the man who sold team parts and built the frame (chassis) of our race car. He had two fully uniformed County Sheriffs with him. As they began to walk over to our hauler I saw they had paperwork and they were asking one of our crew members where the owner of the team was. Another Deputy Sheriff came forward and was trying to tape off the area. I knew we had trouble. The press started getting curious and came nosing around with their notepads and cameras (this was before everyone had an iphone)......

I went up to the parts man and I said, "Sir, I represent this team, what is this all about?"

He said that he was there to confiscate (re-possess) the race car and he had an outstanding bill for over $50,000 that was owed to him for building that race car chassis and all the parts that were on it. He had a court order and the Sheriffs were there to seize the car. Right there and then in front of everyone during a huge NASCAR race event at Charlotte Motor Speedway!

I knew instinctively in my spirit I had to step into action. The media was getting curious. I had a major PR crisis on my hands for my sponsor, my team, my driver.

I said in my heart, God help me, I need your help right now, give me a solution here, give me wisdom! I took a breath and said out loud: *"Sir, can you give me one hour? Let me talk to my team owner and we can get this all straightened out. I am asking you for my team, my crew - these are good hard working guys and this would devastate them. They have been through a lot."*

He agreed! They said they would be back. The Deputy stopped with the tape, and went away with them. I went to the media and said all is well, we have everything under control. Then the media walked away too! Phewwww…..

Deep breath. Ok Lord. I have a major moment here, guide me on this! I ran into our huge race hauler all the way to the air conditioned lounge area. My team owner was hiding out up there. He knew what was happening. He did not have the money to pay the man. They would take the race car, right in front of everyone before the race.

I said to him; *"Where is all the money from the sponsors that we have been bringing in to you?"* He just shrugged his shoulders.

Another deep breath. I had to pull from the reserved fuel of my faith. *My reserve tanks!* I felt Holy Spirit Boldness take me over. I said to the team owner: *"Ok I will tell you what. I know someone who wants to buy a race team. He is here with his wife as a guest at the Spam (yes, that Spam in a can) Hospitality tent, I knew him from when I worked at the #55 car. He used to be one of our sponsors."* I continued. *"His name is Joe Falk, he owns Little Joe's Autos in Virginia, If he can pay off this bill today, will you sign over ownership of the team to him?"*

The team owner looked at me for a minute, and he must have seen the boldness in my face. I was not playing around. I was serious. I stared back at him not flinching and said: *"Well? You are about to be shamed in front of your entire team, your driver, NASCAR and the media is out there wanting to film the entire thing on ESPN! You will never be able to do business in this garage area again! It's not looking good here! I asked them to give me an hour! They will be back!"*

"Ok", the team owner said. *"Go get Joe. If he can write a check to pay this off in full to the parts man, I will sign over the team to him, I can't do this anymore."*

I nodded. Then I shot out of that hauler like a bolt, told my crew chief just keep everything calm and normal I will be right back!

I ran so fast to that Spam tent, like I never ran so fast in my life. My reputation was on the line too, but the love for my team members was on my heart, and the faith fuel reserves from the months I spent with Miss Jackie at Bible Study were being tapped into. "Lord Jesus help me run faster!" I knew the clock was ticking.

I ran through the crews, cars and crowds of fans and officials in the infield all the way to the fenced off VIP Hospitality area. I had an all - access pass for all areas so I easily walked through. I was trying to look professional when I got into that area because it was filled with corporate executives and major sponsors. I saw the Spam tent. Oh Lord, please let Joe be there! I looked at my watch, it was 12:15 pm lunch time. Still had approx. 45 minutes before the Sheriff would be back. I ran to the tent, there were a few people in line to get in. I went around to the side where the open tables were, I looked in and I saw Joe and his wife happily munching on BBQ ribs and potato salad (yes Spam is owned by Hormel and they make ribs but they have Spam burgers too....) The area was bordered by a plastic picket fence and sponsor banners. I waved over to Joe. Trying to get his attention. His wife Shirley saw me. Thank you Holy Spirit! She waved back and they both looked over and waved me in. I climbed over the plastic fence (it was only knee high). They wanted me to join them for lunch, then they saw me out of breath, red faced and sweaty from running and of course the intense look on my face! "What's up Anna Banana?" (Joe always called me that, and yes this is the same Joe that 15 years later I got my miracle truck from)....

"Joe," I began. (trying to catch my breath...), "I have an offer here for you to buy a race team today, right now."

He looked at his wife, "Ok." He said, "I am listening."

I told them both the current situation and that time was of the essence.

They looked at me and then at each other.

"Sweetheart," Joe says to his wife Shirley, "Did you bring the checkbook?"

"Yes, I did." She answered.

"Ok Then." Said Joe. "Let's go. We are buying a race team today!"

I wanted to sigh of relief, but then I realized we only had 30 minutes to get back to the team hauler, draw up a quick agreement and have Joe write a big $50,000 check to the parts man.

Joe's wife stayed at the Spam tent and Joe and I quickly walked back to the team hauler. We had 20 minutes left when we got there. We walked past the team working on the car and did not have time to say a word. Straight back to the lounge area of the hauler Joe and I put the fastest deal I have ever seen in all my career in motorsports. It was a literal handshake deal. My team owner called the parts man on his flip phone and asked for the exact amount owed and that Joe Falk would be writing him a check and bringing it to him shortly. That he is now the new owner of the team. Joe pulled the checkbook out of his back pocket and wrote the check to the parts man for the full amount. I then took out my media notepad, wrote the date and a simple agreement that they both signed. Joe said he would get with his business attorney that week and draw up the official paperwork. The now 'former' team owner agreed.

Joe and I then walked over to the parts man's booth inside the garage area of the teams next to the NASCAR inspection area. The Sheriffs were still there. We had 5 minutes left!

Joe handed him the check and we showed him the paper. We asked him if he would keep this confidential for now, and everything was being made legal that week as Joe as the new team owner. The parts man agreed, took the check, wrote a receipt, gave it to Joe - and *called off* the car confiscation. He then shook hands with Joe and said he was looking forward to doing business with him. The Sheriffs then left.

I finally sighed with relief. I had been running on my faith reserves. I then felt elated. I could not believe what had just happened. I did not know I had that in me. Joe just looked at me and smiled and said: "I am gonna go back to eating some BBQ ribs, I have a race team on the track this afternoon that the wife and I will be cheering for. Looking forward to coming to the shop and meeting the team this week."

I was so moved by this gesture. Joe knew that it would be too much on the team right before qualifying for them to take this all in and they had to have their mind on racing and winning. Not all this drama and distraction. I knew then he was going to be a great team owner in NASCAR. He is still a Team Owner to this day! It's been close to 20 years now! (I know because I could never run that fast now, haha!)

As for me. I went back to the hauler. Told my team all was well. I finished my job at the Charlotte Speedway that weekend and then made sure Joe made a smooth transition as team owner in the next few weeks. Spam became the sponsor of the team, and brought in their own marketing and PR people. I needed a break anyway. I decided to step back from the team PR and marketing trackside and work as a consultant from my home office. This was a good start to my consulting and coaching career.

Looking back at that defining moment - needing immediate solution in an emergency. WOW - did GOD really come through BIG TIME. While writing this chapter and remembering this moment, God is reminding me to get intentional when you are needing an immediate breakthrough or miracle - go back to these moments where God did it before, and He can do it again and even greater!

After that moment with God saving our race team from the confiscation and embarrassment, I wanted to get back to work on my faith and my relationship with God and learning His word. I wanted to get back to Miss Jackie and Ladies Bible Study, I wanted to get tapped back into my faith fuel resource and get filled up.

Miss Jackie welcomed me back with open arms. I wanted Jesus, I wanted more of what kicked in for me that day at Charlotte. I wanted to have Holy Spirit solutions that when

I heard Him speak, I had the fuel to carry it out by faith. I wanted to stay FILLED UP.

I began to see that when Jesus is calling you He will put Holy Spirit filled mentors and teachers around you and in your path to grow you. You have to *stay tapped into* those teaching and mentoring resources as a baby Christian. It is crucial to your growth. If not you can backslide quickly. I learned that and now that is why I am a mentor today. In the early church, Timothy had Paul. He stayed connected to that fuel resource. The fuel is faith that comes from the work of the Holy Spirit inside you, Jesus made that connection for you. But there are resources to get filled up, to keep your tank full. Like a filling station for gasoline!

Resources For Filling Up Your Faith Tank:

- Holy Spirit filled mentors and teachers! Ask God to bring one into your life! This is why I became a mentor.
- Churches and Bible Based Ministries that operate and teach in The Gifts of The Holy Spirit.
- Bible Studies that encourage You to get revelation from the Holy Spirit on what you are reading, learning and applying - focusing on GROWTH

I remember the Lord told me to get a very plain King James Version Bible. He told me to get this Bible as I would have to rely on the Holy Spirit as I read it to help me understand it. Once I asked the Holy Spirit to do this for me, I was astounded at how the word of God opened up for me! Don't hold yourself back because you are afraid you won't understand. This is why the Holy Spirit is your teacher and helper - He is waiting for you to ask! It's His job! He is your coach and crew-chief! Ask Him to give you understanding of the Word.

Faith begins as a seed and must grow, a drop in your tank that expands and soon begins the overflow to others. You must have good soil to be rooted in and be thirsty! Don't be afraid to leave a Church where you are not being filled! Ask God to bring you to the right church, or even bring you to the right teachers and mentors. He did it for me He will do it for you!

These are some resources. The source is the work of the Holy Spirit - the living presence of God within you. Once you become born again in Christ, the Holy Spirit works to help you grow your faith and guide you into a deeper relationship with God, Jesus Christ makes it all possible. You become of His Kingdom. You belong to Him. Once that happens He will never forsake you. Even if you back-slide, He will keep calling you back to him. No matter how far gone you are, He *never* forgets you. You will face challenges and you will have to call upon those faith fuel reserves. But who wants to have to keep tapping into the reserves when you can have the full tank all the time! I want the full tank! I want the HIGH OCTANE stuff! I want to go faster, further, deeper with my faith! How about you?

The only way we can complete our purpose on this earth, and even if you want to be accelerated into your dreams it's going to take faith. There is no way around it. Without faith, the tanks are empty and the enemy is going to fill it with fear, the opposite of faith! How are you keeping yourself filled?

I remember Miss Jackie saying to me one time: *"Faith and Fear cannot operate at the same time. You are either faithful or fearful. Pick one."*

Again, like Esther. We are faced with a choice. Faith or Fear? What will it be, the choice is up to me, and one will set me free!

I will never forget this lesson in faith. You must have it for this race in life. You must have a resource or resources around you to come in for your "faith pit stops" to get refueled. We cannot just 'wing it' through life and just rely on 'passion'. You will be stuck on the side of the road without a gas can more than once. Faith is the answer to keep you moving ahead successfully.

Don't run out of faith fuel! This is a long race. When you run out you get laps down! We don't need setbacks, we want setups!
We have to look to Jesus and His Word as our Faith Source. He is the author and finisher of our faith, and He wrote the best most awesome story for your life! It's a Victorious story! The Holy Spirit leads you to the earthly resources, the places, the strategies and the right people to help keep you filled up! God is the Source of ALL things. Jesus is the way to ALL things of God and the Word of God. When we come into alignment and agreement with that, we want more. We get filled, then the overflow happens! Our cup overflows. The faith has filled us to the point of overflow where not only do we have reserves but we are flowing on to others abundantly. Our cup runneth over! We have enough faith for everyone around us and help them finish their race strong and get them through the rough times!

I remember when one time my husband said he was unsure that we would be able to pay our taxes one year. I said don't worry honey - God will do it, I have enough faith for **both** of us right now. Guess what! God did it! That grew my hubby's faith, but I needed to share from my overflowing faith fuel tank for my husband at that moment.

When our faith overflows we become the resources for others, we become the mentors, the teachers the encouragers.

This is why we have to be rivers, not lakes. Faith is an unlimited fuel source! It must flow and keep filling and overflowing into other 'vessels' so that we all stay filled and faithful. We flow this faith fuel onto our children too. It's like the mamma bird feeding the baby bird. We have to fill each other up with faith! Pass it down through the generations.

Each family has a destiny and a purpose too, and when one person has a full and overflowing tank of faith it passes on from generation to generation.
One thing I loved is when my grandpa used to say to me: *"Annamarie do you have gas in your car?"* *"Yes, Grandpa."* *"Well just in case you need it, here is $20, keep that in a safe place in your wallet for gas so you never run out."*

This is like our Heavenly Father. He does not want to see us stranded on the road side! He wants to make sure we have everything we need to make it and even more!

When we use our faith it multiplies and grows, and it grows stronger. We begin to accelerate in all things and people take notice! Soon you are going from regular to high octane, to jet fuel!

Miss Jackie definitely runs on jet fuel faith! I am getting there! I am so glad and grateful God set it up so a wonderful mentor like Jackie was able to pour into me, so I could get faster and stronger in my own race, and now I am doing the same for others.

I asked her one time: *"Miss Jackie, why do you do all this?"* *She said, "Because I love Jesus and I want Him to tell me* *"Well done good and faithful servant."*

I want Jesus to tell me that too. How about you?

What faith fuel are you running on? Where do you want to be with your faith? Are you keeping your tank full? What legacy of faith will you overflow to those who come after you? Who is pouring into you and who are you pouring into?

I started this chapter with an old hymn, and another one I used to love to sing is; *"Let All Who Come Behind Us Find Us Faithful"*

I love to think about that. How will others, after I have gone to heaven, be inspired by my faith? Have you asked yourself this question?

This is a powerful revelation about faith that God has given me - when it comes to our race and those who will come behind you.

Gas Pedal Faith: For The Roads Already Set Up Before You!

LIKE A GAS PEDAL - THE APPLYING OF YOUR FAITH DETERMINES THE SPEED OF YOUR ACCELERATION TO YOUR BREAKTHROUGH

Trail Blazing Faith: For The Roads That You Are To Clear A Path and Build a Highway For Others!

WHEN YOU BLAZE A TRAIL TO THE LEAD THAT GOD CALLED YOU TO DO - DON'T WORRY WHAT ANYONE THINKS OR SAYS - KEEP GOING! LATER YOU WILL SEE HOW MANY PEOPLE WERE BLESSED AND FOLLOWED IN BY THE TRAIL YOU SET IN OBEDIENCE TO GOD!!

Your faith can accelerate things in your life and the lives of others! This is a word the Holy Spirit gave me to encourage me one day when I was praying for more faith. He wanted me to realize how much my faith had already done in my life and how my faith was moving to God's heart. He encouraged me to keep decreeing the things I wanted to see in my life by faith. The more I called it forth, the more it would be accelerated to me by believing it was there already!

I have done what He told me to do and I have seen amazing breakthroughs and miracles in my life. Answered prayers for loved ones coming quickly - and acceleration of the growth of my ministry.

HOLY SPIRIT SAYS:

- LOOK AT WHAT THE FAITH OF ONE PERSON CAN DO!
- FAITH MOVES GOD
- DECREE IT AS YOU WANT TO SEE IT SAYS THE LORD
- CALL IT FORTH
- TAKE THE FIRST STEP AND THEN WATCH WHAT GOD WILL DO!

"As it is written, I have made thee a father of many nations, before him whom he believed, even God, who quickeneth the dead, and calleth those things which are not as though they were. " - Romans 4:17 (KJV)

WE ARE INSTRUCTED TO CALL THOSE THINGS FORTH THAT ARE NOT AS THOUGH THEY ARE BY FAITH

That, my friend, is acceleration. Your mouth is the gas pedal!

Faith is the fuel and you must activate your mouth to decree what you see by faith.

I used to not think it was so funny back in school when I talked too much in class and they would call me "motor mouth" But now it has a whole new meaning! Our words have the power of acceleration. Yes!

An example of accelerator faith speech according to Romans 4:17 would be speaking this daily by faith: *"And just like that _____ happened! God did it!"*
Faith is the fuel, our words release the faith. Angels and the Holy Spirit go into action to carry out the words we speak in faith. This is Kingdom Activation. God designed it this way!

I heard a great quote that explains this perfectly: *"Faith is the possession of something you can't see yet, knowing full well you have it." - Pastor Gary Keesee*

This is the truth! God promised the Israelites the land of milk and honey when He delivered them out of Egypt. While in the desert, God had Moses send a group of 12 men ahead to scout it out! He told Moses to tell the people it was all theirs, all they had to do was move forward in faith! God told them to go up and POSSESS The Promised Land! Yes, not just believe in it, pray for it, he told them to go and POSSESS it! Take ownership of it! It was all theirs! Like I have already taught you in the previous chapters, when the scouts returned, they reported there were some "giants" (big armies and powerful looking people) squatting on these lands that God had promised His people. Only Caleb and Joshua saw past the giants (they kept their eyes on the promise). Caleb and Joshua went to the same exact place the other scouts did, but they saw it with their FAITH EYES and they were ready to POSSESS IT. Now how is that for acceleration to your promise! These guys would have been in the promise in a matter of weeks!

Say out loud right now: *"Father, I see it, I believe it, I am ready to possess it! Bring me the opportunity God, I know when you present the opportunity everything will be ready for me to receive it and take possession of it in Jesus name!"*

No matter what you see in nature right now, remember what God said! Your promise is there and it's REAL! Stand on His promises no matter what and move forward to Possess your promise in Faith! GOD is with you all the way!

Your example of faith has a profound effect on the people around you. You may not see it, but you are an influence everywhere you go!

Understand that Joe had a desire to own his own race team, he was patient, kept his vision intact and made himself accessible to the opportunities. When the opportunity presented itself, everything was there to receive it, including the checkbook and the finances! This is already pre-ordained by God for your destiny and Joes! I might add Joe's wife Shirley is a woman of strong faith in the Lord and Joe is a giver, a generous giver to the community. God sees these things and rewards them. God rewards faith and the cheerful givers! Always!

Look at me with Miss Jackie! My hope is that like her, I am an example of faith to you! Then you become an example of faith to the next person! I remember that first day I saw her, I said, I want to know Jesus like Jackie does! I realize now that my mouth spoke it and God accelerated it to me and I took ahold of it and now I am living it! I love Jesus so much and my relationship with Him is so beautiful and precious that people tell me that they want that kind of relationship with Jesus I have! He is MY Jesus but I want everyone to have Him as their very own precious Jesus too!

It is so incredibly awesome when I think about my relationship with Him I can hardly put into words - it's an experience that I want you all to have! I can't help but shine it out of me! People stop me and say, "You have a light and joy on you, what is that?" I say to them, "It's Jesus!" Then I hold their hand and ask them if they want it too! YES!

Faith is fuel, Fuel is Faith and it Multiplies! It never runs out if we keep filling ourselves daily and pouring out the overflow onto others.

Who has shined their light into your life? Whose life are you shining your light? Faith is fuel that burns a light so bright in us it never dims or goes out!

Jesus intercedes for us so our faith will not fail so we can strengthen others around us!

"But I have pleaded in prayer for you, Simon, that your faith should not fail. So when you have repented and turned to me again, strengthen your brothers." - Luke 22:32

Wow. What the faith of one person can do. You are that person! Jesus is interceding for you right now that your faith will not fail! Because He wants you to encourage those around you, He is counting on it! Your faith is being prayed over by Jesus and you can ask Him for more! WOW!

Faith Prayer/Decree:

"Thank you Lord Jesus for praying for my faith! I agree with your prayers for me Jesus! I want more faith, I want my tanks filled up with faith and overflowing to others! I want to grow in my faith. I want to finish my race strong and by faith I want to see and call forth those things that are not as though they are right now as written in Romans 4:17. Lord Jesus, You are the author and finisher of my faith and I know you have written my story for a victorious finish! Send your Holy Spirit to train me up in faith, to guide me to divine resources, teachers and mentors - help me in my prayer life, guide me in the word and bring me closer to you Jesus! I love you Lord and I want to leave a legacy of faith to those who come behind me! I want to hear those words from you Lord, well done good and faithful servant! Teach me the ways of faith Lord, lead me to the faith paved roads, so I can accelerate fully into my purpose, then show me how to blaze a trail for others! I love you Lord and I want to become all you have called me to be and do for your Kingdom and Glory, for such a time as this! I declare this all by faith in Jesus' Name, Amen!"

CHAPTER 8
DEFEATING DELAYS & ADVERSITY

Earlier in Chapter 6, I touched upon having an 'Overcomer Mindset'. This is crucial for you, especially once you have launched out into your purpose, calling and assignments for your life. One of the biggest issues people face when running their life race and possessing their promise is delays, waiting on God's timing and dealing with adversity, setbacks, distractions and spiritual warfare.

The keys that I am going to give you in this chapter is:

1. Discerning what is causing the delay or adversity
2. What tools and strategies you can use to overcome it swiftly
3. How to keep these delays or setbacks from ever happening again
4. Understanding that God is already ahead of you and has prepared your victory

In the auto racing world, we have something called "lap traffic". Lap traffic is the slower race cars going around the the oval shaped track that the faster leaders have to keep dealing with. Each time they have to get around a lap car, they have to do it wisely so they don't allow that slower car to hold them up to the point that the guy in second place goes around them both into the lead. Or even worse, if the lap car does not stay down on the bottom of the track and gets all squirrely and takes out the lead cars. The official flag man has to make sure that these lap cars stay low so the faster leaders coming around them can get by quickly. He waves a "lap flag" at the lapped "slower" car to make that driver in the slow car gets down lower on the track so the faster lead cars coming up can quickly get by with no hold ups.

It was interesting over the years to watch who were the leaders and who were lap cars. Most of the guys and girls who started out as lap cars, stayed as lap cars. But a few of them would soon emerge to become contenders with the leaders, and eventual winners.

I loved to study these lap cars and the drivers in them because I realized it was not so much because their car was a bad car, it was because the driver had not yet come into alignment with the track itself, or the driver did not yet have the confidence or experience to know how to win. If the car had a wreck or had to go in the pit area for repairs and came back out to "ride around for points', that was a whole different story. That car originally had a chance to win with the driver. I am talking about the cars and drivers who were lapped cars in the beginning, but eventually **overcame** being lapped traffic and accelerated to being front runners and eventually race winners.

I will address the wrecks and and blowouts in a few minutes, but hear me out on this part first. Not everything that causes setbacks and delays is spiritual warfare. You might be frustrated right now because you want to accelerate ahead and you think you are getting hit with attacks from the enemy. But what if, just what if these delays, blow outs, spin outs and attacks on your life have everything to do with your mis-alignment with your divine assignment, and not so much demonic warfare?

Your delays and lack of delays first and foremost begin with you, and your willingness to come into alignment/agreement with God.

Look At Yourself First

I remember when it seemed my house was full of chaos with my family. I was trying to run a business from home and it seemed like nobody wanted to support me. I blamed everyone else for my stress and problems and I wanted them to change! It was them (I thought) that was holding me up, keeping me from being fulfilled, they were making things hard on me! In my mind they were holding me back. Did not anyone else in my family think to take out the trash, do the dishes and keep up with the laundry? I was too busy! (bla bla bla wa wa wa).... I was whining and complaining all the time. I would wake up, worried about all I had to do that day and then walk into the kitchen and get mad at my husband and daughter because they did not think of me, care enough about me to do the dishes or take out the trash. *I was yelling at them and saying stuff like; "How can you guys just walk by these dishes and not see them? The trash is overflowing! What are you blind? Doesn't anyone think of my feelings, what I am going through, what I am trying to do for this family? Why is it always up to me?!"*

Have you been there my friend?
I was pointing the finger at everyone else, but there were four fingers pointing right back at me. I knew I had 'stinkin thinkin'. What was wrong with me? Why am I miserable and stressed all the time? I love God, but am I *really* living the abundant life Jesus came to give me and my family?

I had a life changing revelation from the Holy Spirit. When I applied what I am about to share with you, my life was truly made victorious, and so was my family and business. I got up in the morning with joy and expectation never complained about dishes or laundry again. As a matter of fact - I now look at it as time with the Lord!

This is what He (Holy Spirit) taught me:

- It ALL begins with YOU!
- Change Yourself - Change Your Outcome
- Do Everything As Unto The Lord
- He is working ALL things for Your Good!
- Learn To Rule and Reign Through Christ - "Authority"
- Employ Your Angels and Holy Spirit To Help You
- Victorious Mindset is a KINGDOM Mindset
- Agree With God - >> God Says You Are A Winner!
- Obedience - Put God First and Obey What Tells You To Do Promptly and With Joy

"Set your minds on things that are above, not on things that are on earth." Colossians 3:2

Why did Paul the Apostle tell us to do this? Because he was telling us even though we are on the earth, we have to think and live as we are of the Kingdom of God, where there is no lack, no pain, no adversity - only victory!

Jesus even said, as I have already pointed out in these chapters that the "Kingdom of God is within you". You carry and operate in the Kingdom. You are a Glory Carrier!

This means you must NOT look at your life, even daily circumstances in adversity, delay or defeat. That everything is aligned in your favor to excel and win. You just have to switch over from *'stinkin thinkin'* to **'Kingdom MINDSET'**!

As Born-Again Believers, We are *seated* with Christ, according to Ephesians Chapter Two. We are *already* raised above all this junk and debris on earth! I keep telling my students, you should be looking down on all problems! They are under your feet! You have already been put above anything on this earth that could possibly come against you! It's time to rule and reign and live a life of victory!

When I applied this to my life, my entire family changed. We do more fun things together now, we enjoy doing household chores and because I don't complain, they have stopped complaining. I stopped trying to force people to help me and sent the Holy Spirit to those people to open their hearts to help me, and give me opportunities to help them. He can do way more with them than I can! I even learned to send my Angels on assignments! In the prayer/decree at the end of this chapter I will give you a strategy on this. This is what it's like to truly operate in the Kingdom of God! On earth as it is in Heaven means *right now* for you and me!

You might be saying; *"Annamarie, that's easy for you to say, I have more problems than most people, everything seems to go wrong for me, the enemy is attacking me, I have so much warfare, I just can't get away from it. My family does not have money, I am so busy and I have no support from anyone." Etc etc...*

Well, let me tell you a story. It's a "Coach Annamarie Story" with one of my young promising racing driver students I used to coach before I was in ministry. I loved to teach these up and coming professional racers about having a victory mindset. That once they had this 'shift' in their thinking, and saw the victorious results from it, they would never go back!

Kodie's Story

In 2012-2014, I had a coaching program for up and coming professional race car drivers. I called it the B-Main Bootcamp. The drivers that applied for this program had to meet a criteria that they were serious about their career and were willing to apply the strategies I gave them with a no-excuses attitude. I had some great talent in that program from ages 12-22. These kids were very promising and they were on their way to the bigtime leagues of NASCAR and IndyCar racing. One of those students was a 13 year old race driver from North Carolina, Kodie Conner. Kodie was a bright, intelligent, hard working young man with a very supportive family. They were not wealthy, but they built their own cars, and had a good crew around them, who all believed in this boy and his future. Kodie, was a race driver since he was seven years old, already had many race wins, and championships coming up through the ranks of the sport. He had all the "right stuff" as they say. He was a very well spoken, 'straight A' student and very marketable for sponsors. That year however, Kodie had made the move up into racing super late models. This was a much more competitive and expensive series. It was going from $30,000 a year budget to $150,000 a year budget. A big jump, but Kodie had the talent to make this jump. It was like going from amateur to pro and it was a make it or break it time in his young career. The super late model car racing is a series loaded with up and coming hopefuls trying to make it to the big leagues, and everyone was trying to get noticed. Let's just put it this way, plenty of beating and banging cars on the track, cheating and even blatant un-sportsmanship among these young racers, even spinning someone out to win.   Sort of an "American Idol and Survivor" for up and coming professional race car drivers. All the big time team owners scout drivers through this series. It was crucial for Kodie to showcase his winning skills on the track for his resume' and I was teaching these kids how to be true leaders and good sportsmen and women.   In professional motorsports you have to find a way to stand apart - have an edge on the competition - this is a battle for the big leagues and only the best will make it even to the end of the season. Not to mention they were all trying to attract big name sponsorship.

It was about five or so races into the season, and after my online B-Main class - I had noticed that Kodie had not been in class.

I texted and asked him why he was not in class. He asked if he could call me on the phone, on Facetime. I said OK.

When I answered the Facetime call I was surprised because my normally well spoken student was practically crying, more like whining in his greeting.   "Um, Coach Annamarie I am not gonna be able to come to class anymore because everything is going wrong for me right now...."

Then calmly I said, "Kodie, what is wrong? Tell me what is going on."

"Uh, well..." He hesitated then explained (or complained LOL) "I keep getting wrecked on the track, other drivers spinning me out, hitting my car into the wall, and we also keep having mechanical stuff go wrong on the car!" Kodie lamented.   "Then last weekend we blew a tire and other stuff is breaking on the race car! I have not been able to finish up front or even chase points for a championship!"

I paused for a minute, and said to him; "Kodie, what do you do in a faithful expectation of victory?"

"What do you mean?" He questioned.

The 'coach' rose up in me and I said: "Kodie, where do you keep all your trophies from your past wins?"

"In my room." He said.

Then the 'mom' came out in me.

"Kodie, take your phone and show me a video of your room and your trophies please!"

"Uh, well it's kinda messy in here." Kodie hesitated.

"Kodie, please do this so I can help you." I encouraged him.

"Yes ma'am." He said respectfully.

Kodie then took his phone video as I viewed and he panned around the room, then over to where his numerous racing trophies were from his past victories.

I was shocked at what I saw.

The room was a mess alright. I understood that he was a teenager, but Kodie Conner was not just a typical teenager!

He was a champion race car driver who had the dream, the talent, the desire to go to the top levels of NASCAR.

He was also my student and I believed in him, and had taught him the strategies to be a winner and leader along with hundreds of my other young racers. I had discerned Kodie was special and set apart to do great things. But what I saw that day through his phone video was not reflecting that!

(Note: Take a minute to look around your room right now - what are you reflecting? hmmmm)....

What shocked me the most with Kodie was how he treated his trophies. They were covered in dust, clothes thrown over them haphazardly and some of them even knocked over.

"Kodie!" I exclaimed. "Do you want to win more races? Do you want to win more trophies?" I asked him very directly.

"Yes, Coach Annamarie, I do." He answered.

"Ok then." I said. "Kodie, why are you treating your past victories with such disrespect? Why are you treating them like trash?" I was not yelling, but I was upset to see this in a young man who had so much potential.

"I guess I've just been so busy with school and working on my race car I don't have time to clean my room." He tried to give me excuses.

However, I am a 'no excuses' coach.

"Kodie, as your coach I say this to you and I say this with love. Don't give me your excuses. You are a champion, and this is not champion behavior. How can you expect to win more trophies and championships when you treat the ones you have like crap?" I got real with him.

"Kodie, listen to me! Success is a mindset. It's an attitude of excellence and expectation!" I exhorted.

"I'm sorry Coach Annamarie, I guess I have been discouraged." He said flatly.

"Do you want me to help you fix this?" I asked.

"Yes Ma'am!" He perked up.

"Ok. Here is your assignment for this week." I began.

"Tell your dad you are taking a day or two off from working on the race car in the shop, if you want me to call him for you I will, to back you up."

"OK." He said. "Then what?"

"First," I instructed. "Take all your trophies, get them up off the floor. Separate them out to the ones that were the biggest wins and marked the biggest milestones in your career. Put them all together in one spot. Those are to be cleaned and shined up and ready to be put on a special shelf."

"Then," I continued, "Take the smaller trophies from smaller wins, and clean them up shiny and put them into a box. These trophies you will give to the people that have supported you with a personal thank you note, that you want them to have it as a keepsake. The rest give to children you know who need encouragement."

"Ok, awesome! That's a great ideal!" He started getting excited.

"Now, vacuum, dust and clean your room, get your closet and dressers cleaned out for more room for your clothes. Your trophies are not clothes hangers. Got it?"

"Got it." He confirmed.

I continued.   "Go to the hardware store and get some strong shelving for your walls that can hold trophies. OK?"

"OK, I can do that!" He was really perking up now.

"After the room is clean and the shelves are up, I want the special win trophies placed nicely on the walls, the ones that are as tall as you, keep on the floor space, but arranged according to year." I added.

"Then I want a space in the room for this year's trophies that you are in *expectation* for. I want the shelves up and ready and I want you to put 'post it' notes on those shelves, Win #1, Win #2, Win #3 and this year's date, in faithful expectation of these coming victories." I continued.

"Yeah!" Kodie exclaimed. "I am even gonna make a shelf for the season championship trophy for this year! I am gonna win this championship!"

"That's what I am talking about kiddo! Let's get fired up about this!" I cheered him on.

"Now you have until Friday to get this done." I gave him a deadline. "Then you are to call me on Facetime and put me on the video and show me everything completed."

(Note: Do you give yourself deadlines? It's a good thing and gives you accountability! No accountability - no growth! No growth, no fruit, no harvest, no Glory for God - Jesus is all about the fruit - why? Because it gives God Glory in your life!)

"I will do it!" Kodie said, as I could feel his spirit and the true Kodie I knew rising up in him.

"Kodie, you don't have to have all the little trophies distributed by Friday, just have them in the box ready to go, but everything else has to be done. Are you understanding this assignment?" I asked.

Yes, I understand Coach Annamarie, Thank you so much! I can't wait to get started!

"Kodie, to be a winner you have to act like one." I said firmly.

"Yes." He said. "I am a winner!"

"YES!" I repeated. "Now get 'er done driver!" I said like a Crew Chief on the radio.

As a coach and a mentor, I had to 'snap' Kodie out of his excuses and get his eyes and mind back on who he truly is. Get him back into the right mindset. A winner, a champion.

Champions are not like everybody else. They are set apart for greatness, but they must see it, act like it and believe it.

Just like the Chapter earlier in this book, you have to SEE the VICTORY and build a shelf in advance for it.

This strategy is for you and me and not just Kodie. My friend, you would not be reading this book right now if you were not called to be a winner and a champion. The Holy Spirit put this book and this story in your hands and heart for this very reason. YOU are a KODIE too for the Victories meant for your life! What past victories do you need to respect and honor? What shelf are you going to build for your future victories? This is honoring what God has done in your life and faith in what He is about to do!

The next day I called Kodie's Dad. He was excited too. He said he knew all about my call with Kodie because *that very evening* Kodie was cleaning and vacuuming his room! Kodie's mom was so shocked that she ran out to the race garage to tell Kodie's dad! Hahaha!

(Race moms loved me!)

Now I will tell you, when Mama is happy everyone is happy and so Dad was then easily on board with the plan. He was taking Kodie to Home Depot that afternoon to go get shelving and help him put it up in his room!

(Note: when one person changes their mindset to a victory mindset it causes a positive ripple effect on the people around you.)

Kodie with Dad's help got them both in the winning mindset. Teamwork makes the dream work!

I was excited for Kodie's Facetime call on Friday to see all that they had done. I was pleasantly surprised when I got an early call on THURSDAY evening. It was Kodie.

He was very excited to show me what he had done to his room and trophies and he got his assignment done early!

"Coach Annamarie! Look!" He exclaimed. "I made the three shelves for the wins I am gonna get this season and I made a nice big shelf for the season championship! I got my "post it notes" on them! See?" He was so proud to show me what he had done and in record time.

"That is so awesome Kodie, I am so proud of you!" I said. "Now, This is the Kodie I know! You are a champion and you will do this!" My heart was so full for my student, I could barely hold back the tears.

"Thank you Coach, You woke me up to my mind being in the wrong place." He admitted. "I am so glad you told me to do this, my Dad even helped me! We are totally pumped up for this!"

"Oh and guess what!" He continued, "I gave a couple of my small trophies I picked out to give to some kids who are just starting out racing, back when I started when I was 7 years old. I am going to give them one of mine to encourage them that they can do it too!"

Ok, now I was crying. Kodie was seeing victory not just for himself, it was now flowing out to other kids through him.

This is why I coach. I love my job!

Kodie was smiling and had a complete new attitude and mindset.

I did not want him to see me crying so I moved the phone away from my face, and quipped over to the phone speaker:

"Kodie you just needed someone to light a fire under you, Kiddo, now you are lit up as that red hair on your head!"

We both started laughing.

"Now, let's go win these races!" I cheered.

"Yeah! I am so ready!" Kodie exclaimed. "Dad and I will be at the shop tomorrow we will have the car prepped and ready for next week's race and I will send you a picture from Victory Lane!"

"Sounds great, Kodie! I am confident you will do it. Wish I could be there with you, but I am there in spirit." I said.

When we ended that call, I did not realize what we had begun. It was more than a coaching assignment for Kodie, it changed his life. What happened in the weeks and months after that call with Kodie Conner, I keep in my testimony of one of the many miracles and moves of God that I had experienced during my years of race car driver coaching.

Kodie Conner not only won three races after that call, he won FIVE races. Then he proceeded on to win the SEASON CHAMPIONSHIP that year. The trophy for the season championship was a beautiful bronze eagle sculpture that fit perfectly on the extra strong shelf he had prepared for it.

When he sent me a picture of that Eagle Season Championship trophy, I texted him and told him how proud

I was of him, and we talked about his mindset change and his new faith. I thanked God for that moment. It's amazing how God knew I would write this book and use this Kodie Conner testimony and lesson for you all today.

I asked Kodie to come and speak that January at my annual "Suit Up" Conference for my racers and to tell this story. When I brought him up to the podium he gave a motivating speech to all the young up and coming racers who were there, and his Dad was beside him, speaking to the other racing parents about how even as a racing dad, a car owner and mechanic he also had to change his mindset too.

After his speech as we stood up in front of all those wide eyed hopefuls and their parents I said to him: "Kodie, when we had our first call you were upset and discouraged. You had the worst of the worst happening in your career, crashes, wrecked cars, blown motors, money running out, Dad frustrated, you frustrated, you were very overwhelmed…"

I paused and took a breath.

"… and you were about to give up coaching with me." I stated.

"Yes, ma'am that's true." Answered Kodie as his Dad shook his head in agreement towards the audience.

I continued. "Then things changed dramatically for you after our call, Kodie. You started winning, your engines ran great, you had no more wrecks." I continued as the audience watched and listened intently.

"Yes, ma'am that's true, too." He answered again.

"Kodie, let me ask you a question here in front of all these racers and parents: What change did you make after that call?   Did you get new race cars?   Did you get new engines?   Did you get more crew members?   Did the competition get out of your way and let you win?" I asked him directly.

"No ma'am." We had all our same equipment and crew." He responded.

"So then Kodie - please tell us, what was the one main thing you changed on your race team for this success that brought you a championship?" I asked him.

Both Kodie and his Dad immediately pointed to his head, now topped with his neatly cut and combed red hair, complete with gel style on point for a professional athlete (he was even taking better care of his appearance)....

He looked directly at the audience with his sharp blue eyes and stated confidently: "The only thing that I changed was *my mindset*."

BOOM THERE IT IS!

Then something powerful happened. Kodie tapped on his forehead and then pointed his finger across the audience of up and coming racers, and spoke to them with passion in his voice: "I am telling you all right now, take your excuses and your complaints and put them in the junk pile and leave them there.   Focus on who you are, winners. You are only going to win if you believe you will and you respect what wins you already have." He affirmed.

That was a defining moment for Kodie, and for all of us at that conference, and a moment I will never ever forget as a coach. It changed many lives that day and many mindsets for the better.

I knew that God was saying something powerful here from this experience I had with Kodie. I am so grateful for this time I had with him and his family and racing career, the special moments that I was able to be a part of. I treasure that.

When God called me out of motorsports and race driver coaching and into ministry, He said to me: "Annamarie I want you to teach MY people how to win, how to be victorious in the purpose that I have called them to, just like you did your race car drivers.

"Yes, Lord." I answered.

AND HERE WE ARE.

We all as Believers in Jesus Christ, are instructed to renew our minds, and expand our thinking. In the Bible, God instructs through His word, breathed by His Holy Spirit for all of us today, right now. This is KINGDOM VICTORY and this is for YOU. You are God's Champions for this time!

Romans 12:2 says:
"Do not be conformed to this world, but be transformed by the renewing of your mind. Then you will be able to discern what is the good, pleasing, and perfect will of God."

God's perfect will is declared to us in Ephesians 3:20...

"Now to Him who is able to do exceedingly abundantly above all that we ask or think, according to the power that works in us."

What this means is, God wants to pour out to you abundance based on what you believe (the power of your faith working in you) and not only does God want to give you what you ask for and are believing for (your mind/thoughts/desires) He wants to give you even more than what you are expecting because it pleases Him to do it!

WHAT? Yes! Believe God and expect him to do even more than you expect because that is who GOD IS and that is His will for you!

A very wise man once said to me (who was also a multi millionaire businessman): "Show me a man's closet and I will show you if they can be a millionaire." I never forgot that advice. It's all about your level of expectation and excellence. Not perfection or being OCD. He was talking about having an attitude of excellence and expectation. Wanting to be excellent, having that desire, and being the person now that you want to be in the future! If the closets were neat and organized, with some empty shelf areas in expectation of more and empty hangers ready to receive! Then you have the readiness to become greatly successful.

Or in the words of my very wise, good 'ol country boy and my hubby Michael Strawhand: "Don't talk about it, BE about it." Ha! Yep!

Both are great words of wisdom! This is BIBLICAL truth my friend!

Before I had that experience as a coach and teacher with my race driver student Kodie Conner, Jesus himself had an experience with a man who made a bunch of excuses and blamed others too for his problems. It was the man at the Pool Of Bethesda. Jesus, the ultimate teacher of all teachers, was not going to stand for any excuses and people who blame everyone else for their problems and setbacks. I love how Jesus teaches us all something very powerful here with this story during one of His more well known miracles in the Bible.

The Pool of Bethesda - John Chapter 5

"Some time later there was a feast of the Jews, and Jesus went up to Jerusalem.

Now there is in Jerusalem near the Sheep Gate a pool with five covered colonnades, which in Aramaic is called Bethesda. On these walkways lay a great number of the sick, the blind, the lame, and the paralyzed.

One man there had been an invalid for thirty-eight years. When Jesus saw him lying there and realized that he had spent a long time in this condition, He asked him, "Do you want to get well?" [Side Note: Jesus asking the man about his Mindset - what do you really want? Is this man even thinking victoriously? Jesus was establishing this in front of everyone!]

"Sir," the invalid replied, "I have no one to help me into the pool when the water is stirred. While I am on my way, someone else goes in before me." [Side Note: Man Blaming Others and Complaining, 'Stinkin Thinkin']

Then Jesus told him, "Get up, pick up your mat, and walk." [Side Note: Jesus Commanding, ruling and reigning over the problem!]

Immediately the man was made well, and he picked up his mat and began to walk.

Now this happened on the Sabbath day, so the Jews said to the man who had been healed, "This is the Sabbath! It is unlawful for you to carry your mat."

But he answered, "The man who made me well told me, 'Pick up your mat and walk.'"

"Who is this man who told you to pick it up and walk?" they asked.

But the man who was healed did not know who it was, for Jesus had slipped away while the crowd was there.

Afterward, Jesus found the man at the temple and said to him, "See, you have been made well. Stop sinning, or something worse may happen to you." [Side Note: Jesus establishes here that the man's 'stinkin thinkin' and his excuses, blaming and negative behavior is actually sinful! Jesus makes a point for him to stay in this new "Kingdom Mindset" and not go back and gives him a strong warning! This is how important it is to do this and stick with it!]

And the man went away and told the Jews that it was Jesus who had made him well."

 WOW…

My friend, you will stay in lapped traffic, spinning out, wrecking and never get to the front of the race if your mind does not change! You will never win if you don't really want to win! It all begins with YOU! I asked Kodie, "Do you want to win?" Jesus asked the man at Bethesda, "Do you want to get well?"

As a KINGDOM teacher, it was my responsibility to bring my student to the realization that their victory begins with them and what they really want! No more blaming others, no more excuses, and no more complaining! Kick that 'stinkin thinkin' to the curb! Thank YOU Jesus for teaching us this powerful lesson of Kingdom VICTORY Mindset and telling us to stick with it!

"And when the people complained, it displeased the LORD: and the LORD heard it; and his anger was kindled."
- Numbers 11:1-3

Are you getting this? Are you with me here? GOOD! This is very crucial to your acceleration and your overall success! If you want to complain or blame, stop and ZIP YOUR LIPS!

The biggest enemy you can have is yourself! Engaging your mouth to speak the stinkin' thoughts literally manifests delay, adversity and setbacks over your own life, therefore coming against the plans and purposes of God! No wonder Jesus made a point to warn this man about it! Jesus wanted to see the man fulfill His purpose (which gives God Glory) and not fall back into cursing and complaining over his own life, (which gives the devil a foothold). Your mind is a battlefield, that tries to push your mouth to speak out lies and negativity... but YOU must take authority over it, like Jesus just taught you and me right here!

Understanding "Waiting On God"

It's not always you waiting on Him, He is waiting on you! Get out of the pits and on the track! God's timing is on YOU coming into agreement and taking action steps according to His promises by Faith.

One of my favorite Biblical Success teachers is Dr. Clarice Fluitt. She sings this song: "Who will agree with God?"

Will you agree with God? When you speak the word of God over your life, you activate the creative will of God that is already in place for you!

The most powerful form of worshipping God is speaking His own words and promises in the Bible back to Him!

This is how I do it - I open my Bible to God's promises - for example and I point to the promise and declare it to my Heavenly Father:

Pray: "Father God, You said I could do all things in Faith and through Christ - this promise of Victory, wholeness and abundance in your Word, You said I could have this, You said that You promised me this and I agree with You and I receive it now! Thank You Father!"

How does this get you into alignment with your assignment and accelerate you? How does this overcome every delay and setback?

You are made in the image of God! You have the creative and aligning power in your mouth when you agree with HIS creative and aligning word!

But you might be thinking, "Annamarie - I still don't know what my assignment is, I don't know what God's will is for my life and I don't want to say anything that is not His will for me, because I am not sure."

How do you know and receive your assignment?

Pray: "Father God, I thank you for the assignment you have for me and I say YES in faith. I ask your Holy Spirit to reveal my assignment to me and lead me on each step in Jesus name, provide, equip and guide me in Your will to fulfill this assignment for Your Glory in Jesus name, Amen!"

Then have a notebook to begin to write down dreams and things that God starts to show you and desires He puts in your heart. Then go to the word of God and begin to see how God speaks to you from His word to give you exact clarity with exactly where you are at that moment!

I have good news for you, my friend. God's word is His will.

You should not beg God, or try to manipulate God to move on your behalf because of striving, performing or good works. You can however, remind God of His word and promises in the Bible and prophetic promises - that He will act on those words and promises on your behalf!

It's your faith that pleases and moves God. It's the agreement with HIM and who He already is and what He already said in His word and through the revelation of the Holy Spirit to you and what Jesus paid for for you to have on the Cross!

That's why Jesus came to redeem and confirm this covenant "agreement" God made in the beginning with His creation. We have an everlasting agreement with God, all we have to do is believe it and enforce it in our lives thanks to Jesus.

Jesus purchased God's children back to Him so we could get back into the original intended relationship with our Father and Creator!

Let's not forget God spoke the world into creation. Jesus is the "word" and the Holy Spirit 'hovered' over the earth waiting for the "word" to be spoken to create! We connect the two and we come into alignment. What does alignment do? It brings clarity, stability, speed, acceleration, and most of all the fruit of the Holy Spirit into our lives like we have never experienced before!

So the word, spoken by us in the authority of Jesus' name, through the power and anointing of the Holy Spirit, brings together the creative power of God to activate what we ask for into our lives! It is already hovering over us waiting for us to come into agreement with it by speaking the promise!

It's like the spark of the spark plug combined with oxygen and fuel to fire up that engine! You gotta turn the KEY. It takes action on your part.

Jesus made this possible to ASK the Father for what we want and believe Him for according to the promises in His word.

Jesus explained this to us many times, that by faith if we ask and believe we will receive - in every single Gospel this is mentioned - sometimes twice!

- "Therefore I tell you, whatever you ask in prayer, believe that you have received it, and it will be yours." - Mark 11:24
- "Whatever you ask in my name, this I will do, that the Father may be glorified in the Son." - John 14:13
- "If you abide in me, and my words abide in you, ask whatever you wish, and it will be done for you." - John 15:7
- "Whatever we ask we receive from him, because we keep his commandments and do what pleases him (faith). " - Matthew 21:22
- "And without faith it is impossible to please God, because anyone who approaches Him must believe that He exists and that He rewards those who earnestly seek Him." - Hebrews 11:6

Ask, Seek, Knock - Matthew 7:7-12

"Ask and it will be given to you; seek and you will find; knock and the door will be opened to you. For everyone who asks receives; the one who seeks finds; and to the one who knocks, the door will be opened.

"Which of you, if your son asks for bread, will give him a stone? Or if he asks for a fish, will he give him a snake? If you, then, though you are evil, know how to give good gifts to your children, how much more will your Father in heaven give good gifts to those who ask him!

- OPEN YOUR MOUTH AND ASK, SPEAK IT BY FAITH
- YOU HAVE NOT BECAUSE YOU ASK NOT
- GOD'S WORD IS HIS WILL FOR YOUR LIFE
- GET AWAY FROM RELIGION AND RULES AND GET INTO RELATIONSHIP AND REVELATION
- REALLY BELIEVE IT'S ALREADY THERE BECAUSE GOD SAID IT WOULD BE
- AGREE WITH GOD - AGREE WITH THE GOOD PROMISE
- DON'T BE AFRAID - GOD ONLY GIVES GOOD GIFTS
- HOLD UP YOUR BIBLE AND REMIND GOD OF HIS WORD AND PROMISES TO YOU

Removing Roadblocks

I taught you many chapters ago about when you are in your "garage time" to get the soul wounds and trauma of your past healed. These are some of the biggest hindrances to your success.

Another "Coach Annamarie" Story...

When I was coaching in motorsports, one of my very talented and promising female race drivers, Maddy Ryan who raced here locally at the famed Langley Speedway, had a major crash with her newly painted race car on opening day for the season. She was not hurt, but the entire front and back end of her beautiful pink and silver race car was destroyed. The car had to go back to the shop and a new front and back clip (frame) pieces had to be completely replaced. It took three weeks to get the car back to good as new racing conditions. Maddy however was taking longer. She got back in her car no problem but she was not really "back". She was not running the fast lap times she normally would, and usually a leading and winning car - she became 'lap traffic'.

Her entire crew was perplexed. They knew the car was fully fixed even better than before, and in that time they had even upgraded her to a faster racing engine. They went to the track during the week and tested and tested. Maddy could not get back up to speed and she was convinced that it was something wrong with the car.

Her crew chief said; "OK, can I bring another driver in here to try it out and see?" Maddy agreed. The other race driver got in her car and instantly began to turn very fast lap speeds, close to what Maddy had done with the car before her crash on opening day. The other driver actually came in the pits and told the team it was one of the best race cars he ever drove. Maddy was upset. She did not understand what was happening. She knew she was a good race car driver. She loved to race. She had many race wins and Championship already under her belt at Langley Speedway. What was she doing wrong?

The sponsors of her team began to call with concerns, they wanted to see results. Everyone was getting stressed and

Maddy and her family called me in for an emergency meeting.

I arrived at their home and race shop in Chesapeake, Virginia - not too far from me on a very hot afternoon. I had grabbed a large iced tea from McDonald's because I did not know how long I would be there. I had a feeling (discerning) that this was a trauma wound in Maddy's soul/mind from that crash that was affecting her performance on the track.

I went around the table and I let each of them tell their opinion of the situation. Then I asked her Dad (who is also her race car owner) if he had any video of her recent testing laps on the track that we could compare with her fast laps last season.

He said he did and we pulled up the video. I said let's listen to where Maddy lets off the gas pedal around the track and compare both videos.

Dad looked at me and smiled - he knew where I was going with this.

Maddy however was sitting back in her chair from the whole thing and was getting upset. That was not like her at all. I discerned she was shoving down a painful emotion.

As we watched the first video of Maddy's fast testing laps from last year (before the crash) we listened as she stood on the gas pedal almost all the way around the track, barely letting off the gas even in the corners. She was smooth, fast and confident - you could tell by listening to the roar of her racing engine - powering around the track, only lightly feathering the gas pedal once or twice as she entered a corner, but boldly standing on the gas and she powered down the straightaway. This girl had guts and no fear - this is who she really is.

We then looked at the next video, the one from the past week of Maddy's testing laps. As I watched the video of her going around the track in her car, listening intently to the sound where she was on and off the gas pedal.

As she came around the track, she was on the gas strong, until she got to the spot where she had her wreck a few weeks ago. Normally that would be a place where she would come off the corner and power down the front straightaway - however it was now a place where she was noticeably slowing down and letting off the gas - gingerly going past the spot of 'memory' of that wreck. You could hear it in the video. She was letting off the gas in that spot where she had the wreck a few weeks before.

I sat up in my chair, made eye contact with the dad and he knew that I realized what she was doing in this race car now. Maddy was afraid of that spot where she wrecked on the track and it was affecting her performance and speed now.

Maddy had a trauma wound in her soul memory from that wreck, that was causing her to slow down at that spot, even when nobody else was on the track with her!

There was nothing wrong with her car, crew or equipment. It was in her mind (soul), and needed to be healed, so she could get back to 'full speed' and into winning form.

You see, we all have traumas in our lives. Soul memories that caused us pain and grief - that if not healed hold us back from success with our dreams. These trauma wounds are like sandbags weighing you down! Sometimes we do not even realize these wounds are there! They also open up the door for the enemy to put lies in our minds of fear and doubt. Maddy was a professional athlete, one of the best female racers on the east coast of the USA, she was dealing with something that could jeopardize the rest of her career - everything she worked for all her life - came down to this make or break moment - I had to ask the Lord to give me wisdom to say the right words to her.

I said to her; "Maddy, what do you see and hear when you watch that latest video of yourself on the track?"

"Well…." she started as she wiggled uncomfortably in her chair…. "I think there is something wrong with the engine, it has not been the same off that corner since we got the car back together."

Her dad jumped in about the other test driver coming in and having no problems with the engine.

I saw Maddy starting to get upset and defensive and I knew I could have a family problem on my hands let alone a race team problem. Her Mom was beginning to get tears in her eyes. This is so understandable because most short track race teams are family owned - it really is a wonderful family sport. Especially this family. They were amazing together - so much joy and fun to race with them - they were all frustrated and heartbroken over this situation. They loved their daughter, and they were fully behind her dreams of professional race car driving in NASCAR's top levels someday - at eighteen years old, racing a full size stock car, with her talent, she was very close to making this dream happen.

I asked mom and dad if they could go outside for just a minute so I could speak privately with her.

"Maddy," I began. "I believe we are dealing with a traumatic memory of your wreck and I want to help you get healed from this. You are a champion and an overcomer. Do you still want this dream? Does it still mean something to you? Do you still want to win races?"

"Yes, I do." She burst into tears.

"Good. I said. "I know what to do - you have to trust me on this, OK?"

"Yes," She wiped her tears, mascara smudging onto her fingertips.

"Now, Maddy I am going to record you some words that you will listen to while you sit in your race car, before your test session, before a race and even sit in the car at the shop when nobody is around. You listen to these words, and repeat them out loud OK?" I instructed her.

"OK." She confirmed.

"Now the first thing I need you to do is forgive everything about this wreck, forgive the other driver that spun you, and forgive yourself." I told her.

I then led her through the forgiveness process.

"Now let's thank God for all His goodness in all this - we have to remember He uses all things for our good. You are safe, healthy, nobody was hurt and your car is fixed."

I then called in Mom and Dad, told them the plan and we hugged and said a prayer together asking Jesus to heal Maddy and this family.

They all seemed relieved and rejuvenated.

Since then, I have learned so much more about soul healing and trauma wound healing. Two books I highly recommend for this, is Healing the Wounded Soul By Katie Souza and Healing the Broken Heart By Joan Hunter.

Katie's book focuses on healing the wound by repentance, forgiveness and applying the blood of Jesus to the wound in the soul, then asking the resurrection power (dunamis) of the Holy Spirit to heal the wound. Joan Hunter's book also explains these same soul strategies, but she also goes into an extra step - commanding the cell memory to heal in Jesus name. Spiritually there is a memory and also in your physical cells that hold trauma.

I was not versed in these author's teachings yet when I was helping Maddy heal - I was being led totally by the Holy Spirit, thank goodness He gave me the basics to help her at the time. Thank You Holy Spirit!

Because I am teaching you right now about how to overcome setbacks and delays - I have to address this subject of trauma wounds. I am asking you to take a moment (bravely) and ask the Holy Spirit to bring to the surface any trauma wounds from your past that need to be healed. I know this can be painful, but once this is dealt with you can get this healed and pick up speed to your breakthrough that will make you say - wow I wish I had done this years ago!

I made Maddy's recordings of powerful decrees that she would speak over herself to bring her back to a winning mindset behind the wheel of her race car. It took about a month, but she did it, and I am grateful to say that not only did Maddy return up to speed and back to top five race finishes but she blew past that 'ol spot on the track like it was nothing! Our champ was back in winning form! I was so proud of her!

(Note: At the end of this chapter, I have an example of winning decrees that I gave to Maddy that you can use for yourself.)

How to heal a trauma soul wound/memory:

- Allow the Holy Spirit to bring the trauma memory to the surface - don't be afraid this is necessary to deal with it and get it healed once and for all.
- Decree: "In the name of Jesus I curse and renounce all trauma in my mind, body soul and spirit and command it to be loosed off me NOW in Jesus name!"
- Repent to God for any unforgiveness/bitterness surrounding the incident that caused the trauma.
- Forgive all people and situations surrounding the incident that caused the trauma.
- Forgive yourself
- Ask Jesus to wash you and your sins in His Blood
- Apply the Blood of Jesus to any trauma memory and the soul wound
- Ask Jesus to wash all memory of the trauma from the record books of heaven and from your memory with His Blood
- Ask the resurrection power of the Holy Spirit to come (dunamis) and erase any remnant of wounds in your soul and put your hand on your mind and

command all negative cell memories to be erased in Jesus name

- Take your hand and grab your heart (for heartbreak or grief) and release all grief, pain, bitterness on to the cross of Jesus Christ (do the motions)
- Decree: "My mind, body, soul and spirit are a temple of the Holy Spirit of God therefore no trauma, pain, grief or bitterness can dwell in me in Jesus name! I command my mind, body, soul and spirit to yield to the power of the Holy Spirit! I command the dunamis power of the Holy Spirit to be activated in me now and restore my mind, body, soul and spirit to divine order in Jesus name!" Amen.

Discerning What God Really Wants

God actually tells us to test Him on His word (Malachi Chapter 3)! So when we do this, we do OUR part in faith! Understand it could be that your delay was caused by our own lack of belief or even in our own lack of faith in action through God's word. I tell many of my students, if you think you are waiting on God to move, He is waiting on YOU! We have to put our feet to our faith. Almost all delays are not caused by the enemy, many times it's because we sit and wait while God is actually waiting for us to take bold action with our faith.

This happened to me. I was not discerning what God wanted, and it was because of doubt, my own fear, allowing distractions and unbelief. Yes, me the 'Faith Coach' Annamarie dealt with this exact thing!

I always tell my students, I don't expect them to do anything that I would not have done myself.

So, when God called me to ministry, I was at first on fire very excited. I was in a learning season, deep into the word, prayer, declarations, reading every book from every established Bible teacher I could get my hands on. Then the Holy Spirit spoke to me about doing a YouTube Channel and beginning my own teaching videos. "Going Public" and take my spare bedroom, and use that as a video studio.

In obedience I started my Channel on YouTube "Annamarie Strawhand - Life in the Faith Lane TV." This is how many of you found me and why this book is in your hands right now.

In the beginning I did a few short videos and hardly any viewers. I thought well, I am going to get better equipment, I invested in a nice microphone, a fabric backdrop and some lighting. I did a few more videos. I used all my marketing skills too to promote. Still only a few viewers, maxing out at about 20 total. So, with a few hundred dollars, I hired a producer and shot five 30 minute episodes with some graphics, music intro and some bold covers that looked like what all the other 'youtubers' were doing.

Still even with that I was only maxing out at about 30-50 viewers. I began to doubt myself. I began to doubt what God told me to do. I stopped doing the videos. I did not go back into the studio for weeks, then weeks turned into months. At the same time my daughter was going through some rough things as a teenager and my husband was not working, getting another knee surgery and we were trying to make it on his disability checks. Out of worry for finances and family I fell backwards on trying to build the ministry and then all my prayer time and devotion to God was about what was going on in my family.

My studio lay dormant for almost a year.

One day I was in deep prayer about God helping my husband and daughter, and I heard loudly from the Holy Spirit:

"ANNAMARIE YOU ARE IN DISOBEDIENCE TO ME!"

What? How God? I tried what you told me to do and it did not work and my family is struggling. I am struggling!

Then I heard loudly from the Holy Spirit: "Your window of opportunity is coming to an end soon - get in that studio and show up every day and watch what I do!"

Oh my goodness. I was undone. I started repenting immediately.

Then I really messed up! I let doubt and unbelief come out of my mouth! I said: "But Lord, I can't do this unless I know my family is gonna be OK."

I thought I was gonna hear a reprimand again from the Holy Spirit....but this is what He said:

"Have I not called you to ministry? Your obedience will bring the breakthrough you need for your family. Have faith! I will take care of Landry and Mike. Now get in there on that microphone right now and just speak what comes from your spirit through what I give you!"

BOOM. There it is. Show up every day for God, and trust Him to take care of your needs. No Excuses.

It's one thing if you put limits on yourself and other people and even your own marketing skill, but don't put limits on God. When I really started understanding this I was so sorry I ever doubted or put limits on His greatness. This is something you may have to search yourself on right now. You have so much grace from God and I know this will be a blessing to you when You go to Him with a repentant heart.

OBEDIENCE BRINGS BREAKTHROUGH.

FAITH IS ROOTED BEING OBEDIENT TO WHAT GOD SAYS NO MATTER WHAT YOU SEE IN THE NATURAL

We all struggle with unbelief and doubt of God's power. Jesus dealt with it in His ministry. A man who wanted his son healed from seizures came to Jesus after His apostles could not heal the boy. Jesus was frustrated by their doubt and unbelief!

I want to share the powerful teaching of Jesus when He Heals a Boy Possessed by an Impure Spirit - Mark Chapter 9:

"When they came to the other disciples, they saw a large crowd around them and the teachers of the law arguing with them. As soon as all the people saw Jesus, they were overwhelmed with wonder and ran to greet him.

"What are you arguing with them about?" He asked.

A man in the crowd answered, "Teacher, I brought you my son, who is possessed by a spirit that has robbed him of speech. Whenever it seizes him, it throws him to the ground. He foams at the mouth, gnashes his teeth and becomes rigid. I asked your disciples to drive out the spirit, but they could not."

"You unbelieving generation," Jesus replied, "how long shall I stay with you? How long shall I put up with you? Bring the boy to me."

So they brought him. When the spirit saw Jesus, it immediately threw the boy into a convulsion. He fell to the ground and rolled around, foaming at the mouth.

Jesus asked the boy's father, "How long has he been like this?"

"From childhood," he answered. "It has often thrown him into fire or water to kill him. But if you can do anything, take pity on us and help us."

"'If I can'?" said Jesus. "Everything is possible for one who believes."

Immediately the boy's father exclaimed, "I do believe; help me overcome my unbelief!"

Jesus was adamant about the man's faith and choice of words to Him "IF I can?" IF? Like hello, I am Jesus the Son of God and I have been doing miracles here for three years, and my disciples have been taught how to do these miracles too by their level of faith and belief and even they are not getting this! How much longer do I have to tell and show you people how to operate *by faith in the power of God*?!

I mean think about Jesus and step in his shoes (sandals) for just a minute here, can you feel His frustration? Have you ever prayed like that? IF you can Lord would you ….." NO!! Jesus called those people an unfaithful generation! It was frustrating to Him!'

Are you praying doubtful prayers? Change the way you pray right now. Pray BOLD believing prayers. "God you *will* do this!" "God *when* you do this!" "I *believe* in your power God!" "Nothing is impossible with YOU God!"

Start praising God and celebrating in Faith ahead of time.

In the Old Testament God dealt with this as well with His people of Israel and His leaders and prophets.

Did you know that God is waiting on **You** to Speak what you want to see by Faith so He can perform it? Yes!

"Moreover the word of the Lord came unto me, saying, Jeremiah, what seest thou? And I said, I see a rod of an almond tree. Then said the Lord unto me, Thou hast well seen: for I will hasten my word to perform it."
- Jeremiah 1:11-12

Just like the Prophet Jeremiah God has put words in your Spirit before you were born when He knit you in the womb. These are words that you are expected to speak and declare over your life and others lives. God is ready and waiting for the day you will speak the words, coming into agreement with what He has meant and already spoken for your life.

It's time! Let's do this!

DECREE OUT LOUD:

"Heavenly Father, Your word says in Jeremiah 1:11-12 that You are asking me to see by faith and that when I speak what I SEE you will perform it quickly. So, I see now by faith _____. I believe Father that you are faithful to your word. That you will now hasten this, accelerate this to me in the natural even right now. You say Father, in Jeremiah 1:11-12 that you are waiting on Your word to perform it and I am in faithful expectation to see this word come to pass quickly for your Glory in Jesus name! Thank You Father for the promises in Your word I stand on this today! I speak this in Jesus name, Amen."

Stop shaking your fist at the devil and exhausting yourself in warfare, stop looking for other reasons why something is not working and start raising your hands up to God and declaring His faithfulness and protection over you! Start showing up for God and know He is showing up for you!

These are some powerful decrees I begin my day with, you can speak these too every morning!

DECREE:

- THE GLORY OF GOD IS MY COVERING!
- THE FAVOR OF GOD SURROUNDS ME AS A SHIELD!
- I HAVE BEEN CREATED IN GOD'S IMAGE AND DESIGNED FOR VICTORY
- THE ANGELS OF THE LORD ENCAMP AROUND ME AND PROTECT ME AND ASSIST ME!
- THE LORD GOD GOES BEFORE ME HIS HORNETS DESTROY THE ENEMIES OUT OF MY PROMISED LAND!
- THE LION OF JUDAH ROARS OVER ME AND BEFORE ME!
- ME AND MY HOUSEHOLD SERVE THE LORD THEREFORE WE ARE CHOSEN AND HIGHLY FAVORED!
- I AM MORE THAN A CONQUEROR THROUGH CHRIST JESUS!
- I HAVE GODLY WISDOM OF THE HOLY GHOST HE IS MY GUIDE AND CONFIDENCE!
- I AM SEATED WITH THE LORD JESUS CHRIST! THE NAME ABOVE ALL NAMES!
- I RULE AND REIGN THROUGH CHRIST! I PUT ALL DARKNESS AND DELAY UNDER MY FEET!
- THE BLOOD OF JESUS COVERS ME AND I WALK IN THE GLORY LIGHT OF JESUS CHRIST!

- THE ENEMY SCATTERS AT THE SOUND OF MY VOICE BECAUSE OF THE AUTHORITY IN CHRIST I CARRY!! IN JESUS MIGHTY NAME!!

I want you to understand not everything you are dealing with is NOT spiritual warfare or from the enemy. It's NOT your circumstances! Once you know who you are, a Victorious Child of the Most High God - you realize the enemy has no power over you, and neither does your circumstances. Most of what you need to happen your breakthrough can come from you changing your mindset, your level of faith and your words - and your obedience to God and His MIGHTY POWER. I have seen great miracles and breakthroughs happen over and over again in my students and myself and I want the same for you!

Your loving Father God, wants success and victory and abundance for you even more than you do. He sees you Victorious, so you should too!

Who would agree with God? Me! You? YES!

CHAPTER 9
FINDING THE GROOVE

'Groove', 'the line,' 'on a rail,' 'hooked up,' 'grip.' 'scrubbing speed,' 'drafting'... These are words I heard racers use when they talk about getting that perfect ALIGNMENT for SPEED on the racetrack. This is what they live for - getting in that perfect groove, where the race car is perfectly hooked up to the track. When that 'groove' happens, wooo baby you are fast and smooth - ain't nobody gonna catch you and you are driving through the obstacles like a hot knife through butter!

Do you want to get in the groove? Where things are moving forward smoothly and speedily with barely no interruptions or warfare?

Alignment. This is an automotive word, but it's also a 'spiritual' word. A life word. We all want alignment, alignment with God, peace and knowing we are on the right track. Our soul, mind, body and spirit in alignment with hearing God's voice and knowing what He wants. Alignment comes with tweeking, constant adjusting. Wanting to get more tuned in to God and you Keep Asking, Keep Seeking, Keep Knocking, Keep Adjusting until you see it come to fruition. Jesus said you will KNOW things by their fruit. If you are not seeing good fruit, you are not in alignment with the Holy Spirit.

Scrubbing Speed: Warming up all four tires before the race starts, and keeping them warm in between green flag runs and during caution laps. By keeping your tires hot they will keep their "grip" when the green flag drops and you can start out fast and stay fast, even on the 're-starts.' Are you staying hot with the Holy Spirit even in times between your breakthroughs? Are you staying alert, prepared and ready so you never lose your 'grip' (You never backslide away from the Lord or go lukewarm - always hot and ready for the Lord and your Kingdom Purpose.)

Drafting: This is like getting into a 'slip stream'. Two or more cars on a super speedway tag behind each other to push the lead car to the front, thus the cars behind the lead car go to the front of the pack too. They are picking up speed because the lead car is piercing through the 'dirty air' (air that has resistance) and creating a 'clean air stream' for the car behind them. It's like if you are on the highway and you see several semi trucks in a row and they are in the passing lane going like a train, one after another. Something to ask yourself - are you truly following Jesus and the right people? Are you following strong Holy Spirit filled leaders? Are you in unity with your brothers and sisters in Christ? The leader must be bold and pierce through the 'dirty' air to make everyone that follows him faster in a clean stream.

(Note: This would be a good time for me to sing my favorite song that I always sing on my broadcast - Smokey and the Bandit movie fans know - I sing this song so much that the Holy Spirit told me to make it about Him and one of my students said that it came on the radio one time and all she could hear in her mind was my voice singing it! LOL)

Here ya go... change the words of 'bandit' to "Holy Spirit" and that's how HE likes me to sing it!

East Bound and Down
By Jerry Reed

> *Eastbound and down, loaded up and truckin'*
>
> *Oh, we gonna do what they say can't be done*
>
> *We've got a long way to go and a short time to get there*
>
> *I'm east bound, just watch ol' Bandit (Holy Spirit) run*
>
> *Keep your foot hard on the pedal, son never mind them brakes*
>
> *Let it all hang out, 'cause we got a run to make*
>
> *Eastbound and down, loaded up and truckin'*
>
> *Oh, we gonna do what they say can't be done*
>
> *We've got a long way to go and a short time to get there*
>
> *I'm east bound, just watch...*

Who would have ever thought that song about truckin' could be prophetic - but now that it's stuck in my head and in yours, let's talk about how this brings us to scripture. The Holy Spirit loves when we sing and put Him as the forerunner because He is!

He is your best buddy running ahead of you, making the way in your life's race! The Holy Spirit has got everything you need to get in the GROOVE and pick up speed, jump over obstacles, and kick in that TURBO BOOST.
Whooo hooooo! Yeah Buddy!

Here is the revelation on this "Groove" and the 'Super Speed Highway of Holiness' that is for the redeemed believers in Jesus Christ. You and me! We have access to this HIGHWAY and it's a road that there are virtually no enemies or hindrances.

Get On The Highway of Holiness:

"And there will be a highway called the Way of Holiness. The unclean will not travel it, only those who walk in that Way and fools will not stray onto it. No lion will be there, and no vicious beast will go up on it. Such will not be found there, but the redeemed will walk upon it." Isaiah 35:8

Many people even Christians especially think it's when you suffer more you are Holy. However, the word of GOD in Isaiah 35:8 above is clear: To be Holy is to be redeemed by Christ and cleansed from your sin, and moving forward easily and unhindered so you can fulfill God's purposes on earth, which is your purpose. You are an overcomer through Christ, and you know you are! You move in this glory day and night!

Disciples and Apostles of Christ who are moving forward advancing the Kingdom understand this. Anyone who is called for a purpose must understand this too, *I really want you to get this today.*

Apostle Paul's suffering did not make him more Holy. It was the fact that he *overcame* the suffering by believing in the power of God, knowing His identity in Christ and he operated in Glory.

Apostle Paul was not Holy because he suffered a snake bite. Paul was Holy because he was able to easily shake it off. (Acts 28:5)

No beast could bother him or hinder him.

Paul had a promise from God, he believed it and it got him in the "glory groove" - The Highway of Holiness.

Reminder: Jesus took all the pain, sin, suffering and hindrances for us onto The Cross. It's the ultimate victory so we can have continued victory! The Cross is the Key. Jesus is the Door, The Holy Spirit is the Guide to Glory.

Paul wrote in Hebrews 12:1-3 *"Therefore, since we are surrounded by such a great cloud of witnesses, let us throw off everything that hinders and the sin that so easily entangles. And let us run with perseverance the race marked out for us, fixing our eyes on Jesus, the pioneer and perfecter of faith. For the joy set before him he endured the cross, scorning its shame, and sat down at the right hand of the throne of God. Consider him who endured such opposition from sinners, so that you will not grow weary and lose heart."*

One of the most important things to get speed out of a race car and to get in that groove, is to get as much weight off it as you can. You cannot carry the extra weight of sin and ascend to the top of the mountain of the Lord and onto the Highway of Holiness.

You already have all that you need inside you! The finished work of Jesus Christ confirms your victory and through Christ you have the authority to go after it!

You also have the authority to trample on the enemy!

WOW. This is the confirmation of Christ and what He confirmed and fulfilled you have in the old testament promises and even more!! That's what Jesus meant by "it is finished" when He died on the Cross. It's all been done *for* you. All you have to do is believe it and receive it and walk in it!

Father God created you with your gifts and talents already inside you. He's given you the power to use those gifts and talents to become successful to give HIM Glory. Ask Him to reveal, train and activate you to use this! It's exactly what He has given you inside that will bring wealth and abundance in your life! It's His promise to you!

Just a reminder from what I have told you earlier, Deuteronomy 8.18 says that God has given YOU the power to GET wealth.

You got the power, the authority, the gifts, the talents and the Holy Spirit to help you all the way!

THE GROOVE IS THE WAY TO GOD'S ALIGNMENT - TAKING POSSESSION OF THE PROMISE AND ENTERING GOD'S REST.

How do we 'get in the groove' so we are working so smoothly with God we can only have victory after victory and we finally are there - living in our promised land?

"So the Lord gave to Israel all the land of which he had sworn to give to their fathers, and they took possession of it and dwelt in it. The Lord gave them rest all around, according to all that He had sworn to their fathers" - Joshua 21:43, 44

No Shortcuts to Victory Only Holy Spirit Race Strategy!

I have learned along the way there are no shortcuts to your breakthrough. There is only strategy. Strategy from the Holy Spirit. Shortcuts come from impatience. Strategy comes from wisdom. Wisdom comes from God. Wisdom makes you better, faster, keeps you from pitfalls. Wisdom makes competition irrelevant. Wisdom brings secret knowledge from God, to give you ways to that victory that nobody else can see or give you.

"I wisdom dwell with prudence, and find out knowledge of witty inventions (strategies/ideas)" - Proverbs 8:12

Maybe you wanted to read this book because you hoped I would reveal a "shortcut" to your breakthrough? A "quick and easy method" is what so many people want to succeed.

I am here to tell you I used to read volumes of "get rich quick" books, listen to hours of speakers, for success in business, wealth, marriage, family - you name it.

I tried some of these strategies and some of them seemed to work on the surface, BUT if there was no *Biblical and Holy Spirit inspired* wisdom in it, there would be no long term good fruit (results).

Sort of like shaving your eyebrows instead of plucking them... (I am sorry for that example but that's what the Lord just popped into my mind, LOL)

Listen to me!

You might think that shortcut is clever, fast and easy - but....

I used to work with a race car crew chief that had a sign over his toolbox at the shop that said: "You can't fix stupid."

Maybe you have heard that saying before. I don't look at people as 'stupid'. I only see a *lack of wisdom*. They are lacking the wisdom of God that can be fixed if they want it to be.

If you think someone is acting foolishly, or you have done something foolish or made a mistake, remember how to pray God's word over them and yourself.

"And he hath filled him with the spirit of God, in wisdom, in understanding, and in knowledge, and in all manner of workmanship" - Exodus 35:31

Wisdom is given when we ask for God to FILL US with it, and liberally (a lot)!

"If any of you lack wisdom, let him ask of God, that giveth to all men liberally, and upbraideth not; and it shall be given him." - James 1:5

Wisdom brings strategy to win, and win *repeatedly* to come into your promises and stay there with no recourse or do-overs. This is victory that multiplies into lasting fruit and more fruit, fruit that comes from the Holy Spirit is the only good fruit that lasts and brings more good fruit in your life and the lives of others. Then and only then can you be the right groove to your personal track on this race of life and staying in that groove!

That is why both John the Baptist and Jesus said that God would chop down every tree, and pluck up every seed that did not produce *good fruit. (Matthew 3:10)*

What this means is that God will judge and remove *influences* in the world and those around you that are not using Godly wisdom to bear positive results in others lives that are good for the Kingdom and God's purposes!

DECLARE: LORD GOD FILL ME WITH MORE OF YOUR WISDOM SO I CAN BEAR GOOD FRUIT AND LASTING WINNING RESULTS THAT MULTIPLY FOR MY LIFE, OTHERS LIVES AND YOUR KINGDOM IN JESUS NAME!

(You can even declare another person's name there who is in need of Godly wisdom!)

There are a five things that try to knock you out of your groove and upset your winning strategy:

1. **Other people's opinions**
2. **Distractions that DO NOT need your time or attention**
3. **Your own fears and doubts**
4. **Allowing negative influences to control you and hold you back**
5. **You are afraid of taking a risk**

Remember this with your life's journey: Keep your eyes on the road ahead, your hands firmly on the wheel and your foot on the gas!

*"You will never reach your destination if you **stop** and throw stones at **every dog** that **barks**." Winston Churchill.*

What this means is:

DON'T STOP FOR DISTRACTIONS AND DON'T LET THE HATERS AND THEIR COMMENTS AFFECT YOU. IGNORE THEM AND KEEP GOING!   GET MOMENTUM IN THE GROOVE! DO NOT BE INTIMIDATED!

However if you need to, make a move out of the groove and take a risk   *... there are moments when you just gotta do an "Earnhardt Pass in the Grass..."* - *1987 All Star Race in Charlotte, NC*

THIS IS WHEN YOU HAVE "FAITH MOMENTUM" FROM BEING IN THE GROOVE OF GOD THAT YOU CAN EASILY TAKE A RISK IF SOMETHING TRIES TO KNOCK YOU OR BLOCK YOU!
If anything tries to knock you out of your groove or take over your groove that is when you just gotta do an "Earnhardt Pass in the Grass..."

You pull from everything God has given you, your gifts, your talents, your knowledge and the authority and boldness to take that risk no matter what! You will not be stopped or hindered! YOU know you got this!

You pull yourself up in the seat, tighten your belts, get up on the steering wheel and mash the gas!

You look for an opening even if it looks 'unpaved' and you go for it. You have the speed, the momentum, the trust in God and all that He has given you!

You take it, take it because it's your *rightful place*. Victory is your rightful place! Don't let anyone or anything hold you back! Your groove is in God!

Declare: *"I take my rightful path and place of Victory that God has ordained for me and nothing shall come against it in Jesus name!"*

CHAPTER 10
TAKING THE WIN

The great NASCAR Champion Dale Earnhardt Sr. once said: *"Second place is just the first place loser."*

Earnhardt also is also quoted saying: *"Finishing races is important, but racing is more important."*

How can you have both of these mentalities? Well let me explain: **This is actually *one* winning mentality.**

The late Dale Earnhardt, Sr. was the greatest race car driver I have ever witnessed in my lifetime. He won numerous races, set many records and won many Championships.

If you look up Dale Earnhardt Sr on Wikipedia it says: "Regarded as one of the greatest drivers in NASCAR history, Earnhardt won a total of 76 Winston Cup races over the course of his career, including the 1998 Daytona 500. He also earned seven NASCAR Winston Cup championships, tying for the most all-time with Richard Petty and Jimmie Johnson. His aggressive driving style earned him the nicknames **"Ironhead"**, **"The Intimidator"**, and **"The Man in Black"**. Also, his success at the restrictor plate tracks of Daytona and Talladega earned him the nickname, **"Mr. Restrictor Plate"**.

Wow. I gotta tell you my personal funny story of the first time I "met" the great Dale Earnhardt, Sr. - but first I have to get this important teaching to you on *'Taking The Win'*. I want you to have a good understanding of this - for your own life and goals.

I know I have a lot of analogies and examples of the great NASCAR Champion Dale Earnhardt, Sr. in this book. I was honored to be able to be around him many times in my professional motorsports career and know people who were very close to him. I did not understand it at the time, but the greatness and boldness I recognized in Dale Sr. was his *God Given Anointing*. (The anointing is the power of the Holy Spirit on a person and on their gifts and talents). We are all born with gifts, but when the anointing comes on it, that's what makes the gift extraordinary, and there is *always* a purpose of God behind that anointing.

Isaiah 45: "This is what the Lord says to his anointed to Cyrus, whose right hand I take hold of to subdue nations before him and to strip kings of their armor, to open doors before him so that gates will not be shut, I will go before you and will level the mountains, I will break down gates of bronze and cut through bars of iron, I will give you hidden treasures, riches stored in secret places, so that you may know that I am the Lord, the God of Israel, who summons you by name."

All my life I felt and saw that 'special something' on certain people and now that I know what the *anointing* is because of my revelation of the Holy Spirit. I now see people like Dale Earnhardt and other greats in history as to why God anointed and used people like them to teach us each something in their area of influence on earth for the Kingdom.

God used Dale Earnhardt Sr. to teach us how to win and at the same time enjoy the race of life.

Another 'man in black' the great singer and country/gospel musician Johnny Cash said: *"I love to go to the studio and stay there 10 or 12 hours a day. I love it. What is it? I don't know. It's life."*

These two men are American Icons, they both had some hard life journeys - but had immense success - they lived the American Dream. They were both known as 'rough around the edges'.... But one thing I know for sure they both gave glory to God for their lives and they LOVED what they did. It was not stressful work or striving for them.

You become victorious not by every hit record, or every race win, you become victorious because *you know* you will get one, and the story on the way is your favorite part.

Taking the WIN is inevitable. You WILL get it. Why? Because you live your entire life and everything you do as a winner. It's not what you do, it's who you are.

Have you ever heard the saying: "Don't postpone joy?" You should NEVER say, "I will be happy when this happens or that happens…" (I think we have all been guilty of that).

Instead, thank God for the journey He has you on. Take joy in every moment up to and the moments of Victory. Then have discernment when to grab ahold of that victory and savor it!

Just because you might have time plowing your field and breaking a sweat does not mean that there will not be those moments of eating your beautiful harvest. They work together for your ultimate good. Your ultimate victory.

I want to remind you again of my favorite Bible verse and promise from God in Romans 8:28: *"We know that God makes all things work together for the good of those who love Him and are chosen to be a part of His purposes."*

ALL THINGS ARE BEING USED FOR YOUR ULTIMATE VICTORY. RIGHT NOW.

Once you understand this - it changes everything!

I have taught you in the chapters of this book how to overcome adversity. That is the *winner's mindset.*

"You win some, you lose some and you wreck some" - *Dale Earnhardt Sr. (another great quote!)*

Dale had some of these in his career, but he never gave up. Why? Because he knew the 'win some' was going to happen and he never doubted it. It was an inevitable part of his life.

For Dale Sr, Winning happened and would happen again and again for him. He knew this and never stressed about it. Not because he was arrogant, because he truly "got it". He understood life was about the journey to each win, and being in expectation of the next win, it will surely come. This is for you to "get" too!

Now here is what Coach Annamarie says: "Get over the 'lose some' and 'wreck some' and get back behind the wheel and win some! Get back at it and pick that guitar back up or whatever is PICK IT BACK UP!! Your purpose, your gift, your calling, your vision, your goal!" THIS RACE IS NOT OVER! The win will come!

Winners never quit and quitters never win.

Just because the journey can be tough does not mean you should give up! It means God is creating your winning testimony and training you and equipping you as a winner.

Understand your Victories are part of God's purpose not just yours - He wants them for you more than you want them yourself - because what God does through you is part of His bigger plan for His people. That ultimately gives God the Glory. Don't be the part of this plan that holds it up for everyone else. If you are the hold up, God will push you and prompt you with His Holy Spirit. If you keep ignoring it then He will give you a hard shaking to wake you up into obedience - it's for your good and His!

I remember a powerful prophetic vision I had recently about walking into a storeroom in Heaven and seeing many mantles (special anointed purposes for people that look like colorful scarves). I was told by an Angel to pick up mine (it was gold for ministry and marketplace) and I asked God for it to be activated first and fulfilled so that the many more that were stored up for others there could be activated. Many mantles were waiting for those who were going to be activated through what I do in obedience to my calling.

This is not just about you. It's about the many people that will be affected by you fulfilling what God has called you to do.

Do you want that? I do.

Stop waiting for other people to do it for you.

BE YOUR OWN STUNTMAN.

Ha ha! I always joke that I do my own stunts. Sure these are risks, to be out front and boldly going for your goals.

I also have another saying, *"No Risk It, No Biscuit."*

Don't be afraid of boldly asking God for these things. He is waiting for you to ask, and Angels are ready to be activated on your behalf to assist you!

Going boldly before God, asking for what you want and then jumping in with two feet by faith can be intimidating. I get it. Jumping off a "known" path of doing things that are uncomfortable to you can be scary. That's where the excuses start. "Well this is the way my family always did it - or this is the way my Church always did it....."

LISTEN TO ME...
The "known" path of man can be very worn with good intentions of many people. It does not always mean they are *winners*. Most of the time it just means they were survivors.

Trail blazin' is where the traction is. It's the trail that leads to the Highway of Holiness that I talked about in the last chapter. Many times you gotta blaze a trail to get traction, to get momentum, *get some side bite in them back tires* as my race drivers used to say!

Trail blazers are anointed by God to be winners. I have asked for this anointing and He gave it to me. I asked God for this winner anointing and He said to me: *"I will make you a TrailBlazer!"*

Blaze the Trail and don't worry for others to catch up to you! God will eventually bring them through behind you!

Now, Don't make this mistake (thank God I learned my lesson). I asked for the Trailblazer anointing from God, then I was too scared to use it! Not only that once it was given to me, I had an assignment to do and I would not do it until I thought my husband and daughter would do it with me. But they were not ready. God was still working on them. But that did not mean I was supposed to wait.

My assignment from the Lord was my YouTube Broadcasts. God wanted me to blaze a trail there. He gave me everything to do it. He had people waiting on me. But, I was letting everything else hinder me, spin me out and using excuses why I could not do it right now. The microphone sat silent in my studio for months while I cried on my face to the Lord to move my husband and daughter into ministry with me *so I* could move forward.

So for weeks and months, my microphone was collecting dust in my studio, and I was daily putting my face in the carpet (sometimes dog or cat hair was there but I did not care, I was determined to get God to move on my behalf!)

But God was waiting on me to move.

- GOD HAS PEOPLE WAITING ON YOUR OBEDIENCE
- DO IT EVEN IF THE CONDITIONS ARE NOT PERFECT
- DO IT EVEN IF YOU ARE AFRAID
- KNOW GOD HAS GOT YOUR BACK
- IF YOU ARE BEING STRETCHED OUT OF YOUR COMFORT ZONE YOU KNOW IT'S FROM GOD

Now, many of you would not have even heard of me and would not be reading this book if I did not step out into obedience to the Lord the very next day after He spoke to me and told me to move. I fired up that microphone and began to do daily live broadcasts on YouTube. This was in August of 2017.

I sat my butt down in front of that Microphone and started talking, teaching and encouraging my listeners. I showed up every day just like God told me to. I had to rely completely on the Holy Spirit and the gifts and anointing He had given me for daily messages.

It was rough, it was 'grass roots' broadcasting. Nothing fancy. It was quilts on the walls to help the sound and chicken lamps from Tractor Supply rigged up as my camera lighting. I had no moderators on my live chat on the broadcast. There were many interruptions and trolls coming on the chat posting inappropriate stuff we had to try and block. I had a few loyal listeners that showed up almost immediately that were responding well to my teachings and I stayed focused on helping them get a breakthrough to encourage the others. Many of these early followers of my broadcast told me that my teachings and encouragement was exactly what they had been praying for.

We are given gifts by God to serve and help one another!

If we do not use our gifts faithfully and obediently, others could be delayed in their need. There are people praying you into their life right now. This is why we cannot wait. It's not just about us. The picture is so much bigger.

Those first weeks of broadcasts I was pulling from everything inside me and everything the Holy Spirit flowed to me. Keeping my foot in the gas and hands on the steering wheel so to speak. The seat and wheels under me felt squirrely, there were distractions BUT I had to push myself past it by faith and know God would never lie to me and *God had faith in me.* He was going to make sure I won, that my 'team' won (family). I just had to trust him and stretch myself - doing whatever it takes to do this. Life In The Faith Lane TV with Annamarie was being birthed!

God has faith in YOU.

The window to victory opens - take this moment in time.

IT'S WHEN YOUR ANOINTING KICKS IN....

YOU are reading this book for a reason. There are no mistakes with God. Just by the timing of you reading this book, God is telling you: "Time to Win with Me!"

Don't be afraid to do the pass in the grass! What this means is YOU have been equipped and anointed to take a risk for victory - even on the unpaved roads! You are so 'in the groove' that you can make the pass even if the ground is shaky or slippery! You are gonna fly right through with your divine momentum! God brings you to these moments so you have to rely on these things He has given you to give him glory! Then you discover all that you really have been given to use on this earth! It's eye opening and it brings you into another level of glory. You learn how to use your anointing and how to be obedient and trusting in God. You become fearless. You become the winner God destined you to be.

Don't be afraid of boldly asking God for these things. He is waiting for you to ask, and Angels are ready to be activated on your behalf. But once heaven is activated on your behalf you have to do your part too.

This is about YOU and GOD and your assignment and purpose and how many people out there will be impacted by it.

Your Victory is celebrated in Heaven, too!

We all meet God by ourselves, not with our stuntman or our husband, or wife or kids. We stand before God alone.

"Did you fulfill what I called you to do and gifted you to do on earth?" I believe we are asked that question.

I had to learn this. I had to come to my moment. My pass in the grass was getting on that microphone and staying on it. Now you are here. You are getting victory because I went for it. Others will get victory because you went for it too! Do you understand?

What is your pass on the grass? What trail do you need to blaze?

God did everything He promised me He would do, when I did what I needed to do by faith.

GOD IS FAITHFUL. HE SEES YOUR EXPECTED WIN AND ALL THE ACCOLADES THAT GO WITH IT. HE WANTS YOU TO SEE IT AND TAKE IT!

Were you obedient when called? Did you use faithfully what was given to you?

ASK YOURSELF HOW BAD DO YOU WANT IT? Let me make this clear, that desire you have in your heart to be a winner at what you love to do, and reach your goals is from God. He is the one who put that in you. It's not selfish to want to win. It's not selfish to want success. It's not selfish to want VICTORY.

It's not frivolous or self-serving to ask God to be a winner or successful in your life's purpose. It's actually more selfish for you not to. Because your victories and wins are serving God. He will use them to activate others. There are people lined up behind you - waiting for you to go for it so they can.

To take the wins, you must first:

1. **Have the vision**
2. **Trust in God and your gifts**
3. **Ask God to anoint you (set you apart from the rest)**
4. **Allow the Holy Spirit to train you and equip you**
5. **Enjoy the journey there**
6. **Know you will succeed**
7. **Discern when to take a risk and go for it**
8. **Celebrate and savor each victory**
9. **Give God Glory by showing others what He has done through you**
10. **Ask God to multiply it in your life**
11. **Expect more**
12. **Teach others to be winners**

Years ago I wondered about re-incarnation. I know now that is a lie from the devil. The reason there are similarities in certain great people throughout history is because of the *ANOINTING of the Holy Spirit* that is on them!!

Many winners and successful people have a certain anointing. It's from God, combined with the gifts God has designed in them, a special anointing comes on them from the Holy Spirit to be exponentially victorious in what God calls them to do.

THE ANOINTING SETS YOU APART FROM THE REST

I also noticed the winning anointing is always connected to that person's journey, the belief in their gifts God gave them and most of all a knowing they have in their spirit, maybe even since childhood. It also is connected to that person's trust in God.

You may be wondering, how do I get that winning anointing? How do I get the victories I want?

You ask God for it in Jesus name. Then you show up for the Holy Spirit to train you up in it. Then you know that you know that you know He has equipped you and His divine power and grace is working through you. It's KNOWING in your spirit. Then you GO FOR THE WIN - God gets the GLORY through your STORY.

In John 14:13-15 Jesus states this to His disciples: "Whatever you ask in my name, this I will do, that the Father may be glorified in the Son. If you ask me anything in my name, I will do it."

Jesus repeats this twice. I think He was making a POINT.

If you ask Me (Jesus) anything.

What? YES. Anything.

Declare with me NOW:

"Lord Jesus You said in your word in John 13-14 that if I ask for anything in Your name You will do it. I believe you Lord Jesus so this is what I am asking for today!
I want to WIN Lord.   I want a trail blazing winner's anointing from The Holy Spirit and By Faith I receive it right now! Thank you Lord!"

"Lord Jesus in Your Name I declare that I am anointed to _____ in and be exponentially successful at _____such a way that the world has never witnessed before all for the Glory and Kingdom Of God!"

Declare: *By faith, these are the Victories I am asking You for Father God for in Jesus name:*

1)._____
2.)_____
3.)_____

"Show me Father God where the Victory is, train me up and show me how and when to take the wins for Your Glory! I ask this and am in faithful expectation to receive in Jesus name! "

What is your win? Your Victory?

Your marriage restored?
Your new home?
Your children's salvation?
A business or career goal?

A book being published?
A movie script being accepted?
Your complete healing?
All your debts paid?

I want to make this point to you my friend right now. Cast off all old religious thinking and I am here to tell you that God created you to WIN and ask to WIN and expect to WIN.

You want victory? You want to Take the Win? Ask for it! Want it!

Know it is YOURS and do not be ashamed to be a winner and to BOLDLY go after your wins. Victorious living belongs to you through Jesus Christ!

Jesus was clear when He said: *"I came so you can have life abundant." John 10:10*

Let's look at the word Abundant - it's a winner's word.

English meaning:
a·bun·dant
/əˈbəndənt/

adjective
existing or available in large quantities; plentiful

Hebrew Translation (Jesus' language):

שׁוֹפֵעַ
abundant, bountiful, copious, superfluous, flush, bounteous

עָשִׁיר
rich, wealthy, affluent, well-heeled, abundant, heeled

OK, are we clear? Jesus wants you to be a *winner*. An abundant, blessed winner with the prizes to show for it. He died and rose and was ascended at the right hand of God so we could win and take territory on the earth with Him, for Him and through Him. Don't take this for granted.

Now it's time to ask for and take the win. You have Jesus' permission. You have asked for everything you need on this journey. Now let's go for the WIN with no shame! You have it in your sights. You can do this! Your Father God is proud of you! He enjoys the wins with you!

What victory do you have in your sights? It's time to **take it by force.**

Yep. That's what I said. There is a moment where you see the Victory by faith, and you know God has your back and He has prepared you for this moment. There has to be a moment in you in this journey where the bold move has to happen in your life.

In my experience, victories can come in two ways - they are either taken by force by a bold move of faith or happen as a "suddenly" from God because you have stayed faithful.

When you have decided to follow Jesus you have decided to take the win. Faith is the Victory, Jesus is the Reward. The life you then have is in the Kingdom of God. The Kingdom of God advances in the earth because of our bold acts of faith. When you are a Kingdom advancer you have greatness on earth and in heaven. You are a winner.

Matthew 11:12 states: "And from the days of John the Baptist until now the kingdom of heaven suffers violence, and the violent take it by force."

This is good violence, bold people of faith taking bold steps of action in a moment taking the win and being in expectation of wins that could come any moment by God.

"Take The Win" Instances In The Bible:

Sudden Wins: Joseph! He went from the prison to the palace in one day! This came from a sudden move of God because Joseph stayed faithful and joyful in his journey, and kept His eyes on the victory that God promised him years before. He kept using his gifts faithfully knowing the win would come. When the opportunity came, he took it confidently! He was in expectation.

Take By Force Wins: Esther! This is the greatest take it by force story in History. This is "If I Perish I Perish, but I gotta go for it story! This is "You were born for such a time as this, and God positioned you right here at this very moment and the Victory is yours you just have to trust God, make a bold move with no excuses and take the Victory!

Wins Are Meant For Believers in Christ: The Apostle Paul Instructs that we are to go for the win, go for the prize, race to win! There are winner's crowns waiting for us! 1 Corinthians 9:24 - Run Your Race to Win: "I do all this for the sake of the gospel, so that I may share in its blessings. Do you not know that in a race all the runners run, but only one receives the prize? Run in such a way as to take the prize. Everyone who competes in the games trains with strict discipline. They do it for a crown that is perishable, but we do it for a crown that is imperishable." (A Crown in the spirit given to you from Jesus Christ! We must desire to win and win bigly for Jesus on this earth, so it's OK to desire and go for this prize! In fact we are being told to do this as believers.)

Do you realize God is positioning you to take the win right now? He actually has a hold of Your hand moving you forward as He fights for you with the other one.

"I brought you from the ends of the earth and called you from its farthest corners. I said, 'You are My servant.' I have chosen and not rejected you. Do not fear, for I am with you; do not be afraid, for I am your God. I will strengthen you; I will surely help you; I will uphold you with My right hand of righteousness. Behold, all who rage against you will be ashamed and disgraced; those who contend with you will be reduced to nothing and will perish." - Isaiah 41:10

Take note of your position in your personal race at this very moment! Are you understanding you are not alone? God is with you every step of the way on this journey!

God is with you in the trials and the victories. When you are not enjoying the practice runs and the building and trail blazing days - you are missing God in all of it!

EMBRACE YOUR RACE AND YOU WILL STAND IN THAT PLACE! THE PLACE OF VICTORY!

Jesus wins, You win! When God looks at you He sees His son, His daughter. God is the biggest stage mom and soccer dad you have ever seen. (I call them racer moms and racer dads and trust me I have dealt with many of them as a racer coach! They are like fierce lions, tigers and bears when it comes to their kid succeeding and don't get in their way LOL...)

This is your FATHER GOD for you! He wants to brag about you! He is fiercely fighting for your success so He can throw it in satan's face!

God says in His word: "Then the Lord said to satan, 'have you considered my servant Job? There is none on earth like him, he is blameless and upright, a man who fears God and shuns evil'" (Job 2:3)

WHAT? God bragged about His servant Job to satan?

I Love that!

Think about this for a second. Don't you want to win so your Father God can brag about you and what a kick in the teeth it is to the devil? Come On!! That is totally awesome.

I can just hear Father God bragging about His Children to the devil: "Well let me tell you about my daughter Esther. She lost both her earthly parents, but she did not despair, nope. She stayed faithful to ME and even all the other girls who were jealous of her - it didn't phase her, and even when her husband the King was not even speaking to her, she did not care - she went straight up to him and asked him for a favor on MY behalf and on behalf of MY people. Ha! She even out smarted your old buddy Haman! Hahaha!"

"Oh and hold on there devil, I gotta tell you about My sons Joseph, and David! So much to brag on those boys!"

"Of course you'll never forget My Son Jesus Christ who kicked your butt for good devil on behalf of all my sons and daughters! Hahaa! I have great kids!"

How is God going to brag on you? How are you going to brag on God?

I want to give you a very wonderful encouraging word that the Holy Spirit gave me. He said to me: "Annamarie, when you boldly go for the win for Me - with no fear, thousands of other sons and daughters will get victory, too because of you."

WOW. It really puts it all into perspective. That word is not just for me - it's for you right now, today my friend, my sister, my brother.

My DALE EARNHARDT Sr. Story:

I promised you I would tell you my funny (and impactful) Dale Earnhardt, Sr.   story and my very first and embarrassing and (very encouraging) meeting with him, so here we go…(but a little back story first leading up to that moment.…)

In 1995 I worked my very first major NASCAR race at Daytona International Speedway for the Daytona 500 week.   I had been given an amazing opportunity to manage the Marketing and Public Relations for RaDius Motorsports, a top Pro NASCAR team that competed with two drivers in both Winston Cup and Grand National Series running at Daytona at that time.   I was a total rookie at doing Public Relations and Marketing at a big time National event like this. I was like a deer in the headlights. But this team believed in me, they had sought me out for my talent and paid to move me down there. I wanted to do a good job for them. Daytona was an intimidating place to start though! It was like getting thrown into the deep end of the pool and it was sink or swim - at the biggest most important race event of the year, and it's your first. I was gonna have to fly by the seat of my pants because I had nobody showing me what to do and I really did not know hardly anyone yet. It was like the scene in the movie, "Coal Miner's Daughter" when Loretta Lynn (Sissy Spacek) finds herself standing on the stage of the Grand 'Ole Opry for the first time and told to just get up there and sing - after only performing in 'ol honky tonks for the last 8 years.

I was trying hard to learn the ropes as a newbie here in the big leagues and look confident and professional at the same time (and try not to get run over, ha). To explain to those who do not know much about NASCAR Racing - the Daytona 500 week in February of each year brings the best stock car race drivers and teams in the country to this place. Fortune 500 Corporate Sponsors, Major Automotive Manufacturers including Chevy, Ford, Toyota.... All the top driving stars are there, all the big television networks are there, celebrities and movie stars like Tom Cruise and the (late) Paul Newman. Rock Stars like the band Aerosmith, Gene Simmons of KISS and Cheryl Crow are seen being escorted around by PR Reps like royalty with their entourages and security at this event. Not that I was all googly eyed over these celebrities, I am just trying to give you a mental picture here.

Here I was, 31 years old - with experience of working in the grass roots levels of motorsports at the local short tracks - to getting a "sudden" opportunity to work for a top national race team at the highest levels of the sport.

NASCAR. I had made it. I could walk just a few steps and be standing in Victory Lane at Daytona International Speedway!

It truly was emotional for me to witness my white tennis shoe clad feet standing on the tarmac at the famed Daytona International Speedway Garage Area. Not to mention my name and a professional team title custom embroidered on the upper right front of my new light blue polo shirt. My Hot Pass and Media Credentials jingling from my 'official' lanyard around my neck. I was "Team P.R. Girl" uniformed and all geared up. My back pocket of my pressed navy blue khaki pants held my mini notebook, two Sharpie markers, and a small pocket tape recorder. Clipped to my belt I was issued a team radio and headset. My long brunette hair pulled back and clasped neatly in a Goody Barrette. I sure looked the part I was set to play!

Daytona Speedway in Daytona Beach, Florida - "The Daytona 500 "Speedweeks" - it was a beautiful, bustling, busy place. Engines roaring, race cars pulling in and out of the garages, TV news helicopters hovering over the track, careful to work around the Goodyear Blimp's airspace. Reporters and camera people running around chasing down interviews with the drivers. I was a bit overwhelmed, nervous and wondering how I got here.

Did I deserve this? Can I really do this job?

I remember that first day on the job at Daytona - looking through my team sponsored Ray Ban Sunglasses, flipping them up on top of my head, trying not to pull on my mini gold hoop earrings. Taking it all in.

I took a deep breath. Yes! I was born to do this!

Biblically, my story in my motorsports career - it's a JOSEPH and ESTHER story combined, with a bit of JOSHUA in there! To understand this "Daytona" winning moment in my life - let me give you a little back story...

I started my 'professional' career in motorsports as a young and naive 22 year old, I was young, pretty and slim (slimmer) LOL, with big blue eyes and a brain filled with auto mechanical knowledge. I loved to talk about horsepower and cars - I had a great passion for motors and motorsports! You could put a blindfold on me and fire up an engine and I could tell you the make, model and sometimes the cubic inch and cam in that thing. Ha! Yepper! That was me. I was good lookin' gal in a size 8 Jordache Jeans - all 5'3" of me and I was a 'motorhead'. This came from my years as a child sitting with my earthly Daddy in his garage handing him wrenches and working on his race cars, soaking in all this knowledge like a sponge.

At the age of 22, in the early 1980's I was noticed by the owners of Brewerton Speedway, a local dirt track by my home in Upstate New York- where many of my dad's old friends still raced. They thought I was an attractive girl, with racing knowledge and a friendly personality that would be a good representative for the Speedway. They asked me to be a trophy presenter there. I accepted. Soon, I was presenting trophies in Victory Lane for more local short tracks, and local racing magazines, wearing cute jumpsuits, bathing suits with high heels, big hair and silk sashes. As I started to get known in motorsports, I entered and won beauty contests and then represented regionally many corporate sponsors in the North East US - particularly in New York where I was born and raised.

I had many "titles" back then in the early 80's including: Miss Miller American for Miller Brewing Company's race events, Miss Parts Peddler for the Parts Peddler Newspaper and continuing as Miss Brewerton Speedway and Miss Oswego Speedway Classic. These "spokesmodel" "presenter" opportunities then expanded into mainstream businesses and corporations in New York State. I modeled for advertisements for telephone companies in Syracuse, NY, represented and did spokesmodel appearances locally for Executive Airlines, and won the 1986 Kodak Most Photogenic Model Search in Rochester, NY.

I had an impressive modeling portfolio that was growing and many respected corporate clients that I was working with. I could stand around and look pretty, approachable and sell your product at the same time because I had the gift of gab. I loved people too, and I still do! Auto Racing Sponsors benefitted from my bubbly personality as I represented their brand - and because I had grown up around racing, I could talk engines, spark plugs and gears and easily answer questions for their corporate guests at events for both women and men! I talked with everyone and made them feel welcome at the races and events - this was in between applying fresh lip gloss every hour or two and of course hair spray to my big 1980's hairdo (the bangs had to stand up real puffy ya know...)

Anyway - back then in 1987 I was on my way to the BIG TIME baby! I knew I was going to the top. I had that knowing in my heart. I 'saw' myself presenting trophies and standing in Victory Lane at Daytona someday. I saw it and I wanted it! I dreamed it all the time! I was going to be in NASCAR! I was on my way.

Then, like young Joseph in the Bible I had some wicked and jealous people try to come against my destiny. With Joseph it was his own brothers, with me it was people in my own racing circle of acquaintances. Like Joseph, they threw me in a proverbial pit.

I am not telling you this story to highlight all the 'titles' I had or would have. Titles mean nothing on earth unless God places you there for His purposes like He did for Joseph and Esther. YOUR desires for your future and vision is important however to have in your heart - because God placed it there.

Stick with me here. You will understand how this all comes together with my Dale Earnhardt encounter years later as I tell this back story. Some of you will go through something like this in your journey - maybe some of you already have. This directly connects to our "Taking The Win" theme of this chapter. Let's keep reading….

When I was on top of my modeling game in Upstate, NY in '87 I was already submitting letters and photos to larger modeling agencies in New York City and particularly the agency in Winston-Salem North Carolina that handled the trophy presenters for Winston Tobacco Company - NASCAR's title sponsor.

I wanted to be "Miss Winston". This was the top Victory Lane and Spokesmodel presenter in the motorsports world. It was like Miss America for Auto Racing. I had to have three recommendations from leaders in the sport to even get considered for the title. I was so excited. I was lining up good connections that would vouch for me.

Please don't get religious or judgmental on me here. Yes, they are beer and tobacco companies. But what people do not know is there is a clean-cut image that you must be held accountable to as a spokesmodel and presenter for these companies. They wanted representatives for their brands that did not drink or smoke or party believe it or not. They wanted All-American fresh faced and classy women who were good ambassadors even in their personal lives and would not be subject to anything trashy that could hurt the brand name and company.

God can use anything and anyone He wants to get His purposes done and get you to where you need to be in your destiny. God used pagan leaders and influential unbelievers the time to fulfill a plan for HIS chosen ones and HIS plans, that is you and me and our divine path!

I held up being a class act in my life, always. Even though I was not walking with the Lord the way I am now - I loved God and I wanted to make my family proud of me. I especially wanted to honor my late father Carmen's memory through his dream of racing at the top levels of the sport. I was determined to get there in a way that would fill that void in my heart.

So, here I am, 23 years old at that point, bright eyed and bushy tailed (hairdo'ed) - expectantly waiting for phone calls from top modeling agencies - when my phone finally rings.

"Annamarie Malfitana?" The caller asked in a deep man's voice.

"Yes, this is her." I replied.

The man's voice continued: "I am calling from St. Catherines, Canada with "B" Racing Parts Incorporated, and we were looking to do some advertising promotions with you through motorsports publications for our new race car designs." He began.

"Yes," I replied. "I am interested in working with you, I know you are a great professional team and company."

"Well, Annamarie..." He hesitated. "It has come to our attention that you are appearing and dancing at a Canadian Stripper Show in Niagara Falls, is this true? Because we were shocked to see your picture in their advertisements that are in our newspapers up here in Canada. If you are doing this kind of thing we would reconsider not working with you - but you have such a good reputation that we wanted to call you and ask you about it - frankly we find it hard to believe. We wanted to give you a chance to explain what is going on."

I could barely breathe. His words on the other end of the phone were like sledge hammers coming down on my heart.

"Sir," I said. "I have no idea what you are talking about. This comes as a shock to me too! I am not a dancer nor would I ever consider being a stripper anywhere!"

I was trying to hold it together.

"Oh," He replied. "That's good to hear Annamarie. We did not think so, that's why we called you directly."

"May I ask you a favor?" I asked calmly. "Could you please send me a copy of this ad you saw and the paper it is in? I will give you my address. I would like to get this taken care of and tell them to stop using my photo for their ad."

"Yes." He answered. "I will be happy to do that. I have a copy right here and I can mail it right out to you."

"Thank you so much." I told him. "I appreciate this phone call. I will let you know when I get this issue taken care of."

I gave him my mailing address and hung up.

My friends, those were the days of snail mail, we did not have email yet or I-phones where he could have sent this ad in question to me immediately. The waiting to have this ad in my hands was agony. I wanted to stay calm and believe it was just a simple mistake, I did not want to accuse the advertiser or make a call until I saw the ad myself.

I got the ad in the mail. It was worse than I thought. It was the modeling picture of me in my bathing suit that I used to sign autographs for at my beauty title and race presenter appearances. I had signed thousands of these photos, but this one had no signature and this was the days before photoshop. Somehow they had got that clean photo and used it in their advertising for their strip joint. It was my picture for sure. The ad was very misleading. It did look like I was appearing at that place.

HOW COULD THIS HAVE HAPPENED? I needed to put a stop to this.

I showed my Mom Marlene and her brother my Uncle Guy who I looked to for wisdom to see if they could help me. My Uncle Guy suggested writing a letter telling them to cease and desist using my photo. He helped me write the letter and sent it. I also called their office in Canada and told them to please stop using it. They laughed at me.

I was shocked. Then I got mad. I called up the people who had been behind me in my career, the Miller Corporate reps, the track owners, my photographer. Seemed nobody wanted to back me or get involved.

I could not get a job working as a spokesmodel after this. I was dropped from Miller Brewing Co. and some other titles.   No matter how much I tried to explain I was not dancing in a Canadian strip club. Nobody cared. They shut the door on me.

I tried to go on living my life and focusing on keeping good contacts in the sport.   I kept going to races to see old friends looking for support and possibly some work.

Fans and racers came up to me at the short tracks around NY State where I was there attending with friends, asking me if I was 'dancing' at this strip place.   I could not understand why people in my state would know about it. I was constantly trying to clear my name. It was getting very upsetting!

Then I found out the strip club in question had used the same advertisement in newspapers in the United States side of Niagara Falls and surrounding areas. The owner of the strip club, was a very wealthy man in Canada that also owned a large dirt speedway facility in Ontario.   He was very connected in racing circles in New York as well as Canada.   I am going to call him "Mr. Dupe" for privacy purposes and to continue my story.

Not only did his strip club NOT stop using my photo they were expanding their ads with my photo into the state, my state. New York State.

I got a copy of the ad they used with my picture in a New York State "Nightlife" magazine. I had this as evidence.

I sat down with my Mom to help me pursue legal action against this strip club and against Mr. Dupe. I had nowhere else to turn at this point but to my family.

My mother Marlene is a praying mother. She has a very strong faith in God. She always prayed for me and all her children practically from the day of our conception. The most powerful prayers in the world, I believe are the prayers of a Mother. For this I am very grateful. Because I relied on her to pray for me and guide me with this.

If your faith is not strong enough during times of trouble, find and connect with someone who is strong in the Lord. This is why I became a mentor because I know people need strong people of faith in their lives to help lead them to Holy Spirit solutions.

My mom helped me secure an attorney. Her name was Linda Cook. Linda believed I had a strong case to sue the strip club and Mr. Dupe. She took my case for free. She would only get paid if we collected a settlement.

Linda Cook was like a little bulldog. She was a good lawyer. She was a short, compact lady with square, thick rimmed glasses, a slight overbite, sporting a brown page boy haircut and a really sharp mind. She reminded me of "Thelma" on Scooby Doo. She was on this case right away and she sunk her teeth into it, gathering evidence to make sure we had a winning case in court. She had the Sheriff in Niagara Falls (USA side) serve Mr. Dupe with a subpoena. Justice would be served.

Our court day came. I wore a very professional dress, shoes with a low heel and a matching jacket. I had a jury of both men and women. I was called up on the stand to state my case. I did have some good witnesses come up and testify on my behalf who I had worked with in racing.

Linda Cook did an amazing job presenting evidence, proving my modeling and spokesperson career was on the rise, and that I had an excellent professional reputation. She proved that I never gave Mr. Dupe or his business permission to use my photo or my name in his advertising. She proved that I had never agreed to work for him or gave him my photo to use in any way.

Then it came time in court to cross examine Mr. Dupe. He did not show up for court. He was a no-show coward.

I held up my head and stood strong in that courtroom. I had lost a lot. They had tried to throw me in a pit and lie about me. But God came to my rescue and reminded me who I was. A winner.

The jury ruled in my favor and awarded me 2.5 million dollars in punitive damages. This was a huge sum. The local Syracuse Post Standard Newspaper reporters did a big story on me and winning this case. My name was cleared.

I was never able to collect that money. Years went by and Mr. Dupe kept evading us. To this day I am grateful for Linda Cook. I pray God blessed her and her household immensely. She was there at the right time.

Even though my name was cleared, I decided I did not want to go back into modeling. I had found a passion for motorsports and I wanted to work in the management and marketing side of the sport. I wanted to have a solid career that could last for years, that was not based on how I looked, but on my skills, knowledge and gifts.

I started doing marketing and sales for the National Parts Peddler Newspaper. Working the phones behind a desk. I was grateful they were one of the companies that stood by me. I was one of their top salespeople. I began to also volunteer working behind the scenes at several speedways in the area selling race event sponsorships and billboard ads. Soon I was volunteering on race teams and working on the race cars themselves, turning wrenches, running fuel and helping with tire changes. I was not afraid to get my hands dirty.

I became a "Girl Friday" of every job you can imagine in motorsports. You needed something done, I tackled it with gusto. Painting grandstands? No Problem. Being a back-up announcer for the races? Sure! Get me on the P.A. Working in the souvenir trailer? I am your sales gal, service with a smile. Need an extra pair of hands in the concession stand? Get me on the grill and I'll sling some burgers. Team needs an engine picked up? Get me the truck and the tie downs and a tank of gas and let's get 'er done. No matter what I was asked to do - I could do it and I was happy to.

The money was not as good as modeling, but I was happy and learning a lot, making great new contacts along the way. God was building character in me.

I did not know that the right people were watching me at that time. Be encouraged when you are doing the hard jobs! Do it as unto the Lord and with joy - because He has the right people watching you that are going to give you your next opportunity! I am living proof of this!

Soon my skills at selling and signing sponsorships landed me a job at Sandusky Speedway in Ohio. I had my own office, a phone and a fax machine. The track had just changed owners, the new owner was Racing Legend Bentley Warren. He had seen my hard work and talent and asked me to take over the sponsorships for the Sandusky track. They had no sponsors secured for the season. It was January and they would be opening in April. They were a "NASCAR" sanctioned short track. Meaning they got support from NASCAR on some levels - sort of a subsidiary.

I saw the opportunity and I went for it. I wanted to make Bentley proud because he believed in me.

I was learning to be fearless. I knew that in my spirit I was still going to the top levels of NASCAR. I did not know when or how, I just knew someday I would be there. This is so much like Joseph's story in the bible. He stayed faithful to his gifts even in the prison because he still saw that victory and dream God had shown him years ago. So many of you are on this same journey right now. This is why we cannot give up the dream!

I was beginning to understand that somehow things were being positioned around me and I had to take a hold of it. I did not have time to sit around and wait. My gifts, what God had put inside me were beginning to shine. They were always there. Now God was giving me a chance to use them.

Sandusky was cold and snowy in the start of January and the speedway was located not far from the shores of Lake Erie. It was actually a tourist town, famous for Cedar Point Amusement Park. I had a challenge in front of me here: What could I do to make a BIG SPLASH, get the fans excited about the speedway and attract enough sponsorships to cover a whole summer racing season in less than three months while everything outside was frozen and under two feet of snow?

Even in the middle of winter, you can feel the need, the need for speed!

I got the idea to have a "Speed Show" in January, at the Mall, in the middle of Sandusky, Ohio. I would get all the local drivers and teams there, I would let potential sponsors have free booth space to promote their products for free to give that incentive of goodwill so they will want to become a sponsor. (Jesus said give and you shall receive!)

Now I knew I needed something big to get attention to get the fans there - to pack the place. That was the year that the huge blockbuster movie with Tom Cruise "Days of Thunder" was hitting the theaters. Talk about timing!

I was going to find a way to get the race cars from that movie in my speed show, heck I was gonna try and get Tom Cruise himself!

I sat at my desk and started making calls. I was like a girl on fire - I was working those phones until I got to the decision makers. When I heard 'NO', it only meant Next Opportunity. My dialing fingers kept going. I got through to movie studios and acting agencies. I called the NASCAR teams and the sponsors that were part of the making of the film and their promotion companies. I was shooting for Tom Cruise and he was not available but I was persistent like a bulldog! Eventually the promotion companies and the NASCAR teams made a way for me to get the actual race cars that Actor Tom Cruise drove in the movie to come and be displayed there at my event! They would haul up the cars all the way from North Carolina to snowy Ohio. I negotiated for free "Days Of Thunder" movie swag (official merchandise) for giveaways - the film production companies sent me cases of official posters, pins, and stand-ups! I thought; *"Well if Tom Cruise can't be there we will do the next best thing..."* We did a Tom Cruise look-alike contest! I had the local TV news station come out and did a big feature story. The official "Days of Thunder" movie cars were a huge hit and drew thousands of fans to the event at the local Sandusky Mall!

Families with kids got to sit in the cars and get a photo. We had many companies and even bigger corporations such as Pepsi, Wendy's and Chevrolet with their regional midwest Reps and Dealerships come and set up booth spaces. It was exciting, memorable and everyone from the community supported it. The local racers finished up their race cars for the season early and displayed them and they even picked up some new sponsors! Everyone at Sandusky Speedway and the city area benefited in some way.

Because of the success of the event - I was then able to pull in all the sponsorship dollars needed for the upcoming race season within 60 days. Bentley was very happy with my work. My confidence was growing in my abilities - I could now see things in myself that I did not know I had before.

Understand something: This was a situation where I had to pull deep from everything God had put inside me. My gifts to do this were already there. It was a testing moment. You will have these testing moments in your journey for God to reveal what He has *already* put inside of you! The anointing is the favor and authority God bestows upon you to do it in an extraordinary way!

1.) You will understand what gifts you have so you can tap into them at any moment.

2.) Other people will witness your gifts in action and remember it when God is ready to advance you.

- NO MAN CAN STOP OR STEAL THE GIFTS THAT GOD HAS PUT IN YOU!
- GOD IS POSITIONING YOU IN YOUR CURRENT SITUATIONS AND GETTING YOU TO YOUR DESTINY!
- THE HOLY SPIRIT AS YOUR DIVINE COACH WILL SET UP THESE TESTING MOMENTS TO TRAIN AND PREPARE YOU FOR THE COMING BIG WINS
- YOU WILL NEED TO TAKE ON CHALLENGES ALONG THE WAY FOR YOUR GIFTS TO BE REVEALED AND EXPOSED TO THE RIGHT PEOPLE

I loved my job at Sandusky Speedway. It was a challenge, but I was thriving in it. I did not get big accolades or pats on the back from my successful event from the racers or the industry, but my boss Bentley was happy, so I was. I went fully to working behind the scenes at the track keeping sponsors coming in and making sure they were satisfied. I was in my element. You know you are fully using your gifts when your spirit is fully engaged. It's coming into alignment to what you have been created to be and do - and the Holy Spirit is rejoicing inside you.

I know now that if you take on, thrive and complete certain challenges presented to you by God, even if they are not public victories, God will reward you in public in the future. He is faithful like that!

I also understand now that even if you struggle or suffer loss with a challenge, God will redeem you in the next season.

This is all for Him to fulfill His great purpose in you and He will bring you to it if you don't give up on Him! Stay in FAITH.

I tell you my story is similar to those in the Bible like Esther and Joseph - but there also comes a time where you will see yourself as a David the Shepherd Boy being trained in in the fields of sheep by learning how to kill the lions and bears to be able to take on the giants, and then to be honored as King!

This is who we all are! I want you to see this in yourself!

I love this quote by one of my favorite Kingdom teachers:

"Every David of God is hidden for a season with an assignment that may look like "only a few sheep." But in that process--a King is being born." - Lance Wallnau

We are all Kings and great people of influence being shaped, trained, raised up for our assignment for the Kingdom of God. We may not be in the limelight right now, and maybe only assigned to a smaller group or territory, but God is building you up for something bigger. Much bigger.

Through these smaller testing challenges you are being prepared for your David and Goliath moment. Your moment to take the BIG WIN.

That season at Sandusky Speedway I became good friends with one of my track officials, Brent Seelman. Brent operated one of the push trucks for our Supermodified events and he also was an official for some of our special stock car events. Brent's mom was Diane Seelman-DeWitt and she and her husband owned and operated two NASCAR teams in North Carolina, as well as some short track stock car teams in the midwest. Their team was known as RaDius Motorsports. One of the young drivers they were developing for NASCAR was out of Michigan named Tim Fedewa. They came and ran a few races at Sandusky and I was always willing to be a part of our promotions there if I asked them.

Brent and I worked together on many events and he was an outstanding official. I did not even think about the fact that his family was connected to NASCAR, we just worked together to make sure we put together the best events possible for the teams and the fans at Sandusky.

Eventually, Brent moved to North Carolina to help his family grow their NASCAR team and I lost touch with him.

At the time I was also dating a race driver that was racing at Sandusky Speedway. Looking back I should have not had that conflict of interest. But the lesson was learned. Because of this, I was asked to leave my job at Sandusky.

I was devastated, and went to live with my boyfriend and his family in the Columbus, Ohio area. It was a tumultuous relationship to say the least. I thought I was in love and I was going to "marry" a race car driver and we were going to have our own race team and race all over the country. I worked hard for his team, landed him many sponsors and marketed his career.

I loved his family. They were a true racing family. I learned so much from them, especially his mom, Brenda. She was such a mentor to me to understand how being a racing mom and wife should be, a skill I would need later when I coached racing families.

But I was not meant to marry a race car driver. Things were not going well in the relationship. I was very depressed. I got a job working at the local High School Cafeteria. I was very unhappy and my self-esteem was struggling. I was constantly trying to 'fix' this relationship and this went on for a few years.

One night I got on my knees and I cried out to God to help me. I did not have anywhere else to turn. I had lost myself completely. I really did not know who I was anymore. Is this it? All those years of hard work and dreams of making it to NASCAR and I am here working as a lunch lady - I know God had so much more for me! (No offense to lunch ladies)...

I was still young, strong physically and had a desire for something greater in my heart! I knew God had something more. But I was stuck.

Have you ever felt this way? Do you even look back and think God, why did I allow myself to stay in the wrong place for so long? Sometimes it's our own bad choices, sometimes God will keep us hidden for a season to remind us of the desires He has put in us and to cry out to Him - so He can show His glory. When this happens - He redeems all the time you have lost and even more!

A few days later, while I was working in the school cafeteria. I went into the large walk-in cooler to get something. The door slammed behind me. It was the first time I heard the audible voice of God.

"Annamarie! GO HOME!"

It was like a bolt of lightning that shot through into the deepest of my spirit. It was loud but not in my ears loud, it was loud into every ounce of my being.

I stopped. I could not move. Somehow I knew it was God or an Angel - it was a supernatural voice and it meant business. It was a COMMAND.

I was shaken awake. Awake in my spirit. I knew it was time to get out of there and leave this relationship behind and go back home to Syracuse, NY. But gosh I was 31 years old and moving back in with my Mom? That would be humiliating! Everyone who saw me leave NY for a bright future in motorsports would see me come home like a lost puppy with my tail between my legs. How could I do this, I had invested so much in this relationship with my boyfriend and his racing career and I loved his family! Excuses swirled in my head.

Then that VOICE, that COMMAND kept reverberating inside me.

I sat alone in our apartment, my boyfriend was out of town racing. The longer I sat there the more I felt the push of that divine command. I stood up and began to pack my things.

I left the apartment and went to stay with a friend for a few days while I sent for money from back home for gas to drive back to Syracuse. My family was excited to welcome me back home.

I did want to say goodbye to my boyfriend's family. I loved them, they had been kind to me. I went to their house to tell them I was going back home. It was very hard to say goodbye to Brenda. I adored her. I knew they loved their son. He had a bright future as a race driver and I did not wish him any bad. He just was not ready to settle down. I could not change that only God could. I did not want to cause any drama, I just wanted to leave quietly. I wanted to thank the family for all they taught me about life in racing - and how they looked after me over the last few years.

I had my clothes, a few personal items and an Old Pontiac Bonneville. It was a huge car. My racing buddies would call it "The Land Yacht". It was a gas guzzler and my family had sent some money as well with what I had with my final pay from the school cafeteria. I was ready to go.

As I woke up early that morning, jumped into the Bonneville, I was sad. Grieving my failed relationship with a man I had been very much in love with - but it was not to be. My stuff loaded up in the back seat and the trunk, I had just enough clear space to see in my rear view mirror.... It was time to go, on to the next chapter and I was not looking back. I pulled out of that Mid- Ohio town and onto the highway back to New York State. I felt an urge to change the radio station. I turned the dial and the song "Independence Day" by Martina McBride was playing. I felt my spirit rise up in me. I knew it was right. I knew it was God, it was time to walk in freedom - freedom in HIM.

GOD WILL BRING YOU TO THE END OF YOURSELF SO YOU CAN BEGIN ALL NEW WITH HIM

Hours later I pulled into my Mom's driveway in Syracuse. My family ran out to greet me. I cried. The hugs felt good. It was unconditional love. I was gonna be alright. My grandmother next door had Italian bread and cold cuts ready to make me a beautiful sandwich. My grandpa joked with me and made me laugh.

It was hard though. I still had wounds in my soul that I had to deal with from my breakup. I did not feel victorious at the time. I took time to heal and rest for a few weeks. My old boss at Parts Peddler Newspaper gave me my old sales job back. I was able to reconnect with some of my Upstate NY racing contacts. I was working in the sport, but laying low. I tucked away my NASCAR dream. The dream started believing I could be Miss Winston, then that crashed. Then I thought through working my way up the ladder at Sandusky Speedway I could earn a position with a large NASCAR track, then that crashed. I thought maybe my boyfriend and I were going to make it together to NASCAR and I would be a NASCAR racing wife. Then that crashed.

I was like a racer in a race! Gosh life can be rough! I did not know if I could take any more wrecks. This is how I learned about "Victory Mindset" that I would teach my student Kodie Conner someday!

Now I know what Earnhardt meant when he said, You win some, you lose some and you wreck some... but Earnhardt was not phased by any of those things - he kept his mind on winning.

I was not there yet, I was not at that mindset yet.... I had to get snapped out of the defeated mentality!

We have to know by faith at these times, that God will use those losses and wrecks to bring you to the life of a Champion that He has waiting for you.

But, I did not understand that at the time because I was having a hard time rebuilding my self esteem while I was back home. Parts Peddler was not as successful as it had once been as everyone was going to a new and bigger magazine called Performance Racing Industry. Sales were not good at the paper. I needed to find another job to supplement my income. I could not live at my Mom's forever. I felt like a loser. (Never ever rely on your current emotions - I have learned this!)

While living back at my Mom's I got out the Syracuse Post Standard and looked for employment. The same paper that had reported just a few years ago that I won a million dollar lawsuit. But now, I was in need of a job, any job. I wanted something close because the Bonneville was not an "economy car". There was a job available at a book and paper factory up the street in East Syracuse. I went for a quick interview and they just needed people in their "binding" department and I got the job. I started the next day. I had to take stacks of printed paper and paint glue on the back, then run it through a machine. I was miserable and it was messy work, but I decided to put on a smile and do a good job.

I went home to my Mom's each night, sometimes to my Sister Marcia's babysitting my niece and nephew while she went to her night college classes, and getting a meal or two there at her place.

It was family, It was a job. It was good. But something inside me kept saying that this is not all for you - factory work is not what you were designed to do.

MY SPIRIT WAS CRYING: THERE IS MORE. I WAS MADE FOR SOMETHING MORE. (This is your spirit crying out too?)

A few weeks later, just after Thanksgiving Day, my Mom knocked on the door of my room and told me I had a phone call.

A couple of friends had reconnected with me here in Syracuse and I thought maybe someone wants to go see a movie or hang out or something.

I went to the phone and put it to my ear.

"Annamarie?" A woman's voice on the other end asked. "Yes this is she." I answered.

"This is Diane Seelman-DeWitt, calling from North Carolina. My son Brent and I have been trying to track you down for days."

"Oh, Hello Diane! Good to hear from you. How are you?" I asked cordially and was a bit surprised.

"I am great." Diane started. "The reason I am calling is to offer you a job working for my NASCAR teams here in North Carolina if you are interested."

Shock went into my ears. I was speechless.

Diane continued. "Brent thinks very highly of you and we saw the great job you did at Sandusky Speedway. We feel you would be a perfect fit for our NASCAR team to handle all the Marketing and Public Relations."

Shock again. I could not believe what I was hearing on the other end of the phone.

"Oh, Wow, Diane, I am so honored you would ask me! I am um…. well I am back here in Syracuse and I am embarrassed to say that (nervously stuttering and I don't normally stutter) I would have to drive to North Carolina and I don't have the money to do that right now." (That was a really dumb response but my confidence had taken a hit and I was trying to grab at it and could not muster the words…)

"I would be willing to pay your expenses to get you down here," Said Diane. "You can stay with me at my home until you get on your feet. Do you know how much you would need?"

"Oh my goodness, Diane you would really do that?" I was shaking in disbelief. "That is so generous of you! I am very interested! Can I call you back Monday (it was Friday afternoon) and let you know for sure?"

What the heck was I thinking? Why did I not say YES I will take the job and whatever you want to do, wire me up Western Union for gas money I will get there I don't need to call you back? What the heck was wrong with me? I should have thrown my clothes in the car and headed south that very next morning without even blinking.

I was scared. Yep. I had fear. My confidence had taken such a hit the last few years that deep inside I was afraid I did not deserve the job (my dream job) and worse - I thought I did not have what it takes to do this. I was in denial of my gifts. The gifts God had given me for such a time as this.

The enemy had beat me down. I had allowed it. Now I was getting the Victory handed to me and I did not recognize myself in it.

Maybe some of you have been here. You get the opportunity of a lifetime, and your own fears, and years of being in a negative atmosphere has damaged your God given identity that when someone else sees who you truly are you cannot see it yourself - and you allow these opportunities to pass you by.

"Ok, then. Let's talk Monday." Agreed Diane. "But I need to know by noontime. We have to get ready for Daytona in February and we have a lot to do. Brent and I have been doing this for a month because our former PR girl moved to another team and we need to get sponsor proposals out and contracts signed before the end of December. I need someone right away who has experience like you who can handle jumping right in and taking over for us." She said.

"Yes, yes, I understand." I said. "I will get back to you promptly Monday before noon! I promise! Thank you so much Diane!"

I hung up slowly - still not believing all this.

I turned and saw my Mom looking at me. She had heard the entire conversation.

"So, you got a job offer?" She asked.

"Yes Mom, it's a big deal. It's NASCAR and they want me to move to North Carolina right away." I said still in disbelief.

"Oh that's wonderful, Annamarie!" She clapped her hands together and sprung up on her toes. My Mom was always my biggest cheerleader and still is!

"Mom. I don't know if I can do it." I said, shaking my head at the floor.

"What! What do you mean? Mom exclaimed. "Of course you can!"

I started to cry. I was so mad at myself - my heart knew I could do this - but what was wrong with me?

"Is this the daughter I raised to go for her dreams?" My Mom had her hands on her hips calling me out. "Is this the daughter that did a Horse Show and raised thousands of dollars in her senior year of High School for the football team when you had everyone not believing you could do it and you were determined to show them you could?" She reminded me.

"Annamarie! This is your dream! I believe in you. I never stopped praying for you!" My Mom was giving me a passionate pep talk and knew this was an answer to her prayers for me too.

I said: "Mom I know all that. I just don't know if I can do this! It's really a big deal - I don't know if I have what it takes."

I ran into my room, and cried for hours. What had happened to me? God how did I get to this point. I prayed in my pillow. "Help me God. I want to be myself again!" I layed there for hours staring at the ceiling. Wondering what I should do. Playing ping-pong in my head of all the possible failure scenarios. What if my ex-boyfriend finds out and gets mad that I had an opportunity and not him? I was letting my past failures control my thoughts! My brain would not shut up. I kept thinking what if my car breaks down on the way? What if those big time race team guys would make fun of my big old car? What if's are always so stupid when you look back them.

I was on brain overload. I was supposed to be thinking about the reasons I should take this job and the amount of money I needed Diane to wire up to me for gas and expenses and let her know when I could leave to come there. I had until noon Monday. My gosh, Brent and Diane had tracked me down - it took them days, they must think I can do it, or they would not have gone to all this trouble - what am I afraid of?

This is what happens when you allow the enemy to try and steal your identity. When the enemy can steal your identity and your confidence, he can steal your destiny by causing you to reject it. God is still going to stay faithful to you and bring you divine opportunities - you cannot allow the enemy to work in your mind to steal it from you!

It's one thing to take the win, but you first have to recognize it! Know that it's for you and yes, you deserve it and you have been gifted to do it!

The next day, I called one of my old racing mentors Linda Holdeman who had been the manager of Oswego Speedway where I used to do trophy presentations. Her daughter, Kymberly and I had been good friends at the track, Kymberly had just graduated college with a

Marketing Degree and moved to North Carolina. I knew she was looking for work and maybe she would be interested in this job, I mean she was already down there. I got her number from her Mom Linda and then I called her.

"Hey Kymberly! It's your old buddy Annamarie!" I greeted her as she answered my call. "I talked to your Mom and she gave me your number. She said you have been looking for a Marketing job with a NASCAR team."

"Hey Anna Banana!" Kymberly answered. (That's what my close buddies used to call me.) "Yeah, I am looking for work. I have some applications in some teams and agencies. I am hanging in there for the right opportunity." Kymberly explained.

"Yes, I talked with your Mom about you moving down there to NC," I said. "She told me you were needing supplies because things were tight and she sent you down a couple of rolls of that giant toilet paper that they use in the ladies restrooms at her speedway, hahaha!" I laughed.

"Hahaa! It's true!" Kymberly laughed with me. "Those big rolls of TP sure helped me out and they will last a while! So are you back in Syracuse?" She asked.

"Yes." I explained. "I broke up with my boyfriend and came back home a few months ago. I am thinking of coming down there to work though, but I am not sure. I was offered a job doing team PR and Marketing for RaDius Motorsports, you know Diane DeWitt? She called me and wants me to start right away and pay me to come down. But I don't think I am going to be able to handle it, I don't know if I have what it takes to work at that level with sponsors and everything, I ……. Ummm ……. (long pause) …...So, I was calling you to see if you would be interested in it and I can connect them with you, because well you are already down there and you could help them out because you are looking for a job right?"

(I know what you are thinking right now, am I totally nuts? I just was about to give away my dream job….)

"Girl!" Kymberly exclaimed. "That job was offered to you! Now you get your a--- down here to North Carolina and take that job, it's not mine it's yours!"

I was shaken awake again. To my core - I felt God's voice and it was a COMMAND. The Holy Spirit had just spoken through one of my old pals and snapped me back into reality. Reality of who I am. Realty of how foolish I had been acting. Reality that I must take this win, it is mine and only mine. To go and TAKE IT.

God will send His Holy Spirit to speak to you through divine encounters. Some that you have are very supernatural experiences and hear His audible voice like I did in the walk in cooler at the school cafeteria. He can also speak the message to you through anyone you encounter. God is not a respecter of persons and you don't have to hear God by going to a minister or prophet. God is onmi-present and if He wants to speak to you He will find a way to. That day it was my old pal Kymberly through a long distance phone call. For you, it could be through your child, a neighbor, or even a cashier at a store. God will get your attention however He has to, and yes He said the word a--- (He knew that was Kymberly's style)! It was a moment I will never forget. I was grateful for my friend and her heart and wisdom at that moment, and it forever changed my life.

"You know what Kymberly?　You are right!" I exclaimed back on the phone.　"You are exactly right!　I am going to take that job.　I am going to call Diane right now!" I was pumped up, I could do this!

"You do that!' Kymberly replied.　"Let me know when you get down here and we will get a bite to eat and celebrate!"

"You got it girl!　I can't wait to see you!" I said.　"You are the best, thank you so much!"

"No problem.　Now call Diane, OK?" She confirmed again.

"I am doing it as soon as we hang up, I have her number right here!" I confirmed.

"Ok, Bye!" Kymberly said.

"Ok, Bye!　" I said and hung up.

I was fired up and excited.　A flame had been re-kindled in me.　I grabbed Diane's number and called.

"RaDius Motorsports, this is Diane,"　She answered her direct line.

"Diane, It's Annamarie, I am so glad I caught you at the office on a Saturday." My voice was excited.

"Hi Annamarie!" Diane said.

"I called to confirm that I will be taking your offer of the position of Team PR and Marketing and I can leave right away - I can be down there this week!" I said.

"That's fantastic! Wait till I tell Brent he will be so happy!" She exclaimed.

"Diane, I do need some help with expenses, but just for gas to get down there. I have a big car and I am coming with just my clothes. I will pack some food and drinks for the trip. Should be about $500 for the gas and hopefully no toll roads, is that sound OK?" I asked.

"Sure, that sounds fair!" She said. "You should not get into any toll roads, just come down Route 81 all the way to I-77 then to Route 150 to the Mooresville, NC exit. I will have Brent call with directions to the house. Should take about 10-12 hours. Leave early so you can arrive at dusk. Do you want me to wire you up more in case you need to stop and rest and get a motel?" Diane offered.

"No, that's Ok." I replied. "I will drive straight through. I am ready to do this and get down there as soon as I can."

"Good," Diane replied. "I will wire this up to you, and get your room ready at the house. Brent has your office ready too! We are so glad you are going to do this! I know you will do a great job for us!"

"I am grateful for this opportunity and I will give you my best!" I said with all my heart.

Then I gave Diane my information where to wire the money and ended the call.

I ran with the cordless phone still in my hand to my Mom and told her what happened.

She gave me a hug and we were thanking God together. She immediately started doing laundry and getting all my clothes together helping me pack. Because that's what Mom's do.

Looking back, I see God in every detail of this moment. You will have moments like this. They are your Joseph "Prison to Palace" moments. They are your Esther getting the "Favor of the King" moments. They are your moments that God created you for such a time as this. We just have to recognize and seize that time.

Monday morning, I loaded up the Pontiac Bonneville again, this time with just my clothes. Diane had sent the money wire and I had a full tank of gas and cash in my wallet. I checked my oil and put in a quart. While I was loading up in the driveway, my Grandpa Arthur came over from next door and grabbed my hand and put a couple of crisp $50 bills. "You might need this." He said. "Grandma Elsie has something for you too in the kitchen."

My grandmother had packed a beautiful box of sandwiches, cheese and fruit for the trip and homemade cookies. My Grandpa grabbed a roll of paper towels and put them in my car, because he never ever went anywhere without paper towels. It's the little things you remember.

My mom had a small cooler packed with water bottles and ice and fruit drinks and more snacks. I was good to go!

Final check over everything, and hugs to the family and at 8 am I was rolling out the driveway and this yankee gal was heading south!

It was a crisp, cold fall day in November when I left Syracuse, and soon I was driving past the Mason-Dixon line in Maryland. I stopped at a rest area for a break and pulled a sandwich out of my Grandma's care package. The temperature was getting warmer as I got further down Route 81, soon the interchange for I-77 to Carolina would be on the border of Virginia and West Virginia.

Driving down the highway through Virginia in my big old Pontiac I was singing John Denver's song at the top of my lungs:

"Almost heaven, West Virginia

Blue Ridge Mountains, Shenandoah River

Life is old there, older than the trees

Younger than the mountains, growin' like a breeze

Country roads, take me home

To the place I belong

West Virginia, mountain mama

Take me home, country roads...

As I sang that song, I felt I was always meant to live in the South. I was getting a strong feeling in my spirit that this would end up being a permanent home for me. I was no longer the New York girl. I was going south to stay there. I just knew this in all of my being.

I was really doing this. It was really happening. I was on the road to North Carolina. I would be working at the top levels of the sport, NASCAR. The best of the best in all of motorsports make it here.

I was getting excited and nervous at the same time. The joy of the Lord had refilled my spirit. It was a long ride, I had a lot of time to think and talk to God. I thought about how much I had wanted this for so long, but what I thought would get me here did not get me here. God had an even better way there.

I told God I was sorry, that maybe He was trying to get me here sooner, maybe I should have made some better choices and decisions. I thanked Him for never forgetting me even through my own mess-ups. He never forgot the dreams of my heart.

GOD WILL REDEEM THE TIME YOU MISSED - EVEN IF YOUR OWN POOR DECISIONS CAUSED IT - AND GET YOU BACK ON TRACK!

I want to encourage you my friend with my experiences! I know many of you need to see and understand what I went through and how God was so faithful. I promise you HE WILL do the same for you. Believe in His goodness.

I arrived in North Carolina that evening about 7:30pm. I easily found the DeWitt home. Diane welcomed me at the door and Brent helped me get my clothes trunk and bags into the guest room.

It was Monday night and we would be at work first thing tomorrow. We talked a bit in Diane's huge kitchen and I went to bed.

The next morning I left my Pontiac Bonneville in Diane's driveway and rode to work with Diane in her Lincoln Continental. They were a Ford team and everything on the team, even their personal vehicles were Ford and Lincoln. Soon, I hoped I would be able to trade in the Bonneville for a Ford Thunderbird! I was grateful to the big old faded wine colored Pontiac Bonneville though, she got me to where I needed to go - she never let me down!

When I arrived at the RaDius Motorsports shop, I was welcomed by a very friendly, very southern receptionist at the main front entrance named Ruthie. I had never heard such an accent since I heard Loretta Lynn in Coal Miner's Daughter and Ruthie was from the mountains of Kentucky too. She grabbed my hands warmly and hugged me right away. We would become lifelong friends.

Brent then showed me where the coffee was (it would prove important for late nights at the office) and the copy machine. He escorted me to my office which was adjacent to his, and just outside the 2nd car race team shop and showroom area. I would first be assigned to the Grand National Team, the #55 Ford - Driven by Tim Fedewa.

Knowing what I know now about Biblical meanings of numbers and how the Holy Spirit speaks through numbers "5" means "grace". I was getting that in double portion for sure!

I sat at my desk and got settled. Brent went over everything with me. We had always worked very well together when he was a track official at Sandusky - like brother and sister and we thought alike so I was able to pick up on the work quickly and get things done the way the team needed.

I was immediately comfortable there. It felt right. Then Brent said: "Let's go introduce you to the team."

Ok - now this was a little nerve racking because you never know, as a girl on a team how the 'guys' are going to act towards you. I was still pretty cute, long brunette hair, a little plumper than my trophy gal days. But I wanted to be taken seriously as a professional. I knew this was a woman owned race team so I had that in my favor.

The driver, Tim Fedewa was one of the nicest people I have ever met and had the most beautiful and kind smile I have ever seen. I liked him right away. He was supportive and loved his team. He had a successful short-track background so he was very down to earth and not an arrogant bone in his body. He was looking to finish top in the points this year so he was under some pressure to attract a major sponsor - which was part of why I was there to help him with. There were times when Tim was very serious, and there were times he was very laid back and joking around. I had to learn his ways and his personality so I could be a good Public Relations and Marketing person for him. He was always good to me and trusted me - we hit it off right away.

The #55 team members were almost all from Michigan and transplanted to North Carolina from when Tim raced short track with the DeWitt team up north. So we all had a lot in common. It was their third or fourth year racing in the NASCAR Grand National Busch Series and they were a very promising up front and competitive team. They had good people that were hard working and wanted to win together. They all accepted me and tested me with a few jokes to see if i could take some jabs and I think I passed pretty good cause I jabbed right back - everyone laughed and I earned my first team stripe so to speak!

I headed back into the office and started to organize my desk. I waited a bit and called Kymberly at about 10 am.

"Hey Girl! I'm here! I am in North Carolina and I am sitting at my desk!" I gushed excitedly as she picked up the phone.

"That is awesome!" Kymberly exclaimed. "Listen I don't want to rush you off the phone, but I just got a call and I have an interview to get the position of PR for Jeff Gordon and the DuPont team and I have to get ready!"

Note: The Jeff Gordon, DuPont Team at that time, was the biggest, best team you could possibly work for. A championship team in NASCAR. DuPont was a multi-million dollar sponsor with an extensive marketing and corporate entertainment program. Jeff Gordon was a HUGE rising star at the time - becoming a household name. Kymberly had done the right thing by telling me to take this job at RaDius because God already had a wonderful opportunity waiting for her just days later!

I encouraged her like she did me, and she got the job!

WOW. Only God could have seen that coming!

Weeks went by and I was getting in the flow at work at the office. It was like riding a bike, I went right back into using my gifts and talents and everything God had equipped me with easily. We were ready in time for Daytona in early February. I was going to drive down to Florida with the team, and meet up with Kymberly as soon as we got to the track to park the team haulers (transport truck and trailer).

The Grand National teams parked up on the hill behind the backstretch grandstands the evening before they were allowed to come inside the track and get their assigned garage space. Daytona International Speedway was an immense facility - bigger than any track I have ever been to. It had a lake in the middle of it and there was a boat pulling a water skier. I am not kidding. The place is HUGE.

I was taking it all in - a tiny bit nervous about the next day. It was almost sunset, and Kymberly met me at the top of the hill, we hugged and walked and talked back to my race team hauler. She had already been inside the track because her team got there two days before. They had already raced the Bud Shootout and there was still a week's worth of races before the 500 on Sunday.

My friend Kymberly, who was younger than me but so much wiser at that time - had a powerful talk together that evening. We were both women in a man's sport. We had both grown up in motorsports in many different ways but we both shared a passion for it and wanted to make our mark in a very positive way. We were both very good at what we did and we knew we were both new at the big time levels. We were being thrown into our first big race with new teams and we were both inexperienced with the big league NASCAR track etiquette - she had done some interning with NASCAR in college and me with my short track savvy .... we were both determined to do well, but we were working on opposite ends of the speedway that week, we needed to have each other's back.

This was way before "I"phones and texting and we had to create that commitment to check in with each other when we could.

We looked at each other and made a pact. If I was doing something stupid that would get me in trouble or make me look unprofessional, she would reel me in and set me straight, and I would do the same for her. We promised each other that we would always keep it classy and stay out of drama, partying, and don't date anyone in racing so we can keep our reputations as professionals.

We were going to help each other succeed and be honest with each other always. It was easy to get tempted by unscrupulous things in this big money, traveling sport.

There were a lot of temptations for single women and men on the NASCAR circuit and back then only a few of the really wealthy race drivers could afford the big motorhomes to bring their wives and kids to the events. So the men were just as much to blame for unprofessional behavior, infidelity and yes there was some sexual harassment that happened in the workplace - this is a traveling race show and things can happen on the road.

However, Not all of the people in NASCAR were like that, a small handful of bad eggs and most people knew who they were. The main people in the sport were good, God fearing Christians who were loyal to their families and kept good team rapport. Many of the teams prayed together and had curfews and behavior clauses in their contracts.

Kymberly and I did not want anything to do with any of the sleazy side of things we had heard about. We wanted to do well at our jobs and be respected for it by men and women alike. We wanted to stay wise, vigilant and known for our work ethic.

We made that promise under a beautiful Daytona sunset in the early 1990's and have kept it all our lives. We both did very well as professionals in NASCAR and to this day Kymberly remains one of my most trusted friends.

I stood on that hill on the backstretch of the great Daytona Speedway with my dear beautiful friend who helped me get there at the pivotal moment. It seemed like it happened so suddenly for both of us. It was surreal.

I felt my feet on the sandy ground. It was real. I was here. What a process it had been!

Looking back, God was teaching me, training me, preparing me for this VERY moment. He made sure He had positioned the right people at the right time around me - and me for them.

HOW GREAT IS OUR GOD?! His timing is truly perfect.

The next day started early at Daytona International Speedway my #55 Team was now parked inside the track and race cars unloaded. It was time to get it done. I was on the job! No time to waste standing around looking confused. I had to dive right in! I was on my own. I was looking at the part of "PR Person" with my neat khaki pants, tucked in polo shirt, radio on my belt and hair pulled back tightly in a barrette. Yes, I was entering the stage looking like a poster girl for Public Relations and 'Sports Illustrated - Khaki Pants and Polo Shirts Edition'...LOL!! A far cry from my beauty queen bathing suit poster days - but I was happy as a clam in my new outfit!

Now let's return to the funny (and poignant) Dale Earnhardt, Sr. Story...

About mid-morning that first day at Daytona Speedway, I set out with my new white tennis shoes and an armful of blue Press Kit folders neatly stuffed with copies of my team stats and press releases through the parked haulers and into the special Hot Pass Only areas, with security guards at each gate. I held up my Media Credentials and Hot Pass clipped to my lanyard and flashed my biggest smile to the guards, they nodded at me as I marched confidently to the red and white building in the entrance to the Daytona Speedway "Winston Cup" Garage Area. I saw the sign over the door that said "Media Center". I knew that was the place I was to distribute my press releases and team info to all the big time TV, Radio and Newspaper reporters.

I stood there for a moment taking it all in; revving up my confidence to enter the Media Center. I did not know I was about to have one of the most impactful encounters of my career.

With my left hand I went to grab a hold of the handle to the solid wood red door to the building, carefully balancing my stack of folders with my right arm. Suddenly and powerfully the door swung out and knocked me backwards. My neatly stuffed folders went flying all over the pavement spilling out all my stats and press releases I had prepared for the media. My name on each paper as the new PR rep for the team now scattered everywhere. As I rebalanced myself I looked down and standing toe to toe with my white tennis shoes were a pair of shiny black cowboy boots.

I slowly looked up to the neatly pressed and creased black Wrangler Jeans, then pressed black button up shirt. I smelled the scent of men's cologne - it was a nice scent not too strong. I lifted my eyes big and wide right into the face of the great Dale Earnhardt, Sr.

"Excuse me darlin,'" He says to me a Carolina drawl. "You alright?"

"Uh, Umm...." I could not speak. All I could do is look at this legendary man. It was like standing before a King. I was face to face with the "Intimidator".

I peeked over his shoulder and Dale's PR guy who is just as tall as him, if not taller. The PR guy is giving me a look and rolling his eyes and me like "what a rookie this girl is."

I felt so humiliated and unprofessional. But Dale and his tall PR guy had come out that door leaving the Media Center and I was on the other side of it! I did not know the door swung out! Who designed that doorway anyway - The Three Stooges?

Sorry... I digress. Let me continue. I was standing there, a rookie PR girl - my very first hour on the job at Daytona - now face to face with the great Dale Earnhardt Sr. - and he was taking the time to ask me if I was alright.

I replied to Dale, "Oh, thank you, I am fine. I was just trying to get in this door and I did not know it swung out instead of in."

Dale smiled and said to me: "Here let me help you." He then bent down, balancing on his shiny black cowboy boots and helped me pick up my folders and papers on the ground.

WOW. What a gentleman! I was pleasantly surprised!

"Oh thank you so much Mr. Earnhardt." Thank you, thank you is all I could say as we stood up together and he handed me what he had picked up and I grasped the bunch of papers and folders tightly to my chest with folders going every which way.

He nodded and smiled, put his hand on my shoulder and patted it and walked away. The tall PR guy walked by and looked at me shaking his head as I sat there stunned for what felt like hours - but it was only minutes.

The smell of Dale's cologne stuck with me the rest of the day, but his kindness stuck with me the rest of my life. Every encounter I had with Dale after that seemed God wanted to point out the true heart of this man and the anointing God had on him, and I am not talking about his cologne. I did not realize it then - but I do now that I am walking closely with the Holy Spirit. God was teaching me at that moment how to look at the heart of people and how to recognize the 'anointing' - the God given uniqueness that sets them apart from the rest.

You might think the PR guy was being mean but years later, Dale's PR guy John would end up being one of my best friends. We laughed a lot about that first day. He said to me: "Hey, we all have that embarrassing moment, Annamarie and yours brought you smack into Dale Earnhardt - not bad for a first day." He said he was used to Dale stopping and doing things like that for people. But my episode was actually kinda funny. I do laugh when I think of it, but more so I feel it was a divine meeting arranged by the Holy Spirit, to help comfort me that big first day.

Could Dale's winning anointing have been released onto me that day? I don't know. We know from the Bible that the anointing can be passed on to another person in many ways. Peter released healing that way through his words, (Acts 3:6) Paul released on to his church leaders that way and even the fabrics Paul touched released an anointing on to the next person that touched it. (Acts 19:12)

When I talk about the anointing on a person I am not talking about their cologne or oil they have applied. What I am talking about is the gift, talent and authority God put in them and the power of the Holy Spirit that was on them that set them apart from everyone else. It's something very special and it's supernatural - only from God.

I felt the anointing on Dale, and I learned to appreciate it. I believe God was saying something though our 'impactful' meeting for sure. Did I feel different after that? Yes. I felt at ease right after that meeting. Like it was OK if I was not doing everything perfectly and by the standards of every other PR person, that there will be good people there to help me and people of influence who God positions at the perfect moment. I was there to do what I was gifted to do! That I am to keep enjoying the journey - God is letting my story fold out with these incidences. I was to be confident, bold and go for it. I knew that I did deserve to be here at the top and I will have favor with God and man and to RELAX. Chill out - you got this because of God!

WHEN YOU KNOW YOU DESERVE VICTORY BECAUSE GOD IS GOOD - YOU ARE TRULY OPERATING IN GOD'S REST.

Dale Earnhardt, Sr. was a winner on and off the track. It came easy to him. He was operating in his anointing and in God's rest all the time. Because of that he was able to hear God when he needed to help someone. He was not all caught up in worry that kept him distracted. He knew who he was and fully operated in it - and that is true greatness.

How many times are we so focused on our own issues that we ignore God telling us to stop and help someone?

When we decide that we are winners, more wins will come freely, frequently and easily because of the help of the Holy Spirit in our lives - we are fully operating in our gifts and special anointings. We have this confidence. It's not a day to day struggle. We are not annoyed or offended when God asks us to take a minute to help another person. We know God will make up the time. That we are on our way to a win and we are in tune with God every step.

Jesus said the Kingdom of God is within you. We are GLORY carriers. We are created to win and be a way of life. We cannot do that without a full connection to the Holy Spirit and walking in the authority of Christ every day. It's who we are and what God created each of us to be.

My friend this story is my story, but God is taking you through your story and it's just as amazing and wonderful. Each moment that you have on this journey to the Win and WINS is important and it's the training ground for your victory and how to stay victorious. For those of you wondering, Dale Earnhardt, Sr. was a believer in Jesus Christ. The day of his final race when he left this world for Heaven, he had a Bible verse in his race car taped to his dash that read:

"The name of the Lord is a strong tower: the righteous runneth into it, and is safe." - Proverbs 18:10

That verse tells me that Dale looked to God for strength. Yep. 'The Intimidator' looked to God for strength. This verse was all over the news media after he died in a racing accident of all places, at Daytona Speedway years later. God was there in everything right to Dale's final moments on this earth, as God will be with you.

I don't care how famous you are or how much money you have, we must each stay connected to the power of the presence of God. He is our source, everything else is a resource. The strong tower is the high place. The fortress of our God. His walls surround you and His Glory dwells in your midst! (Zechariah 2:5)

"Take The Win" It is yours. You must recognize and step into it and God presents it. But you must understand these things:

- YOUR PROCESS TO YOUR RESULT IS DIFFERENT FROM EVERYONE ELSE'S

- WHAT YOU THINK ARE FAILURES ALONG THE WAY ARE ACTUALLY LEARNING MOMENTS AND GOD USES THEM TO ACCELERATE YOU IF YOU STAY FAITHFUL THROUGH THE FAILURES

- COMMIT ALL YOUR WORKS TO THE LORD AND YOUR THOUGHTS (HOPES-DREAMS-GOALS) WILL BE ESTABLISHED

- NEVER GIVE UP - YOU COULD BE TAKING THE WIN TOMORROW "SUDDENLY"

- NEVER COMPROMISE TO MAN'S OPINIONS (POLITICAL CORRECTNESS IS VILE!)

- GUARD YOUR CONFIDENCE AT ALL COSTS

- STAND FOR RIGHTEOUSNESS AND ON GOD'S PROMISES

- DON'T FALL VICTIM TO EXCUSES

- DON'T WAIT FOR LOVED ONES TO LINE UP WITH YOU - KEEP MOVING ON - GOD WILL CATCH THEM UP

- DON'T BE AFRAID TO BE REAL - BE YOU - BE UNIQUE - IT'S YOUR ANOINTING

- GOD SEES WHEN YOU WERE REJECTED BY MAN - HE SEES WHO STOLE FROM YOU! HE WILL BE THE ONE WHO WILL RAISE YOU UP FOR THE WIN AND RESTORE EVEN MORE THAN BEFORE!

- WHAT GOD HAS PUT INSIDE OF YOU WILL FUEL YOU ALL THE WAY TO YOUR DESTINATION

- WHEN THE WINDOW OF OPPORTUNITY OPENS GO FOR IT!

- YOU ARE MADE IN GOD'S VICTORIOUS IMAGE

- WITH GOD YOU CANNOT LOSE! WHEN YOU REST IN HIM HE ANOINTS YOU FOR MORE!

- REST CAN BE AN ACTION WORD WITH GOD. IT'S A LIFE WITH HIM IN EVERYTHING YOU DO!

God will get you to your winning destination in a way that you would have never thought and even better than you expected. He will make the journey a testimony of His great love for you! God is leading you to that moment of taking the WIN. Ask the Holy Spirit to help you recognize when to take the win and not let it pass you by. Your God given destiny is YOURS and nobody can take it from you or stop you unless you stop yourself. Trust God to get you there and keep you there! Take the WIN it's yours and there will be plenty more!

CHAPTER 11
KINGDOM PUBLIC RELATIONS AND MARKETING

Now that you have learned how to "Take The Win" we must learn and apply how to stay in a winning position, occupy it and keep advancing and growing, for us and for others. We must learn how to PROMOTE what God called, assigned and designed us to do in an effort to bring more people into the Kingdom and advance God's purposes. This is directly connected to your purpose. You promote God - He promotes you.

As I taught you earlier in this book, God is your divine sponsor. The sponsors on a race team get great benefits, advertising, promotion and growth of their company, mission and message because of partnering with you as their spokesperson.

This is why God promoted Joseph in the Bible, and this is why He wants to promote you! Every Christian on earth should be a walking advertisement for the goodness of God!

This is why these goals and dreams are inside of you. God lights a spark in you to become a flame of burning desire and passion for your purpose. You cannot help it. You cannot stop thinking about it. This is no mistake. God put this in you for a greater reason, and we must fearlessly and faithfully see it done. To do this we must not be afraid to go public with it.

I have written in this very book and have been teaching and speaking prophetically through my own public platforms on the timing we are in as God's people on the earth. We as Christians have been called to use our gifts, talents and anointings to be shining lights in the Seven Mountains of Influence of society for the Kingdom and Glory of God.

Seven Mountains of Society: Family, Religion, Government, Business, Education, Arts and Entertainment, and Media.

If you are a teacher, a business owner, a farmer, an athlete it does not matter - you are in ministry! Your ministry is your message through what you are divinely called to do. When you use your life and platform, wherever it is, to give God glory - He promotes you and protects you.

"Do you not know that you yourselves are God's temple, and that God's Spirit dwells in you? If anyone destroys God's temple, God will destroy him; for God's temple is holy, and you are that temple." - 1 Corinthians 3:16

Jesus also instructed us to get out in public in Matthew 5:13-16: "You are the salt of the earth. But if the salt loses its saltiness, how can it be made salty again? It is no longer good for anything, except to be thrown out and trampled underfoot. You are the light of the world. A town built on a hill cannot be hidden. Neither do people light a lamp and put it under a bowl. Instead they put it on its stand, and it gives light to everyone in the house. In the same way, let your light shine before others, that they may see your good deeds and glorify your Father in heaven."

Jesus commissioned us to go to the 'mountains' and the nations for Him.

The Great Commission:

"Now the eleven disciples went to Galilee, to the mountain to which Jesus had directed them. And when they saw him they worshiped him, but some doubted. And Jesus came and said to them, "All authority in heaven and on earth has been given to me. Go therefore and make disciples of all nations, baptizing them in the name of the Father and of the Son and of the Holy Spirit, teaching them to observe all that I have commanded you. And behold, I am with you always, to the end of the age." - Matthew 28:16-20

Jesus gave us the power and authority to crush the enemy in all the places we go!

"Behold, I give unto you power to tread on serpents and scorpions and over all the power of the enemy, and nothing shall by any means hurt you." - Luke 10:19

This means we are a remnant in this time for the plans and purposes of God. You truly were born for such a time as this to be the top influencers of society and the nations for God's Kingdom!

We, followers of Christ, God's people are to be the 'salty' ones. The ones that bring all the flavor of life abundant for everyone else! Salt also preserves. We are the ones called to preserve life! We are to be the light, not seek the limelight, but BE IT.

We are supposed to build up the cities and restore the waste places (Isaiah 61:4). We are supposed to own and operate the movie studios and universities and go into government service and shine. To use these areas to be our platforms for God and reflect His goodness.

How can we fund missions and feed the poor and bring souls to salvation in Christ without money and influence? It takes money to feed people, to travel to these places, to rent stadiums for revival meetings, to make a Christian movie, distribute it and advertise it. It takes money and promotion to campaign for public office to bring Christian values into our government.

The Lord has commissioned me to activate you out of your fears, get you unstuck, rev up your spirit, and help equip you to fulfill your purpose and shine for the Kingdom of God. IT IS TIME! No more waiting. It's a time of great acceleration and we must jump on the Glory Train!

Do you think God did not plan for the good His people for this time? Do you think God sent His only Son to tell us to do a great commission in all the mountains and nations, give us all authority to do it so we can just sit in our little pews in the four walls of the church, keep quiet and just wait for the rapture? Like "oh Lord, the devil us run amok in this world, our leaders are doing evil things, just beam me outta here!"

NO!! The devil was already running amok in Jesus day! Yeah, things seem to be escalating but that's when we are to come into our finest hour as the Ecclesia! The Church! The Body of Christ is not meant to lie down. Christ ROSE and we rose with Him. He rules so we rule! (Ephesians Chapter 2).

God has put great things in YOU and me and our children to fulfill His purposes in the earth in these last days. He has set the stage for us. He is with us all the way, and given us all authority to take it all from the devil! Thus God's people are bringing the Kingdom to every place in society and we will not be affected by culture, man's ways or any agenda of the enemy. We were created to shine, take it for God and prepare the way for Jesus' return!

Are you excited? I am! Jesus also said we (as his followers and disciples) will have everything we need to do what we have been called to do for the Kingdom here on earth including financial backing if we go and occupy these areas of influence as Christians until He Jesus) returns.

Luke 19:13 says in the King James Version of the Bible: "And he called his ten servants, and delivered them ten pounds, and said unto them, Occupy till I come."

Another version of this word from Jesus says:

Luke 19:13 (Amplified Bible) "So he called ten of his servants, and gave them ten minas [one apiece, each equal to about a hundred days' wages] and said to them, 'Do business [with this] until I return.'"

We can ask God for the finances we need to market, advertise and promote, do business, serve and minister powerfully in the mountains of influence for Christ according to this word. This means anything that God has called you to do and where He wants you to do it. This includes money for anything you need which is directly related to your assignment, calling and purpose - even if you need it to feed your family and pay your bills while you are starting up and building!

Prayer:

"Father God, you have called me to this place to do business, minister, _____ and according to your word in Luke 19:13 You will provide everything I need financially to make sure I can occupy and be influential in this place

for your Kingdom. I am asking for $_____ to build and promote. I am also asking for $_____ for my own wages to take care of myself while I build and promote. I ask this in your name Jesus, Amen. "

Do not worry or fear as you launch out. God has set the stage for you. He has sent the Intercessors ahead into these mountains and areas of influence. I know because I am one of these intercessors. Myself and my ministry and many other ministries have been praying for people like you and the purposes God has through you to come forth and to be powerfully influential in all areas of society for Christ and the Kingdom. This will be fulfilled with Angelic protection over you, through your purpose/assignment and the power of the Holy Spirit upon you. We have also prayed for the transference of wealth prophesied in the Bible to come forth for the righteous who are ready to launch into these mountains of influence and are needing the finances, and Christian benefactors will put marketing dollars behind you to do this. I see it already happening! (Proverbs 13:22)

Everything belongs to God. He can move money, homes, buildings, land to whomever He wants. We have sonship through Christ Jesus and we ask the Father for what we need to do the work of the Kingdom the same way Jesus would. This includes if you need to advertise on social media, pay for a website, hire good people and even pay your business taxes!

Our source is God and He is unlimited! He wants us to ask. So He can move funding to us where we need it, exactly when we need it. Remember, God is our source, everything else is a resource.

It's a time where we must push through and persevere on every platform for the Kingdom, this includes all social media platforms.

I have many people who say to me they want to stay off social media because it's evil and negative. Listen to me! God needs and wants HIS PEOPLE on these platforms reflecting our Godly values and influence. Jesus went to the worst places in His ministry and He did that on purpose. WE carry the authority in Christ Jesus and we must not be afraid to be influential on all social media platforms. This is why the enemy has run amok in these places! God's people need to stand and not run away - even when we see unpleasant things. Don't let that intimidate you. Be the LIGHT on social media.

Intercessors and prayer warriors have been rising up calling upon the Angel Armies of God to destroy satan's influence and have God's people reclaim each of the Seven Mountains of society: Family, Religion, Government, Business, Education, Arts and Entertainment, and Media. The enemy has fought us tooth and nail to keep God's people from taking the mountains of influence in the earth. But the enemy will not prevail. Jesus said to Peter that upon him He will build His church and the gates of hell will not prevail against it. Peter was a disciple but he was the foundation of all of us. Peter was also a businessman (commercial fisherman), a husband, a teacher, healer and a minister. He had influence in many mountains of society. These are the words of Christ and they mean forever. We, now as followers of Christ, are to take these mountains of influence. Our influence brings the Gospel of Jesus Christ to all the peoples of the earth in every area! We will overcome any hindrances of the enemy.

INFLUENCE IS PUBLIC RELATIONS - HOW THE PUBLIC PERCEIVES YOU,   RELATES TO YOU, LEARNS TO TRUST YOU, RECEIVES YOU AND THEN ULTIMATELY ALIGNS WITH YOU!

But for you to advance up to the top of your mountain and gain influence in the public, market your product, service, business or ministry you might feel intimidated, or have dealt with some hindrances. Today we are going to crush any fear, worry, hindrances or intimidation! It's time for you to take your mountain and shine at the top of it, and draw people to your light!

Now you might be asking right now: "Annamarie you are good at marketing and public relations, but that's something I am natural or good at.   How do you get noticed for an opportunity or get influence and followers? What if I am afraid of public speaking?   What if I am not comfortable in getting out there in a big way?   What if I don't know how to market and promote myself faithfully without bowing to the culture of man and sin?   What if I don't have the money to promote my message, ministry mission or business? How can I do this and get to where I am influential for God and the Kingdom - and promote myself or my business?"

I understand all these issues and questions as I have had to deal with this myself and overcome to take my mountain for my purpose and for the Lord.   I know you want that right?

In this chapter I am going to teach you how to do this.   I have some important things we must address first with you and your potential for Kingdom Marketing and Public Relations.   I want to ensure that we have dealt with any pitfalls, wrong thinking and fears first that would hinder your success at this at such an important time.

Through my many years of coaching pro race car drivers and aspiring business leaders and (now ministry leaders) for success I have found common issues that hold them back.

1. **Afraid of being in the public eye**
2. **Afraid of rejection, failure or doing it wrong**
3. **Afraid of lack of support (from family or friends)**
4. **Afraid of what people will think or say (fear of man)**
5. **Afraid of success (you worry about the responsibility and accountability success brings)**
6. **Afraid of leaving others behind (sense of guilt and false burdens)**
7. **Afraid that you won't be as good as someone else**
8. **Afraid of being by yourself in the work (lack of understanding of the true help of Holy Spirit)**
9. **Afraid or confused that it's not the will of God**
10. **Afraid of looking prideful or greedy**

So because of reasons 1-10 they stay frozen and stuck, and their gifts, talents, anointings and what God has called them to do never get off the ground and never get to where it is blessing the world and advancing the Kingdom of God.

Tragic! Don't let this be you!

Maybe you are this right now?   Are you dealing with reasons 1-10? Maybe you are stuck. You know what you want, maybe you even have a word from God that promises you will fulfill a certain goal or vision. But you have no idea how to move forward on it. Or you are waiting on God.

I am here to tell you something very wonderful about partnering with the Kingdom of God for Public Relations and Marketing. As a believer in Jesus Christ, the Kingdom of God is available to you and all the benefits associated with it.

God has a "Kingdom" PR and Marketing plan in place ready for you. All you have to do is partner with it. I have learned this and I am excited to teach it to you in this chapter.

You might be thinking: *"That's great Annamarie, give me the strategy!"* Ok I will. I will give you the strategy. It's a proven strategy too even from my own life! But, first we must address any fears or bad beliefs you have and get those removed off you before I give you the strategy. This is crucial we do this before we move ahead with strategies.

I tell you this with love - as your coach and mentor through this book - I want you to get this and truly be able to successfully use it. This might sound a bit harsh, but as a coach and mentor for many years, I have taught Marketing and PR strategy to many people. But they don't end up using it because they never dealt with their fear issues and never destroyed them at the root! So these issues could hold you back or cause you to go backwards! I know you don't want that. This book is about accelerating and that's what you will do if you take this and apply it.

Let's put this in simpler terms. It's like buying that expensive treadmill in the beginning of the year because you have an intention of losing weight and getting into shape. You really want this and you are determined to do it. You get on the scale and you only lose a pound or two. You think wow I have to really be accountable to this and do it every day to see the results I want. I have to persevere on my own willpower and then when I lose the weight and reach my goal I have to keep myself accountable to keep the weight off. You try to do this on your own power without the help of the Holy Spirit and without allowing the Holy Spirit to show you before you start that you have a root issue that will keep you from success if it's not dealt with. You fade on your own willpower and then just end up using the expensive treadmill once or twice. It collects dust and it just becomes a worthless piece of equipment taking up space in your house.

Do you know it's actually FEAR not laziness or excuses that keep you from using the treadmill to get you to your very best? Fear is a root issue and must be dealt with.

The Holy Spirit showed me this! Why does fear not laziness keep you from using the treadmill or sticking to that diet, or fulfilling your Kingdom assignment?

FEAR OF SUCCESS.

What? I want to be successful you say.

We all say that. But what comes with success? Accountability, Responsibility. You might get success and you are afraid you don't have what it takes to stay there. You have to show up every day. You have to be *accountable*. That can be daunting.

Why does that happen to so many people? Why do we buy equipment, or take a bunch of classes, go to hundreds of conferences, read a gazillion self-help books, chase hundreds of prophetic people online for a "word".... but never put any of it into action and follow through with it?

"It's not what you've got, it's what you use that makes a difference." - Zig Ziglar

Yes! We need to use our gifts, not let them collect dust!

If you have a gift to use, and you try to use it without the help of the Holy Spirit and you begin without dealing with root issues of fear - you are going to struggle, get discouraged and sadly many people give up. This will not be you! Not on my watch! This is why this book is in your hands! Thank You Jesus! But I have been there - I understand where you are! I had to overcome fear and discouragement.

Let me give you my example. Say that you want to do a YouTube Channel and start a Ministry to help many people and Teach the Word of God. You know God has given you the gifts to teach. You even feel the anointing of the Holy Spirit to do it. You love Jesus so much and you have a deep faith in Him. You want so badly to serve Jesus. You even have a bigger vision of writing books and traveling and speaking at churches and conferences. You even have a promise from God that you will build a Christian Retreat Center someday. You have an amazing vision board of these promises on your wall. You know God has called you to do this. You set up a spare room at your house to get started. You buy all the equipment to do great videos, tripod, camera, lights, podcasting microphone.... You even get your husband to put up quilts on the walls to help the sound and royal blue fabric behind you so you have an appealing background for the camera. You get a comfortable office chair and a table. You go online and set up the website, the social media pages. You are good to go! Boy you are hooked up for this race baby! Lights, camera......

What comes next. Yup. ACTION

You know you gotta bite the bullet and do the first video. You have enough faith. You can do this.

You sit in the other room asking God to help you. To launch you. You decide to jump in there by faith.

So you go and do a few videos. Only a few people show up. You feel a little rejected....maybe this is not going to work? Maybe I don't have the right stuff?

Fear of failure rears its ugly head in your mind. You allow yourself to think "lack" thoughts.

Then, these HINDERING words start to come out of your mouth:

"If I just had _____ or just had_____ I could do this and keep doing it."

OR

"If _____ happens or _____ happens then I can get started."

HINDERING WORDS are actually cursing yourself! You are highlighting what you don't have instead of what you do have.

Hindering words cause more lack instead of abundance and breakthrough to fulfilling your destiny!

The root of lack is fear. Fear brings excuses. Excuses keep you from God's abundance.

You can have the knowledge, the equipment, the gifts, the anointings, the prophetic words but you are not able to apply it - you start to rationalize in your mind why you are not able to apply it. Those thoughts become words.

Rationalizing why you can't apply these things right now gives fear and lack a place to operate and you have agreed with fear instead of abundance.

What you agree with takes root and the longer you agree with it the more of a stronghold it becomes on your life.

Your words of lack and fear give the enemy the devil an open door to cause hindering spirits of lack and fear to hold you hostage!

Let's reword this now to come out of your mouth in KINGDOM speech.

Declare:

"Because I have _____right now I am doing _____and I love the difference this has made in _____."

YOUR KINGDOM MARKETING AND PR STARTS WITH YOU BEING YOUR OWN GOOD SPOKESPERSON - YOU MUST HAVE "KINGDOM SPEECH"

My friends we have to watch our words - it's the most important part of launching us out and accelerating us and our purpose for the Kingdom of God. Do not let the enemy control your speech - your speech speaks to your future and fulfilling God's promises over your life!

Proverbs 18:21 says: "The tongue has the power of life and death."

The stakes are high. Your words can either speak life, or your words can speak death. Our tongues can build ourselves or others up, or can tear them down.

You might be thinking to yourself: "Well if I speak highly of myself isn't that arrogant? Isn't that prideful? If I want success, fame and fortune isn't that greedy, fleshy, self serving and against God?"

It's not about speaking highly of yourself, it's about speaking highly of the message and purpose God placed in your heart. People are moved by your message. They see you in your message, they see GOD in your message. You carry a word. I carry a word. We all have a word in us! It's our message and God put them in us even before we were born! Your message is there to bring value to others in some way.

The book of John says Jesus is the Word that became flesh. Jesus lives within us. We carry the Word. We carry the Author and Finisher of our faith. He wrote our story, we have a book to fulfill in heaven on the earth. You have to trust that Jesus writes the best stories for you!

I have learned this and I want you to remember this: It's not just about you. It's way bigger than you. It's about what you carry in you. It's bursting to get out there.

Let me say one thing to those of you who are afraid to speak in public and never forget this:
WHAT YOU HAVE TO SAY IS IMPORTANT AND LIFE CHANGING TO SOMEBODY GOD HAS PLACED TO HEAR YOU SAY IT.

Here is another truth: We all have been called to take our place of influence for God's Kingdom. If you don't do it because of excuses or wrong thinking - you will find yourself in disobedience to God and have to answer to Him for this.

Let's put it this way: You have been praying for God's favor, breakthrough and promotion and it's not coming. You think that the reason your breakthrough is not coming is because of outside opposition. The conditions do not look ideal for you to launch out. You are spending a lot of time in warfare against the enemy and on your face crying out to God. Still, your breakthrough is not coming. What could you be doing wrong? Why the delay?

Delay can be directly connected to your disobedience.

People may bypass you but God is the One who promotes you! God does not delay! Your destiny is already pre-written for you in Heaven by God for your life and it's a good future.

"For I know the plans I have for you," declares the LORD, "plans to prosper you and not to harm you, plans to give you hope and a future." - Jeremiah 29:11

Some versions of that verse say to get you to your "expected end."

So why would God delay it? The answer is He does not delay it. He already has ordained it to happen, it's your faith that accelerates it or hinders it. God has set it to come forth when you come into alignment with Him. Then He immediately moves the "chess pieces" needed around you in your favor. Sometimes those moves take some time to align, and God is calling others into obedience to be a part of what you are doing. You see this in God's plan for Jesus' perfect birth timing: First John the Baptist's Father, Zechariah had to come into obedience and agreement with the Angel Gabriel. This was so John the Baptist could be conceived and born exactly six months before Jesus. The Angel even took away Zechariah's ability to speak until John the Baptist was born! This was to make sure there would not be any hindering speech coming from Zechariah's mouth to try and delay God's process and timing! (Luke 1:5-7)

The Holy Spirit's job is to help you fulfill your assignment and calling according to God's will, timing and plan. WE are the ones who get in our own way and cause delay!

God leads and guides through His Spirit that is working with us and we must listen and follow. Jesus said, "My sheep hear my voice," If you believe in Jesus Christ and have asked Jesus and the Holy Spirit to come live inside you, you are hearing the voice of God.

The key question is are you recognizing His voice, and are you obeying it?

Do you think all your delays are being caused by outside opposition? Maybe you are not hearing God correctly?

If you have been experiencing delay, Please save yourself a lot of heartache and go directly to God and ask Him what you are doing to hold up your own breakthrough and ask Him if you have been in disobedience in any way. Then ask the Holy Spirit to correct you quickly.

God knows what's on the other side of your obedience and it's awesome! Do not be afraid even if things are not perfect when you start.

If we seek the Kingdom and the Kingdom alone all things will be added unto us, including bringing our families and any opposition into alignment with God's plan and purpose for your life and theirs.

"When a man's ways please the Lord, he maketh even his enemies to be at peace with him." - Proverbs 16:7

So, it's actually more fleshy, selfish and arrogant to NOT speak publicly and to NOT create and serve publicly! God wants us to get out there so that someone who needs it can discover you and can benefit and be blessed by you! God has people waiting on your actions of obedience.

If you are struggling with family members not understanding you or not supporting you, it's because you, not them, could be in disobedience to the Lord. Once you come into obedience to God, He causes all those difficult people who were once a problem to become a blessing and they get blessed too!

Look at all the doubt and opposition surrounding Jesus (even neighbors and relatives in Nazareth) and His ministry and fulfilling His purpose for the Kingdom (and he only had three years to complete it!) You are in good company if you are getting some opposition and if the circumstances are not perfect.

If we wait until everything is perfect that would take no faith.

I repented to the Lord for my disobedience and not trusting in Him to take care of the personal situations surrounding me, so I could start my broadcasts. He was actually waiting on me to step into obedience.

The very next morning, I went into my spare bedroom and got on my microphone and webcam, and began live streaming every morning on YouTube at 11am.

In obedience to God, I showed up every day!

Just like the Holy Spirit promised, He gave me the words to say to the people who came on the broadcast. The YouTube channel grew quickly. God prospered it.

Amazingly, the more obedient I was, the more I partnered with the Holy Spirit, the more I saw the Lord working in what I needed in my family. They started to support what I was doing. Mike has appeared on my broadcasts and Landry has helped me in many ways surrounding the ministry.

HE IS FAITHFUL IF WE ARE!

Many of you are here reading this book, or mentoring with me because you found me on my YouTube live stream, which I began in obedience that morning. Many of you have benefited greatly from the teachings and words the Holy Spirit wanted to speak through me on that microphone. Many of you have stepped into your calling and have been activated because I did.

This is the will of God for our lives. He is a God of multiplication. WE are His vessels to be poured into but we must pour forth into where He wants us to. He works in seasons. There are seasons of PROMOTION. We cannot miss these!

If we miss a season of promotion, we can repent and ask the Lord to give us another chance. He will do it. I have helped my mentoring students do this, and God is always faithful and gracious to them, and brings a new season of promotion for them.

When you use your gift faithfully, connecting the message God put in your heart with it - and dedicating it to God - you have the Kingdom covering. It's God's product. How much more is God going to prosper a Kingdom product more than a secular one?

Think about this! This is KINGDOM THINKING!

Our SEASON OF PROMOTION comes when you have an understanding of these things:

1. You know what your gift is
2. You know who would benefit most from it
3. You begin to get ideas and vision
4. You take the first steps in faith
5. Get into dialogue and listen to the Holy Spirit
6. You Obey and Take Action
7. Divine Promotion Kicks In

Proverbs 18:16 is a powerful statement that reveals the answer: "A man's gift makes room for him".

God has put a gift or talent in every person that the world will make room for. It is this gift that will enable you to fulfill your vision. It will make a way for you in life and also is what will create income for you. If you pray for these to come forth, the Kingdom of God is behind it. But you have to put your feet to your faith.

Sometimes we feel we don't have enough faith to do this. You can ask for more from God. You can ask the Holy Spirit to fuel you with His fire. So that you want to do this with so much passion you start commanding things to come forth so you can start running with the ball. Put the pedal to the metal!

Pray like this: *"Father I thank you for the gift you have given me to _____. I call forth _____ you have waiting for me in heaven to _____. I dedicate this _____ to you. I want to partner with You Holy Spirit for all the Public Relations and Marketing of this _____, please help me to be obedient and act quickly on what you guide me to do. I ask for more faith Father! Fuel me with a burning passion to run with this and not stop through your Holy Spirit! I ask you to prosper _____ and the message of this _____ for your KIngdom and Glory in Jesus name!"*

Take that prayer for yourself and add in whatever you have been gifted to do!

This is how those operating in God's KINGDOM are meant to prosper! Your books, businesses, ministries, movies, songs, podcasts, paintings, inventions and creations are already products in heaven waiting to be fulfilled in the earth through you!

The only thing that keeps them from coming forth and promoted and prospered is if you are getting in the way of it because of fear and wrong beliefs!

What are you amplifying in your life? What you amplify will be the voice that leads you.

SHOW UP WITH THE BEST OF YOURSELF FOR GOD!

Sometimes we are so influenced by society, political correctness and religion that we cannot see the KINGDOM of God is here already working through us powerfully.

This is exactly what Jesus was trying to tell the Pharisees of His day. They were blind to who He was and they could not see the Kingdom of God was right in front of them. Why? They knew the Bible, they were scholars of the Torah! Why did they not understand Jesus and the Kingdom and judge Him while He was teaching in Jerusalem. Jesus was fulfilling the exact prophecies of the Old Testament and Torah and they were so wrapped up in their own political agenda that they missed the season of their MESSIAH right in front of their faces.

JESUS HAD TO BRING PEOPLE INTO A NEW WAY OF THINKING TO BRING FORTH THE KINGDOM OF GOD ON THE EARTH.

Some people were stuck in their old ways (Pharisees) and even got jealous of Him because they thought their power was threatened because of His fresh message and popularity of His teachings.

Have you dealt with that at work or at church or in an organization? Nobody is open to fresh ideas and instead they are threatened by you or want to shut you down?

Time to move on and go where you are needed and can use what God has given you! That's what Jesus did!

Ephesians 4: 22-24 says: "to put off your former way of life, your old self, which is being corrupted by its deceitful desires; to be renewed in the spirit of your minds; and to put on the new self, created to be like God in true righteousness and holiness.…

KINGDOM MARKETING AND PUBLIC RELATIONS IS ALWAYS ON THE MOVE AND ALWAYS INCREASING

This morning as I write this chapter, the Holy Spirit spoke to me exactly on this! So many Christians have been called to fulfill great things in their lives for the kingdom - but struggle getting themselves out there into the marketplace and taking their mountain or field of influence! This is because of conflicting and wrong beliefs on what God's will really is about promotion and prosperity for your life! I see the struggle and the confusion in so many people called by God! They are faithful lovers of Jesus. They want to walk in humility yet they have a calling by God, and the only way to fulfill that calling is to boldly get out there with it. They need money to do it successfully and they have an issue (wrong beliefs) on what God really says and means about prospering, money, humility and promoting yourself. So they stay conflicted and never launch out. Maybe you have been dealing with this in your own mind and heart.

I want to address the questions and conflicting messages that could be causing these wrong beliefs and keeping you confused:

- What is true humility? How are we supposed to prosper and be humble at the same time?
- How can we be humble in the Lord but still have success and achieve our goals?
- How can we market, promote and get ourselves out there boldly without looking prideful?
- Why so many confusing messages about humility and wealth in the bible?
- Why did Jesus tell us that He came to give us the Kingdom and the Kingdom was "life abundant"? (John 10:10)
- Why did Jesus say the rich man was like a camel trying to get through the eye of a needle and could not get into the Kingdom? (Matthew 19:24)
- Why does Jesus tell the young wealthy man to sell everything he has and follow Him? (Matthew 19:16-30; Mark 10:17-31)
- Why does Jesus say we must pick up our cross to be worthy of Him? (Matthew 10:38)
- Why does Jesus tell us to not worry just have faith? That we can have anything we ask for? (Matthew 7:11; Mark 11:24)
- Why does Jesus tell us to be persistent and we will get the reward? (Luke 18:1-8)
- Why does Jesus say if we don't multiply what we have been given we are called a wicked servant by the master? (Matthew 25:14-30)
- Why does Paul tell us not to seek our own glory or the glory of man? (I Thessalonians 2:6)
- Why does John say pray that we prosper even as our soul prospers? (3 John 1-2)
- Why did Paul tell Timothy that the love of money was the route of all evil? (1 Timothy 6:10)
- Why does God tell Peter to now eat the unclean things that he was raised not to eat by religious traditions? (Acts 10:13)

- Why does Paul tell us we are to race to take the prize? (1 Corinthians 9:24)

I have asked these questions regarding these scriptures and the Lord has given me an answer, this set me free and I know it will help you too.

Here is THE answer to all these "why" questions:

"Pick up your cross and follow me."

Have you thought about what that really means?

What happens after the cross?

We die to worldly life and enter the Kingdom life.

The cross the KEY to a transformation process for each of us to go through to step into the resurrection power of the Holy Spirit and enter to operate in the Kingdom realm of Glory.

Jesus rose out of the grave after the cross and walked in His Glorified body on the earth in front of over 100 witnesses before He ascended to Heaven, where He is seated and we are too.

THE CROSS IS THE KEY TO THE KINGDOM

"I will give him the key to the house of David—the highest position in the royal court. When he opens doors, no one will be able to close them; when he closes doors, no one will be able to open them. He will bring honor to his family name, for I will drive him firmly in place like a nail in the wall. They will give him great responsibility, and he will bring honor to even the lowliest members of his family." - Isaiah 22:22-24

I want you to get this: Every word in the Bible points to us coming into the Kingdom with Jesus Christ. We are meant to shed our worldliness and take up the cross as a key and enter the Kingdom realm here while we are living on the earth. Why? Because we become a part of Jesus family.

Once we make that transition into the Kingdom through the Cross, everything that is given to you from that point comes from God and is under Kingdom jurisdiction through the finished work of Jesus Christ to bring you into His Family and Kingdom realm.

Your ministry, your business, your home, your wealth, your land all came through that Cross from the point of you receiving Jesus Christ.

You see if the wealthy man had left all his worldly accumulated wealth and his camel, trusted Jesus to get him in the gate and followed Jesus, he would have received much more than he had before on the other side of the gate!

THE RESURRECTION IS THE GATEWAY THAT BROUGHT US INTO THE GLORY REALM (KINGDOM)

"But God is so rich in mercy, and he loved us so much, that even though we were dead because of our sins, he gave us life when he raised Christ from the dead. (It is only by God's grace that you have been saved!) For he raised us from the dead along with Christ and seated us with him in the heavenly realms because we are united with Christ Jesus. So God can point to us in all future ages as examples of the incredible wealth of his grace and kindness toward us, as shown in all he has done for us who are united with Christ Jesus. - Ephesians 2:6

You see how we can get so easily confused with conflicting messages, and religious teaching or traditions? They are taking these words of 'humility' and putting into a 'worldly' sense instead of a 'kingdom' sense.

People focus on the suffering and death of Jesus and forget about the resurrection and the glory! The transformation that happens! That Jesus died and rose for us to transform into the Kingdom RIGHT NOW.

When you pick up the Cross, the Resurrection, Kingdom and Glory follows soon after for YOU!

Why does God want us to have the Kingdom and Glory on earth now instead of waiting until after we leave this earth? Because He has stuff we need to get done for Him here!

We can't do the stuff we need to get done for Him on earth if we are sick, broke and have no place to sleep and nothing to eat! If we just stay stuck in our prayer closets forever or being quiet on our little church pew and never get out there boldly for Jesus and stand up for His righteousness in areas of influence outside the church walls because we think we are being 'humble'...

NO! That is not the humility the Bible is teaching - that is religious thinking - a false humility.

Jesus came to teach us and show us the KINGDOM and the ABUNDANT LIFE. He died and rose from the dead to purchase us back to the Father so we can fulfill what God wants done on the earth, and give us access to everything in the Kingdom of Heaven on earth.

While on earth ministering, teaching, traveling and doing miracles, Jesus said to His complaining and worrying disciples in (Matthew 8:10) 'the Son of Man has no place to lay His head'. Why would He say that? Was He teaching them to be poor and homeless? NO! I will tell you why: Jesus was trying to teach His complaining and worrying disciples a lesson! As a coach and mentor I get this!

Jesus was proving to His disciples as they witnessed all that He was accomplishing in His ministry, that He did not even need a house to do it successfully or a nice bed, that He (Jesus) was approaching His ministry with a no-excuses attitude! He was saying to these men and women that He was sending out on a mission: Do this with no complaints and no excuses like I (Jesus) am doing! There is a cost to ministry, there is some sacrifice and changes you must be willing to make - but not because you are supposed to be in poverty! But to do it faithfully and God will take care of your needs! He spoke of this again when He told them God cares for the sparrow and takes care of it, how much more will He care and take care of us! A LOT MORE!

There is no lack in heaven. There is no sickness, there is no pain and suffering. Jesus nailed all that to the cross for us. WE must do the same thing, nail these things you worry about to Jesus Cross, and then follow Jesus the rest of the way after the cross into the Kingdom realm! On earth as it is in Heaven - Kingdom here you come!

PICK UP YOUR CROSS AND FOLLOW JESUS INTO THE KINGDOM LIFE - IT'S WAITING FOR YOU!

The cross is the key to the door into Jesus Kingdom, He closes all the old doors behind you and opens the new ones He has for you that are way better, protected and in the Glory Covering of God's Kingdom.

The rich man could not get into the Kingdom because his money and wealth would not buy him in, only Jesus could bring Him in! He had to unload his worldly stuff, come to Christ and then experience a better more blessed KINGDOM life!

IF GOD DOES NOT GIVE IT TO ME I DON'T WANT IT!!

Now that's what I personally feel in my journey and you may not quite be there yet. BUT...

Here is what I DO know with many students of faith that I have mentored: God may not ask you to give up everything, but He does ask you to GIVE Him everything.

Let me explain. Everything that you have that is not under the covering of God's Kingdom realm is susceptible to the enemy and the world's lack and limited system. It's open to attack at any time.

This is a legal battle the devil fights against you with God.

This is not just stuff, it's your marriage, your children, your purpose.

True humility is surrendering all to God and being obedient to Him no matter what man or your flesh says. Once you and all you have are under the Kingdom Domain, it all comes under the Grace, Blessing and Protection of God.

Romans Chapter 6 perfectly explains this. The old self has died, the new self is in Christ and we have all the Grace and Covering of God that comes with that.

We then get the help of the Holy Spirit because once you accept Jesus Christ, you get under the Kingdom realm and grace, the teaching time begins. Your spiritual eyes open to truth. You are in a process with learning how to operate under grace and in the dominion of the Kingdom of God. You have to learn and adjust. The Holy Spirit begins to reveal to you all the Kingdom has for you and how to be teachable, movable and obedient. This is why we must listen to the leading of the Holy Spirit after we receive Jesus Christ.

Not all of us have the "sell everything and go live in a hut for Jesus" situation. God will use and bless what you already have, but it needs to be dedicated to HIM in Jesus name.

There is a moment of transformation for each of us, where all of a sudden you realize that alot of the stuff we had before does not have much meaning and we want more of God's miraculous gifts. We pass through that gate, and some old things need to be unloaded to get through. Some things need to come through with you, only if they are now to be used for the Kingdom.

Remember, Apostles Peter and Andrew had their greatest fishing miracle right before they started following Jesus. The huge catch of fish came from the Kingdom of God, it paid off their debts and was a way of provision for Peter and Andrew and their families - when they left to follow Jesus. God took care of their financial need ahead of time. God gave Jesus what He needed even for His team and fund them for ministry!

They had an empty boat, with no fish in sight Jesus showed up, the boat filled and overflowed with fish! Kingdom transformation of wealth and abundance. True, sustaining wealth and abundance because it came from God! The conditions were perfect for a miracle! Jesus was demonstrating the Kingdom and how it works to teach them how to be fishers of men and how they will soon be demonstrating the Kingdom with signs and wonders and miracles!

Your boat does not always have to be empty to get this transformation miracle. Many times, He wants us to take what we have at hand, dedicate it to HIM, then it's under the Kingdom jurisdiction/dominion and it can be multiplied by God!

WE GIVE GOD OUR BEST LOAVES AND FISHES AND HE MULTIPLIES IT.

Nothing can be multiplied continually unless it is under the dominion of the Kingdom of God, and you realize Jesus and the Father as your True Family. I have learned this.

True humility is giving everything to God, then asking, listening and trusting Him to bless it and multiply it!

I have my own sweet story about this trust:

One night I was laying in bed and praying quietly. I was praying about our rescue horse Pongo. I knew God had brought him to us, but he still needed to continue his training, and we had been through five trainers who did not ever seem to work out. It was getting very discouraging.

As I prayed for God to bring the right trainer for Pongo that would stick with us, I heard the voice of the Lord Jesus. Jesus' voice is very loving and He always addresses Father God as "Father" so I know it's Jesus. I heard in my spirit Jesus soft and kindly say: "Annamarie, Ask the Father like this; "Father, I have this little horse named Pongo that I give to You, what can You do with him?"

It was so sweet! I started weeping right there on my pillow. I felt the heart of Jesus. He was trying to teach me how to be a child in the Kingdom that would ask like a daughter of her Father who she trusts to do the impossible with something she loves and cares for.

I realized I was not going to God as Father. I was not really treating myself and the things I have dedicated to God and the Kingdom as in the Kingdom of God my Father! I had not really surrendered Pongo to God and into His Kingdom realm the way Jesus did the loaves and fishes. When it's truly surrendered to God, He can do the impossible with it, does even more than expected and it sticks forever. I needed to act like a family member to Jesus! Go to the Father like He does!

Speak this right now with your situation:

"Father God, thank you for _____, I give it and dedicate it to you. Father, what can you do with _____?" I ask In faith in Jesus Name, Amen.

When we keep relying on man's ways and our own strength and the limits of the earthly realm - we stay limited! Whatever is not placed under the dominion of the Kingdom of God, is vulnerable to the enemy.

I do not consider myself a Catholic or a Baptist or any specific denomination. I am a born again believer and follower of Jesus Christ, baptized, filled and led by the Holy Spirit. I do what God tells me to do and go where He tells me to go, no matter what. It took me a while to work on my mind, flesh and heart to get me to that place of obedience and I still have to work at it.

The rewards of obedience are so beautiful! YOU right now reading this book, is my beautiful reward for my obedience to God for writing it! YES!

You will go through this too, and it has nothing to do with what denomination you are. God is no respecter of persons or any specific denomination. He is looking for those who are willing and obedient. To stretch themselves, come out of their comfort zones and take action where He needs you to.

God is looking for those who will work with His Holy Spirit on earth in an effort to promote and advance His plans and purposes. To continue to advance The Kingdom, that Jesus Christ opened for us.

Sometimes your church will support you and promote your message and assignment sometimes they will not.

What I am saying here is that if there is no revelation of the Holy Spirit happening in your church and the church family or leadership does not encourage you to grow in the gifts of the Holy Spirit and focus on discipling you out into the nations and the mountains of influence you need to find another church!

You can also ask God for a Holy Spirit filled mentor that will help get you activated so you can activate your gifts and fulfill your divine assignments. Help you grow in the gifts of the spirit, and get you discipled and moving powerfully into your Kingdom area of influence.

This is why I am a mentor, I am so passionate about helping people get activated!

Many people have come to me asking for mentorship in the gifts of the Holy Spirit because their church leadership did not allow or help them grow in this. One man I mentored this past year who was in a church that would not allow him to grow or use his prophetic gift, left his church. With my encouragement he turned out to be a very prophetic person even prophesied over me and my husband with words that came to pass! I taught him how to take this gift and anointing he had and now has his own prophetic ministry with his wife and is bringing many more people to Christ by freely walking in his prophetic gifting.

The work of the Holy Spirit inside you cannot and should not be quenched! It must FLOW and flow powerfully!

"And not grieve the Holy Spirit of God, by whom you were sealed for the day of redemption."- Ephesians 4:30

Also in 1 Thessalonians 5:19-25 we are told:
"Quench not the Spirit. Despise not prophesyings. Prove all things; hold fast that which is good. Abstain from all appearance of evil. And the very God of peace sanctify you wholly; and I pray God that your whole spirit and soul and body be preserved blameless unto the coming of our Lord Jesus Christ. Faithful is he that calleth you, who also will do it."

FAITHFUL IS HE! Come on let's give the Holy Spirit a shout! Whoo HOO! I love You Holy Spirit! HE WILL DO IT!

Holy Spirit is so awesome and we need Him! We cannot fulfill our purpose and callings without Him! Once the Holy Spirit can move freely through us breakthroughs and blessings happen very quickly.

Decree: *"MY Breakthroughs come easily, quickly and frequently with the help of the Holy Spirit."*

He is our partner in the marketing and public relations of our purpose, Holy Spirit is your Marketing and PR Partner, Public Relations Partner, and R&D "Research and Development" too!

All the major successful race teams I ever worked on had a Marketing and Public Relations Department and a Research and Development Department. They worked hand in hand with each other.

Proverbs 25:2 "It is the glory of God to conceal a matter; it is the glory of kings to search it out."

We must search and research the things we do not know and need to know to advance. The Holy Spirit LOVES to lead you to the secret things!

Keep asking, keep seeking, keep knocking. We are KIngs and Priests through Christ Jesus. We are not supposed to stay stagnant and stuck and dry.

If you are confused, don't understand something, don't keep rolling back to 'what you always did'.

Ask daily for fresh revelation from the Holy Spirit.

We are not lakes, we are rivers of living water! We have to be a constant flow in the spirit as our fresh source!

Seeking the Kingdom and the Glory, Keep drawing from the well deep into uncorking the spirit He wants to get out and flow out to others and to the world through you! YOU are His vessel, His tributary! There are thirsty people out there who need what you are pouring out!

Quenching the work of the Holy Spirit in your life and making it stick to traditions is the spirit of religion and it can be crippling to your purpose for the Kingdom of God! It can give a false humility and block you from receiving all God has for you and your life.

Don't be afraid or scoff if something looks new and different than before. You have to be open to the move of the spirit always.

Isaiah 43:19 "See, I am doing a new thing. Now it springs up; do you not perceive it?"

I was a willing seed ready to spring up and grow into the new thing as fast as I could and plant more seeds all over the world for the Lord. My hubby Mike, he was not understanding it for some time and we even had some conflict over it.

What Mike struggled with was his family traditions with God and the Bible. He would say to me: "This is what I saw my family always do." Those family traditions were a good foundation for Mike, but our God is a God of multiplication, a generational God, that the next generation will do more than the first and so on. Mike did not have an understanding of this for a long time. This kept him stuck from his own purpose.

My husband Mike really struggled with this new prophetic ministry God had called us to because he had been raised in a very traditional church family.

He had never heard much about the leading of the Holy Spirit by revelation, or that people have anointings, assignments and mantles for the Kingdom and commissions to do great financial things for the Kingdom. It was all strange to him at first.

He wanted to be a good person and he is a very good man. He was in the mindset of going to church on Sundays, taking care of your family, taking good care of your home - and being able to pay bills and that was that. He thought that's all what life was, and all God had for him.

Mike would always say to me: "I just want the Lord to give me a peaceful life and enough to pay my bills."

Have you heard that from so many Christians?

The truth is, God wants to provide your needs and even more. He wants you to think abundantly. More than yourself and your needs. Understand God wants to show His Greatness and Glory in your life!

The Blessing is in the provision, the Glory is in the overflow.

One of Jesus' greatest miracles was feeding the 5000. He started with a little boy's lunch of five loaves and three fishes, lifted it up to God, dedicated it into the Kingdom so it could be multiplied instantly. In the Kingdom there is no lack, only multiplication. There was enough to feed the 5000 and even baskets left over - more than enough. What was Jesus showing us here? When we operate in the Kingdom economy there is more than enough.

When I was trying to be obedient to God and start my ministry, my husband could not understand why I would want to give away a successful motorsports coaching business and start completely from scratch to do a ministry. We were easily paying our bills at the time.

It did not make sense to Mike and some of the things I was sharing with him about the Kingdom's abundance that God told me, Mike had a hard time believing.

Nobody has ever said to Mike before that they heard God speaking to them.   He was skeptical that I was hearing God to give away a successful business and start new and fresh with a ministry. But Mike loved me and he was really trying to be understanding. I could tell he was frustrated. Finances were starting to get tight and as I slowly closed down the motorsports business to prepare for ministry he would ask me each day, how many clients are you down to now? He was worried about paying the bills. I kept telling him to have faith that God would take care of us. We had his disability checks coming in and we would just have to be wise with our money until God advanced the ministry to where I could also do some mentoring and coaching, and put out some books and teachings - this would take some time.

My husband was very stressed and worried and said things to me like: "I live in the real world"... and you know all those things people say when you say to them, "just have faith" and they don't (at the time).

I thought; "I will send him some teachings from Holy Spirit filled teachers on Youtube, he will watch these videos, get inspired like me and boom he will be on board!"

I must have sent my husband 50 links trying to get him to watch online videos and teachings. All it did was make him mad.

"Quit sending me all those videos!" He would stomp off.

I was getting frustrated too and cried out to God:

"God, why would you call me to this ministry, give me this assignment, give me a big faith and not my husband?"

Maybe some of you are dealing with this with your spouse.

Then I got revelation from the Holy Spirit.

I was trying to force Mike to come alongside me on my own strength and strategies and not God's.

I was "marketing" to my husband but not in partnership with the Holy Spirit.

I HAVE COME TO THE CONCLUSION THAT THERE IS NO LASTING PROMOTION UNLESS THE PROMOTION COMES THROUGH THE HOLY SPIRIT.

I knew I had to be obedient to God and keep growing and moving myself with the Holy Spirit and move forward building and getting the ministry and my teachings out there, but not having my husband on board with me was really difficult.

Especially when it came to purchasing the things I needed for the ministry and money to promote the teachings I was putting out there. I had to launch into my KINGDOM PR AND MARKETING and I needed Mike on board! I felt stuck.

Mike is my husband and I love him and honor him. I wanted his agreement in the money matters of the ministry.

It costs to have a website, it costs to have the internet, it costs to have electricity to run the internet, it costs to publish and print books, dvd's and have an email newsletter.

Husbands and wives should come into agreement. The Power of Agreement is in the Bible and it accelerates things.

But the enemy can bring strife and division through an open door of arguments and offense between couples. I knew that so I did not want this to come into an argument even though I was frustrated too. The more I tried to convince Mike the more he pulled away from me.

I realized that I had to rely on the Holy Spirit to do the heavy lifting in this situation.

It did not seem like it was happening fast enough on my strength trying to get Mike into alignment with my assignment for the ministry, and get his support,

I was using the wrong "Public Relations" strategy with my family.

The revelation then came to me on how I was supposed to be doing this with Mike. Jesus said the Holy Spirit was our HELPER. I needed HELP. I needed the Holy Spirit to be my PR man and help me promote the ministry to my own family members. To bring my Husband on board.

I prayed this simple prayer:

"Holy Spirit, Jesus said you are my helper. I need your help right now. Please go to my husband and show him all the things you have shown me. Help us come together in agreement in God's plan for each of us in this ministry and our marriage in Jesus name, Amen."

The Holy Spirit immediately went to work on Mike! He started revealing some things that He had put inside of Mike. Things that Mike never thought of before! The Holy Spirit was revealing Mike's divine purpose to him - the desires of his heart began to emerge, to have more money to help the needy! He wanted to put a roof on an elderly couple's home who were in desperate need. This all of a sudden grieved Mike's spirit that he did not have the money to do this. He had not been thinking beyond his own needs before! He had not realized he could believe God for more to do these things that had been shoved down by wrong thinking! The spirit of religion and old beliefs were hindering Mike from fulfilling his calling and the true desires of his heart for the Lord!

The spirit of religion is not a good thing! It comes from people stuck in traditions and being complacent. It is directly related to the Pharisee spirit that came against Jesus with their rules and traditions. Jesus hated it! He called them snakes, vipers, foxes and whitewashed tombs!

If there are people trying to force you to comply with their beliefs, rules and traditions, beating a bible over your head (or sending 50 youtube videos of bible teachers and prophets) just makes matters worse, and tries to block the move of God! The Holy Spirit must flow!

I realized the spirit of religion was a stronghold on me and Mike in two different ways. It can be crippling to your purpose (and theirs) for the Kingdom of God! It can give a false humility or a false sense of superiority and block you from receiving all God has for you and your life.

The spirit of religion is not Kingdom. Jesus made that clear with the Pharisees!

It's clear that the spirit of religion is void of the Holy Spirit.

This is tragic and has caused many people with great callings for the Kingdom to get turned off by 'religion' and church, and never fulfill what God has called them too.

I wanted the Holy Spirit. I wanted the Kingdom of God, I wanted to follow Jesus and represent who He truly is. I needed this religious thinking removed from me too. I always think I am alot like the Apostle Peter, devoted to my Lord and the Kingdom, but still a work in progress of understanding!

Peter, after the Upper Room infilling of the Holy Spirit at Pentecost was boldly beginning his ministry, with no fear. However, (a bit later) Peter (Acts Chapter 10) still struggled with his old religious traditions and beliefs that would limit his ministry for the Gospel! Peter did not want to go to Gentiles (non-jew) homes to preach because they were considered 'unclean' and ate 'unclean' foods according to religious Hebrew law.

God needed Peter to move forward so He spoke to Peter in a dream and said: "Peter, kill and eat, whatever I make clean is clean!" This was God helping Peter understand that now, because of the finished work of Jesus Christ, the Kingdom was here, and Peter was to obediently do his assignment and eat whatever was available - simply dedicate all foods to God! This way the Gospel could go around the world, in all cultures. We pray over all our food, whatever is, (even bacon) offer it to God in Jesus name, and it is made clean and under the dominion of God's Kingdom!

"Jesus did not come to abolish the law but to fulfill the law! His unparalleled work did what you could never do. Therefore, you are no longer under the law of sin and death. Nor do you have to endure the devil's continual condemnation over your failures in keeping the law." - *Katie Souza, Author of Soul Decrees, and Healing the Wounded Soul*

It's hard to do this when you want support from your loved ones and they don't understand. But you cannot make them understand - only the Holy Spirit can! He will show you what to do and say! He will come and give your loved ones dreams and visions and understanding and set people in their path to speak a word to them! The Holy Spirit will reveal what God wants for them too! It's so beautiful - the work of the Holy Spirit - He does all the heavy lifting for us!

Some of you are ready to launch and promote what God has called you to do and you don't feel you have the support of your church, your family or even your spouse.

I know that is so difficult, I have been there! I am telling you my friend I found comfort in the fact that even Jesus himself was not received in His own home town of Nazareth.

I believe that is the true revelation that God called you as a teacher, prophet or leader for this time if you are not always fully received by people close to you, or in your own circles. Don't get discouraged - it's a badge of Honor!

Did that stop Jesus? NO! He kept going. Getting His message out there more and more! He kept the flow going and the right people came around Him and supported Him.

We MUST, as individuals seek our own understanding of the word of God and how it applies to each of us through the partnership of the Holy Spirit. Do not just take a Bible teacher's word for it. Teachers are to light a fire in you to go deeper! Take the word of God and go to God with it YOURSELF.

This happened for my Husband Mike and it was beautiful to watch the Holy Spirit work in him. I had to understand that Mike's faith would not be exactly like my faith, and God would speak to Him through His word too.

Mike and I began to read the Bible together every morning. The scriptures that we were given meant something to each of us. We learned to pray on the word. We came together in the Word. This was the first alignment between us with the Ministry.

Ask: *"Lord Jesus, What does this scripture mean for me and my assignment for your Kingdom? I ask for revelation from Your Holy Spirit. Lord, I do not want to have limiting beliefs from wrong teaching or religion that keeps me from fulfilling what You Lord have called me to do! Lord align me with your word and your Holy Spirit as it pertains to my divine assignment in your precious name, I ask, Amen."*

THE WORD OF GOD MUST BE RECEIVED WITH THE REVELATION OF THE HOLY SPIRIT AS IT ALIGNS WITH YOUR ASSIGNMENT.

Soon, (within weeks) the Holy Spirit confirmed to Mike his assignment in our ministry! That Mike was anointed for finances and that Mike would be in charge of the outreach of our ministry, where we would use the finances to bless the needy and build for the kingdom! YES! Mike was fully on board with me!

THE HOLY SPIRIT NEVER FAILS US! HE GAVE MIKE HIS ASSIGNMENT! THANK YOU HOLY SPIRIT!

The Holy Spirit does the BEST Public Relations for you! What would take you years in convincing a person, He can do in a day! I hope our story will help you and your loved one come together in agreement!

The Holy Spirit must be invited by you to work with you for your public and personal needs.

Ask: *"I invite You Holy Spirit to come work in me and through me. I ask You, the Holy Spirit to be my divine Public Relations Person. In Jesus Name Amen"*

The Holy Spirit is always in movement. So you must be.

The Holy Spirit never does anything wrong. It might be a stretch for you, but not for Him.

He (The Holy Spirit) is the most important voice in your life, and He can speak through all creation. If you give Him a place He will speak. If you send Him ahead to make a way, He will do it!

If you don't know what to say for a speech, a job interview, or even a quick email to someone important? Ask the Holy Spirit for the words! He will give them to you!

He can fill your mind and voice with words you need if you don't know what to say. "Give you utterance" Ask Him for the words in any situation and let Him flow. (I call them "Holy Spirit Downloads".)

The Holy Spirit is your Marketing and PR person and can represent you in the spirit! What happens in the spirit reflects directly in the natural! Send Him to people you need to get understanding from. Send Him ahead in all situations.

For example, you may be nervous about a job interview and you want to make a good impression, you can ask the Holy Spirit to go ahead of you and prepare everything, and even be present in the interview to help things flow and bring God's presence, His wisdom and favor in the job interview! The right things will come to light in the interview for you that you would have never thought to say on your own! The other people in the meeting will also be prompted to connect with you in a more personal way and see things in you that God will reveal to them supernaturally!

I have sent my helper, the Holy Spirit ahead with doctors appointments, before my meetings, speeches and broadcasts and even for my family members and students! We have seen amazing things come forth that could only be the work of the Holy Spirit in that situation! He is your forerunner and your revelator!

This is the job of the Holy Spirit and He LOVES to do it!

"For all that is secret will eventually be brought into the open, and everything that is concealed will be brought to light and made known to all." - Luke 8:17

The Holy Spirit deals with the impossible situations ahead of you! He brings to light and reveals to you everything you need to have solved and helps you solve it! Holy Spirit is the ultimate PR person!

So if you are confused about your mission, calling, purpose, family and you are being held back in any way - these are important things you must have clear answers and solutions to and they cannot wait!

The Holy Spirit is chomping at the bit waiting for you to ask Him! He is like a race horse ready to be let out of the gate for you!

Does praying and fasting help? Absolutely. It helps you hear the answer clearly! Fasting is an act of humility to God. That's where we exercise humility, before God, not the world and not man!

We bow before no man! Only God! Father, Son and Holy Spirit. We respect others and love them, but we do not bow to them. It's God who exalts us and advances us. God can work through the people He puts around you, but take everything to God and His authority. If you don't it could result in 'dead works'! Dead works are things you act on from man's opinion or your own without God in them.

Here are the steps to hearing from God and taking action on what you hear:

- HUMBLE YOURSELF BEFORE GOD
- ASK GOD SPECIFIC QUESTIONS ON THE NEXT STEP
- WATCH AND LISTEN
- RECEIVE REVELATION
- LOOK OR ASK FOR CONFIRMATION
- RECEIVE CONFIRMATION
- ACT ON IT QUICKLY
- SEE GOOD FRUIT AND KNOW GOOD FRUIT IS FROM GOD

"Humble yourselves therefore under the mighty hand of God, that he may exalt you in due time:" - 1 Peter 5:6

What does due time mean? The confirmation from God of the timing of a promotion from God.

"This is the third time I am coming to you. In the mouth of two or three witnesses shall every word be established." - 2 Corinthians 13:1

If you are really stuck and confused on your next step. Do a three day fast, pray and seek God in secret, until He reveals to you the next action step. He will give you confirmation! Then take action on it! Do not wait on this too long. Keep asking for confirmation. We must be intent on this because our season could pass us by and we do not want that!

1. **The first confirmation should be in your spirit, your spirit will witness to it. It will give a sense of peace and knowing.**
2. **The Holy Spirit will send you to a specific place in scripture to confirm.**
3. **The second or third confirmation will either come from a person or a sign sent from the Holy Spirit.**

Is it ok to ask the Holy Spirit for confirmation? YES. It's called 'putting out your fleece' like Gideon did. Gideon was called a "Mighty Man of Valor" by God's Angel Messenger. So if it's good for Gideon to ask for confirmation, it most certainly is for you who are in Christ!

"And God did so that night: for it was dry upon the fleece only, and there was dew on all the ground." Gideon was such a humble man, and as he went to God, he respectfully asked Him to give him a sign to be sure." - Judges 6:40

Your testimony of how God gave you His confirmation is public relations and marketing for Jesus Christ and showing off God's goodness and faithfulness!

Let me give you a true life example of how one of my students asked for confirmation from the Holy Spirit on a big move, that has now become his testimony.

Jeno and Karrie were listeners on my Live broadcast when I first started out back in 2017. Karrie reached out to me via email and said she and her husband Jeno wanted to talk with me. With that first phone call, I discerned that God had a major ministry planned for this couple and also there would be some building, even real estate investing they would do for the Kingdom. Jeno and Karrie had been pressing in with their prayer because they felt the Lord had something greater for them, but they needed more clarity and guidance. They were stuck and not sure what to do. I invited them to start mentoring with me.

Within a few months of mentoring them it was revealed that Jeno had a strong prophetic gifting, and that Karrie was a powerful prayer warrior and carried an anointing to help people birth their assignments for God. As we progressed, Jeno asked me how he could ask the Holy Spirit for a 'sign' that he was taking the right direction with what God was showing him to begin to speak words over people prophetically.

I told him; "Jeno, of course you can ask the Holy Spirit for a sign of confirmation!" He said; "What should I ask Him to show me?" I said; "What about a 'whale'?" Jeno laughed; "A whale?" I said; "Yes, remember Jonah in the Bible?

God put Jonah in a whale to put him in the right direction of obedience."

Jeno agreed and we prayed and asked the Holy Spirit to show Jeno a 'whale' if he was going in the right direction with using his prophetic gifts and should pursue a ministry. I told Jeno that it will take him by surprise and in an unexpected way - because the Holy Spirit loves doing this - it's a true relationship when you start doing these confirmations with the Holy Spirit.

Many days passed and Jeno did not see a 'whale'. He was getting a little concerned. I told him to just be at peace and keep his spirit open and ready to receive - that the Holy Spirit would show him and it may be surprising . Few more days passed. Then Jeno messaged me excitedly one afternoon.

"Annamarie! The Holy Spirit showed me my whale!"

Below his text message was a picture of a child's story book opened to a huge illustration of a polka dot whale.

I texted back: "YES!! Whooo hooo and it's even got Polka Dots!" I was so excited for Jeno.

"Yes!" Jeno texted back. "My daughter brought this book home from school today and wanted me to read it to her. We read together enjoying the story, then I turned the page and all of a sudden there was this whale right in the middle of the book!"

Now, some of you may think this whole "whale" scenario is coincidental. Understand this! There are NO coincidences with God. The Hebrew language, God's language does not even have a word for coincidence. That's no coincidence!

So, here I am with one of my brightest new students Jeno, whom I had discerned the Lord wanted to use in prophetic ministry getting Holy Spirit confirmation. Prophetic ministry is very needed for our times. Those who can see things in the spirit for other people, for regions and for nations are being called up for the Kingdom. Why? Because God wants His people activated and stepping into their assignments, and many people are not hearing God clearly.

Prophetic seers like Jeno can see the hidden and future things quickly, and they must use this gift boldly. This can shift families, businesses, ministries and even speak what God wants him to speak over a church or city! Jeno needed to have confirmation for himself that God wanted him to do this. I am very careful to tell my students to seek God for their own confirmation on things and don't just take my word for it. I do this to kick start them into a deeper relationship with God and for them to begin to speak and hear from God themselves for confirmation. They can use this tool in their future and help others.

That's when you can tell you are working with the right teacher or mentor. They push you to learn how to do these things yourself, so you will not always need them, then you can go out and eventually have those that you will teach and mentor, and so on - that's God's law of multiplication. It's true disciplement. We should never try to keep our students or those we are leading dependent on us forever, or neither should we keep them stuck in the four walls of the church - they must grow, learn, mature, activate and be SENT out.

This was my goal with Jeno and all my students. I wanted him to be equipped with the tools to hear God clearly as he would be sent out for his own ministry.

Jeno asked: "Annamarie - what do you think the Polka Dots mean on the whale? I know that the whale is confirmation of my question. I asked the Holy Spirit - that I am to pursue prophetic ministry, but why the dots?"

I loved that Jeno was wanting to see deeper into this message God was giving him. So, like Jesus did many times with His disciples I put the question back to Jeno, "What do you think they mean?"

"I think it means keep connecting the dots, that He is going to show me more!" He answered.

"Yes! I typed as my heart leapt with joy for my student, then I added; "Jeno, you put out your question, and the Holy Spirit answered, He knows you are ready to have that constant communication with Him and He is ready to lead you to the next step!"

We both had confirmation from this moment.

Since then Jeno has asked the Holy Spirit to show him "signs" of whales to confirm a step.

Once you get the first confirmation, the Holy Spirit begins to move quickly in your life, it's like a flood gate has opened.

Just a week or so after that, Jeno and Karrie were told to go pray on a mountain over San Diego California and prophesy God's promises and purposes over that city! Literally a stranger came up to Jeno out of the blue - in a prayer meeting and pointed to him and said that Jesus had given Jeno a key to go and pray and prophesy over the city of San Diego and that Jesus had asked someone else to do it, but that person did not go and do it! The Lord saw Jeno had an obedient heart and He wanted Jeno to go and pray on that mountain right now! WHAT! Wow!! Jeno called me, and told me all this. In obedience to the Lord we prepared him and Karrie and even their little daughter to go up to the mountain and pray over San Diego for Jesus there. We did not hesitate!

"Surely the Lord God will do nothing, but he revealeth his secret unto his servants the prophets." - Amos 3:7 (KJV)

They had a powerful time of prayer on the mountain. Repenting for the city and the region, proclaiming the land for God and the Gospel of Jesus Christ. I was so proud of them and their faith and willingness for God and the Kingdom.

My dream when I started my ministry was to have a group of prayer warriors being boots on the ground intercessors across the Nation! I was here in Virginia Beach on the east coast, I had already prayed at the First Landing Cross here in Cape Henry, Virginia where there was a large granite cross. It was amazing because there was my disciple, Jeno and his wife and child, praying on the west coast a year later some of the same prayers, declarations and scriptures and on that mountain (Mt. Soledad) there, where they prayed, to their surprise here was a large granite cross on top of the mountain - very similar to the cross where I prayed on the east coast at Cape Henry. Talk about Holy Spirit confirmation! Both Crosses are near the sea on the coasts. Sea to shining sea Jesus has been proclaimed!

This was a powerful act of obedience for Jeno and his family. They were doing this all in private, but obedience brings breakthrough, and what you do in secret, God rewards in public!

If you do not act out in obedience to what God needs done on the earth, God will find someone who will do it.

Jeno was willing and ready. Are you?

It was about to go big for Jeno. His public debut was happening - God was preparing a launch for his ministry and the steps (the dots) were all coming together....

For the next step Jeno needed a bigger whale.

A few months later, Jeno had been accelerating in his walk with the Lord and beginning to grow in his prophetic gifting with his wife Karrie alongside. He was getting prophetic words and words of knowledge over people in our class, as Karrie was also teaching from the Bible and praying powerfully over our students. They were a power couple for God. I gave them an opportunity to teach a few classes for me and they began to find their confidence in teaching to small groups. I could tell God was going to multiply this quickly for them. I was excited and honored that God had trusted me to mentor this couple and sent them to me to help disciple them.

Now that Jeno had begun to partner with the Holy Spirit for signs of confirmation on each step, the Holy Spirit was accelerating him and his ministry. It was about to take a huge leap.

"For the eyes of the Lord run to and fro throughout the whole earth, to give strong support to those whose heart is blameless toward him." - 2 Chronicles 16:9 (ESV)

One evening soon after, I got a message from another student - "Martyna" - saying she needed to speak to me ASAP.

I called her and she answered on the first ring. "Annamarie!" She was breathless. "What's wrong? I said.

"Nothing is wrong, something amazing just happened!" She replied. "I was walking my property here in (Pahrump, Nevada) and praying like usual, and all of a sudden I fell to my knees to the ground and I heard the Lord speaking loudly to me."

"What did you hear?" I asked.

"That I am to have Jeno and Karrie come move here to Pahrump and help them build."

"Wow!" I asked her. "Have you been talking to them?"

"No," She said. "I only see them in our online classes once and a while... but this was a very powerful experience out of the blue from God and I wanted to call you and tell you first."

I knew what to do in this situation, because I knew God was moving powerfully for Jeno and Karrie's ministry, and when God is moving and accelerating a ministry, a person, a business - He will set up people around you to help position you and give you favor to build and advance - i could feel it very strongly in my Spirit, but I am careful to get confirmation on these words that come from the Holy Spirit however they come. This is not being unfaithful - it's using wisdom in communicating with the Lord.

"Let's pray on this right now," I told Martyna, "and we will ask the Holy Spirit for confirmation, if He wants us to reveal this to Jeno or not. This would be a big step for them and I want to make sure we are in the will of God.

She and I prayed over the phone and we asked the Holy Spirit to speak to her again on this, and to also show me confirmation. As we prayed, simultaneously we both were reminded of the prophet Elisha and the Shunamite woman. It was amazing how we both thought of that. The Shunamite woman recognized Elisha as a man of God and wanted to show him hospitality at her home when he passed through.

Elisha and the Shunamite Woman:
"One day Elisha went on to Shunem, where a wealthy woman lived, who urged him to eat some food. So whenever he passed that way, he would turn in there to eat food. And she said to her husband, "Behold now, I know that this is a holy man of God who is continually passing our way. Let us make a small room on the roof with walls and put there for him a bed, a table, a chair, and a lamp, so that whenever he comes to us, he can go in there." - 2 Kings 4:8-10

Both "Martyna" and I felt the presence of God while we were receiving this revelation from the Word of God about Jeno, and how God was seeing him as a type of Elisha, and her "M" as a type of Shunamite woman. That she was to create a place for them to come and stay and assist Jeno in building his ministry. That Pahrump, NV was the place that Jeno was to come to next.

THE HOLY SPIRIT WILL SHOW YOU SIGNS AS CONFIRMATION AND HE WILL ALSO BRING YOU TO THE WORD OF GOD FOR CONFIRMATION ON WHAT HE IS SHOWING YOU, A STEP, A MOVE OR AN ASSIGNMENT.

The Word of God is the Will of God. If the Holy Spirit brings you confirmation by bringing you to the Word - you can be confident it's in God's will for you and your life.

GOD WILL POSITION YOU FOR YOUR PUBLIC DEBUT AND SET YOU UP WITH DIVINE APPOINTMENTS AND PEOPLE WHO WILL GIVE YOU FAVOR ALONG THE WAY!

Three Forms Of Confirmation From The Holy Spirit:

1. Ask for a special sign (something that is unusual)
2. Send to the word (specific verse in the bible)
3. Send a witness (another person who will confirm what you are also hearing from God)

Martyna and I knew we were getting confirmation from the Word of God on this for Jeno and Karrie to move to Pahrump and that she was to host them and somehow God would use all this to build Jeno and Karrie's ministry.

"So, what should we do now, Annamarie?" She was excited. "I will do whatever God wants me to do in obedience, like the Shunamite woman. I will open my house to them."

I began to explain to her that if she did that for Jeno and Karrie she would receive a "prophets reward".

"What's a "prophets reward"? She asked.

"A prophets reward," I explained. "Is when you do something in obedience to God to show favor to His prophets, teacher and disciples, you and your household will be blessed. You can even expect a miracle.

This is what God did for the Shunamite woman and her family for hosting the Prophet Elisha **in 2 Kings 4:11**

"One day he came there, and he turned into the chamber and rested there. And he said to Gehazi his servant, "Call this Shunammite." When he had called her, she stood before him. And he said to him, "Say now to her, 'See, you have taken all this trouble for us; what is to be done for you? Would you have a word spoken on your behalf to the king or to the commander of the army?'" She answered, "I dwell among my own people." And he said, "What then is to be done for her?" Gehazi answered, "Well, she has no son, and her husband is old." He said, "Call her." And when he had called her, she stood in the doorway. And he said, "At this season, about this time next year, you shall embrace a son." And she said, "No, my lord, O man of God; do not lie to your servant." But the woman conceived, and she bore a son about that time the following spring, as Elisha had said to her."

As I explained all this to Martyna she told me there are many things she had been praying to God for her family and her land and ranch to be a retreat and healing ministry to be birthed there.

"But," She said. "Yes, I have these prayers, and I am faithful God will do it. I just want to do this for Jeno and

Karrie because I feel it strongly in my heart." She began to weep.

I was so moved at her faith. My heart was knowing that God was moving for her right now and had heard her prayers. He was bringing the prophet there to minister to her and bless her and she blessed him.

There are no coincidences with God. We just have to have faith that He sees us and hears us. He is speaking to us and He is moving things, people, and situations to bring us answers to our prayers. This many times is connecting us with other obedient people. We cooperate together for a glorious opportunity for each party or person that God brought in to help you and you help them at the perfect time. Sometimes it seems to come out of the blue, with people you barely know. But God knows their heart. He knows exactly who to connect you to! You may not, but He does! Your perfect connection is ready for you, when you say Yes - God is speaking to those connections for you immediately!

"This is what I will do," I told her. "I will wait three days and pray. If Jeno reaches out to me for guidance on his next steps, I will tell him about this word of the Lord and that He is to move to Pahrump, NV. This is how I will wait on confirmation from the Lord to tell Jeno."

Ok, I agree, 'Martyna' Said. I will continue to pray!"

"Good night and rest well - know the Lord hears your prayers and He sees your willingness to be obedient. You will be greatly blessed." I assured her.

That evening I prayed as I pulled up Pahrump, Nevada on Google earth and looked over the region. Maybe God would reveal something to me.

I realized that Pahrump, was in a desert valley just over the mountain from Las Vegas. Las Vegas was the very last

NASCAR race I attended before starting my ministry three years before.

I had noticed the mountains around the track, I thought about how they built the speedway in the desert where there was nothing and now such a huge and prospering place. The track was one of the finest I had ever been to. It was my last big NASCAR race - Vegas. Since then - God started me on the road to ministry. Something interesting about how I kept looking at the mountains while I was there. Little did I know that three years or so later, God had something amazing He planned to do on the other side of that mountain in Pahrump, with people he had waiting and lined up for me to disciple for HIS Kingdom and Glory!

God will always give you double for your trouble! He has huge things happening for you on the other side of that mountain in the future!!

There was a sense of 'acceleration' over the region of Nevada that I saw prophetically as I prayed over what God was showing me through the Google Earth map.

The Holy Spirit prompted me to look up the meaning of Pahrump.

I found Pahrump is named after the original indigenous name Pah-Rimpi, or "Water Rock," so named because of the abundant artesian wells in the valley.

Water represents the Holy Spirit, and Rock represents Jesus Christ.

Wells represent water that springs forth in a place to sustain and grow life there.

God will send you to the place of a "well" for you to draw from, as He prepares to launch you into the public, where you will begin to pour out to others.

JESUS THE ROCK, MEETS YOU AT THE WELL PRIVATELY THEN COMMISSIONS YOU INTO PUBLIC SERVICE FOR THE KINGDOM.

It's going from stagnant water to living water and it's already trying to bubble up from inside of each of us, cleanse out all the shame, doubt and fears! Then you feel alive and vibrant and can't wait to flow it out to others!

This is a 'spiritual' well but there may be signs at that place where you are or where you are being sent that Jesus is pulling it forth from deep within you in the natural signs around you to confirm it.

We all know the story of the 'Woman At The Well" in John Chapter 4. It is the longest recorded one on one conversation Jesus has with anyone in the Bible, and it's a Woman, and at a Well.

This is a place of major transformation of a woman who is desperately private and with one conversation with Jesus she becomes exuberantly public.

Historically, the Samaritan Woman at the Well becomes the first evangelist for the Gospel of Jesus Christ! She was the first person who Jesus revealed that He was the Messiah. Also it was in a region - Samaria - that was written off by the religious Jews. Ha, kinda like Las Vegas? How many Christians frown upon that place! Vegas and Pahrump (a valley hidden behind it) is the last place you would think there would be a move of the Gospel! That's why it's perfect and prime for a move of God.

I love how God thinks! These things never change with Him! Even today! From Samaria, Israel to Pahrump, Las Vegas! Jesus is springing up wells in His people and into the regions!

Just like Samaria, God knows what He wants to do on the other side of those tracks or around the other side of the mountain, the 'bad' side or forgottens towns - and He knows who He will send to do it, even though everyone else has written it off. That's where the biggest revivals will break out and that's where God will burst forth wells!

Wells bring life, blessing, prosperity and growth to people and a region! Jesus wants you to partner with Him for this.

God wanted Jeno and Karrie there in Pahrump to pray and prophesy to open up, and accelerate the move of the Holy Spirit and something major He wanted to do in the region of Pahrump and Las Vegas. It was very clear to me at that moment. If He sent Jeno to a mountain in San Diego and Jeno was obedient - He could send him to the next place and grow and influence Jeno's ministry. Jesus was going to do a living water transformation from private to public with Jeno and Karrie personally and flow it out from them everywhere they went to others and in the regions they were assigned!

Now how do I reveal this to Jeno and Karrie? This was not just going to a local site to pray, go home and go back to work the next day. This was packing up your entire family, quitting your job and moving to another state!

Approximately three days later, Jeno reached out to me again that He and Karrie were praying and there must be something more, he was tired of his day job, he wanted to do more for God and he was waiting for God to reveal the next step.

BOOM. Thank You Holy Spirit!

I revealed to Jeno everything the Holy Spirit and confirmed with me and "M" about Jeno and his family moving from San Diego, to Pahrump, NV

Jeno was stunned. He did not even think of moving, he thought God was going to continue to use him in San Diego.

He wanted to pray about it and talk with his family about it. This was a huge step.

I told him to pray, and then let me know if he needed me.

A few weeks went by. Jeno reached out to me and said: "Annamarie, my wife and I have prayed about Pahrump, we connected with "M" to talk and pray and fast on this. But I also asked the Holy Spirit if He wanted us to move to Pahrump to show me a whale."

"Jeno, I replied. "I come into agreement with your prayers and in agreement about the whale as a sign of confirmation for this move."

Another few weeks go by, no sign of a whale. We carried on with our online classes, work and life and left it in God's hands.

One weekend, Jeno's wife Karrie had received some free passes to the Fair in San Diego from a friend of hers. She wanted Jeno to take her and their daughter to the Fair for the day.

Jeno was reluctant to go. He was tired from working the evening shift at work, and he was not in a mood to deal with crowds and rides and all that stuff. Eventually he gave into his wife and daughter who really wanted to go.

They got in the family car, parked and with passes in hand, began to walk into the front gates of the fair.

As Jeno and his family approached the gates, what he saw nearly took his breath away.

Painted on the wall arch above the gate, in full color was a huge whale, breaching up and out of painted waves of water. It was a gigantic mural of a humpback whale on a stucco wall over a gateway that was literally almost as big as the entrance to the gate on the walls to Jerusalem! This was the San Diego Fairgrounds and GOD was speaking to Jeno and Karrie LOUD and CLEAR: "Yes, I want you to move to Pahrump!"

Can you say; "Here's your sign?"

Jeno stopped in his tracks. The huge whale mural in front of him. He acknowledged God's sign to Him and took photos of the whale and sent them to me.

I was in AWE of God. Not only did He show Jeno a whale to confirm this next step, it was over a Main GATE.

Gates have HUGE meaning when it comes to Victory, authority and opportunity. When God shows you a door or gate, I think of the number 444. Which means "Open Doors From God"

"God, you are my king. Give the command and lead Jacob's people to victory." - Psalm 4:44

Victorious armies triumphantly come into a 'gate' of a city to take possession of it.

God will always lead you to Victory and He commands the way and opens the gates and doors ahead of you. We just have to trust Him and look for the gates and doors. He will confirm them, if you go forward by faith you will always see the victory because God commands it for you! Go forward BOLDLY the ViCTORY is yours - no matter how unknown it is ahead.

Declare over yourself: "God you are my King! Give the command and lead me to Victory!"

Many times people ask me why they keep seeing the number 444. They wonder what it means. Is God showing them something or is it just a coincidence?

Again - there are NO coincidences with God. He IS talking to you through His Holy Spirit and He is trying to LEAD you to Victory, you have to pay attention and stop and ask Him what it means.

The Holy Spirit will be showing you "signs" to activate you even before you realize they are signs from God.

It is connected to this scripture in Psalm 4:44

One of the first teachings I ever did on my videos on YouTube in my ministry was about this number 444. Because I had been seeing it all over the place. To this day, that "444 Open Door" video has the most views of all my videos on my channel. As of this date of writing, that video has over 41,000 views. God is showing that number to many of His people right now!

444 was one of the first numbers in sequence I kept seeing repeatedly for weeks and months when I was starting up my ministry. I was intrigued. I asked the Holy Spirit why would I keep seeing this number? Is this from Him?

I know now why the Holy Spirit was showing me 444! God wanted me to go through a "door".... or a gateway to the victory. It was my sign, my "whale". That a great door of opportunity had been opened for me in the spirit and in the natural and it was destined to be victorious if I was obedient and walked through it. He had already commanded my Victory - way ahead of me. This door was to my public ministry - a multimedia ministry. The 444 was to be pursued and be a teaching about that number and meaning itself! The video teaching I did on the 444 would become a "doorway" or "gate" that thousands of followers would find and come into my ministry! Many of you found me this way! God was showing you 444 too! It was a door of victory for me and He has a door of Victory for you!

This is what I discovered about 444:

Hebrew is an alpha - numeric language. It's God's ancient language. 4 in Hebrew means the letter "d" "dalet" or "door" The picture of the "dalet" or "door" looks like a tent door open with the corner pinned up (like a corner on a sheet when you fold it down) The Ancient Hebrews lived in tents so they would connect with this meaning. Hebrew is the language and letters God wrote with His own finger of fire on the stone tablets of the 10 commandments, so it's important that we refer and pay attention to these meanings!! This is how He is speaking and leading you as well - through the Hebrew Alphabet-numerical language, through scripture and through the Hebrew calendar too. I will get more into that when we talk about God's timing and Advancing in The Glory in the next chapter.

Jesus is also spoken of in scripture as the "Door" The only doorway to God. Only through Jesus Christ do we have the Victory! Jesus brings us into a personal relationship with the Father.

"As the door (delet), four shows one the Way into the Throne room of Adonai. Yeshua (Jesus) is the door for the sheep. (John 10:7-9) It is impossible to get this close and personal with YHWH by entering another door or way." - *Source: GraceInTorah.net*

God wants you to communicate with Him through His Holy Spirit for confirmation on your steps. Jesus said the Holy Spirit is our helper. You can ask Him to show you numbers in sequence like 444 for confirmation or a 'whale' like Jeno did. Or in my case, God showed me "eagles" for every step of confirmation for my land prayer assignment for America back in 2016. Whatever you feel in your spirit.

Your signs of confirmation with God are personal and between you and Him. As a believer in Jesus Christ, the Holy Spirit is talking to you all the time, leading you step by step! You can only have Victory because God has already commanded for you, time to get up and go go go and get it!

DON'T IGNORE THE SIGNS - GOD IS GIVING YOU THE VICTORY - YOU JUST HAVE TO FOLLOW THE STEPS AND GO THROUGH THE GATES AND DOORS HE HAS OPENED FOR YOU.

Get up on the wheel and get on the gas pedal! God has you covered! No matter what happens He is leading you to VICTORY!

This is confirmed in the word of God for you over and over:

- "The LORD is the one who goes ahead of you; He will be with you He will not fail you or forsake you. Do not fear or be dismayed." Deuteronomy 31:8
- 'The LORD your God who goes before you will Himself fight on your behalf...Deuteronomy 1:30
- You go before me and follow me. You place your hand of blessing on my head. Psalm 139:5 (NLT)
- For the LORD will go before you, And the God of Israel will be your rear guard. Isaiah 52:12

You are being told to step through the gate (or door) and take it by faith! Then the next gate and the next gate! Then you take that mountain of influence and claim it! Eureka! You will post the banner of the Lord at the Summit!

VICTORY LANE BABY!! WHOOO HOOO!!

Glory To God! You have favor all the way! You cannot fail! If the enemy tries to close a door to you, God will smash it down!

"I will go before thee, And make the crooked places straight; I will break in pieces the doors of brass, And cut in sunder the bars of iron." - Isaiah 45:2

God knows how to Get 'er done! You just press on that gas pedal and go by faith, the gates and doors will open before you!

These are both physical doors and spiritual doors! This is if you are believing God for the neighbors to open their doors to you when your teen is selling candy bars for a mission trip, or whether you need a spiritual door to open for a region to take for God! No door is too big or too small for God!

Did Jeno and Karrie victoriously move through the new door God had for them after they saw the sign of the Whale at the Gate? YES! I am happy to say they did. Jeno resigned from his job, they sold everything, packed up their clothes in the car, signed their daughter out of school and drove to Pahrump, Nevada!

God did amazing things there in Nevada and launched Jeno and Karrie into a powerful and blessed public and online ministry. You can follow Jeno's Ministry on Youtube "The Walk with Jeno Shaw."   Amazing things are happening in their life! Since then, God has opened more doors and gates for them into more regions of this nation!

I am so proud of Jeno and Karrie!   Their obedience is being greatly rewarded by God and their testimony is bringing many to God!   I am doing this in my "walk" to make sure as a leader and mentor, I encourage and help more people become leaders for the Kingdom. One of my hopes for this book is that those of you who are called to be leaders can take these testimonies and be encouraged to boldly step into your calling.

I am also excited to say that Martyna who was obedient to God and gave Jeno and Karrie and their daughter a place to stay while they launched their ministry - has seen great rewards and blessings, healings and miracles on her ranch and her land! She is receiving the "prophet's reward" and still as I write this chapter.

My reward in all this is that my ministry and mentoring programs are producing more disciples and leaders for the Kingdom of God!

"The function of leadership isn't to gather more followers. It's to produce more leaders." - John C. Maxwell

With Jesus, He had three years to make leaders out of His disciples and taught them how to be able to lead and depend on the help of the Holy Spirit. The entire book of Acts is a testament to new leaders who were once followers going public. So many miracles of the Holy Spirit partnering with them. We are all in our own book of Acts! That is the goal of the Gospel not just to bring people to Jesus Christ, but to make leaders for Jesus Christ. This is the KINGDOM.

Your success and victory in public or in an area of influence is because of seeking God this way! Your personal obedience attests to the power of God in your life and to all people you encounter after this! You will have a powerful testimony that will bring more people to God!

This my friend is Kingdom Public Relations and Marketing!

WE MUST BE DEMONSTRATORS OF THE POWER OF GOD AS IT HAS WORKED IN OUR LIFE PERSONALLY AND PUBLICLY

Powerless Religion teaches people how to DEFEND the Gospel. The Kingdom of God trains people how to DEMONSTRATE the Gospel in all aspects of your life and brings power and acceleration into all things around you.

When you demonstrate the power of God, His Holy Spirit and Jesus Christ in your life in public, you will almost immediately see acceleration of your goals.

That's what happened to me! The more I shared about my testimony of the power of God in my life the more people wanted it in their lives too - my ministry began to grow exponentially! I see that in all aspects, whether you are in business, or have a product, service or running for public office. Share the power of God in your life! It attracts the people!! They are hungry to experience this power too!

The advancement comes when you are promoting from the heart - then you will be operating in the GLORY.

Now, what if you moved forward on something without getting a sign of confirmation from God?

What if you took another person's word for something and moved forward without praying or seeking God on it?

GIVE YOURSELF SOME GRACE! It's OK!

Go to God now and consult with Him. It is never too late. You have an abundance of grace through Jesus Christ, and God will confirm if you are on the right track, or He will move you swiftly into the right one! Holy Spirit is so HAPPY when you come to Him on these things no matter if you already started or not. This is a process, a journey and a relationship building time as you seek understanding on each step with the Holy Spirit.

Sometimes we need to act swiftly ourselves on something and make a decision. We don't have time to 'put out a fleece' and wait for confirmation. We just have to take that leap. We walk by faith and not by sight.

So you go ahead and move forward by faith even without confirmation signs - and know that God has got you! If you mess up, He will help you correct it! The key here is MOVING FORWARD by faith no matter what.

"Don't let the fear of "MISSING GOD" keep you from MOVING FORWARD." - Lisa Bevere

If someone gave you advice or you followed it and it did not work out - it's OK! Forgive them and go to God and ask Him to restore the situation and get you back on course.

"All people are imperfect and a work in process. Give the grace to others you will one day need for yourself!" - Paula White

This is why, as a mentor, when I advise or have a word from the Holy Spirit for my students - I tell the person to take this advice or word to God themselves, pray about it and if it does not confirm their spirit then it's OK! Don't hammer them about it. You were obedient and gave them advice or a word from the Holy Spirit, they have free will to receive it or not.

If God really wants them to do something He will push them. If they ignore the signs then they will have to answer to God.

If you keep seeing them stuck and making the same mistakes - ask God to give them wisdom and offer encouragement.

Now, if a student tells me they prayed and feel confirmed and they will do it, and they tell God they will - that's when I will push hard as a coach and mentor to keep them moving forward, no excuses. Because they told me and God yes they wanted it - there was an agreement and commitment there. I feel a responsibility to help get them fulfilling that assignment or next step. The same goes for God, don't tell Him you want something and then He brings the answers, the open doors, the people, the equipment and the strategies and then you don't follow through. That's when you will get conviction by the Holy Spirit and He will remind you that you agreed and then did not proceed - that's flat out disobedience. (I have been there - thank God for second chances!)

Everyone has their own journey and process and must build their own relationship with God, and walk in communication faith, and obedience. We also need to know when to back off and give people space and grace. If they won't listen or you see them continually stuck or spinning out - just send the Holy Spirit to help them. He will get them on track! The Holy Spirit does not mess around! He is the BEST coach ever!

All Public Relations Start With An Announcement....

It's OK to come on the scene boldly and set the tone for what you are embarking on in your assignment or purpose. As a matter of fact it's important prophetically in the spirit and in the natural to do this.

Jesus announced himself to the public and proclaimed what He was called and destined to do, He spoke in the Synagogue fearlessly declaring who He was and what He was anointed to do as many who were there got offended at His bold proclamation!

A young shepherd boy named David did the same thing proclaiming he could take on the giant! Then he did.

"David said to the Philistine, "You come against me with sword and spear and javelin, but I come against you in the name of the Lord Almighty! - 1 Samuel 17:45

418

If Jesus proclaimed and did it and David proclaimed and did it, you can too in the name of the Lord! They both ANNOUNCED out loud and in a public setting!

It's fearlessly saying stand back and watch the Glory of God at work through me and you!

YES!!

I have come to believe that God loves it when we announce ourselves and our vision boldly when we pronounce HIs power behind it. It's like a trumpet that awakens the atmosphere and attracts the angelic around you and activates all of Heaven behind you!

Decree a thing and it shall be established for you!

MAKE A FAITHFUL PROCLAMATION OF WHO YOU ARE, WHAT YOU ARE CALLED TO DO, WHO IT HELPS AND WHO GETS THE GLORY!

This is what Jesus proclaimed over himself when He began His ministry. I encourage you to do the same over yourself! I have added in parenthesis how to speak this over yourself in the first person.

Pray: *"Lord, I declare your word Isaiah 61, the same word that you declared over yourself when you announced your ministry over 2000 years ago. You live inside of me Lord, therefore Your word is alive and operating in me and through me. I declare and come into agreement with your declaration, prophecy and word as my own in Your name Jesus, Amen."*

Isaiah 61 (King James Version) Decree out loud:

"The Spirit of the Lord God is upon me; because the Lord hath anointed me to preach good tidings unto the meek; he hath sent me to bind up the brokenhearted, to proclaim liberty to the captives, and the opening of the prison to them that are bound;

To proclaim the acceptable year of the Lord, and the day of vengeance of our God; to comfort all that mourn;

To appoint unto them (ME) that mourn in Zion, to give unto them (ME) beauty for ashes, the oil of joy for mourning, the garment of praise for the spirit of heaviness; that they (I) might be called trees of righteousness, the planting of the Lord, that he might be glorified.

And they (I) shall build the old wastes, they (I) shall raise up the former desolations, and they (I) shall repair the waste cities, the desolations of many generations.

And strangers shall stand and feed your (MY) flocks, and the sons of the alien shall be your (MY) plowmen and your (MY) vinedressers.

But ye (I) shall be named the Priests of the Lord: men shall call you (ME) the Ministers of our God: ye (I) shall eat the riches of the Gentiles, and in their glory shall ye boast yourselves.

For your (my) shame ye (I) shall have double; and for confusion they (I) shall rejoice in their (MY) portion: therefore in their (MY) land they (I) shall possess the double: everlasting joy shall be unto them (ME).

For I (HE) the Lord love judgment, I (HE) hates robbery for burnt offering; and I (HE) will direct their (MY) work in truth, and I (HE) will make an everlasting covenant with them (ME).

And their (MY) seed shall be known among the Gentiles, and their (MY) offspring among the people: all that see them shall acknowledge them, that they are the seed which the Lord hath blessed.

I will greatly rejoice in the Lord, my soul shall be joyful in my God; for he hath clothed me with the garments of salvation, he hath covered me with the robe of righteousness, as a bridegroom decketh himself with *ornaments, and as a bride adorneth herself with her jewels.*

For as the earth bringeth forth her bud, and as the garden causeth the things that are sown in it to spring forth; so the Lord God will cause righteousness and praise to spring forth before all the nations (and my household). I declare and stand on this word in Jesus name, Amen"

You just declared the same words that your Messiah Jesus Christ declared over Himself. You are speaking to Christ who lives within you. It's a powerful proclamation and from my experience you will see a powerful shift for the good in your life shortly after declaring this. Things begin to move in a very positive direction. The word of God is alive and causes things to shift in the spirit and the natural responds!

GOD IS YOUR SPONSOR! HOW ARE YOU ANNOUNCING WHAT HE IS DOING THROUGH YOU?

All of creation responds to the Word of God. That's why we must speak and proclaim out loud.

Notice when Jesus announced Himself in Isaiah 61 what He really announced was a passionate message of what God is doing through Him and with Him. Things were set into action immediately. It's a self-prophecy!

What makes a video go viral on social media? The message!

You must be passionate and faithful about your message. That is Kingdom minded, the message is stored in you, God knitted it into you in your Mother's womb and your message is also written in your book in Heaven - just ask the Holy Spirit to access it and download it into your spirit!

"For you formed my inward parts; you knitted me together in my mother's womb. I praise you, for I am fearfully and wonderfully made. Wonderful are your works; my soul knows it very well. My frame was not hidden from you, when I was being made in secret,

intricately woven in the depths of the earth. Your eyes saw my unformed substance; in your book were written, every one of them, the days that were formed for me, when as yet there was none of them."- Psalm 139:13-16 (ESV)

We have all been given a message through the gift and calling God has given us either in actions or words or both. Fear keeps it suppressed! Ask God for your message! He already wrote it for you!

When the Holy Spirit is in you He gives you the POWER to release incredible messages and your prayers can open your Books in Heaven to release messages that have been written for you! These messages can be downloaded to you if you ask!

You might be thinking: "Girl now you are talkin' crazy, books in heaven? Downloads into my spirit and mind?"

YES! We serve a supernatural God! Stop limiting what God has available and gives to you! I have seen these books and scrolls and the Holy Spirit has revealed to me many things in my own books/scrolls in Heaven. Because I pursued going into the Courts of Heaven.

I could write an entire book on this, and maybe I will. Understand this: Your spirit man is directly connected to the Holy Spirit that is the Presence of God dwelling in you! The Holy Spirit directly flows from the heart of God like a river to your spirit through the power and anointing of the Holy Spirit. It's like you have a conduit or a canal to receive from the Throne Room and Courts of Heaven where Jesus Christ is interceding for you before the Father to make sure you fulfill your destiny! Like turning on a faucet, or opening a dam flowing from the Throne of God right into your spirit. The Cloud of Witnesses, those faithful ones who have gone before you are witnessing to Jesus and the Father for you! The Blood of Jesus is speaking for you as payment for all that was purchased and redeemed for you on the Mercy Seat in the Heavenly Court before God!

Do this now: Picture the Courts of Heaven with God The Father on the Throne, Jesus to the right of the Father speaking up for you, Angels off to the side with tables of ancient books and scrolls that have your destiny written in them along with your family bloodline destiny. I have seen this in my own experiences. I encourage you to see this in your mind and let it come deeply into your spirit. When you do this, strongholds break off you! Your spirit man is yearning to reveal to you these divine things! Jesus said expand your thinking! We are in a time where God is revealing the hidden things and pouring out His Spirit on all flesh.

Pray: *"Holy Spirit please remove the veils and give me eyes of understanding in the spirit! Reveal to me the Courts of Heaven, the Throne Room Of God and show me what is written in my books of destiny that Jesus wrote for me! Reveal my messages and assignments to me for this time in my life. I declare Jeremiah 33:3 and I am fervently asking God to show me the hidden things about my life and destiny! I come into agreement with Jesus' intercession for me and thank you to the faithful witnesses in heaven witnessing on my behalf! I declare I will fulfill all that is written in my book of destiny on earth as it is in heaven! Holy Spirit bring me to repentance for any sin that may be used against me in the Courts by the accuser and I ask Jesus for your Blood to continually speak for me and my destiny. In Jesus Name, Amen!"*

NOTE: I recommend studying up on how to go into the Courts of Heaven. This is so important before you 'go public' because you can make sure the accuser is stripped of His legal rights to try to hinder your progress. I started with author and teacher Jeanette Strauss - her simple teachings got me started and on my way. As I grew into going deeper into the Courts of Heaven, I graduated into the more detailed teachings of Robert Henderson. I highly recommend both authors, and have seen great results with both their teachings.

Receiving Your Kingdom Marketing and PR Message:

Let me give you some strategies that pertain to helping you with receiving your "message" that is from God for you to speak, write, reveal and act upon your area of influence on earth. This comes as a matter of understanding you already may be speaking it....

Have you ever been in a situation, and you say something profound and it surprises you that it came out of your mouth? Like where did that come from? It just came out of my mouth and it's like it was not 'me' saying it.

My friend, that was the Holy Spirit, giving you a download from your books in heaven into your spirit man and out your mouth! You resourced your heavenly book and you did not even realize it!

This is for songs, poems, essays, movie scripts, speeches, prophecies, teachings, inventions, drawings, building blueprints are already written and designed in Heaven waiting for you to ask for them, to birth them in the earth through your life and time here.

In the Bible, many times this would be described as God giving "scrolls" or "books" filled with the words God had ordained for the certain Prophet to speak and they were told to 'eat' the scroll.

"Then he said to me, "Son of man, eat this scroll I am giving you and fill your stomach with it." So I ate it, and it tasted as sweet as honey in my mouth." - Ezekiel 3:3:

What if you think you are not a good speaker to speak God's words or words sourced for you by the Holy Spirit from Heaven?   Maybe you stutter, or feel you are not educated enough, maybe you have other things that come against your confidence to speak.

Moses actually argued with God at the Burning Bush saying he could not be a spokesperson for the people because he had a stutter.   God let Moses know that would not hinder what He had ordained for Moses to speak.   He would even send someone to help him as an 'assistant".

"But Moses said to the Lord, "Oh, my Lord, I am not eloquent, either in the past or since you have spoken to your servant, but I am slow of speech and of tongue."   Then the Lord said to him, "Who has made man's mouth?   Who makes him mute, or deaf, or seeing, or blind?   Is it not I, the Lord?   Now therefore go, and I will be with your mouth and teach you what you shall speak." - Exodus 4:10-11

God will give you the words and you will not even worry about fear of public speaking or even if you have a 'speech impediment'.   The Holy Spirit takes over and God's words that were written for you to say manifest through your mouth to speak, and even through your hands to write! God will send you divine laborers to come by your side to encourage you, assist you and help you!

I love the story of Oral Roberts, who God used to build a powerful healing ministry beginning in the 1950's.   God used Oral Roberts to lay a foundation to the future of how we would spread the Gospel with technology.   He was to go on television and preach the Good News.   To be on television you would have to be a good speaker, right? Well, Oral Roberts like Moses, was born with a speech impediment.

The Los Angeles Times wrote this article about Oral Roberts when he died at age 91 in December of 2009:

"Roberts pioneered the use of television and computerized databases to spread the Gospel and raise hundreds of millions of dollars -- a formula followed today by numerous other ministries. In the 1970s, Roberts' prime-time TV specials drew 40 million viewers, and he appeared frequently on talk shows hosted by Johnny Carson, Dinah Shore and Merv Griffin. The preacher also had a half-hour program -- "Something Good Is Going to Happen to You" -- that aired Sundays. By 1980, Roberts was recognized by 84% of Americans, close behind the sitting U.S. president and fellow evangelist Billy Graham and 40 points ahead of the next religious figure. "Not bad," he once said, "for a poor boy with a speech impediment who was supposed to die of tuberculosis before he was 20."

WOW! Do you think God had all that written in Oral Roberts books and scrolls in Heaven for that moment in time to advance what God wanted to do for the Kingdom? Oral Roberts became one of the most influential Christian Evangelists of the 20th Century!

I still remember as a little girl, with our black and white TV in the late 60's watching Oral Roberts. He would always say at the end of each broadcast:

"Something good is going to happen to you!"

Those words stuck with me all my life and when I started my ministry, I asked the Lord for something to say at the end of each broadcast, like Oral Roberts had. A few days later, I was praying, talking to God and writing in my journal - all of a sudden my pen started writing the words big on a blank page:

"All of Heaven Is Cheering You On!"

That was another instance of a 'Holy Spirit' download. It seems to just come out of the blue, the words to write or speak. That became my cheer for all of you at the end of each of my broadcasts! I say it every time! Thank You Holy Spirit! It's the truth! All of Heaven is cheering you on!

You have a cloud of witnesses, those of faith, sold out believers in JESUS who have gone before you witnessing for your victory and the fulfillment of your purpose on earth as it is in heaven. They surround the throne of God, and witness directly to Jesus' intercession for you. They also witness around you like a cloud, and sometimes appear in your dreams or visions to let you know they are working with Jesus and witnessing on your behalf. It's like having your own cheering section in your race and even joining Jesus in intercession for you in the courts of heaven. A witness who stands for you with Christ. That's what I love to know when I feel alone, like nobody down here seems to be with me or supporting me, I remember I have a HUGE crowd supporting me in Heaven!

I want you to understand even if you have an issue like a speech impediment, or fear of speaking, or lack of education, physical disabilities, accidents or abuse in your past; nothing can stop you from getting out the message God has written in your book in Heaven for you to reveal to the world!

I love horses. Many of you know that about me. I believe God speaks through animals, especially horses. They are the noblest of God's creatures. We know there are horses in Heaven as Jesus will return riding a white horse. Many who have had encounters in Heaven have seen the horses and Angel armies with horses and chariots are spoken of in the Bible. I myself had a powerful encounter and in a vision I saw Jesus' horse in heaven and he is magnificent. I believe that God reveals messages to us through horses in many ways, as well as other animals and nature.

One of my favorite horses in history was the thoroughbred racehorse in the 1930's named "Seabiscuit" A wonderful author who wrote about Seabiscuit in my generation is Laura Hillenbrand. Her book on Seabiscuit became an award winning book and a major motion picture released in theaters all over the world in 2003. It's a true story of an overlooked horse, how his heart to win and amazing speed was eventually revealed through the placement of the right people surrounding him. They believed in this little horse and saw something special that could not be seen from the "looks" and confirmation of this horse. He was plain, small, and liked to eat and sleep in his stall a lot. He did not have the attributes and temperament of a desirable race horse. Early trainers wrote him off as 'lazy'.... Hillenbrand's story brings together how this horse - Seabiscuit - and each person connected to him overcame adversity during the Great Depression era in America.

This little unknown, plain, small bay colt named Seabiscuit - now divinely aligned with new people who saw 'something' in him - did what the other trainers thought was impossible. He raced against and won over all the 'elite' thoroughbreds of his time and became an inspiration for a nation! He was a working man and woman's hero and made his mark in history. Truly it's one of my favorite movies. Laura Hillenbrand has been praised for her knowledge of bringing the history of those times and understanding of why this horse was so important as a message to the people of America. I believe God was using this horse, and Laura's spirit connected with this story for us of these times in America. I believe this was a divine assignment to reconnect Laura to Seabiscuit for her own story too.

Author Laura Hillenbrand suffered from Chronic Fatigue Syndrome. She was not able to finish college because of this illness and eventually was confined to her bed for months at a time. Her body was weak and chronically exhausted, but her spirit was so passionate to get this inspirational story written about Seabiscut, that she wrote almost the entire book from her bed. I believe that in her destiny books/scrolls in Heaven, this story 'Seabiscuit" for her to write was 'downloaded' to her. She was able to overcome her physical issues and her dream was produced as great fruit for all of us who needed it at the time. Thank you Laura! (and Seabiscuit!).

I think that Seabiscuit is in heaven cheering us all on joining the cloud of witnesses! Did you know something amazing about Seabiscuit that Laura discovered and wrote in her book? When he raced he started out of the gate slow. BUT as soon as the jockey would give him free rein and Seabiscuit could see the front of all the horses and the finish line, a burst of energy would come on him like a lightning bolt! Seabiscuit could 'see' the victory and once he saw it he wanted it and nothing could stop him! This little horse had faith that Victory was his, he could see it and he gave it all he had to get it. Like the little engine that could! He became an 'unlikely champion'! I love that!

You know God has His hand on unlikely champions as He did Moses the Stutterer, David the Shepherd Boy, Joseph the Dreamer and Esther the Orphan. They had to *see the victory* and have the faith to get it no matter what the odds. They discovered in an autopsy when Seabiscuit died years later that his heart was bigger than a normal thoroughbred horse. He truly had a BIG HEART! I believe God was saying something very prophetic here through this horse.

"In 1938, Seabiscuit got his chance to go against one of the greatest of all time - War Admiral. With only those two horses in the Pimlico Special, it was a match race for the ages. And, Seabiscuit didn't disappoint, winning the race by four lengths to a standing room only crowd. In the late 1930s, as the Depression hovered persistently over the nation, Americans turned to one newsmaker with joyous devotion. His name was Seabiscuit. One sportswriter

called the nation's addiction "Seabiscuit-itis." Seabiscuit became a "spokeshorse" for hope in a time where it was greatly needed." - *PBS, An American Experience (paraphrased).*

I find even the name of this horse, Seabiscuit, had prophetic meaning for what the people were dealing with lack of food and provision at the time or the Great Depression. A "seabiscuit" or "hard tack", is a non-perishable unleavened bread or cracker that was carried on old sailing ships as food for sailors on a long voyage. It did not mold or spoil and lasted for months. It sustained the voyagers on the journey to get them to their destination.

God was saying here through Seabiscuit the horse, an encouraging reminder about Jesus Christ, "Put your hope in ME, the bread of life, I will take care of you, get you through these stormy seas, provide for you and get you to your destination - you will finish this race strong."

God was doing PUBLIC RELATIONS through this horse!

Jesus ate unleavened bread at Passover and Passover is when the spirit of death passed over God's people. Because of Jesus we never die, we are non-perishable. We have a journey in this life, and it's through Christ, the bread of life that sustains us. The people of Israel during Moses' times of being delivered from Egypt and slavery at the first Passover needed hope. The people of Jesus' time of his last supper needed hope because of Roman occupation and heavy taxation. We need hope in our times. It's HIS BREAD that sustains us and fills us with hope. The bread is the Word of God. We eat it. If we ingest the Word daily, it's our daily bread for our journey to fulfill our assignments and get us to our destiny. God promises us we will be successful in ALL that we do if we meditate on His word. (Joshua 1:7-9) His word gives us the words to speak, write, strategize and live by for a successful life. If we eat of His word we accomplish all what we have been ordained to do in the world. Jesus also confirms this. We also understand from scripture that *healing* is also the children's bread! The children of God!

"But He answered and said, "It is written, 'Man shall not live by bread alone, but by every word that proceeds from the mouth of God."- Matthew 4:4

I have found the more I stay in the WORD of God, the more He fills my spirit, mind and mouth with the words I need to say at exactly the time they need to be said. Not just to others, but what I need said to myself! I think about the Great Depression in America and the 'bread lines' and the hard things the people had to go through. Looking back I see this was a time of some of the greatest moves of faith and the Gospel in America. People were sustained by the Bible. The WORD. The bread to get them through the hardest part of the journey. These are hard times caused by man, not God. But God takes these times and turns them out for our good and the good of His Kingdom. Seabiscuit was a prophetic message from God for His people! He would sustain them with HIS BREAD. It's like the hidden "manna" or "divine bread' that drops down from Heaven for us. Jesus speaks of in the book of Revelation 2:17. There is hidden 'manna' bread all around you. God is speaking to you and through you and you are to receive and release manna! Your spirit pours out feeds many for the Kingdom! Your words can, encourage, teach, build and heal!

Does God want you to be a prophetic message for the times? YES!

Another word for "Public Relations" is "Communications". This is how you become part of God's "Communications" team. Communications bring a clear message to many on a grand scale. God needs willing communicators for the Kingdom. Your message is meant to help God's people. Open your mouth and heart to God and ask Him to fill it!

"I am the Lord your God, who brought you up out of the land of Egypt. Open your mouth wide, and I will fill it." - Psalm 81:10

If you don't know what to say and you feel you don't have the right words or the right message, declare that scripture in Psalm 81:10 . Physically open your mouth, lift it up to God and ask Him to fill it with a message! I have done this many times! He never fails me and He will never fail you!

God's word flows through our heart which is connected to our spirit. He fills you with WORDS. He sees all that is in your heart, your desires because He already put them there and they match what He has already written for you. It's a heart, mind spirit connection to the throne of God and He loves to bring the "unlikely champion" out in you! God brings together the story already written, gives you the words, the people, the finances, the opportunities and even the animals if needed!

If God can use an overlooked horse for a time in history, He can certainly use you! He does not care about the circumstances that you or the outside world would think of as hindrances or disabilities! Those become just part of the great testimony of God working through you and you and God writing and telling the BEST stories together!

YOU are God's superhero for such a time as this, and He is looking at your HEART, not how you look or talk or if you have a college degree! He is only interested in the heart and he wants to raise you up in PUBLIC to encourage many hearts and fulfill your destiny written in your books.

"But the Lord said to Samuel, "Do not consider his appearance or his height, for I have rejected him. The Lord does not look at the things people look at. People look at the outward appearance, but the Lord looks at the heart." - 1 Samuel 16:7

Now don't worry, God will not throw you into something you are not ready to handle. He will train you and prepare you through His Holy Spirit. I remember when I first wanted to start writing books, I was a bit nervous as I had never done it before. God started me with a story, about our real-life rescue horse, Pongo - who helped my daughter overcome the effects of being bullied in school. I had already started on this book, Faith At Full Speed - but God stopped me for a bit and had me write the book about Pongo. It took me only three months to write "Pongo the Rescue Horse, A Story of Faith, Friendship and Miracles". It flowed out of me so easily and I learned all the logistics of self-publishing a book that I would need for this book and to help others publish their books. Interestingly Pongo was a three year old colt 'rejected' at the auction kill pens. We were able to rescue him hours before going to slaughter. Since then, Pongo and his story have been a blessing to many children and teens who read his story and my book, giving them hope and courage after dealing with the abuse from bullying. Another unlikely 'champion' God used! Thank You God! We love our Pongo! I believe by faith God has plans for Pongo's book into a major motion picture just like Seabiscuit!

Not all of us will have a 'horse' to help bring forth our message. But God has something stirring in your heart that you are passionate about. Maybe something from childhood or something that has grown in you. It wants to burst forth into the light, and I want to help you bring it forth right now!

God has placed something around you that is inspiring you too. The world needs what you carry and it must start flowing through you and beaming out of you! Seabiscuit was just being Seablscuit, Pongo was just being Pongo, Oral Roberts was just being Oral Roberts, Moses was being Moses, now it's time for you to just be you and not worry about anything else - God will take care of the details!

Time for the free rein (no man can control you) and time to run to victory (let your heart kick in) you are designated to shine so others can have hope! If you can do it they can too!

It's time to GO PUBLIC! Now understand that Public can be big or small. It's simply sharing what is in your heart with someone other than yourself. It's GOD who multiplies it to the size of the field He intended for your influence and message. But don't be surprised if what you think is a small gesture, God does huge things with it. There are a few apple seeds that were sown by Johnny Appleseed over 180 years ago that have multiplied into huge orchards and bushels of fruit that are feeding thousands today in America. God may need you to do something now as a seed for something big for future generations! Johnny Appleseed did not talk alot but he walked a lot. He went public with his actions. They are both Kingdom Public Relations and Marketing. It's not all 'speaking', 'preaching' or getting on TV. It's where you are called, your field to plant and influence. Jesus is looking for action takers! Big and small!

We cannot worry about what we see in the 'natural world' - even if it looks grim. We must set our thoughts on things above and ahead - The Kingdom. God is on the throne and laughs at the enemy's foolish tactics. You are seated right next to God in Christ. The enemy is under your feet too. Let's start thinking like Christ and partnering with God, our Hope and Glory.

"Even if I knew that tomorrow the world would go to pieces, I would still plant my apple tree" — Martin Luther King Jr.

KNOW THAT THE WORDS AND ACTIONS THAT YOU ALLOW GOD TO FACILITATE AND COMPLETE THROUGH YOU BY FAITH AND OBEDIENCE WILL LAST FOR GENERATIONS AND BEAR MUCH FRUIT.

What will you do for God? Will you allow Him to fulfill great and important things through you? Do you want to fulfill what is written about you in Heaven - on earth as it is in heaven? Do you believe God's promises or are you more afraid of what man says?

"For all the promises of God in Him are Yes, and in Him Amen, to the glory of God through us." - 2 Corinthians 1:20

Do you believe the promises of God are for you? Do you see giant problems or do you see the land of milk and honey that God says is yours? God is telling you to go up and possess the land! Will you possess the promise for your life? Will you boldly go and take your field of influence and sow, reap, harvest and increase in it? It's your inheritance and do not wait any longer!

The only thing that tries to stop or hinder you from doing this is fear and wrong thinking from the enemy. That's an easy giant to conquer with the Blood and Authority of Jesus Christ. You are MORE than an overcomer through Christ and you cannot be hindered or stopped from what God has ordained for you in your life!

Let's kick this fear and wrong thinking out permanently and ask for our message to be released - God has people waiting for you now and in the future!

Renounce Fear and Wrong Thinking!

Declare: *"In the name of Jesus Christ, I renounce all fear and wrong thinking and command it to leave me now! For it is written in 2 Timothy 1:7 For God hath not given us the spirit of fear; but of power, and of love, and of a sound mind. I come out of agreement with all wrong thinking and I renounce all fearful beliefs and put them under the Blood of Jesus Christ!*
I declare I have a sound mind! I have a heart and mind for victory! Rivers of living water flow powerfully to me and through me! I receive the hidden manna! Prophetic dreams, divine strategies and instruction come to me straight from the Throne Room of God! My cloud of witnesses in heaven witness for me to the intercession of Jesus Christ for my life! I come into agreement with Jesus Christ's intercession for me right now! Jesus is revealing what is in my books of destiny in heaven to me! I shall fulfill all that is written in my divine books of destiny on earth as it is written for me in heaven! I renounce all wrong thoughts and I declare I have the Mind of Christ! I command all my thoughts to come under the obedience of Jesus Christ! I see what Jesus sees for my life and I agree with what Jesus has written for my life! I shall take faithful, bold action on these revelations from Jesus Christ as they come to me through the anointing of the Holy Spirit! My mind has been fully renewed in Christ Jesus! I fully walk in the light of the Lord! His word lights my path and I walk boldly ahead with absolutely no fear! Today I embark on my divine assignment, calling and purpose for the Kingdom and I receive the people and breakthroughs you have waiting for me Lord even if this is in a public setting I am ready! I know that you are with me Lord Jesus and the Holy Spirit all the way and in every step to fulfill Your plans and purposes for my life oh Lord! I am excited and ready and I say YES to all You have for me Lord in this life even

if it stretches me, I will not hinder or shrink back - I trust YOU Lord! You write the BEST stories Lord Jesus and you have written my story! So it shall be and so it is in your beautiful name Jesus the author and finisher of my faith! I want to hear, well done good and faithful servant when I meet you in Heaven Lord! Help me fulfill this Holy Spirit, I will be obedient and brave, I know I have your supernatural protection, Father God and I am not afraid! What can a mere man do to me? For the Lord God Himself is my defender and goes before me, beside me and is my rear guard forever! MY destiny is NOW in Jesus name!! Amen!"

Now let's fully OPERATE ON ALL AREAS IN THE KINGDOM for what God will do with you and your gifts in public. Time to get firing up on all cylinders! (engine talk - another form of 'horsepower') LOL....

Understand your gifts, purpose, anointings, and products/ creations/services must be revealed, activated, developed, and promoted - But You Must Agree To Partner With The Holy Spirit to see these to full fruition. God will not force you to partner with Him and the Kingdom. This is a choice. The Holy Spirit will prompt you, encounter you, but you have to respond and partner with Him to bring to fruition what He wants to do through you.

A few months ago, I had a woman listener on my broadcast typed to me in the online chat that she heard the Lord speak to her in a vision and He told her: "I have anointed you." I asked her what has God anointed you for? She said she did not know. That she was just "anointed". I asked her; "Have you asked the Holy Spirit to reveal what the anointing is for and to step into faith to begin to do it?" She said; "No, she was just waiting for

God for more visions and it had been over a year!" I said to her; "You need to put your feet to your faith and get serious working with the Holy Spirit on this." She said; "Well I just want to be able to have visions from God." I said; "That's wonderful, we all want those supernatural encounters, but do you understand what the anointing is and what it's for?" I began to explain that the anointing is the power of the Holy Spirit that comes upon you and sets you aside for a special purpose or assignment on the earth for God to be fulfilled - and it also sets you apart in your gifts to make you special or unique for the Glory of God. When you are using your gifts the anointing comes on it to make it exceptionally powerful because the presence of God is upon it.

For example people will hear a worship song, and will feel the presence of God through that song or through the singer or musician that is performing it. That's the anointing. It has to be used in some way. It has to be RELEASED and POURED FORTH not held in secret.

I asked this woman; "So you want to be anointed for visions from God, what do you want your visions to do? Instruct you, to instruct others?" She said she did not know and she had not asked. Understand If she has a gift for visions, then that is a seer gift, one of the gifts of the Holy Spirit that needs to be developed and be used for God. He has people lined up ready to be blessed by her gift. I could help her get clear on this and guide her so the fruit of the gift of the Holy Spirit can produce much fruit for the Lord in her life and other's lives.

I asked her to come and mentor with me. She lasted one week in my class. She left because she did not want to pursue what God wanted her to do with the 'anointing'.

She told me that she was 'busy' and did not have time to work on her purpose or calling right now.

What?! Really??

"Faith without works is dead." James 2:26

Many people are enamored with the supernatural, they want to have visions and see angels and some even have encounters with Jesus himself. But what comes from that encounter? Is it just for you in your prayer closet?

Elijah was a gifted seer and prophet of the Lord. When he went to hide in a cave the Lord called him out!

God said: "Elijah why are you here? Get back out on the road and go and anoint Jehu King of Israel!" (1 Kings 19:9-18)

God has to get things fulfilled in the earth through his anointed ones, and you get a special supernatural protection from God to do it. The Bible says: "Touch not God's Anointed". (1 Chronicles 16:22 and Psalm 105:15-17)
With the anointing of these gifts you are called to *use* them for the Lord and not hide them or keep them for yourself.
You now serve the Kingdom of God. You are to be on the *move* with them.

You can fast, pray and seek God in secret. But when you receive instruction from the Lord you must come out of your "cave' and take swift action. Many people fast and pray thinking it will 'move' God. I have found that fasting and praying is mostly so you can 'hear' God and He gives you the secret that was hidden that you can apply for breakthrough. He gives you confirmations, favor and grace for assignments also during times of fasting. So YOU can move forward and be accelerated.

Your cave is to receive guidance and instruction from God and then apply it obediently even if it's only for one assignment. Then God will reward you in public and then multiply it. (Matthew 6:4)

It's not all work and no play! You have benefits to this that nobody else has! But you must *use* it.

What happens when you do not use your anointing obediently and bravely for the Lord? Look what happened to King Saul. God lifted His hand of protection off Saul and gave the anointing to another person, King David. Yes, you can lose it if you don't use it!

When you use your anointing and your gifts lavishly for others you have favor with God and man, and when people bless you, they get blessed and have divine supernatural protection straight from the hand of God!

King David speaks to the Lord of his anointing in Psalm 89:20 - "You once spoke in a vision; to Your godly ones You said, "I have bestowed help on a warrior; I have exalted one chosen from the people. I have found David My servant; with My sacred oil I have anointed him. My hand will sustain him; surely My arm will strengthen him. …"

Many people are afraid to use their gifts publicly especially if they are a seer, prophet or healer. They are afraid of being mocked or being called a false prophet. But the reward from God for using your gifts faithfully and in public is worth it! God will deal with your haters. Understand no matter how much opposition you get or how 'busy' you are, you must use your gifts and bear much fruit. Jesus expects it from us!

JESUS IS ALL ABOUT THE FRUIT! HE CURSED THE FIG TREE FOR NOT HAVING FRUIT, BECAUSE IT WAS JUST A BUNCH OF FLAPPING LEAVES, ALL TALK AND NO ACTION. (Mark 11:12-25)

It's time for ACTION Jackson! I am not kidding - Seriously Jesus is all about the FRUIT you produce through the help of the Holy Spirit. He made it clear with the fig tree. I want Jesus to walk by me and find me full of fruit, don't you?

Now don't get worried that Jesus is mad at you if you are not producing fruit. This is why the Holy Spirit put the word of God and this book in your hands right now. To give you guidance and instruction to help you to bear great fruit for the Lord and fulfill your purpose. Jesus promised us the Holy Spirit would help us do this, and you cannot do what you don't know, right?

This is seeking the knowledge and wisdom of the Kingdom from the Holy Spirit to be fruitful. To be fruitful is to be productive. To have a message, a product, service, even an idea or invention. If you don't have one - you ask God to give you one!

Flourishing in The Courts Of Our God:

There are always good opportunities for those who are Kingdom-minded, even in the midst of great darkness no matter how old you are. The problems of the world do not affect us because we operate on God's government and dominion which is the Kingdom of God which you received access through Jesus Christ. You are destined to flourish even in times of great troubles in the earth because you were transplanted and rooted in the Kingdom Courts of God when you accepted Jesus Christ and that's where your source is to keep you strong, healthy, wealthy and flourishing!

"But you have made me as strong as a wild ox. You have anointed me with the finest oil. My eyes have seen the downfall of my enemies; my ears have heard the defeat of my wicked opponents. But the godly will flourish like palm trees and grow strong like the cedars of Lebanon. For they are transplanted to the Lord's own house. They flourish in the courts of our God. Even in old age they will still produce fruit; they will remain vital and green." - Psalm 92: 10 -14

Where are you rooted? Where you are rooted will make the right fruit, and the rewards and blessings still come to you no matter what is happening in the world's economy! You are in God's economy! Even if you are old! It does not matter! It's all about where you are rooted! You can have a successful business and ministry or invention or book or movie even if you are 80 years old and be fresh as a daisy doing it!

Move over botox and liposuction I have my fountain of youth and it's called being rooted in the Courts of our God! I have FAVOR and all of Heaven behind me! Whooo hooo! I have the energy, body and mind of my youth! I am as solid and strong as a Cedar of Lebanon! Cedars of Lebanon were pillars in Solmon's Palace and in the Temple! I am a pillar of strength and wisdom! God promised me this! YES!

Declare Psalm 92 over yourself! This is YOUR promise! You will be successful, prospering and vibrant well into old age. This means everything you are called to do you can still do at any age! Your age is of no excuse! So don't worry if you are starting late! God will make up for the lost time and give you a refreshing spirit to persevere! He will reward you in public for never giving up and trusting in God!

The Reward Of Using Your Gifts Faithfully and In Public:

Not everyone's gift is the same. We have gifts to be used in sports, arts, business, law enforcement, mission work and in those seven mountains of influence we talked about in the beginning of the chapter. All areas we use our gifts should be used for the Glory of God.

I want to address a few questions regarding "public"...

Do we always use our gifts and callings in the public eye or are there times we have to be covert or undercover?

This is a very important question because Kingdom Public Relations and Marketing sometimes requires an assignment where you will have to go 'undercover' or be 'covert' to be able to do this faithfully and successfully

What are the reasons you would use your God given gifts or have a calling that requires you to be out of the public eye?

1. Religious persecution
2. To save others that are imprisoned or victims of evil
3. To fool the enemy or catch them off guard
4. You are still being mentored or assisting another leader

5. God has not 'released' you yet for your public ministry or calling
6. God wants you to give financially to something and keep it private
7. Times of personal fasting (corporate fasts are usually large groups called by God to fast)

Examples of "Undercover" or "Covert" Kingdom Work:

- Missionaries have to work undercover to get the Gospel to people in persecuted countries

- Missionaries working undercover to save women and children from trafficking here and abroad

- Navy Seals work undercover to catch the enemy off guard, especially terrorists

- Special law enforcement agents work undercover to catch criminals on the internet and on the streets

- Corrie Ten Boom and her family hid Jews in their home from the Nazi's, and had to do this in secret. She and her family were caught, put in concentration camps, all but Corrie died and she was released miraculously. God launched her into a worldwide public ministry sharing the Gospel and her testimony.

- Elisha mentored under Elijah's prophetic ministry quietly learning and following until the mantle was passed/imparted to him, then he went 'public' as a prophet / holy man

- Jesus had to be 'covert' for a while in His ministry especially with performing miracles before He went 'public'. It was his mother, Mary who God used to give Jesus the request to do His first public miracle at the Wedding at Cana - I see also that Mary's faith was to encourage the disciples, and not 'tell' Jesus to do it, but believe he can. Many times God will send another person of faith to you to give you confirmation on timing.

Your assignment from the Lord may not always start out public, He may have you working covertly in the beginning, middle or end - but eventually you will be rewarded in public so that you can share your testimony to encourage others to get out there and activate their calling and gifts to serve and advance the Kingdom of God. Many times God will send a witness or word for you to go public with your gifts and calling, as He did for His own Son Jesus. Mary witnessed Jesus' birth into this world and the birth into His ministry. I love that! Witnessing and confirmation from the Holy Spirit through another person of faith is something you can expect when He brings you to another level of Glory in your calling.

We should give our financial offerings and how much we give in secret, according to what God has told us to give. If we tell people we give it should only be to encourage them to be obedient to God's word too, or to ask them to pray in agreement for a seed offering to the Lord - never to "brag".

"So that your giving may be in secret. Then your Father, who sees what is done in secret, will reward you." Matthew 6:4

Many times you will see philanthropic millionaires give financially to someone in need secretly. Then the person who received it made it public because they were so grateful. Or it's known that person is very generous but does not seek recognition. I love to see that - it reminds me of Cornelius the Roman Centurion in the book of Acts Chapter 10. God sends Him and angel to tell him that all of Cornelius gifts and generosity to the Jews and to the Synagogue was seen by God and came up as a memorial before God! God wanted to bless his entire household for it. This was preserved in scripture forever and Cornelius' household was the first Gentile conversion to Christianity, and to be filled with the Holy Spirit! Talk about a reward that the entire world will read about forever! What an honor!

Question: What is it that I should do publicly for the Kingdom?

Answer: You should 'go public' with all that God has called you to do if He tells you to and when He tells you to! The Gospel is meant to go public. You are a walking talking Gospel of Jesus Christ in the area God has assigned you. Big or small, undercover or in the marketplace - if it's to one or more people, it's public.

GOING "PUBLIC" IS SIMPLY SHOWING UP FOR GOD WHEREVER HE TELLS YOU TO SHOW UP AND USING YOUR GIFTS FEARLESSLY AND FAITHFULLY - GIVING GOD THE GLORY TO WHOMEVER IS AROUND YOU WITNESSING - THEN GOD WILL MULTIPLY YOUR EXPOSURE, INFLUENCE AND YOUR FOLLOWERS

We have to start with something and someplace so God can prosper it. We are each like a seed for the Kingdom

Of God; to give Jesus His Harvest reward with the fruit we produce - we also get rewarded on earth and in heaven. "On earth as it is in Heaven"
A seed can only be a seed so long and it must blossom and bear fruit. You must plant into fertile places here on earth that are of the Kingdom.

Our rewards (fruitful harvest) are not just waiting for us in heaven. They are available to us here right now!

Many times I have a student who is so hyper focused on what their gift is they lose sight of WHY God gives us a gift to use in the world. He gives us gifts (talents/anointings) so we can produce GOOD FRUIT. I can usually help a person's gift emerge powerfully when I can help them get their focus off the gift and more on the good fruit they desire to produce from using the gift.

Think about this: WHAT'S MORE IMPORTANT OUR GIFTS OR THE FRUIT FROM USING OUR GIFTS?

I want to encourage you all to use your gifts and focus on the good fruit (results) of using your gifts, instead of the gift itself. Jesus said we shall be known by our fruit (results).

"Ye shall know them by their fruit." Matthew 7:15–20

We see so many talented people out there who (especially celebrities) are very gifted creatively, but what is the fruit of that creativity? Does it bring life, light, truth and joy or darkness, deception, fear, death and division? Does it advance the Kingdom of God and the GOOD NEWS message of Jesus Christ? Are they using their gift righteously?

To discern this and to know how God wants us to use the gift He has given us - if we focus on this prayer:

"Father I want to produce GOOD FRUIT for your Kingdom, your people and the world. I am excited to use my GIFTS and be known for GOOD FRUIT that Jesus spoke of in Matthew 7:15. Thank you Father, I ask this for my Gift to emerge and come to full fruition in Jesus name, Amen."

When you have a desire to produce good fruit, your gift emerges powerfully and you will see the good fruit just as Jesus said you would be known for!

"For everything there is a season, A time for every activity under heaven. A time to be born and a time to die. A time to plant and a time to harvest." - *Ecclesiastes 3:1-8*

Sowing Into A Season of Promotion:

Seasons of Sowing: Planting seeds into strategic places that the Holy Spirit directs you to. Press releases, articles, social media posts, flyers, business cards, advertising, social media pages, websites.

Alignment and Covenant Relationships:

When I was working with major corporations and CEO's of companies that were sponsors in NASCAR, one of the biggest goals of the sponsor was to build B2B Relationships. What is a B2B relationship? Business To Business. This means they wanted to connect their company name, brand and products with another company's name, brand and products in an effort to grow and advance each other in the marketplace. For example:

Mountain Dew (soda) agrees to do a B2B with Lays (potato chips) . They would share logo placement on a race car, put coupons on each other's packaging, do collectable merchandise, share shelf space on a display in a grocery store with the driver and car signage etc. Some that I would work on while I was a Marketer in NASCAR were B2B's with a product and a store/retailer. For example Lowe's Home Improvement Stores does a B2B partnership with Kobalt Tools. They share the cost of sponsoring a full race car, and in exchange Lowes gives Kobalt front of store shelf space for their tools in all their locations. This is mainly now how all sports marketing is done and most companies jump at the opportunity to do B2B. They sign an agreement to support each other and follow through fully with each other goals. It's a "covenant" partnership and they become "aligned" in their goals to help and support each other for the common good of each company - even though they are different in what they do, they become one and more powerful and influential when they partner, and they tend to stay together for years and grow together successfully! They always are able to give more as well to charitable causes when they B2B - they have common issues they care about, so it becomes something that flows into the community. One that I worked on was the Make a Wish Foundation and there were more than two companies that partnered 'aligned' to support and partner with each other on that. We were able to do some really special things for children who were sick and disabled and their families and what a blessing that was for all.

LET'S TALK ABOUT YOU DOING THIS FOR THE KINGDOM - GOD IS LOOKING FOR B2B PARTNERSHIPS FOR HIS PEOPLE AND HIS CHURCH

KINGDOM B2B = BROTHER TO BROTHER BUSINESS

"How wonderful and pleasant it is when brothers live together in harmony! For harmony is as precious as the anointing oil that was poured over Aaron's head, that ran down his beard and onto the border of his robe. Harmony is as refreshing as the dew from Mount Hermon that falls on the mountains of Zion. And there the Lord has pronounced his blessing, even life everlasting." - Psalm 133

When you read that psalm - remember that Aaron was the BROTHER of Moses. The oil/anointing is the HOLY SPIRIT upon him and the setting apart for God and teh FAVOR of God, and its POURING out abundantly. Dew on the Mountain represents freshness, flourishing, green and growing. Mountain represents INFLUENCE. Then we see that the blessing of the LORD has already been pronounced everlasting (forever) on these BROTHER TO BROTHER relationships and partnerships for the ECCLESIA (the church) Aaron was the first Levite Priest. Also ZION (which represents God's Government) and then we have the "robe' or covering which represents the GLORY covering of God.

How can you do 'B2B' relationships with other ministries? How can you partner with other missions and Christian leaders? How can you partner with other Christian media and businesses? How can you partner your mountain of influence with another brother or sister in Christ who has a different mountain of influence to come together in harmony and receive the blessing, favor and GLORY covering of God?

God is all about COVENANT and when you come into covenant with another brother and sister in Christ with your gifts, your calling and your assignments - God comes into covenant with you and the other person! When GOD is the center of your covenant - then you will see huge prosperity!

I have done this in my ministry and wow have I seen the blessing and favor from God! For myself and those who I have partnered with. Yes, it directly flows to the FINANCIAL BLESSING part of this too!
Understand we need each other. That's why God did not leave Adam by himself! But God specifically gave this to Adam to "fit". You have to trust God to do the same for you in ALL your relationships! You do not want the wrong "fit"....

"Then the LORD God said, "It is not good that the man should be alone; I will make him a helper fit for him." - Genesis 2:18-19

Yes this also means Husband and Wife Partnerships in Kingdom Business, Ministry, too!

God already has your Kingdom Partnerships already ordained for you and them. Just like God picked out Joseph for Mary to help raise Jesus and made sure that Joseph's lineage was directly connected to King David - your partnerships and alignments with other people for the good of the Kingdom of God have been perfectly planned out and aligned by God for you and them way before you were even born. God is strategic that way generations ahead of time! These partnerships are actually "assigned" to each other.

Now this does not mean when you first launch out in "public" and are doing "Kingdom Marketing" you will have B2B partnerships right away. God may have you working just with His Holy Spirit by yourself for a while. This is a good thing because it's a preparation time - preparing you and advancing you so you can be a good partner for the other party. You can pray for these alignments and partnerships to come, and ask God to prepare you for them, and to bring the partners that He has ordained for you and you for them. You first must be in a solid and uncompromising B2B with the HOLY SPIRIT and covenant with God through Jesus Christ and the Holy Spirit and Angels on Assignment will bring other individuals who are also in a B2B with Him! Make sure you do not jump ahead in this!

Make your prayer for the right partnerships clear.

Pray: *"Holy Spirit I only want partnerships with individuals, ministries and businesses who are already in partnership with You, if they are not in partnership with YOU Holy Spirit I don't want it! If there is anything around me that is not supposed to be in covenant or in partnership with me according to the will of God, I ask You Holy Spirit to swiftly and gently remove this from me and my ministry/business. I come out of agreement with all wrong partnerships, alignments, and covenants , in Jesus name! Holy Spirit I am in expectation for the true Holy Spirit partnerships, alignments and covenants that You Lord God have ordained for me and them before time! I ask You ,Holy Spirit, to prepare me and my ministry, business to receive Your partnerships, alignments and covenants and brothers and sisters in Christ who are focused on the Glory and Advancement of the Kingdom of God. Holy Spirit prompt me at the right time to come into alignment with others for my gifts, calling and purpose and to be blessed and bless those you have sent me to align and partner with as it is written in Psalm 133 by God in Jesus Name!"*

If you start looking for 'partners' on your own or for the wrong reasons (money/pride/fame), or before God aligns it, you could end up with a bad partnership and potentially open yourself up to an attack from the enemy. Trust me on this - I dealt with this first hand and, it's not pretty - I want to help you avoid this pitfall. This book is all about speeding up and accelerating your breakthroughs and goals - and the biggest wall you can hit is getting involved in the wrong relationships and partnerships for your Kingdom Marketing and Public Relations and your life for that matter! I can take you years to recover from this - but I am here to teach you how to make sure this does not happen to you!

Make sure your business, your ministry is in alignment, covenant and partnership with the Holy Spirit. Do this by lifting up any official paperwork you have for your business or ministry, or you can write the name of it on a piece of paper. Anoint the edges of the document with prayer over Anointing oil and hold out the document in front of you. Declare that your ministry/business or whatever you are doing with your gift or calling (this can also be a product, a book you authored, or even just 'yourself' etc) is in covenant with Almighty God in Jesus name!

To avoid the wrong alignments, covenants and partnerships, and to make sure you get the right ones - do these things:

1. Do not get in a rush - let the Holy Spirit lead you
2. Do not 'compete' with other people. "I'm not running against someone. I'm running for something."
3. Do not compare yourself with other people. Focus on what God wants uniquely for you! "Mind your own biscuits and your life will be gravy."

Ha! Remember that! Your unique recipe is who you are and even if there are similarities between you and another person, there is only one you! There are many cooks out there but not exactly like you! I never compare, I just run my race!

1. Do not bring people into 'help' unless you know their character well! Who can vouch for their character? Don't be afraid to ask for references, or have them intern or do a three month trial run with you.
2. You want "Holy Spirit" filled Christians around you in your inner circle. Test this by asking them what their relationship is with the Holy Spirit and have them share their testimony. Holy Sprit filled people are used to being teachable and willing to take correction without getting offended
3. Before signing or agreeing to any contracts, ask the Holy Spirit to reveal any reason why you should not and you can tell the person you want time to pray on the agreement at least three days. "Having nothing to do with the fruitless deeds of darkness, but rather expose them," Ephesians 5:11.
4. Be careful of people who want to 'have what you have" they want the gifts and anointings without doing the work and partnership with the Holy Spirit. It's one thing if they come to learn how to seek God under your wing and are willing to apply faith and obedience it takes to receive and grow into this! If God leads you in prayer over them to give them an impartation of what He has given to you, then do that in obedience - however be careful if the person overemphasizes on wanting your anointing. It should just come up only while you are praying for them and if the Holy Spirit leads you to give them an impartation.

"Herod deceitfully asked the wise men to search for Jesus, then let him know where He was that he might come to worship Him. Always be cautious of those who want someone else to pay the price to seek and find Him." - Robert Henderson

Discerning, Removing and Avoiding the Spirit of Divination:

Now I am not trying to scare you, I am trying to prepare you for the public life with your ministry or calling. You must have this understanding so you know how to properly and effectively deal with it. It's called a spirit of divination or "python" spirit.

I would not include it in this chapter if I did not think it was crucially important. I want you to be properly equipped. Jesus warned His disciples to be wise to these things.

As soon as you launch out into the public for the Kingdom there is a sneaky evil spirit that will try to mess with you.

You may even be dealing with it right now so let me teach you how to discern it and get rid of it. This spirit is very rampant in our society and we as leaders must be aware.

In 2 Corinthians 2:11 Paul said; "Lest satan should get an advantage of us: for we are not ignorant of his devices."

I want you to be welcoming of people who want to help you when you launch out in public, BUT you must also be wise that the enemy looks for a way in to stop you or hinder you through wrong relationships. He will try to send a person who is operating in this demonic spirit to infiltrate your inner circle and you must know how you discern this - the bigger the impact you will have for the Kingdom - the more this evil spirit tries to sneak in!

I want you to love people and I don't want you to be paranoid at every person you meet that they might be operating with a spirit of divination - that's why you must be careful to discern properly. I have had this spirit try to infiltrate my business and ministry at least three times! The more my ministry and name grew publicly the more it seemed this spirit was trying to attack. Two were women and one was a man. It is not gender specific!

Now please don't be saying, "Gee, Annamarie if there is a chance I might get an attack from the enemy when I launch out in public with my ministry or purpose for the Kingdom, then I'm not gonna do it."

Listen to me! You can get attacks and open a door to the enemy just sitting at home and watching the wrong shows on TV!

Your desire to be obedient to God and your calling for the Kingdom should be so passionate that you will not worry about this at all and I am going to equip you right now to discern it, destroy it and keep it away for good!

First, let's get discernment on the evil Spirit of Divination...

There is a very deceptive spirit that has been operating in the world especially at this time and it's an anti-christ spirit. A lot of people who you may know and many around us in society are under the deception of this spirit. It's based in witchcraft and the occult and stems from idolatry. It's been operating in all the 7 Mountains of Influence. One of the

456

sneaky evil spirits that operate under the anti-christ spirit is the spirit of divination. It's like a python and it targets those who are powerfully and boldly representing the Kingdom of God in these 7 mountains. The spirit of divination tends to target ministry leaders and those in ministry with a prophetic gifting. It sneaks in looking like it's harmless and even flattering then slowly works to squeeze you into shutting down and quitting.

Now, let's reveal the Spirit of Divination also known as the Python Spirit ...

The Apostle Paul dealt with this spirit early on in his ministry when he entered the Greek city of Philippi:

Acts 16:16-20
(KJV) "And it came to pass, as we went to prayer, a certain damsel possessed with a spirit of divination met us, which brought her masters much gain by soothsaying; The same followed Paul and us, and cried, saying, These men are the servants of the most high God, which shew unto us the way of salvation. And this did she many days. But Paul, being grieved, turned and said to the spirit, I command thee in the name of Jesus Christ to come out of her. And he came out the same hour. And when her masters saw that the hope of their gains was gone, they caught Paul and Silas, and drew them into the marketplace unto the rulers, And brought them to the magistrates, saying, These men, being Jews, do exceedingly trouble our city,"

The SPIRIT OF DIVINATION is someone that will placate you when they think things go their way and try to destroy you when it doesn't. You would never know that they are if you were giving them everything they wanted. They expose themselves in different ways.

You have a mission to complete! A mission from God and cannot let anyone hinder that or try to distract that no matter who they are! This spirit has to be *exposed early* before it does too much damage.

You take authority over that spirit operating through them and you set boundaries with them. Even if they are "friends". Some may even say they are "christians". These are people with wicked spirits operating through them. Understand it's not the person, it's the spirit operating through them!

These are the Signs of the spirit of divination or "python" spirit operating in a person that wants to be around you and your ministry or your Kingdom purpose:

- Gives you flattery in the beginning to pull you in - almost like a groupie or "I am your biggest fan"
- Wants what you have but not willing to learn or work for it
- "Acts" like they have the same gifting you have and begins to mimic you to pull your followers to them
- Hogs up your time away from others
- Begins to constantly pull attention to themselves in your public setting and away from your message for the Lord
- Constantly telling you what you should do in your ministry and pushing you away from pursuing God's guidance and they wanting to be your only 'guide'
- Squeezed feeling of pressure that comes on you after you have started listening to them or agreeing

with them, you may even begin to experience shortness of breath, and difficulty swallowing
- Wants you to do everything their way - gets easily hurt or offended
- Works behind the scenes to pull people to "their side" to put pressure on you to do what they want
- They focus on dividing you away from your people and your people away from you
- May have been involved in witchcraft or new age practices and never got fully delivered (you will see the signs - on their social media - take the time to check them out and what they post)
- In group settings, they are not eager to pray for anyone else's issues - they want most of the prayer for themselves
- Tries to prophesy over your followers and counter what God has spoke to you over them without your consent (if you have a prophetic ministry)
- Usually avoids communion time, and any type of worship of Jesus - more drawn to the supernatural stuff
- Trying to compare you and your ministry to what everyone else is doing - telling you should do that
- Crying, weeping alot and using guilt to manipulate you, wants to have access to you even at night to pull you away from family
- Usually a 'loner' type person. Has trouble with relationships has been through many churches
- Focused on getting constant prophetic words and squeezing/pressuring you to give them every day to them - gets overly needy
- Never carries out what you advise them to do - you see no fruit, just more drama
- When they tire you out they try to act in your place, and influence your people and followers

- Sometimes they act like a 'prophet' and giving false prophetic words that are coming from familiar spirits instead of the Holy Spirit
- Tells you they have "angels" talking to them all the time but they do not have a relationship with the Holy Spirit
- Thrives in constant drama and strife
- Brags how they told-off church leaders, pastors or people of authority
- Usually shows up at a time you are close to a breakthrough
- When you try to use boundaries with them they get offended and accuse you of not being a loving Christian
- They profess love for you, but are always questioning your message and your strategies (a person truly sent by God would resonate and support your message and respect you and your strategies.)

Understand the spirit of divination partners with the religious spirit and it will find others operating with a religious spirit to try and gang up on you and accuse you of ruining things for them, and not being caring or loving Christian if you call out their behavior. You must be careful to keep your emotions in check.

Observe all this wisely, stay calm and prepare to strike this down behind the scenes, do not get caught up is the drama around this person.

So what do you do about this situation? What if this person has embedded themselves in your life, business and ministry? How can you deal with this spirit and still love them? How do you discern this before it takes over and squeezes you until you are so distracted you cannot fully function for the Lord and your calling then your faith is struggling?

PLEASE LISTEN TO ME!

When you have faith, even as small as a mustard seed you don't have to compromise 'put up with' anything or anybody that comes against your faith! Jesus Christ is the author and finisher of your faith only! What you do with your faith and calling in this life nobody has any right to try and change, attack, question, force their will, squeeze or twist it in any way!

GUARD AND PROTECT YOUR FAITH AND MISSION AT ALL COSTS!

KNOW NO WILL BUT THE FATHER'S FOR YOUR LIFE! HIS WILL IS FOR YOU TO HAVE ALL THE PROMISES OF HIS WORD! DO NOT LET THE ENEMY TOUCH YOUR PROMISES! CRUSH THE ENEMY UNDER YOUR FEET!

Jesus gave you AUTHORITY to destroy and crush anything that would come against you!

"Listen carefully: I have given you authority [that you now possess] to tread on serpents and scorpions, and [the ability to exercise authority] over all the power of the enemy (satan); and nothing will [in any way] harm you." - Luke 10:19 (AMP)

What did the Apostle Paul do? He took authority over the spirit of divination/python operating through the girl and commanded it to leave! He did not rebuke the girl, he rebuked the *evil spirit*.

Paul discerned it quickly and nipped it in the bud! How did Paul discern it? Read the scripture - the girl kept on pressuring him and even drawing attention to herself while Paul was trying to preach the Gospel, something Paul did to bring "Good News" to a new town. He was usually filled with the joy of the Lord doing this - however when this girl was around it says: "But Paul, being *grieved*".... (that's the opposite of joy!)

Paul began to feel grieved in the spirit - that means this evil spirit was coming against the work of the HOLY SPIRIT operating through Paul!

This is exactly what I went through when I had this happen to me and let me tell you - you will feel this too if you have this situation. The python/divination spirit will cause you to feel grieved, frustrated, and distracted. Even stressed and depressed. Pressure comes around your throat and heaviness on your chest - you begin to feel weary and do not feel like moving forward. If this persists it could cause you to question what you are doing, maybe that person could do it better, blah blah blah... this gets worse the more you agree with this evil lying spirit.

I want you to understand something - people can try to copy you, try to steal your ideas, try to do what you do - but they can never do what God gifted you to do just like you. Never.

People will try to steal your special "recipe", but it will not taste the same when they try to use it without your anointing! Stay focused even when an attack like this would come. The best thing you can do is stand and not be shaken one bit.

Stay focused on the words of Jesus Christ when discerning relationships. Is it building up and creating abundance? Or tearing down?

Jesus made it clear how to discern what was from Him and what was not in John 10:10: "The thief comes only in order to steal and kill and destroy. I [Jesus] came that they may have and enjoy life, and have it in abundance (to the full, till it overflows)."

The spirit of divination will try to play with your emotions, make you feel unsettled, unfocused and try to trip up your work in public and pressure you to make you quit. They will try to shadow your light. It wants to tear down what you are building. You cannot allow it!! You have to take authority over it ASAP and here are the steps.

How To Take Authority Against The Spirit of Divination:

1.) **If the person is being overly difficult you do not have to confront them.** You can take care of this all in the Spirit realm in prayer. Remember it's not the person, it's the evil spirit operating through them.

2.) **Suit Up - Get on your Armor of God,** Take Your Seat of Authority and Apply The Blood Of Jesus to yourself, your family, your ministry and your business.

2.) **Forgive the person who is doing this and repent** for any bitterness or offense you have toward them, ask Jesus to wash your sins in His blood and put all offense and bitterness on the Cross. Ask God to bless the person you are forgiving and for the Holy Spirit to go to them and lead them fully to Christ and remove all veils of deception from their eyes of understanding and bring them to deliverance. If we do not forgive them, the accuser can use our unforgiveness against us and the evil spirit will still have a legal right to operate.

3.) **You can ask God to remove the person and all their influence out** of your business and ministry with His "Ax Of Judgement". Do this prayer after you have forgiven the person. If you can clearly see that this individual is not there to produce good fruit for you or anyone else, you can stand on the word of God in this situation. Jesus said we would know them by their fruit, and the bad fruit is to be removed. Relationships in the bible are mentioned like trees that either produce good fruit or bad fruit. Fruit coming from a relationship should always bear the fruit of the Holy Spirit, if not, that relationship will be removed by God. You must be able to bear good fruit in all your relationships for the Kingdom. If any relationship is clearly coming against that, such as those operating in divination you can pray this powerfully...

The Ax Of God's Judgment Prayer is based on Matthew 3:10 - *"Even now the ax of God's judgment is poised, ready to sever the roots of the trees. Yes, every tree that does not produce good fruit will be chopped down and thrown into the fire."*

Pray: *"FATHER GOD your word says in Matthew 3:10, now also the axe is laid unto the root of the trees: therefore every tree which bringeth not forth good fruit is hewn down, and cast into the fire. Father I believe your word and I want to activate it right now in the spiritual and in the natural in my life and in all my relationships! I do not have to accept anything that is not the will of God for my life and my life, ministry and business. I BELIEVE The word of God is the will of God! I DECREE As for me and my house we shall Honor and Obey the word and the will of God and serve the Lord Jesus Christ for all generations thereof!*

Father in the name of Jesus Christ, I ask You to take your Ax Of Judgement and permanently remove any ungodly relationships around me swiftly, particularly _____ in Jesus name! Chop these ungodly relationships and influences at the root, pull the stumps up out of the ground, shake the stumps with no roots remaining in the ground and cast this relationship and any influence it had into the fire to burn to ashes in Jesus name! I will never eat fruit from this ungodly relationship again! Father let all remaining influence from this relationship be burned up forever by your Holy fire in Jesus name. Let this be swift and calm, with no recourse or backlash, let you Holy Fire burn up any bad seed left from this ungodly relationship and it's the relationship that is removed and burned to ashes and all their influence and not the person. I have prayed for the person to move on and into what you have for them Lord, but far away from me and my _____ in Jesus name! Thank you Father for your word and your promises and the ability to discern good and bad fruit! Father replace any bad ungodly relationships with Holy Spirit filled relationships to bear good fruit together for your Kingdom and Glory in Jesus name, Amen!"

Now, sever all soul ties with that person:
Declare: "By the Authority of Jesus Christ I break the power of and SEVER off ALL the demonic and ungodly strongholds, agreements and soul ties off _____ FOREVER IN JESUS NAME, I NOW WASH_____ IN THE BLOOD OF JESUS AND INVITE THE HOLY SPIRIT TO COME AND FILL THOSE PLACES IN _____ WHERE THE OLD SOUL TIES HAVE DEPARTED IN JESUS NAME"

4.) **Get the python removed off you** if you have been getting a 'smothering or choking feeling'. I would still do this prayer either way.

Stand and Pray: *In the name and authority of Jesus Christ I command the python spirit to drop off my body and on the floor in Jesus mighty name! Python spirit, I renounce you and all your evil and I command you off me and under my feet right now in Jesus name! Drop off me NOW python! I take authority over you in the name above all names, Jesus Christ! Drop NOW to the ground in Jesus name! (then take a breath and raise your sword of the spirit.....) "In the name of Jesus Christ I crush the head of the python spirit (stomp your foot on its head in the spirit) and I take my sword of the spirit and chop this python to pieces! (make a chopping motion on the floor below you) I chop you up python! Your head was crushed by the Cross or Jesus Christ and I crush you! You have been cursed by God you vile python spirit and I curse you and destroy you to pieces! You will never touch me again python! I scrape your chopped carcass into the fire of God to be burned to ashes (do a scraping motion with your sword of the spirit) and let the breath of the Holy Spirit of the Living God to blow what is left of you python into the dry uninhabited place where you will stay forever in Jesus name! I raise up my sword of the spirit and let the Fire of the Holy Spirit cleanse my sword! Let the fresh breath of the Holy Spirit fill my lungs! I breathe you in the Holy Spirit in Jesus name. I am free and delivered from python forever! Holy Spirit I ask you to pour fresh oil on me, so much oil that no python can ever attach to me again, it will slide off me because of the abundance of anointing in Jesus name! I declare I move free, breathe free, in the natural and in the spiritual and whom Christ has set free is free indeed! I am fully free in Christ Jesus! I place myself mind, body, soul and spirit in the blood of Jesus Christ forever! Through the blood of Jesus Christ I am redeemed from all evil and set apart for the plans and purposes of the Kingdom of God and nothing shall come against it in Jesus mighty name!"*

5). Ask for God to assign and station "Sentry Angels" at the gates of your business and ministry to block these evil spirits.

Decree: "In the name and authority of Jesus Christ in whom I am seated, I thank You Father that you send your angels to keep me in all my ways. I ask You Father God to release to me Sentry Angels that will protect all my gateways. Thank You Father God. Therefore, in Jesus name and authority, I command and post my divinely assigned Sentry Angels of the Lord to these gateway areas to my _____ both in the natural gates and the spiritual gates to my _____, including all gates to all the gates of communication, phones, computers, internet, social media, email and websites that I have. I command the Sentry Angels of the Lord that I have just posted to these specific areas to stand and protect these areas from all evil with fiery swords and shields 24 hours a day, seven days a week from this day forward in Jesus name! I command my Sentry Angels of the Lord, to not allow anything that is not of God to enter or come near any of my gates in Jesus name. I apply the Blood of Jesus Christ to all my gateways to my _____ in the natural and in the spiritual. All my gates belong to Jesus Christ! I ask my Sentry Angels of the Lord to also go and locate, arrest, bind and remove any evil spirits that may have come in my gates and block those evil spirits from ever coming in or coming near my gates or near me ever again! I renounce those evil spirits, especially the spirit of divination is strictly prohibited from entering or coming near me my _____ or my gates from this day forward in Jesus name! Thank you Sentry Angels of the Lord for your obedience and faithfulness to God and thank you Father for my authority in Christ Jesus to receive and command my assigned Angels of your Kingdom, for your glory forever and ever, Amen!"

Do these steps until you see the breakthrough!
It's crucial that you do not waiver or let this spirit of divination/python manipulate you for too long! It comes against the good fruit that you are meant to produce for the Kingdom of God!

Ask God to release His Holy Fire into you:

Pray: *"In the name and authority of Jesus Christ, I renounce and come out of agreement with all religious spirits and words and out of agreement with all spirits of divination and words and command them off of my mind, body, soul and spirit right now in Jesus name! LEAVE ME NOW YOU VILE SPIRITS! I send the fire of the Holy Spirit against you! Get out and go to the uninhabited dry place and stay there until Jesus Christ comes and tells you where to go and never come near me again! I close the door to these evil, vile spirits and seal it with the blood of Jesus Christ forever! I invite the Fire of The Holy Spirit of Almighty God to come in me now and burn in every place in me and around me to destroy any remnant of these evil spirits and refine me and make me excellent of soul with your DUNAMIS power Holy Spirit in Jesus name. Holy Spirit I ask You to fill every place in me and stand hold there forever! I declare a divine wall of Holy Spirit Fire is now around me protecting me and if any evil spirit tries to pass through this wall of Holy Fire they will be burned up to ashes in Jesus Mighty name!" Amen*

You will begin to feel a huge positive difference. I am telling you will feel lighter and that heaviness and guilt will be gone! You will begin to accelerate in your public life and message like never before! Myself and my students have had incredible results from doing this. The growth and increase will come almost immediately. It's like burning off the dead grass in a pasture, diving out the snakes to have new green beautiful pastures with nothing harmful hiding that can trip you up! FREEDOM!

The people in question also need deliverance from these evil spirits! Pray that the Holy Spirit will go to them and lead them to full deliverance. You can also pray those deliverance prayers over that person in the natural or in the spirit. In the meantime, don't let one or two deceived people that are trying to upset your mission ruin it for so many more who really need you and are truly sent by God.

Get mad at the devil, not the person. Be *solution oriented* in the spirit realm! These evil spirits are more afraid of us when we come in the name of Jesus Christ - we are their worst fear! Remember that!

The devil can't stop you through any person or situation. You have authority over all of it. You are a representative of the King of Glory who crushed the kingdom of darkness! All you have to do is enforce the finished work of the CROSS and the BLOOD of Christ in the name of Jesus! You have all access credentials to everything the Kingdom of God has!

The Cross and the Blood of Jesus is your KEY but you must use it and enforce it in your Seat Of Authority. The Fire of The Holy Spirit can be called forth by faith to burn up and chase out any remnant of operating in and around you that is hidden.

Flash your badge of the Blood and The Cross and blind the enemy! Make the enemy bow the knee to Jesus Christ!

You carry the authority through Christ! The devil has no teeth!

Jesus already gave YOU victory over all the works of the enemy! You must put it ON the Blood of Christ every day in the spirit and wear it like an official credential to get you through every gate and door of influence you want to get into!

Keep going - do not stop for any distractions! Even people who try to distract you! Do not allow it. Deal with it swiftly!

Where is your focus? Is it on the useless words of the enemy? Or is it on what GOD SAYS?
"Your enemy the devil prowls around like a roaring lion looking for someone to devour. (1 Peter 5:8). That roar can affect your perception of the situation. If you focus on the roar, you will forget who you are in Christ and the promises that are already yours." - Pastor Gary Keesee

If you don't stay focused, the enemy will send distractions through people to try and get you to forget the authority you carry.

NOT TODAY SATAN!

You have Kingdom work to get done you 'aint got time for that!

The way to repel any daily attacks is to "suit up" with your Armor of God every morning without fail and put on the Helmet of Salvation and declare you have the mind of Christ and command every thought that day to come under the obedience of Christ, then take your authority over the enemy command him to bow the knee to the Lord Jesus Christ! Then invite the Holy Spirit to fill up your mind, body, soul and spirit and command your mind, body and soul to yield to the power of the Holy Spirit. The enemy cannot come into a place that is filled with the Holy Spirit! Keep your bodily vessel filled, especially your mind and soul!

I have found also when I pray the "Ax of God's Judgement Prayer" and I ask God to remove any ungodly relationships that I may not see for myself. I am shocked at who suddenly leaves my life and my ministry. You cannot be afraid of God to remove those hidden ungodly relationships even the ones who you thought were OK. God sees more than you do and He will save you future heartache! I pray this over my child all the time! It's amazing to use this prayer over your loved ones, too!

When you invite the Holy Spirit to fill every place in your life - then the enemy has no empty spots to try and infiltrate! This includes your family and finances! Anywhere that can be filled, even your bank accounts, your home, invite the Holy Spirit to fill it!

DECLARE: "FILL ALL MY VESSELS WITH YOUR PRESENCE LORD! I GIVE NO PLACE TO THE ENEMY!"

Now, give thanks and praise and worship God as you go through every public gateway, as you move forward in the public with your calling - it's your praise that brings more blessings and gets you swiftly through each gate with power and favor that brings the *good people* and the breakthroughs and increase in finances!

I love Psalm 100 because it's your Kingdom Calling Card!

I even have a copy of it printed that I save in my wallet! I pull it out and declare it to remind me to keep moving forward in thanks and praise and nothing can stop what God wants to bless me with! You start praising God and the devil will flee from you and fast! Because when you draw near to GOD, he draws near to You! The evil cannot stay in the presence of God!

Psalm 100 Decree:
"I Make a joyful noise unto the Lord, over all the lands! I Serve the Lord with gladness: I come before His presence with singing. I Know that the Lord He is God: it is He that hath made me, and not me myself; I am His people, and the sheep of his pasture! I Enter into His gates with thanksgiving, and into His courts with praise: and I am thankful unto him, and I bless His Holy name. For the Lord is good; His mercy is everlasting; and His truth endureth to all generations unto me and my household, my children, my children's children and all my generations thereof. Amen"

PRAISE BE TO GOD! KEEP PRAISING AND THANKING HIM AND YOU WILL HAVE MORE TO PRAISE AND THANK HIM FOR!

Kingdom Economics: You can expect your finances to grow by using these Kingdom Public Relations and Marketing strategies. You must be a good and faithful steward of these finances, as they are directed to you from God.

KINGDOM MARKETING AND PROMOTION BRINGS KINGDOM ECONOMICS WHICH ARE UNLIMITED AND NOT SUBJECT TO WORLD ECONOMICS

You Have The Abrahamic Promise:
As followers of Jesus Christ we are grafted into the promises of Abraham. This inheritance is from Father

God, He will prosper you, your children, your household and add no painful toil to it! We have to partner with the KINGDOM and be in Covenant with God and HE will prosper everything we do. Abraham was in covenant with God. So are we. We are not on the world economy system. We are on God's Kingdom system. We get the same benefits of Abraham, Issac and Jacob!

"The LORD will make you prosper abundantly--in the fruit of your womb, the offspring of your livestock, and the produce of your land--in the land that the LORD swore to your fathers to give you."-
Deuteronomy 28:11 (God's Promise to Abraham and His offspring.)

"Then Isaac sowed in that land, and received in the same year a hundredfold: and the Lord blessed him. And the man waxed great, and went forward, and grew until he became very great: For he had possession of flocks, and possession of herds, and great store of servants." - Genesis 26:12-33 (Abraham's son Isaac receiving this promise.)

WOW. Hundred fold increase. You can expect that too with this promise for your business or ministry! You can speak this over your first year of business!

You can even ask God for Secret Business Strategies that will get you out of working for the old 9-5 job! This is what Jacob did when he finally got tired of not having his own sheep and taking care of old mean Laban's sheep! Jacob wanted his own business and his own livestock. Do you realize that your 9-5 job is just a stepping stone to greater things that God has waiting for you? You just need to ask God for your own business strategy like Jacob did! God will prosper you even greater than the place you were working for! Why? Because you belong to the KINGDOM! These ideas are waiting for you in Heaven and once you ask God for them, the FAVOR comes to do it!

Let's see what God did for His people regarding 'secret business and wealth strategies'.....

Genesis 30:37–31:16 (JACOB)
"Then Jacob took fresh sticks of poplar and almond and plane trees, and peeled white streaks in them, exposing the white of the sticks. He set the sticks that he had peeled in front of the flocks in the troughs, that is, the watering places, where the flocks came to drink. And since they bred when they came to drink, the flocks bred in front of the sticks and so the flocks brought forth striped, speckled, and spotted. And Jacob separated the lambs and set the faces of the flocks toward the striped and all the black in the flock of Laban. He put his own droves apart and did not put them with Laban's flock. Whenever the stronger of the flock were breeding, Jacob would lay the sticks in the troughs before the eyes of the flock, that they might breed among the sticks, but for the feebler of the flock he would not lay them there. So the feebler would be Laban's, and the stronger Jacob's. Thus the man (Jacob) increased greatly and zhad large flocks, female servants and male servants, and camels and donkeys."

Deuteronomy 28:11 (THE PEOPLE OF ISRAEL)
"The LORD will make you prosper abundantly--in the fruit of your womb, the offspring of your livestock, and the produce of your land--in the land that the LORD swore to your fathers to give you."

Proverbs 10:22: (SOLOMON)
"The blessing of the LORD brings wealth, without painful toil for it."

ARE YOU GETTING THIS YET?

You belong to the Kingdom Of God! You should be prospering! If you are not prospering then something needs to change in your mindset! Where are you not truly in KINGDOM thinking? It's time to check yourself and go to GOD with these promises and prosperity of Abraham, Issac and Jacob. THEY ARE YOUR PROMISES. Your Marketing and Public Relations must reflect these promises being manifest and operational IN EVERY AREA OF YOUR LIFE!

Did Jesus do this? YES! He was demonstrating the Abrahamic Covenant and the PROMISES of the Father to the people the entire time in His ministry! He was teaching us how to become faithful like Abraham, Issac and Jacob and become true sons and daughters of the Kingdom. That all this was available to us and all we had to do was BELIEVE.

Jesus went to the CROSS so He could fulfill the KINGDOM and buy us all back into it with a BLOOD COVENANT! My goodness why would we want to stay in operating in the world system of lack when Jesus paid to transfer us out of it with His own Blood!

I am witnessing the word of God to you and the Scriptures are clear! The Word of God is the Will of God! These promises in His word all intend to prosper you, both spiritually and physically! On earth as it is in Heaven!

Those who scoff at "prosperity gospel" are not understanding the true Gospel and the KIngdom that Jesus Christ came to give us through believing in Him.

The Gospel is GOOD NEWS!   The Gospel is PROSPERITY.

Synonyms of the word 'good' in English: fine, of high quality, of a high standard, quality, superior, satisfactory, acceptable, adequate, in order, up to scratch, up to the mark, up to standard, up to par, competent, not bad, all right, excellent, superb, outstanding, magnificent, of the highest quality, of the highest standard, exceptional, marvellous, wonderful, first-rate, first-class, superlative, splendid, admirable, worthy, sterling, considerable, sizeable, substantial, appreciable, significant, goodly, tolerable, fair, reasonable, tidy, hefty, ample, plentiful, abundant, superabundant, great, large, lavish, profuse, generous, marked, noticeable, close, intimate, dear, bosom, close-knit, inseparable, attached, loving, devoted, faithful, constant, special, best, fast, firm, valued, treasured, cherished, virtue, righteousness, virtuousness, goodness, morality, ethicalness, uprightness, upstandingness, integrity, principle, dignity, rectitude, rightness, honesty, truth, truthfulness, honour, incorruptibility, probity, propriety, worthiness, worth, merit, irreproachableness, blamelessness, purity, pureness, lack of corruption, justice, justness, fairness, benefit, advantage, profit, gain, interest, welfare, well-being, enjoyment, satisfaction, comfort, ease, convenience, help, aid, assistance, use, usefulness, avail, service, behalf, succeed, achieve success, be successful, be a success, do well, get ahead, reach the top, become famous, achieve recognition, distinguish oneself, set the world on fire, prosper, flourish, thrive, advance (Source: Oxford English Thesaurus)

Jesus Christ died for me and you so we could have eternal life and transfer into the Kingdom Realm of God the minute we accept HIM. This is for our time on earth and it's all for our GOOD and the good of God's Kingdom.

It's the only way into the Kingdom and it's right here while we live on this earth - Jesus confirmed it for us, and set us up to continue the good work for the Kingdom on earth.

"May the God of peace, who through the blood of the eternal covenant brought back from the dead our Lord Jesus, that great Shepherd of the sheep, equip you with everything good for doing his will, and may he work in us what is pleasing to him, through Jesus Christ, to whom be glory for ever and ever. Amen." - Hebrews 13:20-21

What does the word "Equip" mean here?

Not only are you saved from your sins and into eternal life in Heaven, when you accept Jesus Christ - but God will give you everything you need to do His will and your work for the Kingdom during your life on the earth.

Equipping you to fulfill your God given purpose HERE ON EARTH. This includes the finances to build, travel, advertise, market and prosper while you do it, Because the word says equip you with everything good. (We established that good also means prosper.)

HE WILL EQUIP YOU WITH EVERYTHING GOOD TO PROSPER IN YOUR PURPOSE TO PLEASE HIM!

This is ROI for God! Return On Investment. God is invested in YOU.

Question: How do sponsors and investors get a return on investment?
Answer: Through good marketing and public relations that see profitable results.

Profitable Results = Fruitful Harvest

FRUIT FRUIT FRUIT! Jesus loves to see the FRUIT!
Fruit of our labors for the Kingdom of God on earth and fruit of the Holy Spirit!
When I was a Marketing and Public Relations Representative in NASCAR my job description consisted of the following: (As you read this, connect how this pertains to you representing the Kingdom of God as your Sponsor...)

1. Research, propose and acquire both monetary and product sponsors for the team
2. Bring in paid endorsements for my driver
3. Grow driver and team fan base on all platforms
4. Grow media following in all mediums (both electronic and print media)
5. Write and distribute press releases and land stories
6. Get television time for driver, team and car
7. Land media Interviews for driver every week
8. Sponsor Activation Programs (carry out sponsor's promotions)
9. Sponsor Business To Business Programs (B2B) (connect your sponsors with other sponsors to build relationships for them)
10. Sponsor Reports (Show them the Return On Investment they are getting by sponsoring you and your team)
11. Sponsor Entertainment at Events (Make them feel valued, special and part of the team)

12. Work On Next Season's Sponsors (Sowing seeds into next season)
13. Continue to grow and prosper the relationships with my sponsors
14. Make the sponsor's brand and message a household name (ultimate goal)
15. Sponsors receive measurable (ROI) Return on Investment and sales are multiplied - $2 or more for every $1 invested in you and your team (multiplication/harvest)

As the race team and sponsors' Marketing and PR Representative, I had to be equipped to do this to properly carry out my duties and I needed the finances, the open doors, the connections, the wisdom, the favor, the office, the vehicles, the phones, computers, and the skills to do it all! I had to answer to the sponsors each week and report to them to show them how they were getting a return on every dollar they were spending with our team and make sure I kept them happy happy happy!

I prospered, and my team prospered because my sponsors were prospering and pleased with my work. They kept coming back with more money each year as we proved to them we could market them well and advance their company in the media and bring them more loyal customers and new business opportunities through a good PR program.

My friend, this is us; this is the church! The ecclesia—the Body of Christ! Jesus is the Head—the CEO—and we are His marketing and public relations team here on earth! The kingdom must advance and bring in more loyal followers. This is what Jesus started and we keep it going.

Just like the sponsors up-leveling each year from fulfilling what they asked and expected of me, God will up-level you to a higher level. This is divine promotion. The Bible calls it going from glory to glory!

"And we, who with unveiled faces all reflect the Lord's glory, are being transformed into his likeness with ever-increasing glory, which comes from the Lord, who is the Spirit." Some translations say, "being transformed from glory to glory." 2 Corinthians 3:18

'Unveiled faces' in this scripture means 'spiritual veils' are removed one by one as we advance in the glory to give us pure eyes of understanding in the spirit realm. We really begin to understand God and the mysteries of God and His Kingdom.

Obedience and growth in your faith pleases God and matures you as a Christian. You begin to understand more how God's Kingdom operates and your eyes of understanding open more spiritually - you begin to transform more into the Glory realm - we will be talking more about how to fully operate and advance in the Glory in our next chapter.

Jesus strategically places you in an area of influence to do this through your purpose and divine assignment. YOU are His Marketing and PR Representative in your assigned area of influence. Your assigned area is no mistake, it's the area that you have the most drive to give value to others, and where God sends or places you.

I could write an entire book on The Seven Mountains of Influence and it's a deep prophetic teaching and great revelation for the times we are in for the advancement of the Kingdom of God - and where each of us fit into this.

Johnny Enlow and Lance Wallnau are amazing teachers of the 7M (Seven Mountain Mandate) and they both have excellent resources on how to know what Mountain of Influence of Society you are assigned or called to. I highly recommend their books and teachings.

I learned that I am assigned to the Media, Education and Religion Mountains. I think you can see that from what you are learning about me. Yes, you can have more than one area of influence that you are assigned to. No matter what area yours is, it is very important to God. He wants to promote you in your area or areas.

For now, let's assume that you know your calling or purpose and what area of influence you are assigned to. The teaching that I am giving you in this chapter on Kingdom Marketing and Public Relations works for any area of influence you are in. It's a strategy that we have seen great fruit and lasting results across the board for both myself and my students.

Kingdom Public Relations should be done with a pure heart, for the good of God's kingdom and for the love of God's people. It's a focus on doing well for Jesus Christ, and only being concerned about what HE thinks. We can very easily get caught up in our own pride and lose focus of the main thing if we begin to see success.

I am sure you have seen this happen - where you were attracted to a church leader, teacher or business because of their pure, from the heart message - you loved that they were focused on pleasing God and the power of God that was on display. Then once they start to get well known they lose sight of that and become politically correct people pleasers and their message gets watered down and they are more concerned on pleasing man than God. Jesus called these people and churches neither hot nor cold and He would spit them out of His mouth. Jesus says this about the Church of Laodicea in Revelation 3:13-20. The church of Laodicea makes me think of the churches and Christians who mix in 'new age' and politically correct' practices into the church. Jesus calls that vomit! Whoa! NOT GOOD PR for His Kingdom at all! So many people are pulled into that, I got trapped in it for a while myself! Thank God Jesus came and saved me out of that!

Once you start on your Kingdom PR and Marketing you must be careful that you stay focused on the leading of the Holy Spirit, stay humble to God and not succumb to what is 'popular' so you can be popular. If you mess up, repent quickly - Jesus knows we are tempted by culture and that's why He came to teach us about building His churches and what He wants for His Kingdom people and ecclesia and what He expects is spelled out in the book of Revelation. He gave each church the option to repent and get back on track with Him and He would return to them and bless them. This goes for anything you are doing - if you get off track with your message and loyalty to Jesus, you can repent and get a second chance. That's why if you see a church or ministry going down the wrong path, pray for them that the Holy Spirit convicts them and brings them to repentance. Jesus wants them back!

My goal is to be like the "Church of Philadelphia" in the Book of Revelation chapter that Jesus gives "Keys To The House Of David" to because of their obedience, perseverance and faith. I believe this is what we need to be as the ecclesia, the body of Christ and ultimately the end-time church. If we all focus on being this with these attributes and apply them into our Kingdom Public

Relations in all we do, we can be confident we are pleasing Jesus!

I want to touch upon what pleased Jesus about the church of Philadelphia (at the time this was located in Asia Minor, modern day Turkey.) This also was meant more for the FUTURE church as a whole - the end time church as Jesus prophesied it would be to the Apostle John who wrote it down for us. This is meant for Jesus church and His people TODAY.

Revelation 3:7-13

(Amplified Bible) Message to Philadelphia: "And to the angel (divine messenger) of the church in Philadelphia write: "These are the words of the Holy One, the True One, He who has the key [to the house] of David, He who opens and no one will [be able to] shut, and He who shuts and no one opens: 8 'I know your deeds. See, I have set before you an open door which no one is able to shut, for you have a little power, and have kept My word, and have not renounced or denied My name. 9 Take note, I will make those of the synagogue of Satan, who say that they are Jews and are not, but lie—I will make them come and bow down at your feet and make them know [without any doubt] that I have loved you. 10 Because you have kept the word of My endurance [My command to persevere], I will keep you [safe] from the hour of trial, that hour which is about to come on the whole [inhabited] world, to test those who live on the earth. 11 I am coming quickly. Hold tight what you have, so that no one will take your crown [by leading you to renounce the faith]. 12 He who overcomes [the world through believing that Jesus is the Son of God], I will make him a pillar in the temple of My God; he will most certainly never be put out of it, and I will write on him the name of My God, and the name of the city of My God, the new

Jerusalem, which descends out of heaven from My God, and My [own] new name. 13 He who has an ear, let him hear and heed what the Spirit says to the churches." - Jesus Christ to John The Apostle

Let this word given Revelation 3:7-13 that comes directly from Jesus to us soak into every ounce of your being! It is a main key for all that you are and all that you do in these times. It is who you are for the Kingdom. Thank You Jesus!

I want to be called a "pillar" by Jesus! (Like the common phrase "pillar of the community," this is a metaphor of great honor, but far more so! Pillars hold up a building, and are set to be a strong part of the temple the place where the Holy Spirit dwells!)

I want the Keys to the House of David! ("The key of David" refers to Isaiah 22:20-23, where the key of the house of David was given to Eliakim, who then had access to all the wealth of the king.)

I want to keep my crown! (My reward!)

How about you?

Let's all be like the Church of Philadelphia that Jesus says is the best in everything we do for the Kingdom! We KNOW from Jesus own words that's what pleases Him! The word of God keeps this clear for us on How we are expected to be with our "PR" and our message! Thank you Jesus for this!!

THE CHURCH IS NOT A PHYSICAL BUILDING IT'S US AS A PEOPLE - THE ECCLESIA - YOU ARE AN IMPORTANT PART OF IT!

The "Philadelphia" also in America is no mistake, I believe it is prophetic and that is what the body of Christ is called to BE like the church of Philadelphia in the USA! It's where our "covenant" was signed with our Founding Fathers and with God. This is why we need to keep praying that this Nation and all the Nations follow the church of Philadelphia's guidelines that Jesus made clear to us in Revelation 3: 7-13

Jesus gave us clear direction - we can do this together!

That is my hope and prayer for my ministry, my business, my Nation, the church and all of you!

If you are doing right by God, you are popular in Heaven and God will exalt you and your purpose in the earth for your faith, obedience and your heart to please Him at all costs.

YOU WILL BE REWARDED!

As I teach you here in this chapter, it would be irresponsible of me if I did not warn you about potential temptations that could spin you out and cause you to be out of the will of God or even pull you into sin. I do not want that for you. Here are some important things to remember:

- STAY TRUE TO THE WORD OF GOD NO MATTER WHAT!
- NO LUKEWARM POLITICAL CORRECTNESS!

- BEWARE OF PRIDEFULNESS!

- DO NOT BOW TO CULTURE ONLY TO GOD!

- STAY ROOTED IN THE KINGDOM!

- STAY CONNECTED TO THE HOLY SPIRIT!

- LOOK TO PLEASE GOD ABOVE ALL THINGS!

- GIVE GOD ALL THE GLORY!

What does God see in your heart right now? Even in your times of great success? Is He pleased with what He sees? Are you doing GOOD PR? Are you staying true to Jesus' words to the Church of Philadelphia as you get out into public with your mission, assignment and purpose?

I love when an unknown person of faith's message goes viral on social media - for the right reasons - and I love to see people on fire for God and standing for their faith no matter what "culture" says!! To me I would rather be in that church, or supporting that business, mission or organization because that leader is truly giving God all the glory.

I know you feel the same way because you tell me that's what you want to see in my ministry!

We see this happening in our society a lot now with Cake Bakers and Bridal Florists - they stand their ground for their faith in Jesus Christ and the Word of God and will not take an active part in something the word of God says is sinful with their business. Culture wants them to bend to their politically correct ways - and they get persecuted in the "press" for a while. But if those faithful ones stand for God and do not bow to 'man' - you see that God prospers them for their obedience, and then the righteous people become their loyal customers. Their reverence to the Kingdom of God is greatly rewarded. Then we see the support from other strong believers and their business does better than before! Because God promises us He will give us DOUBLE FOR OUR TROUBLE!

"Instead of your shame you will receive a double portion, and instead of disgrace you will rejoice in your inheritance. And so you will inherit a double portion in your land, and everlasting joy will be yours."
- Isaiah 61:7

When you set out to take your message, ministry, business or product "public" - ask the Holy Spirit to check you up and convict you early if He sees you begin to get "lukewarm". Then heed His correction. He is NEVER wrong and He sees the pitfalls, traps and temptations ahead and He will help you avoid them.

- STAY HOT! STAY FILLED WITH THE HOLY SPIRIT FIRE!

- STRAIGHTEN YOUR CROWN AND HOLD TIGHTLY TO THOSE KINGDOM KEYS!

- KEEP YOUR EYES ON JESUS!

Stay sweet to Jesus' taste! There will be a season where Jesus will test your waters and your fruit!

Yes! He checks on you and is constantly praying and interceding for you that you will not fall to the temptations of man and the flesh. He is your VINE and we must stay rooted and connected to Him to be fruitful with all we are called to do and in season.

What I want to make very clear here to all of you as we finalize this chapter on Kingdom Marketing and Public Relations is understanding that God works in SEASONS.

Everyone, no matter what you are called to do or where you are called to do it, will have a SEASON OF PROMOTION set in a certain window of time for you by God.

You saw this happen to me as I told you earlier in this chapter. I was in a DIVINE season of promotion and I almost missed my window of opportunity to bear great fruit on my broadcast! I was so self-absorbed, wallowing in my own problems and worries about everyone else (and trying to force God into "my season") that I was totally missing His season! If I had not been reprimanded by God that day to shake me into obedience and get my butt on that microphone for all of you. Boy, has it brought bushels of amazing fruit for all of us!

Are you focused on fulfilling and completing your assignment from the Lord to get the Victory He intends for you? Colossians 4:17 says: "Be faithful to complete the ministry you received from our lord Jesus and don't give in to your problems until they yield the victory God intends for you to have."

Where are you in this? Do you have questions about what you should be completing? Time to ask God if you don't know. You cannot get into a season of promotion if you are hyper focused on your own problems. I know this from experience!

So, how do you get these DIVINE seasons of promotion, advancement, breakthrough and prosperity? How do you properly discern them? When is it the proper time to do Kingdom Marketing and Public Relations for the most fruitful results that please God? Are there times where you don't have to wait and you can get a breakthrough or result immediately?

"For everything there is a season...." Ecclesiastes 3:1-8

The first thing I did after I read that scripture, was ask the Holy Spirit to teach me how to align with God's times and seasons. I really wanted to know how to do this! He is SO Faithful! This is what He taught me....

ALIGN WITH THE HEBREW SEASONS - ACCELERATE INTO NEW SEASONS - AND ACCESS THE IMMEDIATE

Follow The Hebrew Calendar...

This is God's calendar. I began to follow and learn everything I could. Things really started to make sense and I began to align my projects and assignments with His seasons. Especially my land prayer assignments. The more 'corporate' the assignment the more the Holy Spirit pressed me to do it according to the Hebrew Feast Days. For example The Holy Spirit gave me a land prayer assignment to pray in my region at the places that were "water' gateways. Jesus even came to me in a vision on the night of my Birthday on March 22, 2020 and expanded the assignment to "meet Him at the Shore" before Passover.

This was in the springtime of that year 2020 in the US calendar and the year 5780 in the Hebrew calendar. The year 5780 in Hebrew represented the Year of Pey or the Year of the Mouth - words decreed in this year were very significant to the future. At the time I had a lot of classes to teach to my mentoring students. I had taken on a big weekly class teaching and it was getting closer to the Passover season. I had kept putting off the land prayer assignment because I was not prepared for it.

One night while dozing off to sleep I felt a strong sense of urgency from the Holy Spirit to stop everything else I was doing and ONLY focus on these land prayer assignments and complete them before dusk on Passover that was just two weeks away. I had three different water locations to pray and research for the proper repentance and to take communion in the land. God had specific scriptures He wanted me to proclaim there too. The very next morning I informed my mentoring students I had to take two weeks off of class to complete the assignments in obedience to God during this Passover season.

I live in Virginia Beach, these water locations had a history of sinful actions that needed to be repented for and there was a lot of research I had to do to prepare before I went to the specific water locations. I had taken an oath before God last year to be a watchman on the wall for America and Israel. God takes that seriously and I had to as well. Some of my students were upset with me because I postponed class and some left me. Some were supportive and prayed for me and the assignment God had asked to be done.

Looking back I should have appointed someone to teach the classes, but I had not prepared that, and time was short. I will do that next time as I learned from the experience. You can be called to duty by God and He has strategic seasons, not when we feel like it or have the time.

The key here is   my obedience to God first and understanding God has important things He wants done according to His calendar. I explained to my students that my obedience should also teach them something about God for their own lives and assignments! But I could not worry if they were mad or offended.

I could not and would not offend or disobey God!! I had to complete the assignment before dusk at Passover, which was the 8th of April, 2020 by 6pm. So, I prepared in prayer, gathered my notes and went to each 'water" location the Holy Spirit assigned before the Passover time. My husband Michael drove me to each location, especially the shore of the Atlantic Ocean (Sandbridge Beach). I walked down to the beach to the ocean and it was powerful - Jesus met me there in the spirit when I prayed and took communion and poured it in the sand, I looked up and saw a huge bridge in the spirit from the shores of America all the way to the shores of Israel! I was pressed for time but we got it done and so worth it!

I will tell you the positive shifts I have seen in my region of Virginia Beach and along the east coast because this has been amazing! I began to see huge breakthroughs in my own life too because of this alignment with assignment. I teach this to my students who also are now following the Hebrew feasts and doing land prayer assignments.

God is not looking for how gifted you are to pray, He is looking for you to be available when He wants you to be for a greater reason that is way bigger than you at HIS timing! Particularly the feast days and the meaning of each month, we must pay attention to prophetically and their meaning. For example the Hebrew month of Elul (august-sept) is "The King Is In The Field" it's the season where Jesus inspects the harvest, your fruit (results/

products)! Is it ready? Is it pleasing to our King? Is He enjoying looking it over with you? Are you proud to show it to Him?

Elul is a "Season of Promotion" Where all your seeds are to come to a good and blessed harvest time for you! It's a perfect time to act on those seeds you planted and call them to Harvest, a time to expect great results and BIG opportunities!! You will have great favor and influence in your field of influence because the King is in your field with you! YES!! I love following the Hebrew Calendar and I have a better alignment with understanding God and His heart and His plans for my life better than ever before! Things go so much smoother for me and I can plan a lot easier, now!

I am still learning the Hebrew Calendar and Seasons. When you understand how all the Hebrew Feast Days align with Jesus birth and crucifixion you will be in a deeper understanding of the importance of God's calendar and what it means to you as a Christian, and how God perfectly and purposely aligned this with His Son Jesus Christ - Yeshua Messiah! It will change your life for the better I promise! Especially learning how and when to enter God's rest every week!

Study/Stand On The Parables and Miracles Of Jesus Christ.

Jesus taught about "seasons" and "having immediate access" "taking immediate action" in parables and through His Miracles. I had to go deep and ask for understanding and once I got it - I applied it to my own situations, things began to accelerate for me! What took years to do before it happened in months and weeks. Especially in finances. The biggest understanding came to me about multiplication and the kingdom being within me to have the authority to command things that are not as if they are all the time and call things by faith. Also that I was not to wait when it came to constantly speaking these certain things into my life. This had to be a weekly occurrence. I had to be in a constant 'multiplication and see by faith' mindset. That certain things are "already there" and we don't have to wait for a season for them.

This is how it works with Jesus. For example, Peter had to pay his taxes and he did not have the money to do it. He was stressed and went to Jesus about it. The money to pay the taxes was already in existence and could be accessed immediately. He just needed instruction from Jesus to go and get it.

This is explained in **Matthew 17:27; "Jesus said to him, "But so that we may not cause offense, go to the lake and throw out your line. Take the first fish you catch; open its mouth and you will find a four-drachma coin. Take it and give it to them for my tax and yours."**

I have used this miracle in my prayers many times and have called upon it to ask the Holy Spirit to show me exactly where the money is for something I need because I know by faith it's already there, I just need to access it now. Peter did not have to wait to access the money, as believers neither do we. It's already there! I have also done this where I have stood on the parable of the "good samaritan" (Luke 10:27) That Jesus has people that are ready to come into my path to show me favor and bless my needs financially just by the goodness of their heart. These are divine appointments that are to be called forth and they can happen within days. We had this happen with our horse Pongo. We did not have a barn for him and we had no money to build one. We prayed for the Lord to bring us a barn and for the good people God already had appointed who would help us with his care. Within a week, our neighbor offered her beautiful barn and pasture for Pongo to stay, and she generously pays for his care for many things. You see - Pongo's barn was already there. We did not have to wait for a special season. Our neighbor is thrilled because he is a blessing to her too and she was in need of a horse to be a companion to her donkeys.

These are already divinely aligned and ready for you to access if you ask, call forth and see by faith immediately. The Gospel of Mark emphasis is on the "immediate" and the "sudden" actions of Jesus and the sudden results of His actions. This is due to the obedience and full surrender of Jesus to the Father and allowing the full power of the Holy Spirit to work through Him.

The more you yield to the power of the Holy Spirit to work in you and through you the more you will see these "suddenlies" happen. Jesus was baptized by John the baptist, and "suddenly" the heavens opened and the voice of God was heard, "This is my beloved Son in whom I am well pleased." Then the woman with the issue of blood, totally yielded to the power of Jesus, she did not care if she had to crawl over glass or whatever she was gonna touch him, nothing would stop her. She was a totally sold out believer that she was going to receive if she could just touch that power He held she was ready to receive it.

This is the miracle that shows how the Holy Spirit will shoot like a sudden bolt of lightning when He encounters sold out faith. Jesus did not even see the woman! It was the faith and her full surrender that pulled that power from heaven through Jesus and into her, healing her instantly. Jesus even felt the power of the Holy Spirit shoot out of Him and into her. The Holy Spirit cannot help Himself when He encounters a fully yielded soul. It's like lightning to a rod and it's instant! No waiting. You get hit with the power! Sold out faith is always in season.

Pull From Our Own Experiences & Ask For Wisdom:

The Holy Spirit then told me to pull from my own experiences of timing and seasons in my life and also professionally. Use the lessons that I have been taught through the experiences God brought me through. For example Jesus taught Peter on timing and seasons through his experience as a fisherman. Jesus also taught the people through their experiences as farmers, vine dressers, and shepherds. I was told by the Holy Spirit to write this book, Faith At Full Speed in accordance to the seasons and lessons I learned in my 30 years in motorsports and connect that with God's word for you all to run your race strong and be victorious.

One of the things I taught you was your season of "Garage Time" that aligns with God's Season of Preparation. There are other things that the Holy Spirit will prompt you in your professional life and give you wisdom in timing for each day or each situation according to your fiend of influence and how to get the best result - this is wisdom that we all must pray for and apply. Such as, I learned over the years don't send out a press release to the media on Monday morning but wait until Tuesday morning. This is because they get too many emails from the weekend and inboxes are packed on Monday morning, you will get seen better if you wait until Tuesday!

The Bible tells us to seek and use this wisdom in our everyday lives in Psalm 90:12 says: "Teach us to number our days, that we may gain a heart of wisdom." This is what I ask the Holy Spirit every day!

- GOD DOES NOT ALIGN WITH OUR SEASONS, WE MUST LEARN TO ALIGN WITH HIS

- OUR OBEDIENCE AND OUR FAITH CAUSES ACCELERATION AND ACCESS TO MIRACLES AND SUDDENLIES

I know this is a lot to learn. I went through the school of 'hard knocks' on these things so I could gain understanding to be able to share this all with you. Looking back I am so glad I had those "in the trenches' experiences myself. Now I am able to help people bypass a lot of that and get straight to this understanding.

I worked in the "trenches" for years in motorsports in a similar way, gaining this experience and wisdom so I could teach my racers how to do this. It's important we each get experience with these things so we can pass it onto others and generations to come.

I have heard these complaints over the years from my racers: "Gee, Annamarie can't I just hire out a Public Relations and Marketing person to get this all done for me and not worry about it? I just wanna race and have fun."

Ha! If I had a dollar for every time I heard that it would add up to the millions.

This is a race to victory, yes. But to be a Champion and set apart from the rest, you should have more than one victory notch in your belt! This comes with wanting to always be better, faster, more knowledgeable and more effective than the average guy or gal that's just plugging away at life!

God's timing in your life comes with constantly seeking knowledge of His Kingdom, being hungry for more of Him. Going to Your Father wanting to know Him, really really know Him. The more You know Him the more you want to share about Him! Your faith grows exponentially and Your eyes of understanding of the mysteries of God are opened.

Kingdom Marketing and Public Relations is having insider knowledge of the Kingdom! Having that edge! Just like you would with any field of influence that you want to excel in! People begin to flock to you for that knowledge and want you to share and teach them too. It's the way God set it up!

Jesus made it clear: *"But seek ye first the kingdom of God, and his righteousness; and all these things shall be added unto you." - Matthew 6:33*

Jesus said *all* these things will be added.

ALL MEANS ALL. IT MEANS ALL GOOD THINGS THAT YOU DESIRE AND ALL THE KINGDOM OF GOD HAS AVAILABLE TO YOU!

Pursue God and all things of His Kingdom through Jesus Christ, then everything you need will come! Know that it will. Do not give up! Righteousness comes to those who put their hope and trust in Jesus Christ. The Holy Spirit is the helper in your pursuit and confirms all things! Don't stop pursuing!

When I think of the word 'pursue' - I think of the days I had to be that unrelentless PR girl chasing down the media to get my driver and team and sponsor an interview. My job depended on it. I had to land those interviews to give value to my sponsor and make sure they got exposure for their investment with the team. If I did not get the maximum media time I could be out of a job! I can remember running up and down pit road with my white tennis shoes and my notepad and sharpie chasing down the TV guys and telling them I had a good scoop to give them on my team.

I would have to report back to my sponsors every Monday to see if they watched the race and if they were pleased with the coverage they got. It was constant pursuit of media all week too, working the phones back in the office, faxing press releases, trying to come up with creative ways to get a feature story in the news!

One time I came up with the idea to set up a workout class for my team in the shop, set up mats and everything! Had these personal trainers come in and I had the Charlotte newspaper come and do a feature on the "fitness" program of my team. Some of those great big gasman guys were not too happy with me haha! I needed something new, fresh that would get attention!

That was the Coca Cola 600 week at Charlotte Motor Speedway, and it was tough for a team to get press/media attention if you were not running up front for points at the time. Our team was getting better each week but not enough to get the attention of the 'sports" reporters. My newspaper story on our team fitness program debuted in The Charlotte Observer and made up an entire section of the " lifestyle" of the Sunday paper the day of the race! It was all over the media center at the speedway and every media outlet even the TV 'sports' guys picked up on it! It was a huge hit and something unusual at the time that race teams would train for fitness! Now all the teams do it!

The story took off and wow all the other PR people were coming up to me congratulating me! I had no idea this would happen! I was just doing my job and doing it with passion and vigor and pursuing until I got the result I wanted for my people.

My sponsors were thrilled with the media exposure and the personal trainers gave our team a free gym membership for all the crew members! We also attracted a new sponsor who saw the article and wanted to partner with us to promote their products.

This brought me job security and then other teams started giving me offers to come work for them. I earned a lot of respect in the media and among my peers in the sport.

All because I pursued. Relentlessly. It paid off big time!

Be a trailblazer for God! Don't be afraid to do something new and unique in public! God made you to be bold and courageous! Remember it's He who goes ahead of you! He wants to see His Sons and Daughters shine!

TIME FOR YOU TO PURSUE RELENTLESSLY UNTIL YOU SEE A BREAKTHROUGH - NEVER EVER GIVE UP!

Father God is directly accessible through Jesus Christ. Literally when you take Your seat in Christ, that was given to you in Ephesians Chapter 2, you are sitting right next to the Father in Christ Jesus. You can turn your head to the left and talk to Him, ask of Him, love on Him and worship His goodness.

Because of Jesus, Heaven knows you, recognizes you, and is open to you!

Kingdom Marketing and Public Relations is going the extra mile to know Jesus and represent Jesus in all places and areas of your life and in all relationships.

You must learn these things of the Kingdom of God yourself, lay the groundwork, show God you are faithful with little and He will give you more!   Once you have learned to do this yourself, He will advance you and you can hire a team and even a personal assistant - but God expects you as a leader to get them and all your team on this timeline and understanding. If you don't you are going to have all kinds of problems and your fruit will not be sweet or abundant.   Why?   Because you have to keep stopping to fix everyone's mistakes and bad timing issues!

Start aligning your household, family, ministry and business with the Kingdom Calendar.   The Hebrew Calendar, This will transform your life and family, team and employees for the better.   You all learn how to align with God's seasons and get to enter His rest together!   It is awesome!

I will tell you one of the BEST things I've ever done in my life and for my family was to take a Shabbat every Friday night and into Saturday. It's wonderful and you learn how to enter God's rest weekly this way. As Americans we are working 24-7 and we get burned out and worn out.   God rested on the 7th day not because He was tired! God does not get tired! He rested so we could rest with Him and in Him! It's a precious time with God and if you miss some work - don't worry God will redeem the time, He always does for me! Get your family involved in Shabbat, make the bread, get something yummy on the table, sing songs, light candles, thank God for a good week. Invite your team and employees! I look forward to Shabbat every week. Your family will begin too! You get refreshed and blessed for the week ahead! I love Shabbat - it starts on Friday night at sundown and goes until Saturday night at sundown.

God has designed His week, His calendar, and His seasons to help us align with Him and have an abundant life! I LOVE that God works in seasons because I was trained up this way through my racing career! I get it! I want you to get it!

In all my years working in motorsports, particularly NASCAR we operated in "seasons".

First, Seasons of Preparation (garage time). This is when we did our research, built and re-engineered the race cars, assembled and hired new team members, built our sponsor proposals (packages) and met with potential sponsors.

Next, the Seasons of Sowing. Sending out stories and press releases to the media, going to trade shows and car show events, unveiling sneak peek of the new race car. Handing out promotional materials and freebies to the fans. Advertising new sponsors. Doing charity work.

Next comes the Season of Action. Race season. Actively racing each week at different tracks. Earning points towards a championship, working to get better and faster each week, and going for wins!

Then Seasons of Promotion. Getting recognized by the media and the industry for your achievements in the season of action or race season. New and bigger opportunities being offered to you, bigger sponsors, bigger teams, more money, qualifying for the bigger, higher paying races.

The next and most fun Seasons of Celebration. Awards banquets, red carpets. Gathering in fancy ballrooms with stages lined with sparkling championship trophies and big cardboard checks with million dollar amounts! Instead of fire suits and team shirts, we donned tuxedos, and fancy gowns. Place cards on white cloth tables set with special goody bags, gift giving and finely made momentos at each seat. Prime rib dinners, champagne toasts, podium speeches and thanking your team and sponsors. This all reflected in the public via network TV. Then the TV cameras stopped rolling and the dancing began! I loved the dancing part! I had as much fun at the big fancy NASCAR banquets with the prime rib just as much as I did at the short track banquets serving fried chicken and BBQ! Great memories of spending time with wonderful people!

Finally, the Season of Rest. Spent usually away from the public, a time to take a short vacation during the 'off season' for a time of refreshing before starting all over again, and come back stronger and better for the next year of racing. Some NASCAR drivers and teams shared their season of rest with their fans, doing a "Fan Cruise" on a big cruise ship. Those were always a big hit because the fans got up close and personal to the driver, to encourage them and also for the driver to get good feedback on what the fans wanted. Keeping the communication real, fresh and making them feel appreciated on both sides. The drivers that did this had a tremendously loyal fan base that grew into more sponsorships for them. Everyone loved it and it rejuvenated the team and driver and their families to remind them why they do what they do - they felt blessed and appreciated as they gave appreciation during the time of rest. This was enjoying and sharing the fruits of all the seasons leading up to the season of rest!

UNDERSTANDING SEASONS AS THE HOLY SPIRIT WORKS WITH YOU:

Seasons of Preparation:

- Praying and Fasting
- Journaling - Learning God's Voice
- Prayer Closet Time
- Asking - Listening
- "Garage Time" (refer to earlier chapter)
- Packaging Your Seeds (ready to be sown)
- Researching the Good Land (fertile soil/ relationships/ministries and areas of influence to sow into)

Seasons Of Sowing:

- Unveiling The Seed (you, your message, product etc public announcements)
- Seeds of Giving - (using your gifts on people for free)
- Seeds of Future Promotion (asking people to tell other people about you that they are connected to)
- Seeds of Creativity - (make one product, art piece, or invention and showcase it in public)
- Seeds of Testimony - (keynote speaking, posting videos, writing blogs and articles)
- Seeds Of Future Seasons (what's the best way to accelerate a season and move into a new and better one? Sow into the future season!)

Seasons Of Action:

- Putting your feet to your faith
- Sending the Holy Spirit as your PR man
- Weeding and Pruning (cutting off what is not bearing fruit in relationships and old habits)
- Building new relationships (sent by Holy Spirit)
- Holding yourself accountable to finish

Seasons of Promotion:

- Usually happen 'suddenly'
- God opens a window of opportunity that must be grabbed quickly and decisively
- Take it and show up every day faithfully and you will be promoted again
- You will see God's stamp of favor all over it

Seasons of Celebration:

- Hebrew Feast Days (God's seasons or celebrating)
- Celebrating God's goodness ahead of your breakthrough - Psalm 100
- Celebrating Passover, Resurrection Sunday and all the way to Pentecost (Glory Season) Powerful moves of the Holy Spirit happen in this season
- Invite Jesus and the Holy Spirit to your table and have a special meal and dessert and celebrate a breakthrough together

- I have seasons of celebration when I get a victory and I bring others into that to encourage them for their own victories
- Celebrate by GIVING more after a breakthrough
- Give God a big offering in Celebration - I look at it as a gift of gladness for His goodness (First Fruits offering - The first paycheck of a new job, the first fee from a new client or sale, etc)
- Harvests seasons are seasons of celebration, meaning if your "seeds" from a season of sowing come to fruition it's a season of celebration

Seasons of Rest:

- Entering God's rest each week with Shabbat - giving God glory and thanks for all He has done that week
- Entering the "Good Land" and resting there. This is spiritual and physical rest (God gave His people of Israel rest when they reached the Promised Land in Joshua 21:44).
- Relying only on faith and trust in God that your prayers are already answered
- Laying your issues and needs on the altar of God and then going and enjoying life's blessings
- When you feel depleted and need a re-filling of the Holy Spirit - a time of refreshment
- Take these seasons to worship and praise and draw near to God - He will draw near to you
- Taking a rest from pursuing the breakthrough in the natural and giving it to God in the supernatural
- Ask the Holy Spirit to prompt you into this season - He will usually do this when you are more focused on the 'busy' and not bearing fruit!

- I take season's of rest when I see the fruit of the spirit in my ministry needs to be restocked - distributed better - and I know it's time to seek and pursue God and His presence in a time of rest and refreshing to come back stronger. I usually take a full month off the ministry to do this. It is amazing and worth it.
- Your seasons of rest can produce great seasons of promotion because you hear God better
- Get time to sit back and pray for the bigger picture instead of hyper focusing on all the small issues
- Seasons of rest can become a season of "restoration" It's a good time to focus on 'dreams and visions' speaking them forth and re-powering up in faith when you feel your faith is struggling or you feel like you need a restoration of lost time.

Prayer/Decree: *"In the all -powerful name of Jesus Christ I declare a total restoration for all the years that feel like they were not fruitful or when I made bad choices. I turn to My Father God, my Provider, I ask You Father God to restore all lost or wasted time to me as if I had never wasted it or lost it in Jesus name! I ask that all the time the enemy stole from me be fully restored with Your double portion blessing Oh God! For ashes I shall have beauty according to your Word in Jesus name! Father God You promise to restore the years the devour has eaten and then pour out your spirit upon me and my household! I receive and rest in You oh Lord God and your divine power of restoration! Restore me more than before oh Lord God and align me with Your divine seasons for abundance, promotion, increase and fruitfulness my life in Jesus Name!"*

DOUBLE PORTION COMES IN TIME OF RESTORATION! (JOB 42:10) DECLARE THIS IS YOUR SEASON OF RESTORATION AND DOUBLE PORTION BLESSING!

"All of my life, in every season, You are still God!" - Joni Lamb

This is why God promoted Joseph, son of Jacob to be the second most powerful man in Egypt, and this is why He wants to promote you! Every Christian on Earth should be a walking advertisement for the goodness of God! You represent the Glory of The Kingdom in every area of influence you have been placed. God wants His people on social media, television and in government!

Joseph's "Season of Promotion" happened suddenly. This can very well happen for you as well when you continue to use your gifts faithfully, even in the worst and most adverse conditions, ask people to share their testimony to how their encounter with you blessed them, and always give God Glory for it.

Joseph did Kingdom Marketing and Public Relations even in a prison! He interpreted dreams for two of Pharaoh's employees, a Baker and Cupbearer who were in prison at the time with Joseph.

Dream interpretation was Joseph's gift and He was anointed by God to do this. After Interpreting their dreams, Joseph went further and planted "a seed of promotion into the future" and asked them to remember him and his gift to Pharaoh. A few years later that "seed of promotion" came to fruition for Joseph.

"Only remember me, when it is well with you, and please do me the kindness to mention me to Pharaoh, and so get me out of this house." - Genesis 40:10

Two years later, Joseph was remembered when Pharaoh had a dream and needed someone to interpret it. We know God set this up as a divine appointment for Joseph because of His faithfulness - and that there was already a seed there that had been planted in the Cup Bearer by Joseph that needed to come to Harvest.

God will promote you when you faithfully use your gifts in every situation no matter how bad it is and give Him glory!

We must use our gifts faithfully and keep planting seeds into future seasons. God will faithfully bring them to harvest and prosper you into a new season, greater and bigger than before.

Joseph went from the Prison to the Palace 'suddenly'! Because Joseph was faithful and was not afraid to ask those that were blessed by what God did through his gift if they would remember the experience and pass it along to a person of influence. He knew God had a promise for him.

We have to be bold and we cannot be afraid to promote by asking people to share and spread the news of what you do and why you do it, and how others can be blessed by it too!

GET USED TO TELLING PEOPLE TO SHARE WHAT YOU ARE PUTTING OUT THERE!

Don't be afraid to do some things for free using your gifts in the beginning! Or giving away free samples of your product. These are seeds of promotion! Make sure you tell people to spread the word about you! If you don't tell them to remember you and share their experience with you that seed will never multiply! Speak up and speak over your seed! Boldly!

I tell my listeners who follow my weekly free teaching broadcasts on Youtube that if they don't have a financial seed to sow into my ministry, then share the broadcast on their social media pages! I consider the sharing of my posts a seed into my ministry and I speak a blessing over them.

I never ever forget to tell people to share the broadcast and my posts on social media, or forward my emails. Don't be shy about this for your own stuff! God uses this to get your content, your product, your name in front of influential people.

As a matter of fact, share this book with a friend! YES! See what I just did there, I planted a seed of future promotion.

I never miss an opportunity to sow a seed of promotion - now YOU get in this habit - it could be the seed that causes you to go from the prison to the palace in one day!

For years I told my race car drivers: "Get yourself out there in a big way and start GIVING - and be in expectation to RECEIVE!" When you give you are sowing seeds of your character. This gets seen by the RIGHT people, who want to align themselves with people like you. What if that person who is a multi-millionaire and wants to invest in a person like you never finds you because you stayed in your prayer closet forever? There is a season for prayer closets and there is a season for sowing of your seeds into the good land of giving!

"Give, and it shall be given unto you; good measure, pressed down, and shaken together, and running over, shall men give into your bosom.   For with the same measure that ye mete (give) withal it shall be measured (back) to you again." - Luke 6:38

You might be thinking; "Annamarie, I have to be able to make money to pay my bills and get food on the table. How can I do that if I keep giving what I have away for free?"

The time for sales will come if you have first sown some seeds in giving.   You cannot reap anything unless you have sowed somewhere before that!   Do not expect a harvest if you never sow seeds.   Focus on planting and harvest and get your mind off the bills!   This is the KINGDOM mentality!

You start by sowing seeds strategically - into good land and good areas where the people would benefit the most from what you have to offer.

In marketing jargon, we call that your "target market."

Jesus calls it throwing your net on the right side of the boat!

Cast your net!   Jesus will show you where!   He already knows where all your customers are!   You must go to where these people congregate.

This is marketing like Jesus! We are called to BUILD the Kingdom here on earth. Kingdom is a divine government, being led by our King Jesus. In a company sense, Jesus would be our President and CEO. Holy Spirit would be our CMO (Chief Marketing Officer) and our Senior Partner. God is the OWNER who created it all!

Jesus showed me who and where my target market is! He will show you!

Believers in Jesus Christ who have a desire to be used by God powerfully for the Kingdom, and are looking for clarity, guidance and strategies. Most are called to ministry, media or business and want to do these simultaneously. The teachings, products and services that I offer will be geared towards that individual and individuals.

How do you realize and know your target market for the Kingdom and for your Purpose?

When you know what your message or product is and who it helps the most - that becomes your target market.

Ask Jesus to reveal this to you! When Jesus shows you where your customers and followers are - these are like your fish and at the same time as He reveals where your fish are He is revealing His Glory to you! It gives Him great joy to show you where the "fish" are. This is exactly what Luke Chapter 5 reveals and again in John Chapter 21:6. Jesus did this miracle twice for His disciples, The first time to reveal He was worthy of following and the second time to reveal He was alive and glorified! This is to be revealed to you by trusting Jesus and who He is as the leader of your ministry and business, but He will confirm it with His GLORY that there is no mistaking your success is of the Kingdom, and not of your own labors. Literally both times of the fish miracles that was a financial miracle to sell the fish to fund their ministries and their families!

Ministry can align with the marketplace and one supports the other through trusting Jesus Christ for KINGDOM multiplication in both areas. When your marketplace is thriving it sows into your ministry and both thrive.

There is no striving in the Kingdom, only operating in glory. (I will teach you more on the glory in the next chapter.)

Your Message, Experience and Testimony Attracts The Fish! Your followers, your clients, your customers, your tribe.

Do you have a testimony that is your message that will help a certain group of people? Do you have an experience that you went through that you can teach others how to get through? Has God taken you down a path to teach you something unusual that will benefit others in a big way?

My first book, *Pongo The Rescue Horse*, God had me write in only three months in 2018. It flowed out of me very easily. This book and it's content was completely different from my target market! It was geared toward kids and teens who had been bullied or abused. But what I found out from the experience of self- publishing my first simple book, is that you need to have an established Publishing Company behind your book to be able to get into bookstores! Anyone can self-publish and get on amazon. But to get your book into a book retailer or book store you cannot be self-published, your book must be published by a publishing company with a marketing department! I am a marketer. That is my background. After consulting with the Holy Spirit, I launched a business as Publishing and MultiMedia Marketing and Consulting Company, Faith Lane Media, LLC

This company, Faith Lane Media, LLC markets to target markets for Christian Authors and Content Creators in the Media Mountain. These are individuals who are ready to create, publish and promote books, videos, products and teachings for the Kingdom of God! I also offer consulting services to go with that! If God did not have me do my first little book about that little horse, I would not have known this or been prepared for the next books He had planned for me in target markets and for the world! This is to flow on to hundreds of those He is sending to me to help their publishing and media goals!

It's Ministry - Media - Education - Marketplace Mountains of Influence and I am so excited to help these wonderful people God sends me to assist and guide them into publishing their books, getting them on youtube, coaching them for video, blogging and more! YAY GOD!
God already wanted me to start that Multi-Media Publishing company - but I had to have the experience of writing a simple and quick book, going through the issues of self-publishing and getting through it myself. This was important all before I could serve the people God had waiting for me in my target area. These folks will save time and be accelerated now because of what I learned. God knows what He's doing even if to you at the time it did not make sense. God does this for you too! Don't doubt that project you have been called to do right now that you think does not make any sense toward your ultimate goal - if you ask the Holy Spirit to get you to your goal, He begins to put the things in place to do it!

Look back for just a second, think of something that God put you through that did not make sense to you at the time, but led you to exactly what you needed to get to the next step! I know you will think of something!

God also sends people to help you at first, you may think it doesn't fit your goals. Don't write them off! If God sent them they will be devoted to your message! That's how you can tell they are from God. They don't fawn all over you, instead they tell you that your message inspires them. Trust me on this! Do not fall for 'personal flattery', instead discern the right people by how your message impacts them. Then they will want to bring their gifts to the table to help your overall mission.

Did it make sense for Jesus to call Matthew the tax collector as a disciple? I thought all He needed were 'fishers' of men' (fishermen like Peter and Andrew)? Well, to get the fishers of men, Jesus also needed disciples who were also detail oriented and could write the Gospel so the Gospel could be a "net" to catch men and women for Jesus for centuries to come! Matthew had that attention to detail and gifting of keeping good records. I refer to the book of Matthew in my teachings more than any other Gospel because of the detail of the teachings.

The people that will be attracted to you as a follower because of the Holy Spirit connecting and bringing you employees, customers, will be the ones who resonate with your message. They will also resonate with your passion and who you are providing solutions for. It will hit them in their spirit! They will have that common passion and care for the same group of people.

Think back for just a minute and recall an experience or a relationship that you almost wrote off as meaningless that turned out to be a game changer and propelled you to greater things. We all have these!

God already has these people and experiences aligned for you, ready for you to receive them!

You might be asking: "How do I find these people? Where does God already have them waiting for me?"

Network - "Net" Work

Jesus also did specifically choose "fishermen" disciples for a reason! They knew how to "Net" work. Ha! Get it? The Holy Spirit just gave me that cute quip for you all.

Listen my friend. You have to get out there and sow seeds and cast your net and don't be afraid. God has people all aligned for your Network. Jesus knew where the fish were for Simon Peter in the miracle of the fish - Jesus told them exactly where to cast their nets. They hauled in so much fish that their nets overflowed and they had to call for more boats to help them get all the fish in! Jesus also knows where your paying customers are!

This is called Networking. Going to the places where people come together in groups. You cannot be afraid of groups.

Many of us have been hurt in group situations - even in church! This wound from past group issues cannot stop you from networking in new places. Jesus will bring you to your ideal tribe!

One of the things I help many of my students overcome is the hurt they have from being in the wrong groups or from being hurt in church, and helping them overcome and get into "good" groups, and good churches.

If they are not able to overcome the hurt of being in groups, they will not prosper and grow. They must get healed of this.

Maybe you have been hurt by a group? Forgive them, put the hurt, pain and any offense or bitterness on the Cross of Jesus Christ. Let it go so you can flow and grow!

When all the ingredients you need are in the right group and you have the support and guidance there you will flourish. You cannot give up groups! You have to keep seeking the Holy Spirit to align you with the right tribe! Look for those who unite under the banner of Jesus Christ.

I love this quote I saw on social media by Tim Tebow:
"I want you to be successful, but my hope and prayer is that you turn that success into significance. There is a world that needs you. There are people that need you. There are people in your family that need you. They need your talents, your gifts, and they need to hear the reason for your hope. When you live for Jesus, and you love people, I believe you will have a life of significance." - Tim Tebow, Former NFL Quarterback

When I read that I felt so moved in my spirit for how God used a man like Tim Tebow who had been shoved out of a "group" (professional football) for boldly stating his faith in Jesus Christ. He could be hurt and bitter for it and not want to be involved in any more groups for the way they treated him. But Tebow never compromised his faith and gladly went on to do greater things for the Kingdom, including starting more "groups" and organizations that have helped many people, especially those with special needs and children. He also went on to play other professional sports for those who appreciated his gift as an athlete. He is living a life of significance by giving others significance.

God created us to love Him and each other - we complete the body of Christ - the church, Jesus is the head - we are the body. We complete God's family.

"For as we have many members in one body, but all the members do not have the same function, so we, being many, are one body in Christ, and individually members of one another." - Romans 12:4-5

God wants His people in Tribes. Tribes are like small nations. They all have different "flavors" or "specialties" in a way. God loved His people of Israel and he called them a 'peculiar people". He loved the things that made them different from the rest. He created them that way, as we are as Americans, Canadians, Mexicans, etc. Don't you love that about your own children, or even your own family?

My Mom used to laugh about how me and my two sisters were so different from each other and we still are. I am the oldest, then my sister Leesa and my youngest sister Marcia. These differences were funny when we were kids, sometimes we drove each other nuts, and tried my Mom's patience! But now that we are grown women we rely on each other for these differences. We go to each other to support each other's uniqueness, strengths and gifts. In my Mother's life now, she is a senior and needs our help with things - each daughter is there for her needs in different ways, yet we are "one" family. The things that made us each unique as daughters that once had my mom running to three different places to shop for clothes and hobbies that kept her hopping are now the wisdom, skills and giftings that bless her from her three very different daughters now in her later years!

Don't try to make your kids like little cookie cutters! Encourage them to find their unique gifts and ideal tribe early. (as long as it's appropriate). If you see the fruit of the Holy Spirit happening in their lives because of their unique interests, and the groups they join - then God will multiply that in them for the future, that's what He did in you!

What was your 'tribe' when you were a kid?

For example, my daughter is an only child. She has a gift for art and music that was not something I was ever good at or interested in. She picked up a ukulele she signed out from the High School music room and started teaching herself how to play it. She found a great group of kids in school that had this same interest and had an after school "Ukulele Club" - she loved and thrived in it. It built her confidence and she made new friends who were very kind to her and made her feel accepted. Would I have rather seen her do cheerleading and sports the things that most people think shape a kid's confidence? I was a cheerleader, and just because I was does not mean that's what God created her to be. Cheerleading was not her tribe. Ukulele Club was.

Cheerleading was my tribe - and I was drawn to it because now God is using that for you all - I am a spiritual cheerleader for you NOW my peeps! I prophetically see that the tribes you loved and grew from as a kid, are exponentially blessing you for your gifts and talents for the Kingdom of God today!

Just as I see prophetically that God will use my daughter Landry's musical talent and love for musical people for the Kingdom and for Jesus! I speak that over her!

BE UNIQUE FOR JESUS AND LOOK FOR THOSE GROUPS THAT CELEBRATE YOUR UNIQUENESS AND YOUR SPECIAL GIFTS - FORGIVE THE ONES THAT DON'T. THE HOLY SPIRIT HAS THE RIGHT TRIBE WAITING FOR YOU

Did you know you are "peculiar"? Meaning distinctive, different, individualistic, distinguishing, special, set apart, unique, notable and remarkable!

GOD CALLS US A PECULIAR PEOPLE - THAT HE WILL GIVE PECULIAR GIFTS TO AND WE WILL RECEIVE PECULIAR TREASURES!

- Exodus 19:5 - "Now therefore, if ye will obey my voice indeed, and keep my covenant, then ye shall be a peculiar treasure unto me above all people: for all the earth is mine."

- Deuteronomy 7:6 - "For a holy people art thou to Jehovah thy God; on thee hath Jehovah thy God fixed, to be to Him for a peculiar people, out of all the peoples who are on the face of the ground."

- Deuteronomy 14:2 - "For thou art an holy people unto the LORD thy God, and the LORD hath chosen thee to be a peculiar people unto himself, above all the nations that are upon the earth."

- Deuteronomy 26:18 - "And the LORD hath avouched thee this day to be his peculiar people, as he hath promised thee, and that thou shouldest keep all his commandments"

- 1 Chronicles 29:3 - "And again, because of my delighting in the house of my God, the substance I have -- a peculiar treasure of gold and silver -- I have given for the house of my God, even over and above all I have prepared for the house of the sanctuary."
- Psalm 135:4 - "For the LORD hath chosen Jacob (me) unto himself, and Israel (me) for his peculiar treasure."

- Titus 2:14 - "Who gave himself for us, that he might redeem us from all iniquity, and purify unto himself a peculiar people, zealous of good works."

- 1 Pet 2:9 - "But ye (we) are a chosen generation, a royal priesthood, an holy nation, a peculiar people; that ye should shew forth the praises of him who hath called you out of darkness into his marvellous light.

You think God loves what makes us each different? As individuals, as groups and as Nations? YES!

This was intentional of His creation!

GOD WANTS HIS PEOPLE TO STAND OUT! NOT HIDE IN THE FOUR WALLS OF THE CHURCH - LET YOUR HIDING PLACE BE UNDER THE WINGS OF GOD EVERYWHERE YOU GO! HE WANTS YOU TO FLY AND SOAR LIKE AN EAGLE!

We are to join with each other and become Victorious for the Kingdom and the Glory of God on earth as it is in Heaven!

WE ARE SPECIAL AND WE ARE CHOSEN! WE ARE TO BE THIS IN ALL PUBLIC SPHERES OF INFLUENCE

We are each a 'peculiar people' that God so lovingly calls us in the Bible. God set up the Tribes of Israel to use their peculiarities to cross-benefit each other. King David was of the Tribe of Judah, but he consulted the Sons of Issachar (tribe of Issachar) on the timing of a season. The Issachar tribe has the gifting of knowing the times and season for when King David should go to war and when he would have the greatest victories - he combined different men from different tribes and made groups for their certain strengths in his army. This is like running a successful company. Their skills were honed in their specific tribe to eventually come together with the other unique giftings from the other tribes to complete one mighty army with David having the wisdom of God to lead this army and benefit from these different tribes with different gifts that complete the fullness of one powerful army. (1 Chronicles 12).

When I read the Chapter in 1 Chronicles 12, I realized that God had made each tribe special with their unique skills and giftings to fulfill that very moment when He needed them to complete what He wanted TO BUILD FOR HIS KINGDOM through King David in Israel. God will bring the right people around you with the right skillset to complete what He has called you to build for HIS Glory and to advance HIS purposes. He has these people all lined up, ready and prepared years in advance for your certain seasons! David needed these different tribes to come together to complete the perfect Army in the season he needed them. It's like in America we have different ranks and special forces with special skill sets that have had hours of training in their own groups to come together in times of battle to complete what it's needed for a huge Victory.

God's Angelic Army in Heaven is set up the same way. The angels have to work together and have different skill sets. Gabriel who is a Messenger Angel had to call upon Michael, who is a Warrior Angel to help Him fight through the evil principalities to be able to get to Daniel to answer his prayer! (Daniel 10:13).

God set up His people to work together. This is how the Kingdom grows on earth. When you work with the right tribe you will be operating on earth as it is in heaven. God has these people assigned to you, and you to them, sometimes for years, sometimes for just a season.

God will train you in a unique group for a while then release you when you are ready into bigger groups when you learn how to receive and give 'significance". God may also be training you up as a leader in learning how to lead many different groups of people and how to get them working together for a greater good 'AS ONE' in an area of influence, or for an entire nation! These tribes of God make the enemy nervous! Where we go one with God, we go all!

For where you are right now, understand the groups you join to network with for your current goals and help others in the group with theirs. When you can help each other with your current goals, your future goals are expedited!

This is what you look for in a group: Do they share the same ideals, are they in your region or area of influence that you want to prosper in? Are they producing, GOOD FRUIT and the fruit of the Holy Spirit? Jesus said we will know people by their "fruit". This includes prophets and teachers, business people, people of certain interests like music and art and neighbors. All groups, not just in ministry. Is the fruit fresh and fills you up with goodness and nutrition for your life and your spirit, does it cause you to grow and multiply in a good way?

If they want to see me have good fruit and give me a chance to show that I can produce good fruit for myself and others, that's the group for me!

I found this when I was working in Motorsports. I joined Motor Racing Outreach Ladies Bible Club because it was my ideal tribe, Christian women who were involved in NASCAR racing who supported, prayed and encouraged each other on the road and at home. It could be a stressful life in NASCAR, sometimes dangerous. We needed each other who understood all these things that the sport brought good and bad, and we were all passionate about the love of Jesus! Many times that group pulled me through some tough spots in my life and career. I connected with women who also were able to open up big doors of opportunities for me too! I remember the first graphic design project I ever did was for an invitation to the Motor Racing Ladies January Caution event. They believed I could do it. It pushed me to learn Photoshop on my computer. They were so pleased with my invitation design that I did for free, some of them started hiring me to do paid designs for them and their racing teams! It led me to build a graphic design service as part of my motorsports consulting firm.

I grew that design service exponentially and I did many major graphic design projects in NASCAR that supplemented my income when I had to be off the road when I got married and was raising my baby. I still use Photoshop today to do my own designs and - yes I designed the cover of this book in Photoshop myself! This all came to pass because I was in the correct tribe so many years ago!

It's like making a cake. You can have all the ingredients sitting on your counter, but if you don't have the correct recipe, and a group to encourage you and teach that you can bake - your cake is not going to come out very good. You need to take and bake so you can shake and bake!

I remember when I realized I was in the wrong group. Years ago, I had joined a local bible study in my area. I had just bought a new Bible and I wanted to learn! The group met once a week in the morning. All the ladies were older than me. There was always delicious coffee and pastries there every time I went. I had my Bible and bought a pretty cover for it, and was excited to learn. I would get there and they would all be talking about things that older people talk about. I felt out of place, but I wanted to learn the bible so badly. The teacher put on a video for us to watch each week and we had to buy a book that went with the video. We did prayer requests and then everyone went and got coffee and pastries.

The entire time I was there all I could think about was the coffee and pastries at the end of the class. I was not getting anything from the 'video' teaching or the teachers or the women there. I did not even crack open my Bible, it was all from the book we had to buy for class. I stuffed myself with coffee and pastries at each class but still left 'hungry'...

Why? Because there was NO FRUIT of the Spirit coming from that class or group. It was not my tribe and not where God wanted me to get fed spiritually.

Joining groups and finding your tribe brings you around people who have the experience and knowledge you need, the connections, the resources and sometimes the finances. But if you are not being fed spiritually, and getting Holy Spirit strategies that you can apply - that God needs you to have at that time and season - you will go away empty.

GROUPS: GO FOR THE *RECIPES* AND NOT THE CAKE!

The good groups have the 'recipes' experience and sometimes a very special ingredient or key that you did not know you needed that completes your mission, assignment or anything you have been trying to fulfill for your goals and for the Kingdom. You will walk away with real tangible changes, and strategies that you can take with you and will see manifest in your life! What you learn and apply can be passed down to your children, and be part of their inheritance! It's not just money you pass on to your children it's wisdom, knowledge and experience.

The "Tribes" that God has led me to have blessed my family and my daughter! My Mom Marlene is part of my online faith group and she is so blessed by it! My daughter and I do have a love for horses in common and together we volunteered and joined a horse rescue organization that taught us how to rescue and rehabilitate horses, and how to use them for therapy and healing for children. We also rescued and saved our horse Pongo from there - and he will bless many generations through that one horse rescue group we decided to join! We plan on adding a horse rescue and therapy program to our ministry! Even if I did not have an interest in horses, I would have still joined the rescue organization with my daughter to support her. Sometimes we have to do that for the ones we love, until they get confident enough to go on their own. This encourages your children to join the ideal groups and find their tribe - and shows that you are not afraid to either - you are spiritually equipping them for the future - giving them a Godly inheritance.

You are the example for generations to come! If you don't do it for yourself, at least do it for your kids or those youth that will have an impact in their lives!

"A good man leaves an inheritance to his children's children, but the sinner's wealth is laid up for the righteous." - Proverbs 13:22

If you don't have a tribe, create one. That's what I did when I started my ministry. Many of you are part of my free support group on Facebook! We have an AMAZING tribe there! The networking for your gifts, talents, products and services is allowed too - I actually encourage it! So many wonderful things have been birthed, grown and prospered from that group for so many people. Blogs, businesses, marriage and family restorations, home churches, ministries! Everyone encourages each other and helps each other. I love it and it is the reason I do the group!

Jesus created a tribe! *Hello*! He encouraged the members of His tribe (disciples) and guess what - He was a good leader and he set boundaries!

DO NOT BE AFRAID OF GROUPS! THERE IS A GROUP THAT NEEDS YOU! OR CREATE THE TRIBE YOU WANT TO SEE.

If you avoid networking and groups it's holding you back from your breakthrough! If drama or back stabbing or rejection pushed you out of a group - then like I said you were in the WRONG group. Forgive and move on to where God wants you!

Ask: *"Holy Spirit bring me to the right tribe, the group of people you have for me and I for them in Jesus name!*

If you start a group learn how to set good boundaries! This is what I do. It's not mean or hateful to have boundaries, it's good leadership. Get out there and let the Holy Spirit bring you to your tribe and let him bring your tribe to you. We MUST *network* to succeed for the Kingdom. When you help others into significance for the Kingdom - YOU become significant for the Kingdom!

You have to have the *season* of building NEW trusting relationships and you cannot do that if you are fishing in the same small place over and over and over, and by yourself.

You must be open to the new places and people God wants to send you!

Ask: *"Holy Spirit, send me to the places and groups where I will get the most fruitful and abundant results for my life, my gifts and my purpose _____ all for the glory of God! Help me, the Holy Spirit, to properly discern what places and groups are from You and not give in to the pressures of man and religion! I trust You Holy Spirit to send me to the perfect places and people! In Jesus Name, Amen!*

Now, Let's RECAP for Kingdom Marketing and Public Relations based on the understanding I have given you in this chapter.

KINGDOM MARKETING AND PR 'TERMS' WE LEARNED:

- 7M - Mountains of Influence In Society
- ROI - Return On Investment For Sponsor (God)
- B2B - Business To Business (Building Kingdom Relationships)
- 'NET' WORK - Joining Groups (Go where your 'tribe' of believers congregates)

PUBLIC STEPS IN FAITH AND EXPECTATIONS:

1. ANNOUNCE
2. CONFIRMATION
3. STRATEGY
4. OBEDIENCE
5. MESSAGE
6. RELATIONSHIPS
7. GOOD IN - BAD OUT
8. GROWTH
9. GIVE - RECEIVE
10. MULTIPLICATION
11. OVERFLOW
12. INFLUENCE
13. PROMOTION
14. FAVOR
15. EXPANSION
16. INCREASE
17. SIGNIFICANCE

18. RESULTS - FRUIT
19. MORE SEED (FINANCES)
20. GIVE GOD GLORY
21. OPERATE AND ADVANCE IN THE GLORY

CHAPTER 12
ADVANCING IN THE GLORY

The strategies and resources I have shared with you in this book have come directly from my own experiences in my life, my students, and from the revelation of the Holy Spirit in my own race on this earth. As you go through these experiences in your own life and grow spiritually, you will come to a certain point of desiring FULL KINGDOM.

What is FULL KINGDOM? It's living your life operating and advancing in the glory of God with virtually little or no warfare. Your acceleration has so much momentum that demonic hindrances are like bug splatter on your front bumper!

This happens after you have had a string of victories and you get to a point of spiritual maturity to where you are not *satisfied* just going from victory to victory; you want the life of a *Champion*.

We Are Champions for God and His Kingdom:

Great champions get excited about challenges because they know God is with them and they have a chance to display God's glory! Great champions run to win the trophies and crowns and accomplishments for the kingdom because they look for the day they will be among the chosen to cast these trophies, crowns and accomplishments at the feet of their King—King Jesus!

"Don't you realize that in a race everyone runs, but only one person gets the prize? So run to win!" 1 Corinthians 9:23

In motorsports, there are individual races and there are series of races where "season champions" are crowned or awarded. In my experience, I have found that, once a racer knows how to win that "season championship" the first time, they almost always become repeat champions from season to season. Why is this? Because they have an understanding of who they are from that moment and how to take that identity, cherish it, and operate in it fully. Once they have this wisdom and ability, they never go back.

It's like once you have salvation of Jesus Christ, you must trust that you have it and don't keep going back and second guessing whether you are saved or not! It's knowing that *you are* the redeemed of Christ, and you act like it from that day forward—growing, living, operating, and winning in the light! You know *who* you are and you know *why* you are here—to advance the Kingdom as God's Champion through and for Jesus Christ!

This is why you were put on this earth! You are meant to be a Champion for the kingdom and glory of God!

"The beginning of wisdom is this: Get wisdom. Though it cost all you have, get understanding. Cherish her, and she will exalt you; embrace her, and she will honor you. She will give you a garland to grace your head and present you with a glorious crown." Proverbs 4:7-9

In this chapter, I will teach you these five keys to advance and operate in the glory:

1. Dream Interpretation and Prophetic Works
2. Glory Frequency - Higher Discernment

3. Melchizedek - Order of Royal Champions
4. Angelic Assistance - Ruling and Reigning
5. Glory Covering and Prospering In The Glory

Like so many of you, I have pressed in with my faith, prayed, fasted, decreed, fought many spiritual battles, and did my best to be obedient to God, even in great adversity. I have seen victories for myself, my family, and my students. I have had that desire and experience of going from glory to glory. Because of this, I have grown spiritually, like you all seek to do and are doing. I always want more! I want to be a Champion!

I came to a point where I asked God this question in prayer:

"FATHER GOD, HOW DO I STAY OPERATING IN THE GLORY ALL THE TIME—NOT JUST GLORY TO GLORY, BUT FULL UNINTERRUPTED GLORY? I WANT TO LIVE AND OPERATE IN YOUR GLORY ON EARTH AS IT IS IN HEAVEN, LORD. SHOW ME THE WAY TO FULL KINGDOM IN MY LIFE IN JESUS NAME!"

Soon after that, I began to have dreams and visions about "fences" and "borders" and "crossing a road". I knew to seek the Holy Spirit on the meanings of these dreams, that somehow these signs of fences and crossing over pertained to the answer to my question.

The first rule of advancing in the GLORY is properly discerning messages in your dreams and applying them to your life. I taught you in these chapters to have a journal to write down your dreams and date them. Your answers are there. This is when the Holy Spirit is bringing us "coded" answers and strategies that He will help us decode. Some of you have dreams you are not sure are from God, so what do you do?

Dream interpretation Is a key to advancement. What is from God and what is not?

I have a simple prayer for when you wake up and you want to get the proper discernment of a message in a dream.

Pray: *"Holy Spirit, if that dream was not of You, I do not receive it. But, Holy Spirit, if that dream was of You, I receive it and ask for the interpretation, understanding, and application, in Jesus' name, Amen."*

Glory Frequency: All your senses are operating on Heaven's perspective and perception. The presence of God is FULLY guiding you.

Whether awake or asleep, your perspective and perception on what is being shown and revealed to you must be "glory" related. It becomes a lifestyle when you are operating in the glory. You look to *everything* around you as communication from heaven.

Methods of Holy Spirit Communication and Understanding:

1. **Parabolic:** (Be message/storyline focused) there is a message in everything for you. Holy Spirit speaks in imagery and parable like stories to help you understand like Jesus did. Ask: What does this mean Lord? Is there a next step in my story that I must take?

2. **Prophetic:** (Be future focused) this is your language from now on. Ask: How do I speak and ACT on what I am seeing in the spirit realm into my future?
3. **Manifestation:** (See it happening) The actual event and breakthrough happening that God had shown you and you prophesied and now fully operational in the natural realm.

Now use this strategy focusing on staying in a 'glory frequency' or 'heaven frequency'. Frequency is directly connected to "path of communication". Like changing a channel on the radio, dialing in to the clearest and desired station, with no static.

If we look at the dream I had about "fences" I came to the revelation of what the Holy Spirit was saying to me. "It's time to stop playing both sides of the fence and choose one side: FULL KINGDOM. He was answering my question in the dream. I knew Operating in the Glory was somehow connected to this.

Let me tell you, I did not realize I was playing both sides of the fence! I was doing some "Kingdom" ways in my life to prosper, but I kept reverting back to 'Man's' ways when it was not happening fast enough or from pressure from others.

None of us are perfect and that's why we need Jesus' redemption and the guidance of the Holy Spirit. There are pressures in this world, 'outside' influences (demonic and worldliness) that can keep us from fully operating in the Glory and Kingdom and there are 'inside' influences (our flesh and pride) that keep us from fully operating in full Glory and Kingdom. If you are anything like me, you really want this Glory realm 'full time' and you are tired of fighting these inside/outside things. But this dream and revelation was not about fighting anything - this dream from the Holy Spirit was about *choosing*. Making a choice. What side of the fence will you choose?

I WANT FULL KINGDOM AND NO TURNING BACK! How about you? YES!

To get FULL KINGDOM is bringing heaven to earth for your life. Heaven runs on the Glory of God. There is a DIVINE frequency, a sound, sensations, communication, wisdom and knowledge, and Angelic assistance. With all the distractions in today's world how can you connect to the Glory Frequency of God's Glory and Kingdom and operate in it all the time?

You have to first get OFF the frequency of the Kingdom of Darkness.

Here are keys and steps to getting off the frequency of the demonic and getting on God's Glory Frequency. Do this daily and you will see a huge difference!

1. **Play the recording of the shofar in your home.** This is the sound of the trumpet in Zion – to take out any spiritual enemies and call forth the Hosts of Heaven to fight for you and in the atmosphere around you. (Nehemiah 4:20) I put a Shofar recording on loop low in the background while I work during the day. (I do this each morning on loud volume). While playing the shofar in your home, you can also send the Hosts of Heaven, Heaven's armies to fight for you in a specific situation.

2. **Send the Hosts of Heaven** to take you and your household and family OFF the frequency of the demonic that day.
3. **Decree:** "In the name and authority of Jesus Christ in whom I am seated, I ask the Hosts of Heaven, The Angel Armies of Almighty God to assist me today as one of my mighty spiritual weapons. I command the Hosts of Heaven, Army Angels of Almighty God to go now and take me and my household, my family and children OFF the frequency of the demonic in Jesus name! I decree that the demonic cannot see, hear or perceive us today! Hosts of Heaven, Angel Armies of God, drive out and scatter the demonic into the dry places and put them into confusion to fight amongst themselves far far away from me and my household! I decree that the only frequency me and my house and family operates on today is the frequency of the HOLY SPIRIT in Jesus name! Thank you Father for sending your Angels to Keep me and my household in All my ways! Thank You Jesus for my authority through You as a King and a Priest to have access to the Angel Armies and Heavenly Hosts for my protection here on earth. Amen"
4. **Play worship music in the home and worship God out loud** - this attracts the Presence of God and True Angels of God. The Presence of God inhabits the praise and worship, the Angels come and worship with you!
5. **Shut down all worldly chatter,** turn off the news, shut off the TV, limit social media, and watch your own words and conversations - no negativity.
6. **Decree the Word and Promises of God** out loud in the home or play recordings of the Word of God. The Angels of the Lord Harken to the Word of The

Lord and move on your behalf to bring that word to pass in your life.

7. **Pray in your Holy Spirit Prayer Language** (tongues) if you are able to do that. This is a language only between you and God and brings the Presence of God close to you. The enemy cannot understand it.

8. **Do a morning invite to the King of Glory** and invite Him in your home by decreeing Psalm 24. Come in King of Glory, Come in Lord of Hosts!

9. **Invite the Holy Spirit to come** and fill you and fill your home. Command your mind, body, soul and spirit to yield to the power of the Holy Spirit!

10. **Post Sentry Angels** - From your seat of authority in Christ Jesus ask the Father in Jesus name for Sentry Angels to be assigned to you and your home. Thank them for coming by faith and tell them where to stand watch for constant protection. I post Sentry Angels almost daily to my doors, driveway and around my property!

11. **Anoint your home** and yourself with anointing oil (prayed over oil)

12. **Suit Up!** Put on your Armor of God (Ephesians 6:11-24)

Now, shutting down the devil's frequency and getting yourself on God's frequency will give you more clarity with what God is speaking and sharpen your discernment, and cause you to make the right decisions, move forward in faith and confidence in a *peaceful* environment. This is acceleration mode! This is crucial to Operating in The Glory and Advancing in the Glory, which is FULL KINGDOM in your life.

Once you begin to operate in the Glory and Kingdom realm and frequency you have to begin to realize that God is ordaining your Victory in *all things.* You cannot think just because things are not happening fast enough or 'your way' that it's the enemy or a demonic attack! This is a huge mindset shift you need to make!

You get yourself daily into the Glory realm prepared for Victory and in expectation for Victory and it may not come the way you think! But it will come! You just have to know God is doing it and heaven is working on your behalf.

One of my favorite daily decrees is: Psalm 44:4 "You are my King, oh God. who Commands victories for Jacob (Israel)!"

Decree: *"You are my King, oh God. Who Commands victories for_____! " (add your name)*
DO NOT WEARY IN ANY WAITING TIME FOR YOUR BREAKTHROUGH. ONCE YOU CHOOSE ALL KINGDOM IT'S ALL ABOUT THE GLORY!

In the Glory realm, you do not have to keep engaging in constant warfare when you *think* there is a delay. There are no delays in the Glory - only *strategy* for your Victory happening around you. Heaven is doing their part, and you by faith do yours. Keep proclaiming God's Glory in your life and over your situation and that He is commanding your Victory right now!

Even in the 11th hour, when you feel it's almost too late, that's when you must really believe because that's when God is preparing to show his Glory in a great way.

John 11:11 is what I call the 'great awakening verse'. Jesus is awakening us to: "Awaken! Pay attention! You will see the glory of God'!

Some of you see the numbers 11:11 repeatedly, When you see 11:11, proclaim: "Lord, I am awake and at attention and I believe I will see the Glory of God manifest in my life and in my situation, In Jesus Name!"

"After he had said this, he went on to tell them, "Our friend Lazarus has fallen asleep; but I am going there to wake him up." John 11:11

Remember when Martha & Mary were grieved because they thought Jesus waited too long to save their brother Lazarus? Jesus wept. Then he said: *"Did I not tell you that if you would only believe that you would see the Glory of God?"* Lazarus walked out of the grave!"

Jesus - who operated in the FULL KINGDOM GLORY REALM *knew* that He would have Victory raising His dear friend Lazarus from the dead. But He did not come right away after Lazarus died. Why? Because he had to show the GLORY of GOD in the Victory. He wept because it grieved Him to see Martha and Mary so upset!

But something wonderful happened in the Glory as soon as Jesus got there. Jesus asked Martha if she believed before He raised Lazarus.

"Lord," Martha said to Jesus, "if you had been here, my brother would not have died. But I know that even now God will give you whatever you ask."

Martha was awakened to who Jesus really was, "*even now*". She understood the Glory and the Glory Carrier and that it was never too late, even now after THREE days of her brother lying dead in a tomb. Have no fear, The Glory was here!

I used to think Martha was the 'worldly' sister, only caring about her 'worldly' duties when she complained about her sister Mary being at Jesus' feet and she was doing all the work in the kitchen preparing food. BUT she totally changed my mind with what she said by faith to Jesus when her brother was dead in the middle of her grief - she *believed* in the Glory and power of God! Nothing else mattered to her and she "Got it" now! This is faith! Thank you Martha!

The Glory is here! Lord do unto me so all will see your Kingdom and Glory! I am willing to wait and expect you are bringing everything into alignment for my victory right now!

John 11:41-45

"So they took away the stone. Then Jesus looked up and said, "Father, I thank you that you have heard me. I knew that you always hear me, but I said this for the benefit of the people standing here, that they may believe that you sent me."

When he had said this, Jesus called in a loud voice, "Lazarus, come out!"

The dead man came out, his hands and feet wrapped with strips of linen, and a cloth around his face. Jesus said to them, "Take off the grave clothes and let him go."

Therefore many of the Jews who had come to visit Mary, and had seen what Jesus did, put their faith in him."

THIS IS AN EXAMPLE OF THE GLORY ON DISPLAY THROUGH A FRIEND OF JESUS THAT BROUGHT MORE PEOPLE INTO THE KINGDOM

WILL YOUR VICTORY BRING GLORY TO GOD AND ADVANCEMENT OF THE KINGDOM?

When you partner with the Kingdom, and this is your focus - you are advancing too. This brings acceleration in a way that the glory can be revealed. It's worth waiting for. So keep calling it forth!

Declare: *"I call forth my breakthrough _____ now in the name of Jesus to reveal the Glory of God and advance the kingdom!"*

My friend, understand the Glory and the Glory Carrier. He is working on your miracle right now and God's Glory will be seen. Don't spend your day exhausting yourself shaking your fist at the devil thinking your delay is caused by the enemy! When you make the choice to go FULL KINGDOM the Victory is yours. It is rigged in your favor!

Because Jesus is the Glory Carrier, You are a Glory Carrier!

When you operate in the glory, you understand this and, no matter what you see in the natural, focus on the supernatural power of God! Jesus is a glory carrier and so are you!

"Jesus did not react to the devil, He lived and operated in response to the Father." - Pastor Bill Johnson

Here is an amazing testimony from one of my mentoring students who had been praying for her marriage to be restored. Her husband was a prodigal, away from God and living with another woman! We prayed together and I gave her Kingdom strategies. God was growing her in her faith, and although her husband was not home yet, she kept being obedient to God and stood in faith. She was struggling with her self esteem and seeing her value in her identity in Christ. I was encouraging her, and mentoring her. She really wanted to start a ministry. She was in church and could not give a testimony of her faith when asked because of her struggle with confidence. She wanted so badly to be able to do this and Give glory to God in her life in public.

During this time, the Holy Spirit guided her to begin to create some t-shirts with scripture on them and encouraging messages of faith. The t-shirts were a big hit and she began to sell them at church. This built her confidence greatly, and she even started a blog online and did a few live video teachings on Social Media. I was so proud of her. She grew exponentially in her faith and confidence in who she was in Christ! She could not understand though why God did not bring her husband home yet. It had been a year. She was doing everything God asked her to, but no sign of her husband even communicating nicely with her. She got a few texts and they were not promising at all. We stayed in prayer, and kept speaking and prophesying over her marriage. She continued doing her t-shirts and her ministry and confidence grew, and t-shirt business grew. She said to me, "Annamarie, I think God wants me to grow this business right now. So, I am going to sell the bed in my guest room so I can turn it into a craft room to make more t-shirts." I said, "Ok, I support your decision." So, we said a prayer for God to sell the bed for her quickly and for her business to grow according to His will.

Weeks went by and the bed would not sell. We prayed more. Nope. Still would not sell. We did spiritual warfare against delay. Nope, still did not sell.

Finally we were both thinking: "Are we discerning this wrong?" We decided to pray differently - in a full faith surrender to God, full covenant with Him. She went into a time of fasting and giving all she had to God. She dealt with her 'inside' things pride and flesh. Then fully surrendered herself to Full Kingdom. She decided she was done with the back and forth over the fence and wanted only Full Kingdom. She did all the things I teach to get into the Glory Frequency. She then had a prophetic dream about her husband, that he was at her front door waiting to come home but he was wearing little cartoon kid pajamas. We asked the Holy Spirit to reveal the meaning of the dream. We prayed for discernment in Glory Realm. The Holy Spirit guided us how to pray for him and target our prayers towards God giving her husband spiritual maturity and to awaken him to who he is as a man in Christ.

A week later, she texted me: "My husband is home! He is staying in the guest room right now while we work on things. It's amazing why that bed did not sell! God knew that it would be *needed* when He brought my husband home!"

GLORY TO GOD!!

When you make the choice to go FULL KINGDOM and know you can only have Victory because of your *full trust* in God.

God is not *delaying* things He is *arranging* things!

Discerning these things properly can take some time - but God also teaches you in the waiting and teaches you about His Glory. Soon you begin to see what He is *really* doing behind the scenes and you start to ask the same questions Jesus did of the Father.

Pray: *"Father, I know that you have heard me and you always hear me and you are doing all things for me and for the people around me for the benefit of your Glory!"*

God heard my friend's prayer for her husband's return on the *first day* she prayed. He was growing her, preparing her to take her place in the Kingdom and have a testimony of His Glory when the Victory came! Everything that happened or didn't happen was because of GOD working to answer her biggest prayer of her husband returning home.

It was amazing too because her husband said to her: "I see God in you, and I want to know God again."

FAITH - VICTORY - GLORY - KINGDOM ADVANCEMENT

Her husband not only came back to her, but He came back to God!

Never underestimate how God will do this. Just know He will in a way that He can show HIS GLORY.

Don't allow frustration to overtake you in the waiting, and if some of your other prayers are not being answered there is a good possibility you are not discerning things correctly.

In the waiting time, God is moving things around like chess pieces - to bring the desired outcome. Know that the more you believe He will and pray that way - you are coming into agreement with His promises in His word, according to Romans 8:28: God is working all things for the good of those who love him.

Declare: *"God I know you are strategically moving things around in your Glory Realm right now for my situation and I will see my desired result and Your Glory will be on full display!"*

Pray like THAT in the Glory and BELIEVE it!!

Get in the Glory Frequency. This means no frustration, only faith for victory!

So, how do you communicate with God in the Glory Frequency if you are not really sure about things He is telling you? Let's use my friend's example:

"God, why isn't the bed selling? Do you have a plan for the bed? I trust that you will show me because you do everything for my good!"

If you tend to be a very intense person and like to push hard and sometimes get to the point of frustration, that actually causes you to get into the wrong frequency! Frustration can cause you to work from the flesh and pride instead of faith and glory.

I had an example of this in my own life. I was not 'full kingdom" yet. I was still working both sides of the fence. I was not fully in the Glory Frequency. I had not made that choice because a part of me was still trusting in the ways of man and the world. I would hop back and forth over that fence so many times I should have realized it - but I did not. I would get going good with my "Kingdom" faith for a while, I would be on a roll - then when it was not happening the way I wanted it to, or I was not seeing breakthrough according to my timeline, I would slip back and try to do it 'my way' (flesh) thinking I could speed up the process. Classic pride/worldly move. Not Good.

When you put something on the altar of God to trust Him with, leave it there! Don't keep going back and pulling it off! It throws you out of the Glory Frequency and the momentum that God had been building up for you! You become your own roadblock!

However I was not seeing "instant" results - instead more frustration. I was a wishy washy - not really full kingdom even though I was saying and thinking I was! My discernment was off because of some 'inside' things I did not surrender to God. My pride and my flesh.

I had dedicated my ministry social media pages to God, and asked him to bring the followers. That I would be obedient to post what He wanted me to post and bring the messages He wanted me to and that it was for His Kingdom and Glory. I said the prayer and partnered with the Holy Spirit. I was expecting my social media "loaves and fishes" to multiply speedily.

However, it was not happening fast enough for my liking and even though I was 'trusting God' to do this, I decided to 'help it along' by doing advertising on the Social Media site. Next thing I knew I was doing a paid ad for almost every post. I was not trusting God that the words, teachings and videos He gave me to post would be multiplied by Him and getting to the right people. I was buying my way in, (the ways of the world) instead of working with God in the Glory (the ways of His word)... I bought so many ads that I began to get into debt. I was relying on those dumb ads and paid post boosts to gain me followers. My page grew a tiny bit, but people were still not "interacting" or commenting. It was all superficial, no real fruit. Was I really helping anyone? Was God getting any glory from this?

I was fence hopping like a squirrel with my tail in a knot and getting no acorns - nothing was really growing from this except the negative in my bank account!

Then the frustration fires up in me. What was I doing wrong? I am supposed to be your "Faith Girl" God! I have to show people that my faith is powerful and things can happen!"

There it was. My pride. My flesh! "I had to show people my faith is powerful…"

I did not make it about God, the Kingdom and His Glory! I made it about me! I WANTED TO LOOK GOOD TO THE WORLD.

Whoa! BIG CHECK FROM THE HOLY SPIRIT.

I had to get back on the Glory Frequency. I had been on the world system, and got pulled back in so deep back into the world's ways that I was going broke doing it! This was the devil's frequency because he comes to steal, kill and destroy, this is not of God!

11:11 WAKE UP TIME!!

The worldly frequency will put you in a slumber! It will slow you down and even throw you backwards! It's a very tempting pull - like a magnet but you cannot give into it!

It throws off your discernment and you make foolish decisions - upsetting the flow of the GLORY in your life!

What are you tapped into? What frequency are you listening to and devoted to? Are you jumping from station to station?

Now let's get on that GLORY TRAIN and trust the Head Engineer! Jesus Christ!

Thank God He is the perfecter of our faith and we have the grace for second chances when we go down the wrong track.

I repented for my lack of faith, my pride and disobedience and I reset my social media so I could not do another ad. I blocked that option and removed my debit card off the account. I removed anything that would tempt me. I would now fully trust God to multiply my posts according to where He knew they needed to go! If God could multiply Issac's seed 100 fold in a drought, He could certainly do it for my new online ministry with my posts on a social media platform! When I did this, the pages began to grow! Most of all God used my teachings to get in front of the right people at exactly the right time they needed it. My posts and videos were not for me, but for God who wanted to touch someone!

Many of you are reading this book right now who God connected us through those social media posts and videos! Thank you God! I am so glad you are here now!

All that ad money I was spending foolishly going into the pockets of social media moguls, I instead invested into the Kingdom of God! Sowing seeds into fertile ministries, missions and churches for the people and teachings He wants to bring to me! I always see good (and multiplied) fruitful harvests from the KINGDOM financial seeds!

To be a long term Champion for God, and to build more Champions for the Kingdom - you must be good at the long races! Not just the 30 lap sprints! It's the 500 lappers that build your endurance! You have outlasted and outrun the enemy! Those longer races bring the Sweetest Victories, the biggest payouts! Overall that's how Champions are made and teams and drivers become legends!

God has His Legends of the Faith and we are going to understand how we can be too! I had to make the DECISION. Once and for all.

I am not looking back.

FULL KINGDOM FULL GLORY. FULL TRUST - STAYING IN GOD'S FREQUENCY! COME WITH ME ON THIS!

Declare:

- God's Frequency is the heartbeat for my life!
- I do not want any other way - only your Kingdom way!
- In the Glory I will Recover all and Advance!

- I want to thrive in the glory!
- Show me Your glory God!
- I TRUST Your Glory God!
- I want to reveal your Glory to others God!
- Show me how to OPERATE in Your Glory God!
- I desire to become a Champion of the Faith and for Your Kingdom Oh God!
- In the name of Jesus Christ and for Your Glory God for generations to come, will see Your Glory in my story!

Let's get into these Mysteries and Strategies of the Glory Realm and go FULL KINGDOM!

Melchizedek: The Order of Royal Champions In Christ

A few years ago, just when I was beginning my ministry, I was praying for sharper discernment. I was asking God, according to "Jeremiah 33:3" to show me the hidden things that I needed to know right now. I wanted to go deeper into the mysteries of God. I wanted more! I wanted to go to another level of Glory, like the Bible says.

One afternoon I was watching a video livestream with one of my favorite Kingdom teachers, Lance Wallnau. Lance was at a friend's wedding in Maryland and he and his wife, Annabelle were walking from the church to the hotel where the wedding reception was to be held. Lance was talking to all of us on the livestream down the sidewalk putting his friends and acquaintances on camera here and there as they walked to the reception. Lance was asking each person he chatted with along the way to give his (viewers) some 'Kingdom' wisdom or advice. He brought on a "well-to-do" looking man. Lance introduced him as a person he highly respected and who owned several successful million dollar businesses, much land and had a thriving worldwide men's ministry (I never caught the man's name). This man came on Lance's livestream for just a fleeting moment, and the man peeked into Lance's iphone camera and said to us viewers: *"All you need to understand about operating successfully for the Kingdom, is Melchizedek."* Then he walked ahead into the reception. Lance had to go in too, and ended the livestream. The recording was not archived or saved. To this day, (and I have even reached out to Lance's staff) nobody can tell me who that man was!

But that fleeting moment on Lance's livestream changed my life. My Kingdom 'antenna' was alerted and my Spirit at attention. I knew there was something here that was my answer.

Melchizedek? I had heard about him a little in the Bible, that He was the King of Salem who Abraham paid his tithes. But who really is this Melchizedek that this very wise and wealthy man of faith would say that's all we needed to understand about operating in the Kingdom of God successfully on earth?

I went into full research mode. I wanted to learn everything I could about Melchizedek. I was a woman on a mission, like in the days when I had a hot sponsor lead in motorsports I was gonna land that sponsor no matter what! My fingers were hot on the keyboard and pouring through the Bible. I was reading everything I could that had been written and in the word of God where Melchizedek is mentioned. I knew I had a HUGE KEY to the next level of Glory I had prayed for, if I could just unpack all the pieces and have the Holy Spirit give me understanding!

I wanted to get these questions answered...

1. WHO IS MELCHIZEDEK?
2. WHAT IS THE ORDER OF MELCHIZEDEK?
3. HOW DOES UNDERSTANDING MELCHIZEDEK BRING KINGDOM SUCCESS?

The answer begins in Hebrews Chapter 7:

Melchizedek the Priest: This Melchizedek was king of Salem (early Jerusalem) and priest of God Most High. He met Abraham returning from the defeat of the kings and blessed him, and Abraham gave him a tenth of everything. First, the name Melchizedek means "king of righteousness"; then also, "king of Salem" means "king of peace." Without father or mother, without genealogy, without beginning of days or end of life, resembling the Son of God, he remains a priest forever. (Source: Biblegateway.com)

Here is my revelation on Melchizedek with the help of the Holy Spirit I present this to you:

Melchizedek is God's True Priesthood and God's First King on the Earth. I am still seeking more revelation if he was a spiritual being in the flesh right from the Courts of God, placed there by God at that time for Abraham. Melchizedek is very mysterious and divine. But I do know one thing for sure, it all connects to the King of Kings, Jesus who brought us all into the Melchizedek Priesthood.

Operating and Advancing in Glory is Operating in your FULL Melchizedek Authority that you receive through Jesus Christ, your King of Kings and High Priest!

When you understand WHO Melchizedek is, you will understand who YOU are in the Kingdom of God on Earth!

Melchizedek Is The Royal Priesthood Champion Order of Jesus Christ! As a believer and follower of Christ YOU are also of this order!

Melchizedek Priesthood is over and above the "Levite" priesthood. The Levites of the twelve tribes of Israel were only allowed to be Priests. They could not have businesses, or own land or livestock. They relied on the obedience of the Israelites to take care of them. Their lives were focused on being set apart to bring forth the sacrifice in the temple to God. Rabbi's were the teachers of the Torah (the word of God in the old testament). They were connected to the Levite priesthood - they were a "Levite Order". At the time of the Old Testament it was a temporary priesthood, until Jesus Christ finished the final and forever sacrifice of His own Body and Blood and the "Levite" priests no longer needed to bring the sacrifice to God to atone for sins. Jesus was the sacrifice over all sin once and for all! The temple curtain was destroyed at the crucifixion and now through Jesus Christ we all have direct access to God! We can all be priests now and make intercession for ourselves and others. Jesus is our High Priest.

Let's be clear.   The Melchizedek Order is both King and Priest.

Melchizedek Order is the Order of JESUS CHRIST. This is each of us! We became the Melchizedek Order when we accepted Christ, we became a King and Priest through Christ Jesus. The Melchizedek order of priesthood and kingship is very different from the old Levite order. We can have a ministry and a business! You can own land and livestock, you do not have to rely on the 'people' to bring your food, supplies and finances. You can have an army like Abraham! Abraham lived before the Levite priesthood was established. Abraham's High Priest and King was Melchizedek, who is God's High Priest, Jesus Christ! King of Kings and this was the ORIGINAL order of priesthood for God's people!

Jesus' finished work on the Cross *upgraded* all of us in the GLORY! The old Hebrew order of priesthood, the Levite where for the Hebrews to handle their intercession to God through the blood sacrifices at the temple, BUT Jesus came and fulfilled all those sacrifices and all future sacrifices with HIMSELF being a blood sacrifice, that satisfied God for our sins forevermore. Then, we got an added gift - Jesus Christ brought us into His order of priesthood and kingship, which is the ORIGINAL and FINAL order - the MELCHIZEDEK ORDER! It is the only priesthood established by God on earth and in heaven that is both KING and PRIEST. This was confirmed through the New Covenant:

The Glory of the New Covenant:

"Now the Lord is the Spirit, and where the Spirit of the Lord is, there is freedom. And we, who with unveiled faces all reflect the glory of the Lord, are being transformed into His image with intensifying glory, which comes from the Lord, who is the Spirit." 2 Corinthians 3:17-18

It is the worst fear of the enemy when you realize and operate in your Melchizedek King and Priest anointing! It's the Glory Realm here on earth! Let me tell you and teach you here how God revealed this to me and how you can step into this and fully operate in it.

First Understand Who Melchizedek Is: A King and A Priest of God Most High - You are to OPERATE in this role on earth!

1. **What does a PRIEST do?** A priest makes intercession and offerings to God for himself and others. A priest is also a prophet, pastor, teacher and brings the word of God to the people to encourage, guide and increase their faith. A priest serves God's people with things of the Spirit and of the Word.

2. **What does a KING do?** A King rules and reigns over a territory and land. A king orders armies and maps out strategy. A king makes declarations and his subjects (team) carries them out. A king has authority and influence over every area of Government, Education, Marketplace, etc. A king acquires wealth for his kingdom and makes sure his people are prospering and blessed in every way! A good king has reverence to God and God's word and also leads His people in this reverence. King's rule over COURTS and dictate laws to bring order and ENFORCE them. A king sees talent and the gifts in people and appoints them to places of influence of the Kingdom and awards them for their accomplishments. A King assembles and finances missions and expeditions into new territory!

Genesis 14:18-20 - "Then Melchizedek king of Salem brought out bread and wine. He was priest of God Most High, and he blessed Abram, saying, "Blessed be Abram by God Most High, Creator of heaven and earth. And praise be to God Most High, who delivered your enemies into your hand." Then Abram (Abraham) gave him a tenth of everything."

Hebrews 5:8 - "Although he was a son (Jesus), he learned obedience through what he suffered. And being made perfect, he became the source of eternal salvation to all who obey him, being designated by God a high priest after the order of Melchizedek."

Revelation 1:6 - "And (Jesus) hath made us kings and priests unto God and his Father; to him be glory and dominion for ever and ever. Amen"

You are of the Melchizedek order for BOTH Ministry and Marketplace. PLUS any area of influence you have been assigned or called to by God! We are to operate in this glory and dominion on earth.

Melchizedek had no Mother or Father and no origin of him was physically explainable. He just *was*. I believe God placed Him in the earth in a time where His Priesthood was needed to assist with Abraham's covenant.

The Bible is very clear about lineages, but does not give any lineage to Melchizedek. According to the writer of Hebrews (7:13-17) Jesus is considered a priest in the order of Melchizedek because like Melchizedek, Jesus Christ when born through Mary - Mary was not a descendant of Aaron a Levite, and thus would not qualify Jesus for the Jewish Levite Priesthood under the Law of Moses. (Aaron the Levite was not even born before Melchizedek...) It is clear in the Bible that Mary and Joseph were both descended from King David, fulfilling prophecy that Jesus would be of the House of David. A King bloodline (through Mary) so the Jews would understand prophecy was being fulfilled giving Jesus (Yeshua) the right to rule Israel.

What do you think? Could Jesus have gone back in time to rule in Salem and meet with Abraham as King Melchizedek? A lot of supernatural things around Abraham are recorded, including him meeting and having a meal with Angels who looked like men in his tent. Or Melchizadek could just be God's High Priest sent from Heaven to earth at that time to supernaturally reign in Salem. Many Bible scholars believe this! As Jesus Christ is on the throne now next to the Father, Melchizedek is also serving in the Courts of Heaven today. I encourage you to not be afraid, but adventurous to go exploring these mysteries of God!

I know this is heavy stuff, but we are told to seek these things and we will get understanding. Keep seeking, keep asking, keep knocking! I love the mysteries of God!! Seeking these mysteries that's a huge part of Operating in the glory! I will continue to seek MORE and I hope you will too.

Jesus wants us to seek this knowledge! It prospers us to do so! He said: "My people perish for lack of knowledge." I want the opposite of perish and that is prosper!! More knowledge of the Kingdom God! We want more! YES!

God's plan and every chapter in the Bible points to Jesus Christ. I am still studying the word on this and asking for more revelation all the time. The key here for you is understanding the role we have through the Melchizedek priesthood and kingship and how we operate in that role. Let's first go to the word:

Hebrews 7:3 Melchizedek and Abraham
"Abraham apportioned to him (Melchizedek) a tenth of everything. First, his name means "king of righteousness." Then also, "king of Salem" means "king of peace." Without

father or mother or genealogy, without beginning of days or end of life, like the Son of God, he remains a priest for all time. Consider how great Melchizedek was: Even the patriarch Abraham gave him a tenth of the plunder...."

Melchizedek honored Abraham. He was impressed with Abraham's victory and blessed him. He honored Abraham at His table. Like Jesus invites us to His and honors us there. Melchizedek loves Victory of God's faithful people and recognizes it. Abraham honored King Melchizedek with the first 10% of the plunder from the Victory. They shared the Victory and gave Glory to God!

- SHARING YOUR VICTORIES WITH GOD BRINGS VICTORIOUS LIVING - AND GLORY COVERING
- HONORING OTHERS VICTORIES FOR GOD BRINGS YOU KINGSHIP AND TRUE SERVICE TO JESUS CHRIST

Melchizedek was also very impressed that Abraham turned down awards from the pagan kings! Abraham was a man of great character! God looks at character in a person as well as faith! Good character brings FAVOR with God and man.

So why did Abraham have so much favor that Kings wanted to Honor him?

Let's understand first what that Victory all about, why so special? Abraham was helping out his cousin Lot who had got himself into a jam. We who operate in Glory may be called at times to come and fight for that struggling family member. Because God prospered Abraham so greatly,

Abraham had many servants and camels and horses - enough to have his own Army to fight for his family.

Abraham was Operating in The Glory Realm - Victory Realm. This comes for the one in a family who is in a true Covenant with God. You are able to be the one who can easily pull your family out of bondage. Who wants that? I can testify to the fact that the more I go full kingdom and honor my covenant with God, the more I am able to see breakthroughs in all my family members.

ABRAHAM MADE A COVENANT WITH GOD. A FIRST TO MAKE THAT CHOICE OF ALL THE PEOPLE ON THE EARTH AT THE TIME! HE DECIDED HE WOULD NEVER PLAY BOTH SIDES OF THE FENCE. HE WAS THE FIRST TO BE CALLED A HEBREW AND FIRST PERSON GOD CALLED A 'FRIEND'.

Through this covenant, Abraham became the first human to reject false gods in favor of the one true God. It was the start of the relationship between God and the Jewish people. The covenant carries with it the promise of the land of Israel and now all believers in Jesus Christ.

Abraham was also obedient in his faith. God commanded him to leave his birthplace and go ... to the land that I will show you. Abraham did that sight unseen. God promised to make Abraham's name great.

Abraham honored the Angels of the Lord when they visited his home, inviting them in for bread and wine.

Melchizedek, the High Priest of God was honoring and confirming the *covenant* God had with Abraham.
Could it be that the secret to understanding Melchizedek is looking at His relationship with Abraham, and Abraham's

relationship with Melchizedek? That is how we are supposed to be with Jesus? If we faithfully follow the lead of Abraham's faithful actions, obedience and character, combined with how he interacts with Melchizedek that this is the secret for all of our KINGDOM SUCCESS? I really think so.

The FIRST Key here is Covenant. Have you made a covenant with God alone to serve Him and not the 'gods' or ways of this world?

The role you must have with God is a Kingdom Covenant role. You must renounce every unholy ungodly covenant and declare you are only in One Holy Covenant with Almighty God through Jesus Christ.

OPERATING AND ADVANCING IN THE GLORY IS GOING FULL KINGDOM WITH NO COMPROMISING - STAYING FAITHFUL TO YOUR COVENANT WITH GOD - AS HE WILL STAY FAITHFUL TO HIS PROMISES

God prospered Abraham, fulfilled all his promises to him, made him very wealthy, won every battle and gave him and Sarah a son (Isaac) when it was physically impossible. God also honored every promise to Abraham and his descendants to this day.

These promises of the covenant of God and Abraham have been called upon for Victory in Israel's battles for centuries, God has ALWAYS honored His covenant with Abraham and the people of Israel. You and I are grafted into Abraham's covenant through the blood covenant of Jesus Christ - who is of the Order of Melchizedek! Do you see how God brought this all together so brilliantly for you and I? It's a full circle divine confirmation and I love it so much!

Abraham and Melchizedek are a picture of You and Jesus!

You are under the same blessing of Abraham - a Victory Blessing! You bring your tithes to ministries operating in the Melchizedek Priesthood now. Do not judge ministers that also write books and have a business too. If that person, who has a ministry, if their gift is to be an author they are to use that gift and take influence in the marketplace for the Kingdom! If they make a million selling their book, it's because they are a good author! This is the Melchizedek Ministry! This is how Jesus brought it back for us!

The enemy is trying to keep the Melchizedek Ministry hidden or under attack because it will prosper the ecclesia of Jesus Christ - (the church) financially and give us more influence in the world!

Are you getting this? It's all about your *covenant* with God! What you have promised to do and be for Him and His Kingdom - and putting that covenant FIRST in all things!

Jesus is the *confirmation* of our covenant with Father God! An agreement written in His Blood! All we have to do is agree with this and decide we want to honor it and live through this covenant. When we become of this covenant, we receive the promises and blessings of Abraham and ALSO the promises of the Kingdom of God through Jesus Christ. This is HUGE. It is more than even Abraham had!

Let me make this clear, we are NO LONGER under a Levite Priesthood! We are under Melchizedek! Both Ministry and Marketplace. We are as the Body of Christ meant to have all the influence and lead in all areas of society. Jesus took back dominion for us, now we need to step into that and take it back by using the gifts, talents, and fulfilling assignments God gave us in ALL these areas all for the Glory of God.

The Melchizedek Ministry makes the "Levite" Pharisees jealous and judgmental! The Pharisees tried to trip up Jesus all the time with 'religious rules." These Pharisees were corrupt and politically correct 'elite' Levite Priests and Rabbl Leaders. It's not what God expected of these Levite priests when He ordained them from Aaron's bloodline originally! They were supposed to be set apart and holy! They were supposed to see and know and recognize the messiah! Instead, they got greedy, power hungry and corrupted. They went off and started their own movements based on 'agenda'. This opened the door to the demonic Spirit of Religion, which is what caused jealousy and conflict between the Pharisees and Christ. This led to the arrest and crucifixion of Jesus because of the corrupt hearts of these Pharisee's or Levite order of the priesthood. They took their priesthood and made it about politics and control, instead of service and advancement of God's Kingdom! Jesus tried to tell them over and over but they were so steeped in their own self-righteousness they totally missed it! Jesus was trying to show them the new true KINGDOM AND GLORY priesthood! Only Nicodemus and Joseph of Arimathea realized it out of all the priests of that time in Judea. Too bad. We have a lot of religious leaders even today that still don't get it. BUT Jesus paved the way for us to destroy this 'religious pharisee spirit' and we are in a time when it's being exposed more than ever. God is doing a new thing and great awakening is happening across the Nations. I believe we are in the "Kingdom Age". Those who have been called to the Ministry, Marketplace, Government, Education, Entertainment, Family and Mountains of Influence in

Society are going to bring the Kingdom and Glory of God into these areas. The time is now to bring it all together AS ONE. For the Kingdom of God. Yes this includes all we do financially.

ON EARTH AS IT IS IN HEAVEN!

The only agenda of the Melchizedek Order of Priesthood and Kingship is GOD'S KINGDOM AGENDA! Does this mean prosperity for God's people and His church? YES! It also means God wants more people to prosper like Abraham! Melchizedeks and Abrahams! This is God's Order and Jesus came to confirm it and bring all of us into this blessing!

You might be thinking: "Well Jesus was angry when they were selling things in the temple and He overturned their tables. Doesn't that mean churches and ministries should not sell things or make money?"

The Church and Ministries get attacked and judged for doing fundraisers and for ministers selling books and teaching tools all the time in our society. This is the enemy trying to twist our thinking that we are still under a Levite priesthood, that churches and ministries should not do anything for money! Offerings are important, yes - but how can the church and those in Christ do the big things that are needed for the Kingdom to bring more souls to Christ? This takes money and influence! The Abrahams and Melchizedek's are now one team! This is God's success plan for advancing His Kingdom!

The old twisted lie that ministries and those serving the Kingdom of God with their gift are 'supposed' to be poor and struggling has caused many people who are called to ministry and mission work to never fulfill their purpose for fear of being attacked when it comes to asking for money or raising money. Also the 'poor and struggling' image that the enemy has painted scared many away from fulfilling a calling that would need financial backing.

How can we stay faithful to God and bring KINGDOM INFLUENCE AND FINANCES (not religion or corruption) into these areas?

Let me answer that question, because I had that question myself. Why did Jesus overthrow the tables of the 'moneychangers' in the temple? To understand, you must know the Hebrew culture in Jesus time and read the scripture and ask the Holy Spirit for true revelation on why Jesus was so angry and driving the money changers out of the temple. The word "selling doves" really stuck out to me. I have studied deeply on this.

In those days the Hebrew/Jewish people who were too poor at that time to afford to bring a spotless lamb to the temple for their Passover offering would instead bring affordable doves or pigeons. Interestingly that was the offering of Jesus' earthly parents, Mary and Joseph. They brought pigeons or doves when Jesus was a baby to the temple for their offering. The "money changers" who were there selling the doves, were actually foreigners (non Jews) that came to the Sacred Temple and set up tables in the outer court area. This is the area set aside for just the Jews - who were supposed to pray and be reverent in this special area for their sin and prepare their offerings to give to the Levite Priest in atonement for their sins. The money changers (changing currency / foreign for domestic) they took over that sacred area (the outer court) and were selling the doves and other stuff gouging the people and taking their money for doves that were not consecrated for the sacrifice, and taking up the area where the people were supposed to pray. It's like if we were supposed to prepare our offering for church, in an envelope, and set it aside for God, then get to church and there were some hucksters out there trying to get you to spend your offering money on their junk and blocking you from getting in to pray. Like some bully stealing your child's lunch money that you set aside just for your child!

Now, this is my revelation that I received on studying this and why Jesus was so angry and why He put a stop to it then and forevermore. It was not because they were raising money for the Temple needs, they were stealing money away from those faithful and innocent ones, and taking their money away from the Temple, not putting anything back in for an offering! Even worse they were selling them something that was not spiritually clean. There was no reverence to God in it. So like selling porn in the parking lot of your church. Big difference from a bake sale, or a table of books and teachings from a ministry that will grow you in your faith! As long as the money is going to help the church missions or grow the ministry - and the author is obedient to give 10% of sales to God - we are in God's will for this!

THIS IS THE ABRAHAM - MELCHIZEDEK WAY! THE KINGDOM WAY!

Now this need to purchase or raise animals for sacrifice (Levite/Temple) is no longer connected to us now who are in Christ Jesus, We are the Order of the Melchizedek Priesthood through Christ. Jesus already purchased and confirmed any blood sacrifice we would ever need for us on the Cross *forever*. We are living sacrifices to God through Christ Jesus in all we do and give in His Name. We are now the Temple. God's Spirit dwells in us - the Holy of Holies in our Spirit Man. We are not to be defiled and be used by evil and corrupt people or allow ourselves to be used by evil and corrupt people! Christ lives within us. This is a good thing! We are vessels filled with GLORY. Like the pure doves, set aside. The dove is the Holy Spirit, alive in us. Imagine using your body for something sinful while carrying something so precious? That's what upset Jesus in the Temple! That's why when we stay in the GLORY that means we are in constant communication with the Holy Spirit guiding our vessel, our race here must be well stewarded. Have your own little 'flag man' (the Holy Spirit) in your spirit - waving the red flag to your conscience when you are about to wreck yourself! Heed the warnings - if not you could get out of your Glory Flow and it may take a bit to get back in it!

We must be good stewards of prayer, money, our gifts and the faith! We must still bring our offerings to God in humility and reverence. This now is to advance and fund the GOSPEL to go to all the world and for the harvest of souls for Jesus Christ. Ministries do sell books, apparel, etc to fund the Gospel and their Mission work, build schools for discipleship, feed the poor. Big difference from those stealing from God's people to just make a buck! Look at the ministry that is selling teachings and books, is it also flowing out to fund the Gospel in places? Churches after the finished work of Jesus Christ were started in people's homes! Read the book of Acts. So if you operate a home business and a home church it's OK! Paul also worked and sold tents while starting churches, and was very clear on the Melchizedek order is now the priesthood for all believers.

Also I want to be clear. If you dedicate what you do to God and Jesus Christ, you are like Abraham. Whether you are raising cattle, selling cakes or books written to inspire faith, do it in Partnership with your High Priest of Melchizedek's

Order (Jesus). Now you can make money with your gift, abilities or business in partnership with God as long as you faithfully dedicate it to God and give your 10% tithe of all you make to God. Simple as that! You will be in obedience with this, even if you are in ministry! This is the Melchizedek answer I wanted. I hope it answers a lot for you too! This is the Order of Champions for God! We must not be afraid to be this and operate in this role - especially in these days. This is the KINGDOM AGE!

The best teacher I have found regarding Melchizedek - the anointing for ministry and marketplace, and how to operate in the Melchizedek King and Priesthood is Paul Cox of Aslan's Place Ministry. I discovered him when I was seeking out information on Melchizedek.

This quote during one of Paul Cox's video teachings on Melchizedek sums it up...

"What is your God given ability? What did God put in you to do with skill? If your God given ability is to be an occupational therapist and you get paid to do it, then if my God given ability is to pray for people or write books on faith then what is the difference? I should get paid to do it." - Paul Cox, Aslan's Place Ministries (The Melchizedek Teachings)

When I heard Paul Cox say that, I really 'got it'. It set me free to serve the Kingdom with my gift and in a big way. The money I make with my God given gifts as an author and coach I live off that and put aside my 10% tithe for God or more with seed offerings and first fruit offerings, sometimes I flow much of it into our ministry to grow and build what we need here. It's all advancing the Kingdom of God. I operate this way, and I make sure I do my best to be like Abraham and take everything I earn with using my gifts and put it into the ministry and into advancing the Gospel and helping the poor. Mike and I even started our own 'home church' and have our little coffee can where we put our weekly offerings. Before we knew it we had over $1000 in there! We were so excited! We wrote checks to many missions, and gave to new ministries to help them get started. We also made sure to bless a mission in Israel. We are operating in Glory, and God is blessing us beyond anything we imagined! We are excited that we will soon have enough in the offering to do something really big for a needy family - we hope to be able to put a roof on a home for someone. By the time you read this book I pray we are able to do a 1000 roofs for the needy!

Ministry can just be opening yourself up to be useful to God and His Kingdom in every area of your life! It does not have to be complicated.

WE HAVE BETTER PRIESTHOOD IN ALL AREAS OF OUR LIFE!

"But now Jesus, our High Priest, has been given a ministry that is far superior to the old priesthood, for He is the one who mediates for us a far better covenant with God, based on better promises." - Hebrews 8:6

Remember, Jesus said we are to be rivers of living water, not lakes. I want to be Niagara Falls and have the GLORY flow really huge! Get on the GLORY Flow! The only way you can fully do this is really understand the Abraham Melchizedek relationship and what their roles are. God PROSPERED Abraham and he was exceedingly wealthy - much livestock that he bought and sold, plus camels (like a trucking industry for the marketplace) and even had his own Army. Abraham became the Father of Nations. God is prospering us, so we can spread the Gospel to all

Nations! This is KINGDOM! We are all in ministry and marketplace in some way - how does this connect with what God has called you to do?

Prospering in the Glory:

- Glory Source - God and His Word
- Glory Resource - Wherever the Holy Spirit sends you to learn from, teachers, pastors, prophets, coaches, mentors, books, ministries, etc.
- Full Kingdom is the only option, no more playing both sides of the fence
- No such thing as 'balanced' in the Kingdom. The scales weigh exceedingly abundantly and overflowing in the glory
- Desire only things from above and live like you are a citizen of Heaven on earth
- Do not get offended by those who would judge you like the pharisees judged Jesus
- No lukewarm faith and commitment in your life, only hot hot hot! Do not compromise your faith and covenant with God
- Stay filled with the Holy Spirit - No fear of man
- Understand the Glory is for you right now! You do not have to wait till you go to heaven (on earth as it is in heaven)
- Operating in the Glory and Full Kingdom is in the company of Melchizedek - Both Ministry and Marketplace and all the areas of influence in society
- Understand you get paid to use your God-given abilities, even in ministry because you faithfully tithe your 10% like Abraham in obedience and in reverence to God
- Be more motivated by Kingdom than money or fame

- Know if you seek more Kingdom, more blessings and prosperity and advancement will come
- Understand how God wants to use the money and influence He gives you and what He wants to build through you
- Study the faith, character and actions of Abraham, who was accounted as righteous in the eyes of God and Abraham was recognized as a Champion by the High Priest of God and the Kingdom of God (Melchizedek)
- Be a Glory Operation in all you do. Be like Melchizedek! Invite those who are faithful to Jesus and the Kingdom to your table and honor them!
- Invite your High Priest Jesus Christ to your table, your ministry and your business, have bread and wine with Him. Do like Melchizedek did with Abraham. Rule and Reign and Honor the righteous at your table! This is making your table God's table.

Decree: *"I choose to fully step into the Kingdom of God! Because of Jesus Christ, my High Priest and King, I have full access to the Kingdom of God here on earth! The Glory is for Heaven and Earth and for me and my life right now, I do not have to wait for it, I receive and operate in Your Kingdom right now Father God and I receive and operate in Your Glory like MELCHIZEDEK AND ABRAHAM from this day forward in Jesus name!"*

THIS IS SO AWESOME! I AM SO EXCITED FOR YOU!
Supernatural assistance is headed your way, in the name of Jesus, your High Priest of the Order of Melchizedek— the Glory Order! Can we really have it on earth as it is in heaven for our lives? The answer is YES!

Ruling From Third Heaven Authority:

This was a huge revelation for me when I began to truly take my Seat of Authority in Christ every morning.

Seat of Authority Prayer/Declaration: *"Father God, I thank you for your gracious word in Ephesians Chapter 2, and I do now take my seat of authority in Christ Jesus at your right hand. I will rule and reign through Christ Jesus and in Christ Jesus of the Priestly Kingly order of Melchizedek today. I have divine dominion over ministry, marketplace and _____. I ask the Holy Spirit to guide me in being an influence in these places for your Glory Father. I put the kingdom of darkness under my feet and under the feet of Jesus Christ, King of Kings and my High Priest in whom I am seated, far above all powers and principalities in Jesus name! Thank you Father God for your favor that surrounds me as a shield today and Your Favor goes before me in all things! Your glory is my covering Father God, in Jesus name!"*

I rule from my Third Heaven Authority every day. I have an open heaven over me and the King of Glory is with me and my household! It's amazing how much this has changed my life and the flow, the favor, the peace, the joy is evident all around me. I can easily, smoothly and calmly handle anything that comes my way. I am prepared to help others with their problems. I also take a moment every morning to command my mind, body, soul and spirit to yield to the Holy Spirit. That keeps my emotions in check, and sharpens my daily discernment in hearing God clearly all day long.

Taking your seat of authority in Christ means you are ruling and reigning over your life from the GLORY realm! This is the true Kingship that Jesus died and rose for us to have!

What a gift! Read Ephesians Chapter 2 and you will be reminded of this immense gift of authority and seat you have been given by the Father Himself!

I love the Passion Translation of this word in Ephesians 2:6: "He raised us up with Christ the exalted One, and we ascended with Him into the glorious perfection and authority of the heavenly realm, for we are now co-seated as one with Christ!"

HE ALREADY RAISED US UP!

Why would any believer in Jesus Christ keep fighting from the ground level, when you can take this seat and rule over whatever you need to that day?! Take your seat of authority and don't ever leave it! I don't!

We don't fight for a place of victory, we rule from a place of victory! We rule because He (Jesus) rules!

Asking for Angelic Assistance:

Once you make the decision to go ALL KINGDOM and operate in the glory, you will attract the angelic realm of the kingdom of God. It's just a given. We, the redeemed of Christ, who had ministering angels confirmed around Him in both the wilderness and the garden during His ministry on the earth, are now waiting and available to minister to us.

"Are they not all ministering spirits, sent forth to minister for them who shall be heirs of salvation?" Hebrews 1:14

Because you are declaring the word of God and being obedient to the guidance of the Holy Spirit, angels are hearkened to the word of God and the worship of God. They cannot help it; they are drawn to it.

Angels get excited and cannot wait to carry out assignments for you. I have learned there are angels that are assigned to different tasks for the kingdom and you can ask the Father for them and even command them to assist you in a project or kingdom assignment you have. Understanding Jesus said we would do what He did and even greater, that is biblical. Angels assisted Jesus; they will assist us. They announced His conception and birth. They comforted him and strengthened him twice—once in the wilderness, and again in the garden.

Jesus said when He was arrested that if He wanted, He could ask the Father to send twelve legions of angels to fight for Him, but He was to go to the cross willingly. Huge angels rolled away the stone and guarded His tomb at the resurrection. They were witnessed by Mary Magdalene.

Peter wanted to fight for Jesus when He was arrested. Jesus did not need Peter acting up this way because it was God's will He should go to the cross. However, Jesus made it clear to Peter that He could ask for Angelic assistance at any time if He wanted it! I think He was helping them understand His importance of going willingly to the cross.

Matthew 26:53 "Do you think I cannot call on my Father, and he will at once put at my disposal more than twelve legions of angels?" - Jesus to Peter at the time of His arrest.

What? 72,000 Angels that Jesus could have called upon for assistance! That, to me, should give you at least a little glimpse of the immense glory that is around us, ready to fight for us and the protection we can call upon too! The enemy is toast!

John 14:12-14 "Very truly I tell you, whoever believes in me will do the works I have been doing, and they will do even greater things than these, because I am going to the Father. And I will do whatever you ask in my name, so that the Father may be glorified in the Son. You may ask me for anything in my name, and I will do it." - Jesus

We can ask for Angelic Assistance in Jesus' name. We can do exactly as Jesus did. He told us we can! As a matter of fact, God is already promising to send them and already has assigned them to guard you!

Psalm 91: 11-12 "For he shall give his angels charge over thee, to keep thee in all thy ways. They shall bear thee up in their hands, lest thou dash thy foot against a stone."

Do you think just because you cannot see them they are not there? ANGELS are all around you right now! Waiting for you to acknowledge them and send them on assignments! I have seen the Angels and have given them assignments. You will be able too if you ask God to open your eyes in the spirit to see the Angelic realm. To Operate and Advance in the Glory you cannot be afraid of the supernatural. You have to learn that this is an even more real realm than the one we have on earth. God has veiled our eyes from these things because we are not spiritually mature to understand, But we can ask for the veils to be removed so we can see.

The glory realm is a very supernatural place and it's all Biblical. Everything in the supernatural must glorify the Father and The Son and The Holy Spirit or it's not of God!

The angels serve us, because we are of the Kingdom and God promises to send them to us as heirs of salvation. We as believers have authority over the angels through Jesus Christ only. They serve at the pleasure of the King! King Jesus! When you understand how God's kingdom works, you will begin to realize that it's all about Jesus. If any teacher teaching about Angels does not point to Jesus Christ as KING of KINGS and as the Son of the Living God and does not teach that you need Jesus Christ's authority to send angels, run away—and fast!

Understand this: It's the Holy Spirit of God working with you and within you and points you FIRST to Jesus Christ. Then, through Jesus to the Father. If you have angelic visitation or experience, know it's because the Father sent them because of His love for you. However, we are told to test the spirits. We ask the spirit, "Can you say and confirm Jesus Christ is the Son of God and came to earth in the flesh?"

If the spirit leaves quickly without answering you, they were not of God. If the angel is from God, your spirit will confirm it with the confirmation from the Holy Spirit. They will stay with a "yes" or a nod and worship God with you if you begin to worship or continue to give you a message.

I have seen angels of the Lord many times, and they don't always look like the popular angel "paintings." My most powerful angel-of-God encounter happened when my husband and I were sitting in the back of our church service one Sunday. During the pastor's sermon, I was prompted by the Holy Spirit to look up at the middle of the aisle. I saw a guardian/sentry angel standing there and He was HUGE. At least 12 feet tall, all the way to the ceiling. He was dressed in full armor, with a fitted brown leather breastplate, leather skirting, and a huge sword at his side. His wings were white with flecks of brown, and he was very fierce looking and muscular. I could see him clearly with both my natural and spiritual eyes. He wanted me to see him and the Holy Spirit told me that the early congregation prayed at that church and asked God to assign an angel to protect that church. Since then, that angel was assigned to that church and standing at his post! Jesus talks about angels assigned to His churches in the Book of Revelation.

It's great to want to know more of the supernatural, but be careful to first know your authority in Christ and be working daily with the Holy Spirit before you work with angels on assignment or ask to encounter them. This way, you will not be fooled or open a door to something you do not want!

Beware of Familiar Spirits That "Pose" As Angels!

I had a woman in my mentoring group who thought she had seen and encountered her "Guardian Angel" for years. It was actually a female looking familiar spirit (demon), It started out all nice and sweet. Then as soon as she got married, it turned jealous and destructive. It started manifesting in her bedroom knocking stuff off the walls and causing strife in her marriage! This had been attached to her for a long time and she was trying to rebuke it but she did not understand how to really take authority over it through Jesus Christ. Familiar spirits can get attached to a person or place and do not want to leave. True angels of God are assigned to be helpful to us, not possessive or destructive! I taught her how to take her seat of authority in Christ, and command it to leave in Jesus name. It left and did not bother her again! She anointed her home and bedroom and dedicated it to God, she also knows now how to bring the Glory Frequency into her home to bring in the Presence of God and God's True Angels.

I am still seeking the Lord on this, but I have never seen reference to a 'female' Angel in the Bible. They all have male names. So I am careful when people tell me they see a 'female' angel. My red flags go up. I immediately tell them to test that spirit. There have been some references to female looking angels appearing to major figures in history including George Washington. But in wisdom, test each spirit.

If you think you may have a familiar spirit hanging around, In Jesus name, take authority over it, renounce it, tell it's not welcome and command it to leave NOW in the name of Jesus Christ and and command it to go to the uninhabited dry place and stay there. Ask the Holy Spirit to come and fill the area where that evil spirit was operating and stand hold there forever. Familiar spirits (demons) cannot stand the presence of God. True angels of God can and want to be in the presence, and they actually worship God with you! Familiar spirits (demons) flee when you bring in God's glory frequency into your home. Resist the devil and he will flee! Run him over with your glory train. Your blessed drafting partners will come through right behind you! Be the glory leader, and cut through that dirty air and bring the speed to those in need!

The Angel Armies of God:

God has a kingdom. Kingdoms have armies. Jesus said when we pray to say, "Your kingdom come on earth as it is in Heaven." Therefore, God's armies are the way we think about armies on earth—with different ranks, generals, commanders, special commissions, and special forces. The "host" of Heaven is referred to in the Bible as a "great army." Host, in the Bible, refers to "multitude." Many times in the Bible you see where God's angel armies, the hosts of Heaven, have come to Israel's aid against their earthly enemies. There is a powerful noise in the glory realm that the hosts of Heaven make when they are destroying the enemy—"noise of a great host." I love that—scattering the enemy in fear just at their sound! That's a glory frequency that drives out the enemy!

Ask the Father to Send His Heavenly Hosts and Angel Armies to Fight for you and protect you!

Requesting Angels On Assignment:

1. Take your seat of Authority in Christ (do this every morning when you 'Suit Up')
2. Ask the Father for Angels on Assignment to be assigned to your family, ministry, business
3. If you desire, you can ask the Father to assign you Sentry Angels that you can post to gates and doors of your property each night
4. You may also ask The Father to Assign a special forces regiment of Army Angels to you to go out on warfare assignments, with a commanding Angel to work with you (if you are an intercessor for the land this is very good to have!)
5. Thank the Father and Jesus Christ, thank the Angels for coming by faith
6. Speak a command in the name of Jesus for what you want the Angels that are assigned to you to do
7. Example of Basic Assistance: "By the Authority of Jesus Christ in whom I am seated, I address the Angels of the Lord that are assigned to me by the Father God, I command for you to go now and

_____, and complete this fully with the partnership of the Holy Spirit in Jesus Authority to assist me now to fulfill God's will in this matter in Jesus name!"

8. Specific need prayer: "By the Authority of Jesus Christ in whom I am seated, I address the "Employment" Angels of the Lord that are assigned to me by the Father God, I command for you to go now and bring forth ideal employment for _____ that God has ordained for _____ in Jesus name! Go NOW Angels of Employment and complete this fully for _____ along with the partnership of the Holy Spirit in Jesus name to assist me now to fulfill God's will in this matter in Jesus name!"

9. Thank the Angels for being faithful, thank Jesus for the Authority He has given you and Praise God for the power of His Kingdom and His Holy Spirit and Angels being made available to you and your need.

Specific Angels For Specific Need:

I have sent the "Angels of Employment" to help family members and my students for divine job opportunities, and the Angels of Mechanics to help my neighbor get her tractor fixed! It was amazing! My neighbor does not even realize the Angels were working on her behalf! I went before the Father and thanked Him for my kind neighbor who had done so much for us and our horse Pongo. I asked the Father for Angels to be assigned to me to send out to help her and consider her kindness for a blessing from Heaven. By faith I received the Angels and put them to work right away!

My neighbor had been dealing with a broken down tractor that she sent months ago to the service place with no word from them, she was very frustrated and her pastures almost beyond overgrown! I called upon the Angels assigned to me by God to help and I commanded the Angels of Mechanics to go now in Jesus name and get her tractor home! Within days her tractor finally came home from the service place after months of them having her wrong number, they just dropped it off! It was still not fixed! As soon as the tractor returned I kept commanding the Mechanical Angels to complete the assignment and that her tractor would be fixed and run better than ever before. Days later, my neighbor found an old business card out of the blue from a farm equipment mechanic that had a mobile service that would come out to her farm and fix her tractor right there. Within a day the mobile mechanic arrived and repaired that tractor quickly and effortlessly.

The next day my neighbor was happily on her tractor, mowing her pastures! Our rescue horse Pongo and his donkey pals were enjoying the fresh mowed grass with new sweet sprouts to graze on! Since then, my neighbor is so happy. Her pastures look beautiful, and her tractor is running better than ever before! YAY, GOD!

The Holy Spirit taught me something very powerful about the authority He has given us in Christ Jesus and how we have access to heavenly assistance when we go FULL GLORY, FULL KINGDOM! This is a GIFT from God to us because we believe in His Son! YES! The GLORY and the KINGDOM is for us NOW here on earth! We operate here like we are already in heavenly places because we already are seated there!

Are you getting revelation from this? GOOD! I could write an entire book about working with the Angels of the Lord, and maybe I will; however, there are other great teachers out there, such as Kat Kerr that can give you some excellent strategies on how to do this according to the word of God.

Understand that you should never send the Heavenly Hosts and Angels on Assignment to do something that is not in the will of God. How will you know? Ask the Holy Spirit to stop you, check you up if you are doing something that is NOT God's will! Trust me, He will check you up but you must listen. Also, the Angels of The Lord are OBEDIENT to God. They will never do anything against His will. Know that the word of God is the will of God so realize that, along with the revelation of the Holy Spirit, He will train you up to properly do this by faith.

Never send the Angels to force a person to do your will, only to assist them to see God's will and help them to be blessed and prospering. God's will is that we will prosper and be in health and that our soul also prospers. That our households shall receive salvation in Christ and be blessed.

Do I pray for my neighbor to know God and Jesus Christ? Of course! I pray that God gives me divine appointments with her to reveal God's love for her and the Good News of the Gospel of Jesus Christ. Did I tell her about the Angels assisting with her tractor? No. She is not ready for that yet, but I did tell her I prayed to God for help regarding the tractor, and she was grateful.

I just planted a simple seed in her and asked the Holy Spirit to water it. I trust God to take it from there! It can be done without me forcing all my spiritual knowledge on her when she is not able to receive it yet! Understand not everyone is ready for the glory realm. It's like trying to make someone drink from a blast of a firehose when all they can handle is a little tiny garden hose trickle! But God can add more. You opened the faucet.

You operate in the glory. Ask for WISDOM to plant the right seeds as you go. The Holy Spirit will water these seeds if you ask Him. Trust me, these people will see the fruit of glory you carry. They will think upon it. God will grow it in them, and they will begin to want what they see in you. Then stand back and see the AWE of God at work in their lives! Then Niagara Falls, baby!

This is just a piece of the revelation of Operating and Advancing in the Glory. There is so much more, and much that will never be revealed to us in our lifetime because of God's immense greatness and deep mysteries. But I believe many veils are being lifted in our day, Heaven and Earth are coming together and God can reveal great things on the earth at any time to each of us. Personally, I am excited to see what God does next! We can pursue God more deeply and go from Glory to Glory that is promised in the Bible for us. No matter how much we grow in Glory, we still fall short of God's Glory. But we are born to pursue more of God and the Kingdom and His majesty!

"For all have sinned and fall short of the glory of God."
Romans 3:23

I have good news! Even though we all fall short of God's glory, God wants us to come up higher and *operate under* His glory. Even if we cannot understand it or fathom it, we can, as sons and daughters, operate and advance in GLORY through Christ here on earth. It's like you have a special covering on you. I call it the "Glory Covering" and it brings favor and prosperity with God and man. It's reflecting the glory of the Son, Jesus Christ who lives in you, and this can grow exponentially. This is for you and your children. It's called FAVOR!

God loves us each uniquely and differently as creations of Himself. This is called FAVOR for those who carry out what He created us to do. He loves all His children, but FAVOR is for those who seek His kingdom and glory. The 'no respecter of persons' scripture was revealed to me as that we are each called to something unique and special, it does not matter where you were born or your race or your financial status. God can use each of us for something wonderful, and plans to! Even the most unlikely ones! These seem to be His favorite ones to use to show His Glory through! That means you and me!

The FAVOR comes when you allow yourself to be used by God, and that is over and above the 'respect of persons' face in the crowd thinking! If you read the full Romans Chapter 2, the 'respecter of persons' was not about how God loves us equally, but how each person will be judged according to their deeds on earth.

I want to fulfill the destiny and assignments that God has ordained for me here on earth. This means I will be judged righteously and I want to hear those words, "Well Done good and faithful servant." It helps when you understand you can fulfill your destiny and assignments a lot easier when you ask for favor and want to be seen as "special" by God! I think you want this too, right? YES!

Focus on how, through operating in humility to God, you will receive favor, a glory covering and He will reward me in due time here on earth. I know you want my reward in

Heaven too. But Jesus made in clear that God's will for us in the Lord's prayer is 'on earth as it is in heaven".

"Therefore humble yourselves under the mighty hand of God [set aside self-righteous pride], so that He may exalt you [to a place of honor in His service] at the appropriate time." 1 Peter 5:6 (AMP)

Jesus said: "Pick up your Cross and follow me." Jesus did the ultimate act of humility, for all of us at the Cross! What came after His humility of the Cross? THE RESURRECTION AND THE GLORY!

The same spirit that raised Jesus from the dead lives in you now. The glory lives inside you and must be activated by walking with Jesus and following His example. You can tap into that glory. It's the dunamis power of the Holy Spirit.

Jesus rose from the dead, walked out of the tomb and walked, talked, made breakfast, ate, did more miracles with the fish, and gave instructions to his disciples in HIS GLORIFIED body after His resurrection here on earth. He must have looked like a human being when He was walking around in the GLORY because on the Road to Emmaus (Luke 24:13-35), Jesus was chatting it up with the fellas before they recognized Him. This, all before He ascended into Heaven. Jesus was showing us that the GLORY is for us on earth as well as Heaven! Jesus is the only person that ever died for me and you, so we could have glory and everlasting life too, nobody else did that for us, ever or ever will again! That's why He said, "It is finished". The Kingdom plan has been restored to God's people. All we have to do is accept Jesus is the only one who saved us from death and through Him we have eternal life and access to the kingdom, the Father, and the glory!

Jesus was teaching us how to seek first the Kingdom of God and with this, comes the favor of God. Jesus wanted us to desire the Father's favor and have what He has with the Father!

John 17:22–23: "And the glory which You gave Me I have given them, that they may be one just as We are one: I in them, and You in Me; that they may be made perfect in one, and that the world may know that You have sent Me, and have loved them as You have loved Me." Jesus

Glory thinking is seeking and receiving the FAVOR of God —how HE wants you to be set apart from the crowd as a Son and Daughter! But this takes faith and humility to God. The Bible speaks of the 'favored' ones.

- 1 Samuel 2:26 "And the boy Samuel continued to grow in stature and in favor with the LORD and with men."
- Luke 2:40 "And Jesus increased in wisdom and stature, and in favour with God and man."

Decree over yourself: *"And _____ grew strong and increased in Godly wisdom, stature and favor with God and man!"*

In the Bible, we are clearly taught about FAVOR through the lives of Abraham, Joseph, Daniel, and Esther, and that they understood how to advance and operate in the glory —that it was directly related to RECEIVING FAVOR and humbling yourself before the King of Glory.

FAVOR, FAVOR, FAVOR! It's directly connected to operating and advancing in the glory!

You must seek God and ask for favor! God wants to grant it to you, and you must believe God gives it as soon as you ask for it! Start acting like a Champion of Faith—highly favored by God! Seek it boldly, and know by faith you will get it!

The words and actions of these Champions of Faith directly brought them favor, acceleration and prosperity with God and man. They all were then prospered by God through the men God used to prosper them on earth. These Champions of Faith Operated and Advanced in Glory and did not have to wait to go to heaven to get it, we must learn how to go and grow in God's favor this way.

- Genesis 18:3 - "My Lord," said Abraham, "if I have found favor in your sight, please do not pass your servant by."
- Genesis 39:4 - "Joseph found favor in his sight and became his personal attendant. Potiphar put him in charge of his household and entrusted him with everything he owned."
- Daniel 1:9 - "Now God had granted Daniel favor and compassion from the chief official."
- Esther 5:8 - "Esther replied, "This is my petition and my request: If I have found favor in the sight of the king, and if it pleases the king to grant my petition and fulfill my request."
- Mark 11:24 - "Therefore I tell you, whatever you ask for in prayer, believe that you have received it, and it will be yours.

Humble yourself under and in the mighty Glory of God. Ask, seek and receive the Favor of God. Live and operate in the protection and covering of the Glory Realm!

Can you declare boldly and speak prophetically, and still walk in humility? ABSOLUTELY!

Jesus Christ did this! Jesus is the Spirit of Prophecy! To be Christlike is to proclaim the Kingdom and promises of God over your life and other's lives! Jesus said; "I do what the Father tells me to do." Jesus never held back; He was in humility to the Father alone, not man! He only did as man asked when a person showed belief and faith! Jesus prophesied Peter's future! Jesus prophesied the Holy Spirit coming! Jesus prophesied that the woman who poured expensive ointment on His feet would be remembered for generations for her act of faith. Jesus prophesied that the temple would come down, and that He would die and after three days rise again!

Jesus spoke YOU and the world into existence! He is the word and the word was made flesh and the word lives in us! Speak BOLDLY. The favor is there for you to even speak things that stretch your faith. Those impossible things! Jesus gifted this to YOU!

PROPHESY! There are words in you God is waiting for you to speak so they can be performed on the earth. Call forth your future! (Jeremiah 1:11-12)

Through Jesus we live, operate and demonstrate Glory, all while giving God the Glory! This who you are! You are a GLORY CARRIER and KINGDOM ADVANCER. Nothing can phase you or stop you! You Are, Blood Bought, Highly Favored and Set Apart for Great Plans and Purposes of God!

It is *your* time! NOW throw off your beggars clothes and everything weighing you down, and come up to God's Podium of Victory! Your Robe of Righteousness and

Crown of Glory that Jesus Christ purchased for you to have is waiting! You never have to beg God or man for anything again. You do not have to struggle or strive!

YOU my faithful friend have an ABUNDANCE of grace, ability, equipping, victory strategies, anointing and favor from your Father God!

This is your birthright and your inheritance of the KINGDOM and the GLORY! Because of your King Jesus Christ you are royalty and set apart for the Glory of God! Faith brings boldness and understanding that you have been created by God to WIN and you will be GIVEN everything you need to WIN! Much of it is already INSIDE YOU! Stay seated next to the Throne of Grace as a Son and Daughter of the Most High and seek the Father's favor, tell Him you want to WIN for His Glory and His Pleasure! Your Heavenly Father has been waiting for you to realize *who you truly are...*

A CHAMPION OF FAITH!

A CHAMPION OF THE KINGDOM!

"All of Heaven is cheering you on!"

From Motorsports to Ministry: About The Author, Annamarie Strawhand

As an internationally known professional race car driver coach and spokesperson, Annamarie Strawhand's career spanned over 30 years in auto racing, 12 of those working with NASCAR drivers, teams and sponsors. In 2015 God called Annamarie into Ministry and to serve and advance the Kingdom of God. Now she is coaching and mentoring people of faith to Victory with their divine calling and purpose. Annamarie is the Host of the popular online morning show, "Life In The Faith Lane with Annamarie." Her dynamic Bible based teachings combined with humor, inspiration and real life lessons have brought many wonderful breakthroughs into the lives of her listeners. Annamarie's divine calling is to help God's people fulfill their divine calling—something she finds very rewarding. Annamarie also ministers and mentors under a prophetic covering with the Holy Spirit. This has brought words of knowledge, visions and prophetic dream interpretation for both individuals and for the Nations. She is also very passionate about being a watchman and intercessor for America and has launched "American Gatekeepers." Her mobilized intercessors have been doing land prayer assignments across the Nation the last five years. Annamarie lives in Virginia Beach, Virginia with her husband Michael Strawhand. They have a daughter Landry Leigh, a cat named Snickers, a dog named Junior and a rescue horse named Pongo (who also has his own book, written by Annamarie). She and her family hope to grow their ministry in an effort to help abused and bullied children and adults to heal, restore, and rebuild their confidence and faith in God in an effort to discover and activate their divine purpose. Learn more about Annamarie and her ministry, coaching programs and teachings at: **annamariestrawhand.com**

Made in the USA
Middletown, DE
08 July 2021